# Sir Walter Raleigh

# Sir Walter Raleigh

*By* WILLARD M. WALLACE

---

*O! what a noble mind is here o'erthrown:*
*The courtier's, soldier's, scholar's eye, tongue, sword;*
*The expectancy and rose of the fair state,*
*The glass of fashion and the mould of form,*
*The observ'd of all observers, quite, quite down!*

HAMLET, III, ii, 158-63

---

PRINCETON, NEW JERSEY

PRINCETON UNIVERSITY PRESS

1959

TO

**HERBERT C. F. BELL**
PROFESSOR OF HISTORY, EMERITUS, WESLEYAN UNIVERSITY

**S. HUGH BROCKUNIER**
PROFESSOR OF HISTORY, WESLEYAN UNIVERSITY

**GEORGE M. DUTCHER**
LATE PROFESSOR OF HISTORY, WESLEYAN UNIVERSITY

**WILLIAM E. LINGELBACH**
PROFESSOR OF HISTORY, EMERITUS, UNIVERSITY OF PENNSYLVANIA

**SIGMUND NEUMANN**
PROFESSOR IN THE SOCIAL SCIENCES, WESLEYAN UNIVERSITY

**CONYERS READ**
PROFESSOR OF HISTORY, EMERITUS, UNIVERSITY OF PENNSYLVANIA

**ALEXANDER THOMSON**
LATE PROFESSOR OF HISTORY, WESLEYAN UNIVERSITY

→》》 《《←

*Scholars and gentlemen for whom I have felt esteem
and affection through the years,
teachers whose enthusiasm, knowledge, and wisdom
helped inspire in me an appreciation
and a love of history,
mentors of rigorous standards who should properly receive
a good deal of credit
for whatever scholarly virtue may attach to this biography
but who should be promptly and completely
absolved from all its deficiencies*

# *Preface*

LONG ago Biblical authority observed wryly, "Of making many books there is no end." One might also remark, "Of writing many biographies of Sir Walter Raleigh there is no end." What possible justification can there be for adding to the already impressive list? Had I thought it necessary to justify writing another "life," I should have chosen a different subject; however, I am aware that some manner of explanation is fitting.

In the first place, our knowledge of the Tudor and Stuart eras is constantly expanding, and with this expansion has come an increased understanding and appreciation of the roles played by the individuals who helped shape those eras. Raleigh acquires new dimensions as a consequence of recent, detailed examination of Elizabethan overseas enterprises. The studies of Elizabethan parliaments and government published since World War Two afford the biographer of Raleigh a better opportunity than ever before to assess his role and importance.

Secondly, with so much of our heritage being held up for reappraisal in the light of current developments, we have become increasingly interested in the origins of that heritage. In a day when we are deeply involved in discussions of civil liberties, due process of law, and loyalty to the state, both Raleigh's alleged treason and his trial merit reconsideration. Many of his biographers have emphasized—and rightly so—both his innocence and the manifest injustice of his trial. It is true that Raleigh stood not a chance, or only a chance, of acquittal, but it should be pointed out, instead of being virtually ignored or hastily passed over, that while innocent of overt treason, he knew more than he disclosed of the conspiracy for which he was arraigned. Furthermore, attention needs to be called to the fact that the gross injustice of his trial (one of the most cruelly unjust in English history) obtained not so much because of a perversion of the existing law as because of the law itself and the court procedure of the time—and, of course (as no biographer has neglected to reveal), the vindictive spirit in which the trial was carried out. Raleigh's prosecutor, be it remembered, was Attorney General Sir Edward Coke, who—whatever harsh comments can be made of his conduct during those tragic days—was not an unjust man in the legal sense of the term and who continues to be recognized as a legist to whom both English and American law owe a profound debt. In good part as a consequence of Raleigh's trial, court procedural changes and substantive changes in the law of treason were ultimately effected which have become an integral part of the web of justice which we take so much for granted.

Ours has not been the first generation to be curious about the origins of its cultural heritage. Even as the poets, philosophers, and historians of our day venture to describe the tortuous but ever fascinating course that man has pursued and to explain and account for the values that have animated him, so Raleigh, filling all three roles, attempted the hazardous task with an amazing display of versatility and shrewd penetration. We should be arrogant indeed if we did not consider his conclusions to be of more than passing interest.

Finally, most historians—perhaps because Raleigh is difficult to categorize and because he never occupied a conventional and powerful post in government, and thereby exercised only an indirect influence on policy—have tended to let the writing of Raleigh biography go by default to the professors of literature and the professional free-lancers. Their writings have been gratifyingly prompt to recognize him as a writer of unusual ability and a superb courtier. He was these things, to be sure, but more besides. I had long wondered what a present-day historian would make of him. Though I have satisfied my curiosity, I must confess that there are many buckets of water still to be drawn from what appears to be not a well but an endlessly bubbling spring.

W.M.W.

*Wesleyan University*
*Middletown, Connecticut*

# Acknowledgments

FEW books are written without a writer's being aware, in all humility, of what he owes to the many people, living and dead, who have contributed in some measure to his work. Though my indebtedness is widespread, I wish to make a number of specific acknowledgments in addition to the general acknowledgments to the professors mentioned in my dedication. My gratitude and thanks to: colleagues in the History Department at Wesleyan University, Professors Norman O. Brown, Michael Cherniavsky, Eugene O. Golob, and Carl E. Schorske, whose contributions, invariably reflecting sharp insight, enlarged my understanding of Raleigh as an historical figure and a personality; other colleagues at Wesleyan, Professors George Conklin and Robert Knapp, who brought to coffee chats on Raleigh their interest and competence as classicist and psychologist respectively; Mr. Malcolm Stearns of Haddam, Connecticut, for his lively and extensive knowledge of the Tudor and Stuart eras, particularly of overseas expansion; Professor Albert Van Dusen of the University of Connecticut for several useful suggestions; Miss Agnes Latham, Mr. Vincent T. Harlow, Professor David B. Quinn, Professor Ernest Strathmann, Mr. Milton Waldman, the late Edward Thompson, the late William Stebbing, and the long deceased Edward Edwards for their scholarly studies of various phases of Raleigh's activities; the British Museum and the Public Record Office in London, and the Bodleian Library at Oxford, for their cordial assistance; the Olin Library of Wesleyan University, particularly Miss Gertrude McKenna, for patient and untiring procuring of books; Miss R. Miriam Brokaw of the Princeton University Press for her generous enthusiasm and cooperation; the Trustees of the Princeton University Press for their decision that there still was room for the publication of another biography of Raleigh; the Research Committee of Wesleyan University for stenographic funds; Mrs. Esther Carling of Lakeland, Florida, and Mrs. Elizabeth King of Berlin, Connecticut, for invaluable secretarial aid; and my wife, Elizabeth M. Wallace, whose helpfulness has been of such measure that, truly, "my cup runneth over."

# Contents

# Illustrations

*Sir Walter Raleigh*

# CHAPTER 1
# Fortune's Tennis-Ball

SPANISH guns pounded away at the tall ship leading the English fleet into the harbor of Cadiz to battle with the powerful galleons lying under the protection of batteries ashore. It seemed a mad if gallant venture to expose a ship to such concerted fire. But this was the *Warspite*, a notable name in British naval history from Cadiz in 1596 to Narvik in 1940, and she was the flagship of the redoubtable Admiral of the van, Sir Walter Raleigh.

Tall, spare, dressed as elegantly as for a ball, Raleigh disdained returning the fort's fire. He was reserving his broadsides for the Apostolic vessels of Spain, the *St. Matthew, St. Thomas, St. Andrew*, and *St. Philip*, especially the last. For it was the great *St. Philip*, flagship of the Admiral of Spain, that had led the attack which overwhelmed his heroic cousin, Sir Richard Grenville, and his stout *Revenge* off the Azores. Now Raleigh would himself be revenged on the victors of that epic contest.

Still, when would he deal out his vengeance? To his officers standing impatiently at their stations, and to his gunners blowing on their matches, the delay in the order to commence firing must have seemed interminable. And as if recognizing that some appropriate reply should be made to the fort, Raleigh beckoned to his chief musician. Thus the next time the fort salvoed, the musicians aboard the *Warspite* raised their trumpets to their lips and blew a discordant blast. Again the fort fired, and again the trumpets derisively sounded their defiance. It is no strain on the imagination to hear the hoarse laugh that burst from the *Warspite's* decks or to see the scornful smile on the English Admiral's face. He had displayed his contempt by a gesture as spirited as that of the Earl of Essex, who, in his enthusiasm, had hurled his plumed hat into the sea at the prospect of the fleet's forcing its way into the harbor of Cadiz. And in the bloody fight that presently ensued, Raleigh showed the dashing courage and energy that men had come to expect of him. Though

3

he was sorely wounded in the leg, it was his leadership that was chiefly responsible for the destruction or capture of the Spanish fleet.

Cadiz was but one of the numerous exploits in which Raleigh figured, mixing boldness with calculation. If he lost, as he occasionally did, to the intense satisfaction of his enemies, he also won much fame and fortune. He was truly the Renaissance man of Elizabethan England, whose misfortune it was not simply to combine brilliance and versatility with insufferable arrogance and intolerance of lesser men, but to live on into the sober times of Elizabeth's successor, James Stuart. A handsome figure of a man, though with a forehead almost too high, with intense, heavy-lidded eyes of bluish grey, Raleigh could execute wild Irish rebels without a qualm; contribute delicate, rather somber introductory verses to *The Faerie Queen* by Edmund Spenser, whom he introduced at Court; contrive at vast personal expense the settlement of Virginia, which he named in honor of Elizabeth, the Virgin Queen; secure and successfully manipulate valuable trade monopolies; face Spanish guns and the drawing-room sniping of English courtiers with utter fearlessness, yet grovel before James I for his life. Few men in history have equalled him in the number and diversity of his interests. He was soldier, sailor, courtier, Captain of the Queen's Guard, businessman, explorer, colonizer, member of Parliament, devotee of science, ship designer, military engineer, musician, literary patron, historian, and poet.

It is not surprising that such a man made few friends. Indeed, in his drive toward wealth and fame, Raleigh became the most hated and feared Englishman of his time. Jealousy was not alone the reason, for women as well as men felt uncomfortable in the presence of this brilliant, ruthless, sardonic creature.[1] Successful though he was, he never attained the pinnacle he sought. When triumph was almost his, his Queen died, and her successor threw him into the Tower, where he spent thirteen long, irksome years dashing his splendid feathers against the cage that held him securely on a charge of treason. If this descent from grace rejoiced his enemies at home, it brought no

[1] Francis Bacon reported Raleigh as saying of the ladies of Queen Elizabeth's Court, "They were like witches; they could do hurt, but they could do no good." *The Works of Francis Bacon*, XIII, 335.

4

less joy to the Spaniards, to whom his name had become a terror almost as dreadful as that of the late Sir Francis Drake. It was Spain, through her influence at the Court of James I, which, two and one-half years after Raleigh's release from the Tower, brought him at last to the scaffold.

Then, with England fallen from her greatness under Elizabeth and guided into an unpopular foreign policy by an unpopular king, the English began to realize what a rare and remarkable individual had been this last of the great Elizabethans. Generations who never knew the spell of his incisive, compelling personality or heard the sharp, arrogant voice speaking in a mouth-filling Devonshire accent have marveled that the greatness of Raleigh could have been so poorly appreciated by his contemporaries. Posthumously Raleigh has come into his own, perhaps more than his own. Each age must rewrite its past, and, in the three centuries since his execution, biographies, many of them unqualifiedly favorable, have tumbled over one another in their haste to interpret this remarkable person.

This biographical profusion is no cause for wonder. As long as the spectacle of an individual struggling to break away from the conforming influence of custom and policy stirs the human heart, so long will men and women want to read of Raleigh. When, as in his case, the individual happens to be a person of superlative ability and his principal enemies are almost as gifted and even more powerful, interest has indeed a high potential. An enigma in his own time, he has remained hardly less enigmatical to posterity. A member of King James's Privy Council, a position to which, during Elizabeth's reign, Raleigh had vainly aspired, wrote of this man whom his royal master had executed, "Sir Walter Raleigh was one, that (it seems) Fortune had picked out of purpose, of whom to make an example, or to use as her Tennis-Ball, thereby to show what she could do; for she tossed him up of nothing, and to and fro to greatness, and from thence down to little more than to that wherein she found him, (a bare Gentleman)."[2]

In an age like ours, one in which a tennis-ball existence is all too prevalent in view of the nuclear threat to civilization, even to life itself, it may be edifying to look again at Raleigh and his

---

[2] Sir R. Naunton, *Fragmenta Regalia*, 47.

world. The era was one when absolute monarchs ruled, when Spain was regarded by a large part of Europe with much the same fear as is the Soviet Union now, when religion excited as much heat as the current struggle of the "isms" and conformity was literally the law, when America was a wilderness, the Caribbean, Mexico, and South America were Spanish, and the quick way to fabulous riches seemed to lie in finding a gold mine or, better still, seizing a Spanish treasure galleon. This was a world far different from ours, but the hazards were great, and men and women, though perhaps more inured to hardships, were the same flesh. There are lessons still to be learned from the past, and not the least of these is how and why a man behaved as he did in the course of a life filled with accomplishment and peril. Such a man, for example, as Sir Walter Raleigh.

# CHAPTER 2

# Education and Early Years

RALEIGH came of an old Devon family that had, in years past, five knightly branches. His branch had lived at Fardell near Dartmoor for two hundred years. His father, also named Walter, at one time possessed four manors and, in addition to managing his estates, may have been a merchant, for he owned at least one ship working out of Exeter. He established his residence at Hayes Barton, a farm in the vicinity of Budleigh Salterton, where Raleigh was born in 1552 or 1554, probably the former.

Walter Raleigh of Fardell married three times. His first wife was Joan Drake of Exmouth, a cousin of the great Sir Francis. His second was a daughter of a London merchant named Darrell. His third, Sir Walter's mother, was Katherine Champernoun, who had been previously married to Otho Gilbert and had had three sons by him, John, Humphrey, and Adrian. Widowed, she married Walter of Fardell before 1549 and bore him three children, Carew, Sir Walter, and Margaret. The Champernouns were a distinguished seafaring family, Katherine's brother, Sir Arthur, being Vice Admiral of Devon. In fact, Raleigh was related to a number of distinguished West Country families such as the Courtenays, the Drakes, the Grenvilles, the Russells, and the St. Legers. There were to be occasions in his career when this kinship, however remote, was to be of considerable significance.

Raleigh came naturally by his independence of spirit. With the spread of the Protestant faith during the reign of the young Edward VI, his father dared uphold the new creed in Catholic Devon and was lucky to escape with his life when, on two occasions, he was assailed by mobs.[1] Another time, he helped Sir Peter Carew, his cousin, to flee to the Continent in the Raleigh ship when Sir Peter opposed the marriage of Mary Tudor to Philip II of Spain. For some inexplicable reason,

[1] R. Holinshed, *Chronicles of England, Scotland, and Ireland*, III, 94.

7

Walter of Fardell escaped punishment. Similarly, Katherine Champernoun Raleigh, described by a contemporary writer as "a woman of noble wit and of good and godly opinions," visited and comforted in Exeter Castle one Agnes Prest, who was burned in 1557 during the Marian persecution.[2] Like her husband, Katherine espoused her religion with courage and persistence. Though little is known of the elder Raleighs in later life, it is presumed that they moved to Exeter and were both dead by 1584.

It is unfortunate that we know practically nothing of the formative stage of Raleigh's life. In fact, what his boyhood was like is largely a matter of speculation. In a celebrated painting Sir John Millais portrayed him as a young lad sitting and listening to an old salt spinning the yarns of the sea. That such tales stirred Raleigh's imagination is likely, for all his life he followed adventure, and it must have been obvious to any Devon boy of the time that the sea was the great highway to excitement, wealth, and fame. In his maturity Raleigh was a great reader, a habit undoubtedly acquired when young, but whether he went to school or received private instruction is not known. The regrettable fact is that less is known of Raleigh's early years than of those of many contemporaries inferior to him in ability and importance.

Only when he enters college does Raleigh emerge from obscurity. In 1568, according to Anthony à Wood, he enrolled at Oriel College, Oxford, as a commoner and remained there for three years, after which he left without a degree. Wood says that, while at Oriel, "his natural parts being strangely advanced by academical learning, under the care of an excellent tutor, he became the ornament of the juniors, and was worthily esteemed . . . proficient in oratory and philosophy."[3] This sounds like Raleigh.

What else is known of him during his Oxford days is confined to two anecdotes, one told by Francis Bacon, the other by that unreliable but often-quoted commentator of the seventeenth century, John Aubrey. Bacon relates that a cowardly undergraduate who happened also to be a skillful archer asked

[2] J. Foxe, *Acts and Monuments*, III, 748.
[3] A. à Wood, "Ralegh," in *Athenae Oxonienses*.

Raleigh how he could revenge himself upon a student who had insulted him. Raleigh replied, "Why, challenge him to a match of shooting."[4] If this is not a brilliant display of intellect, though cited as such, it is at least illustrative of Raleigh's own tendency to play from strength. As for Aubrey, he remarks, "I remember that Mr. Thomas Child of Worcestershire told me that Sir Walter Raleigh borrowed a gown of him when he was at Oxford (they were both of the same College), which he never restored, nor money for it."[5] One might add that rare is the person who does not have some object never returned to its rightful owner. In any event, both anecdotes demonstrate that Raleigh attended Oxford despite the fact that his name appears only once on the Oxford Register and that in 1572 when he was far removed from the peaceful Oxford existence. Possibly, though he was absent in person, his name was continued on the record on the payment of a fee and an expressed intention of returning.

During 1572, and probably for much of the three-year period he is presumed to have been at Oxford, Raleigh was in France serving with the Huguenots against the Catholics. One of his cousins, Gawain Champernoun, was the husband of Gabrielle, daughter of the Comte de Montgomerie, a Huguenot leader. Henry Champernoun, Gawain's brother, raised a troop of one hundred English Protestants, many of them from Devon, to assist the Comte, and Raleigh is usually considered to have joined the troop. On the other hand, Raleigh was probably in France already. Though the English volunteers reached the Huguenot camp as early as two days after the Huguenot defeat at Moncontour, on October 3, 1569, Raleigh, in his *History of the World*, speaks of himself as present not only at that battle but also at the severe Huguenot repulse at Jarnac, on March 13, 1569, where the Huguenot Prince of Condé was killed.[6] All of which one can be reasonably sure is that Raleigh fought on the Huguenot side during the conflict and was not one of those Englishmen who took refuge in the Parisian residence of the

[4] F. Bacon, *Apophthegms*, in *The Works of Francis Bacon*, XIII, 384.

[5] J. Aubrey, *Brief Lives*, II, 179.

[6] *History of the World*, in *The Works of Sir Walter Ralegh* (hereafter referred to as *Works*), bk. v, ch. ii, secs. 6, 8 (*Works*, VI, 157-58, 211). I have used the Oxford edition of Raleigh's works, and have referred, respecting the *History*, not only to the volume and pagination of this edition but also to the book, chapter, and section number common to all editions.

English ambassador, Sir Francis Walsingham, during the dreadful massacre of Huguenots on St. Bartholomew's Day, August 24, 1572.

Raleigh was introduced in France to a type of warfare that had nothing glamorous to it whatsoever. While the trappings of war may have color and appeal, the eight wars in about forty years between Catholics and Huguenots were of an especially nasty variety. If the Catholics could not exterminate the Huguenots, neither could the latter hope to eliminate the Catholics. In fact, not until the Huguenot leader, Henry of Navarre, turned Catholic to become Henry IV, King of France, and then issued, in 1598, the Edict of Nantes giving Huguenots official toleration, could the Huguenots hope to survive without molestation as a separate religious sect. Until Henry's conversion, the most frightful kind of internecine strife prevailed. Raleigh speaks of hunting Catholics in the caves of Languedoc, caves "which we knew not how to enter by any ladder or engine, till at last, by certain bundles of lighted straw let down by an iron chain with a weighty stone in the midst, those that defended it were so smothered, that they surrendered themselves, with their plate, money, and other goods, therein hidden; or they must have died like bees that are smoaked out of their hives."[7] The effect of this war experience was to make him a hardened veteran, hardened, that is, to the hazards of battle and somewhat callous to its wreckage of human life.

From this grim conflict Raleigh returned to England after the Comte de Montgomerie was captured and then treacherously beheaded in June 1574. At least, Raleigh's name is listed for February 27, 1575 as a member of the Middle Temple. Whether or not he paid much attention to the law at the Middle Temple is another uncertainty. He said at his trial in 1603 that he had read no law.[8] This may have been modesty, though Raleigh was not one to whom that virtue is commonly applied, or it may have been the truth. The Inns of Court were fashionable finishing schools for university men. They provided a thorough training for those interested in the law as a professional career and afforded young men who might one day inherit

[7] *Ibid.*, bk. iv, ch. ii, sec. 16 (*Works*, v, 355).
[8] T. B. Howell, *State Trials*, ii, 16.

estates an excellent opportunity to learn the laws of property. They were also a meeting place for youths from all over the kingdom, and Raleigh was never one to neglect an opportunity to make the acquaintance of anyone who might prove helpful to him. That he read some law is likely; that he took its study seriously is doubtful. The Inns of Court were a rung on the ladder, and Raleigh was probably there simply for the climbing.

While at the Middle Temple, Raleigh devoted at least part of his time to poetry. One of the fascinating aspects of Elizabethan men of action was their interest in literature, particularly drama and poetry. Throughout his life, Raleigh wrote poetry, much of it of a very high order. Usually it lacks the ornateness and cool detachment so common to Elizabethan poetry; it is strongly personalized, emotional, and often somber. The fact that Raleigh cared little about its publication and rarely signed his name to a poem has left scholars a task at once exasperating and exhilarating in establishing what he really wrote and what has been incorrectly ascribed to him or to others. Fortunately we now know with a fair degree of assurance the poems that are his;[9] but one of which there has never been much doubt is the eighteen-verse poem entitled *Walter Rawely of the middle Temple, in commendation of the Steele Glasse.* The poem, not especially notable, contains two lines which Raleigh may have written with a strange prescience:

> For whoso reaps renown above the rest
> With heaps of hate shall surely be oppressed.

*The Steele Glass,* published in 1576, was composed by George Gascoigne, a poet adventurer who enjoyed the favor of Robert Dudley, the magnificent Earl of Leicester. Sir Humphrey Gilbert, who commanded a small English force that assisted the Dutch against Philip II of Spain, their rightful sovereign, knew Gascoigne well and probably introduced Raleigh to him. Gascoigne, in turn, may have introduced Raleigh to Leicester, for, while in London, Raleigh tried hard to secure the friendship of the Earl.

Presently Raleigh moved to another quarter of London. This we know because two of his servants, William and Richard

[9] The best edition of his poems is by Agnes Latham.

11

Paunsford, evidently half-seas over, quarreled with the London watch on a December night in 1577 and sent for their master to bail them out. Raleigh was quick to comply, signing himself for one as "Walter Rawley, Esq. of Islington," and for the other as "Walter Rawley, Esq. de Curia."[10] He might indeed have been "of the Court," though it is difficult to be certain whether Leicester actually introduced him or the expression signified a goal to be achieved. Furthermore, how he had acquired an estate sufficient to maintain servants remains unanswered. Possibly he had not returned from France empty-handed. Possibly, too, he had already turned to that popular Devon and Cornish pursuit of the sixteenth century, privateering, and had enriched himself with spoil from Spanish ships or those belonging to French Catholics.

Through Gilbert, his half-brother, Raleigh embarked on a venture more enterprising than mere privateering. For many seamen of Devon and Cornwall the unknown lands across the Western Ocean possessed a kind of magical allurement. If attempts to discover new lands failed, there were always Spanish towns to be sacked in the West Indies and Central America and Spanish ships to be captured on the high seas. These were the great days of Hawkins and Drake and their perilous and swash-buckling adventures with the Spaniards in the New World. Gilbert was interested particularly in discovering a northwest passage to China and wrote a *Discourse* to prove the existence of such a passage. Gascoigne published the *Discourse* in 1576. In June 1578, Gilbert received a patent to discover and annex territory in the northern part of North America not already occupied by any Christian people. It was only natural to associate his brother, Sir John Gilbert, and Raleigh with himself in this enterprise.

Even before weighing anchor, the expedition had an encounter with the government. Gilbert had in mind an alternative project of appearing to set out on a voyage of discovery in order to deceive the Spaniards but with the actual objective of destroying Spanish shipping in American waters and seizing both Newfoundland and the West Indies. This was a little too strong even for the Queen and her ministers, as was Sir John Gilbert's

[10] Quoted from the Middlesex Registers by W. Stebbing, *Sir Walter Ralegh*, 13.

action in confiscating a Spanish merchant's craft in Dartmouth harbor along with its cargo of citrus fruit. Authority spoke very firmly to Sir John, ordering him to restore both ship and cargo to the merchant or otherwise compensate him. Sir John was also instructed to advise Sir Humphrey and Raleigh to remain at home to answer for damages committed by their crews.[11] But evidently Sir Humphrey and Raleigh slipped to sea before the Queen's officers could prevent their sailing, for, in 1579, they paid fines to the government.

Had Raleigh been a superstitious man, he might have taken fright from the result of this expedition and turned his back forever on America. From the start, the ship captains quarreled with their leaders and among themselves, and Raleigh later charged one at Plymouth with deserting the expedition. Meanwhile, instead of driving westward at once, the ships prowled about the Bay of Biscay, naturally discovering little new land but many Spaniards, then headed toward the Azores. One English ship went down before the guns of a powerful Spanish squadron, while Raleigh, commanding the *Falcon*, fought a desperate struggle in which his crew suffered numerous casualties; he was lucky to escape with his life. Though most of the English vessels thereafter scurried back to port, Raleigh kept to a westward course until lack of supplies caused even him to turn his ship's head about and sheet his sails home for England.[12]

Once back, and his fine paid, he itched to make his mark in some significant manner that would commend him to those in high places. He found his opportunity in Ireland, a land where the tragedy of its relationship with England was continually taking on a deeper color. Since the time of Henry II in the twelfth century, England's relations with Ireland had been vexed, and those relations became worse throughout the sixteenth century. The problems were mainly three. In the first place, the Irish Parliament had little independence, its acts having to be approved by the English Privy Council. Secondly, the English were in the process of introducing into Ireland a different conception of land tenure. By custom immemorial,

---

[11] E. Edwards, *The Life of Sir Walter Ralegh, together with His Letters*, I, 79.
[12] An account of this voyage, as well as of Gilbert's other voyages, is given in D. B. Quinn, *The Voyages and Colonizing Enterprises of Sir Humphrey Gilbert*. See especially the brilliant introduction to Vol. I.

lands of the Irish were considered to belong to the whole clan and not to individuals. When Henry VIII seized the monastic lands as part of his break with the Pope, he distributed many of them to the Irish chiefs to assure him their support, giving the chiefs hereditary title and making them individual owners. Other members of the clans resented this change and a number of them revolted, some against their own chiefs, others against the English. For the rest of the century Ireland knew little peace, thanks not only to these two problems but also to that of religion. When the enforcement of Protestantism in Ireland became a part of Elizabethan policy, loyalty to Catholicism became identified with patriotism in the minds of the Irish, and they eagerly accepted assistance from the Spaniards, whether in munitions or men. The fact, first, that the English, rarely able to spare many troops for Ireland, regarded the Irish as little more than savages in the pay of Spain and in Papal favor and, second, that the Irish looked upon the English as hateful oppressors who were also heretics helped make the fighting in the Emerald Isle notoriously bloody and cruel. Sir Humphrey Gilbert, who had served as President of Munster in 1569-1570, had successfully crushed an uprising there in two months but with a rigor that startled even the English government, which was not noted for its clemency toward the Irish; Gilbert was recalled. To this unhappy land Raleigh presently came, bearing, like his half-brother, no olive branch.

Before he left for Ireland, Raleigh had several altercations. One was with Sir Thomas Perrot, son of Sir John Perrot, Gilbert's successor as President of Munster. What was the real cause of the quarrel that February day in 1580 is not clear, possibly a dispute over the Irish methods employed by Gilbert and Sir John. In any event, Raleigh and Perrot came to swordspoints, and the Privy Council placed both men in the Fleet Prison, to cool their heels for six days. A month later, Raleigh quarreled with a man named Wingfield beside the tennis court at Westminster, and the Privy Council this time sent him to the Marshalsea Prison to repent. It is interesting to observe that Raleigh did not hesitate to hurl himself into a rough-and-tumble encounter. Not only did he cross swords with Perrot and Wingfield, but earlier he had cut a tavern brawler, one Charles

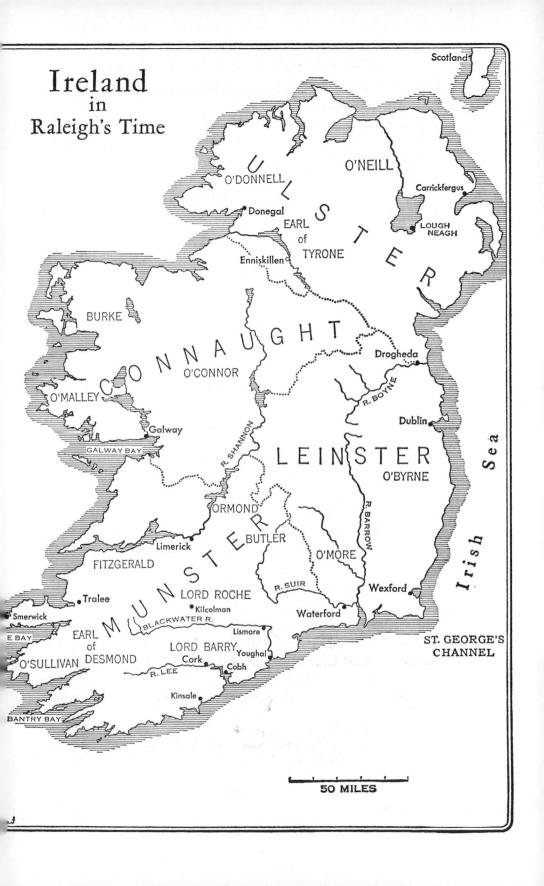

# Ireland
## in
## Raleigh's Time

Scotland

ULSTER

O'DONNELL    O'NEILL

Carrickfergus

Donegal

EARL
of
TYRONE

LOUGH
NEAGH

Enniskillen

CONNAUGHT

BURKE

O'CONNOR

Drogheda

R. BOYNE

O'MALLEY

Dublin

Galway

R. SHANNON

GALWAY BAY

LEINSTER

O'BYRNE

ORMOND

BUTLER

R. BARROW

Limerick

O'MORE

MUNSTER

FITZGERALD

R. SUIR

Wexford

Tralee

LORD ROCHE

Kilcolman

Waterford

BLACKWATER R.

Smerwick

Lismore

E BAY

EARL
of
DESMOND

LORD BARRY

Youghal

ST. GEORGE'S
CHANNEL

O'SULLIVAN

Cork

Cobh

R. LEE

Kinsale

BANTRY BAY

Irish Sea

50 MILES

Chester, down to size and stopped his mouth by tying together his beard and mustache.[13]

The time in prison evidently had little effect on Raleigh's fortunes, for in the summer of 1580 he was commissioned a captain of an infantry company for service against the Irish rebels revolting in Munster. From July 13 on, he received four shillings a day, certainly not a lucrative emolument; in fact, his appointment hardly afforded him food and clothing.[14] Still, though the pecuniary reward might be meager, Raleigh was rich in ambition. He could make a start in Ireland, but since it was folly to expect any significant recognition from his work there, he seemed to feel that it would be well to get it over with as soon as possible. Gilbert's policy of "no quarter" suited him nicely since it promised to end the revolt in a hurry.

Raleigh had just arrived in Ireland when he had an opportunity to participate in subduing the uprising. An Italo-Spanish force landed at Smerwick in Kerry, where it was joined by Irish forces and assailed almost at once by the English. On the Irish side James Fitzmaurice was killed and James, one of the brothers of the Earl of Desmond, was captured. Raleigh then assisted Sir Warham St. Leger at Cork in trying and sentencing James Desmond to be executed as a traitor. This task accomplished, Raleigh found himself with a new commander, Earl Grey of Wilton. Unlike the Earl of Ormond, whom he succeeded as Deputy, Grey believed in the rigorous use of force to settle the Irish difficulties. Raleigh agreed with him.

Eager to distinguish himself, Raleigh took charge of a number of the guns during the siege of Smerwick which was conducted that fall by Grey with the assistance of a small English squadron. In fact, Raleigh handled his heavy culverins so effectively that the defenses speedily crumbled and, after several sorties, the garrison surrendered on November 9, 1580. The garrison consisted of four hundred Italians and Spaniards and about two hundred Irish men and women, all of whom, insist the contemporary records, Grey promised to spare if they gave

[13] J. A. St. John, *Life of Sir Walter Raleigh*, I, 48; *Acts of the Privy Council*, XI, 421; Aubrey, *Brief Lives*, II, 184.
[14] *State Papers* (hereafter *S.P.*), Public Record Office (hereafter PRO), *Ireland* (Elizabeth I), 99/84; Edwards, *Ralegh* (*Letters*), II, 7-8; Naunton, *Fragmenta Regalia*, 48.

themselves up. To this assertion Grey declared that he had demanded an unconditional surrender. The upshot, however, was that Grey dealt with his captives as Samuel had treated the Amalekites. With the exception of a few foreign officers and a renegade Irish nobleman whom he saved for ransom, Grey ordered Captains Raleigh and Mackworth, officers of the day, to dispose of the rest by marching their companies into the fort and putting the Italians and Spaniards to the sword and hanging the Irish. The English alleged as reasons for this atrocious act the difficulty of guarding prisoners in an enemy country and the approach of the Earl of Desmond with a large relieving force. Catholic Europe, forgetting the St. Bartholomew massacre of 1572 and recent Spanish atrocities in the Lowlands, raised a cry of horror. As for the Queen's reaction, Francis Bacon said she was displeased. Actually the principal fault she found with Grey was that he had neglected to let her decide who should be killed and who should be saved. Nowhere in Grey's report was Raleigh mentioned, but there is no reason for thinking that Raleigh, a veteran of the fearful Huguenot wars and a sympathizer with Gilbert's Irish policy, shrank from executing Grey's order.[15]

The year following the Smerwick massacre was for Raleigh a period of reckless displays of courage, of violent disagreements with his superiors, and of constant fretting to be back in England. In the winter of 1581, while he was stationed in Cork, his restlessness got the better of him, and he yearned to take the field again against the Munster rebels. His only significant activity, however, was a trip to Dublin, where he persuaded Grey to let him try to surprise the disloyal Lord David Barry in the latter's castle. To Raleigh's disappointment, Barry burned his property and fled. Still, Raleigh had a slight diversion which must have pleased him. His route lay across a ford between Youghal and Cork, and as he and his escort of six were crossing, they were attacked by Fitz-Edmond,[16] seneschal of Imokelly and one of Desmond's followers, with fifteen horsemen and sixty foot soldiers. Despite the enemy's numbers, Raleigh cut

---

[15] Grey's report is printed in *Calendar of State Papers* (hereafter referred to as *Cal. S.P.*) *Ireland, 1574-1575,* lxix-lxxvi; the Queen's letter to Grey is condensed in *ibid.,* 274.

[16] John Fitz-Edmond Fitzgerald, one of the innumerable Geraldines. The family's lamentable history is related by B. Fitzgerald, *The Geraldines.*

his way through to the other side of the river. Then, seeing one of his men, Henry Moyle of Devon, floundering in the mud, back he went into the stream. Though he saved Moyle, he lost his horse. Undaunted by the mishap, Raleigh made his way safely to the river bank and faced Fitz-Edmond and his men with pistol and quarterstaff until all of his escort reached dry land. Why the seneschal let him escape is not clear, but Raleigh possessed an intimidating presence; besides, one can be fairly sure that Fitz-Edmond, whose courage was more a matter of tongue than heart, was probably convinced that, with Raleigh's pistol aimed at him, he would not long survive the order to take the Englishman.[17]

Impressed by Raleigh's energy, the Earl of Ormond, departing for England in the spring, appointed Raleigh, a Captain Piers, and Sir William Morgan to administer Munster in his absence. In this capacity Raleigh made a daring seizure of Lord Roche of Bally, a nobleman residing in his castle twenty miles from Cork and suspected of aiding the rebels. Determined to bring him to Cork for investigation, Raleigh headed for Bally with a small troop of horsemen. Somehow the Irish got wind of his plans (Irish espionage was usually good), and Barry and Fitz-Edmond tried to ambush him with eight hundred kerns. But Raleigh's own agents informed him of the ambush so that he was able to elude it by a night march. He reached Roche's village at dawn only to find his way blocked by five hundred angry townsmen. Cleverly Raleigh induced them to let him and a half-dozen of his troopers into the castle. Roche declared his loyalty and invited Raleigh to dine with him. Raleigh accepted, then secretly instructed his small detail to let into the castle the rest of his troop, which had been ordered to rendezvous at the castle to avoid suspicion. The plan went so well that, after their meal, when Raleigh demanded that Roche return with him to Cork and Roche refused, Raleigh revealed to the surprised nobleman that his troopers were already in possession of the castle. Recognizing defeat, Roche, with his family, accompanied Raleigh to Cork under cover of darkness. Raleigh had first persuaded Roche that his own loyal townsmen should help serve as an escort against the forces of Barry and Fitz-Edmond. Though nothing could subsequently be proved against Roche,

[17] Edwards, *Ralegh (Letters)*, II, 9-11.

Raleigh's reputation for skill and courage scarcely lost by the incident.[18]

Perhaps the individual most impressed with his methods was Raleigh himself. He wrote vividly to Sir Francis Walsingham of his services and solicited Barry's castle as a reward, offering to rebuild it at his own expense. Though he received, purely on a temporary basis, the entire northern wing of Cork harbor and the island where Cobh stands, the Queen, possibly on Lord Burghley's advice, refused him permanent possession and permission to rebuild the castle. It was a severe blow to his hopes and added to his increasing dissatisfaction with his situation. To Walsingham he had sharply criticized the moderation of Ormond and pointed out how Gilbert, with one-third of the present garrison in Ireland, had ended a dangerous rebellion in two months; he was also critical of Grey, the Deputy, who seemed to have been won to inactivity.[19] Finally, Raleigh decided to remind Leicester of his existence and of his readiness to serve the Earl in any capacity. "I have spent some time here under the Deputy," he wrote caustically, "in such poor place and charge, as, were it not for that I knew him to be one of yours, I would disdain it as much as to keep sheep."[20] Truly, as Aubrey wrote of him, years later, he was "perpetually differing."[21]

The letter, which Raleigh sent over his superior's head in the fashion of many an Elizabethan subordinate, was a thinly disguised appeal to be recalled from Ireland, "this lost land," as he described it. Whatever the reason, possibly because Leicester interceded for him, possibly because the Munster rebels were subdued by the late fall, Raleigh won the release he sought. Grey ordered his company disbanded and, in December, sent him to London with dispatches. On December 29, 1581, Raleigh received a payment of £20 from the government in London as expense money. He was now a free agent, and, in his newly gained liberty, must have thoroughly enjoyed what was left of the holiday season.

[18] Raleigh's seizure of Bally and his experiences with Barry and Fitz-Edmond are related in detail by John Hooker in his *Continuation* of Raphael Holinshed's *Chronicles of Ireland*. A more modern account of his Irish career is that by Sir J. Pope-Hennessy, *Ralegh in Ireland*.

[19] Raleigh to Walsingham, Feb. 23 and 25, 1580-1581. Edwards, *Ralegh* (*Letters*), II, 9-13.

[20] Ralegh to Leicester, Aug. 25, 1581. *Ibid.*, 17.

[21] Aubrey, *Brief Lives*, II, 180.

# CHAPTER 3

# Raleigh at Court

RALEIGH's return to London was that of a veteran of warfare, regular and irregular, and an expert on Irish affairs. As such, he was sought after by the Queen and the Privy Council for his advice on Irish policy. In fact, he was thereafter regarded as a man of rare knowledge of the problems and people of Ireland.

But Raleigh was not acknowledged as an authority without protest. The objections were largely voiced by Lord Grey. The Deputy "neither liked Captain Rawley's carriage, nor his company," and he denounced Raleigh's scheme for transferring the Irish garrison from the royal to the provincial budget without offending Ormond, the principal landlord, as "framed upon impossibilities for others to execute."[1] Although this controversy was subsequently bruited as having occurred within the Council meetings between a cocky Raleigh and an angry Grey,[2] subsequent research has pretty well established the altercation to have been indirect and at long range, Raleigh's answers to the Privy Council's questions being submitted to Grey for comment.[3] Even so, there is no doubt that Grey was thoroughly annoyed and Raleigh insufferably confident.

That reason existed for Raleigh's confidence, quite apart from his experience, does not admit of doubt; he was accepted at Court. How he managed to win acceptance has puzzled people, since even an ambitious, adventurous warrior needed a sponsor. It is possible that Leicester introduced him, considering this favor an answer to Raleigh's letter from Ireland entreating a change of employment. It has also been conjectured that the blunt old Earl of Sussex supported him as a foil to Leicester, the current if aging favorite of the Queen. Even granted that either Leicester or Sussex, or both, introduced him, the introduction alone could not account for Raleigh's swift ascent to royal favor.

[1] Grey to Walsingham, April, 1582, and to Burghley, Jan. 12, 1582. Quoted by Stebbing, *Ralegh*, 22-23; PRO, *S.P. Ireland* (Elizabeth I), 88/12.
[2] Naunton, *Fragmenta Regalia*, 49.
[3] Stebbing, *Ralegh*, 23; M. A. S. Hume, *Sir Walter Ralegh*, 25-27.

What was required was some occurrence that would dramatize his appearance at Court; and here one is led to the famous anecdote of the cloak and the puddle. Thomas Fuller, whose compilation of biographies of great Englishmen enjoyed a great vogue in the seventeenth century, described the incident many years after Raleigh's execution, but, given Raleigh's flair for publicity, it has the ring of truth. Though neither proved nor disproved, and possibly apocryphal, it is as likely an explanation as any for Raleigh's catching Elizabeth's attention. As told by Fuller, one day when the Queen and her courtiers were out walking following a shower, Elizabeth, "meeting with a plashy place, . . . seemed to scruple going thereon. Presently Raleigh cast and spread his new plush coat on the ground, whereon the the Queen trod gently, rewarding him afterwards with many suits, for his so free and seasonable tender of so fair a foot-cloth."[4]

It was a gallant gesture, and a wise investment. The fact that, in the absurd chivalric behavior of the day, it was a not uncommon practice in Spain and France and therefore possibly known to the Queen, detracted not at all from its effectiveness. The English courtiers, if they knew of it at all, may well have considered the custom a fantastic waste of good cloth, or—and this is more likely—they lacked the quick imagination to perceive what would appeal to the sensibilities of the Queen. Though no lady's man, in the usual sense, Raleigh possessed in extraordinary capacity the ability to realize what would please Elizabeth. This occasion was a great opportunity, and he is said to have followed up his first gesture with one even more intimate. As the party continued on its way, he suddenly stopped and scratched on a window the line:

Fain would I climb, yet fear I to fall.

To this, Elizabeth, borrowing the same diamond that Raleigh had used, wrote:

If thy heart fail thee, climb not at all.[5]

Raleigh soon discovered that Elizabeth took neither her duties nor her pleasures lightly. Taking over the throne after

---

[4] T. Fuller, *The Worthies of England*, 133.
[5] *Ibid.*, 133.

the death of her sister Mary—she whose memory was forever tainted by the blood of three hundred souls sent to the stake to the greater glory of God and of the Catholic faith—Elizabeth found England torn between Catholicism and Protestantism. That she succeeded in keeping the country steady by establishing a broad basis of belief to which all but extremists of both faiths could repair, is evidence of her wisdom as well as of the secularity of her nature. She cared not at all, she said, "to open windows into men's souls";[6] so long as men complied outwardly with the terms of her religious settlement, she let them alone. But toward Catholics who persisted in the outward forms as well as the inward tenets of their belief, and toward Protestants who refused to compromise and accept the 39 Articles, she pursued a rigorous policy of persecution, which, however, generally stopped short of the death penalty until the bitter years late in the century.

Even as she followed in religion a course essentially of compromise, in foreign policy she hesitated to make an irrevocable commitment of herself and England. Her condition of unwed blessedness, her celebrated virginity, she exploited for all it was worth. Its value was high, too, if one can judge by the number and quality of her suitors, who included, for some time, none other than King Philip II of Spain, her dead sister Mary's husband. When Raleigh appeared at Court, the Duke of Anjou was about to leave for the Continent, a rejected swain who had proved by no means so attractive to Elizabeth as had his suave and fascinating secretary, Jean de Simier. Her increasing years seemed not to wither the charms she possessed, for she was too much of a realist not to know that her greatest inducement was her realm; and this she zealously sought to preserve inviolate against all possibility of invasion.

Though her objectives were the security of her throne and of England, her methods to achieve that security were sometimes the despair of her counsellors, particularly the two men who rank among England's greatest ministers, Sir William Cecil, the Lord Treasurer, who became Lord Burghley, and Sir Francis Walsingham, her Principal Secretary. She made a virtue, or

[6] Quoted by C. Read, "Good Queen Bess," in R. L. Schuyler and H. Ausubel, *The Making of English History*, 181.

at least a policy, of vacillation. Refusing to admit that England's future was inextricably bound with that of Protestantism, she hesitated to stake England's destiny on the outcome of the religious struggle. After long persuasion, she furnished a measure of help to both the French Huguenots and the Dutch rebels, but for nationalist and dynastic rather than religious reasons. The Huguenots she assisted because internal strife weakened France and occupied the Court faction there most dangerous to herself. As for the Dutch, their Protestantism did little to recommend them in her eyes, for they were in revolt against their rightful sovereign, Philip of Spain, and Elizabeth felt by no means so secure on her own throne that she could endorse without qualification any political revolt. She supported the Dutch because they diverted Philip's growing power and postponed what was acquiring the semblance of an inevitable showdown with that crafty monarch. In the years to come, she was to vacillate on whether or not to put to death her rival, Mary Queen of Scots, who, though held in protective custody after her flight from the angry Scottish lords, became, with her own connivance, the focus of international Catholic plots to overthrow Elizabeth; in the end, the English Privy Council practically took the decision out of Elizabeth's hands. Elizabeth's reign was one of the most glorious in England's long history, and in good part because she kept her country at peace until it was strong enough at home and on the high seas to repel assault.

Throughout her reign, Elizabeth maintained a splendid Court, which was an adornment and an expense, but one expense she was willing to tolerate. An assemblage of about fifteen hundred people, the vast majority men, the Court was a collection of brilliant, colorful personalities who clustered about the greater radiance of their Queen. She commanded the most abject servility, her courtiers bowing and kneeling thrice when passing her vacant seat in the Whitehall chapel, and even her ministers remaining on their knees for hours, if necessary, while in counsel with her. Such obeisance she regarded as her due, even as she delighted in the repartee, now rapier-sharp in its deftness, now stuffy in its fulsome elegance, but always correct when addressed to her, always deferential to her as woman and

Queen. Red-haired and hatchet-faced, Elizabeth could be as profane and obscene as any fishwife, but she tolerated no such display of versatility in those whose duty it was to worship at her shrine. Oaths and slippers, flung in royal rage, elicited only a deeper obeisance to the royal will. The Court was a mirror of her own splendor, and she was at once its despair and its inspiration.

The older Elizabeth grew, the more she adored the subject of love, an interest her favorites played up to in conversation and poetry. It was largely a convention, a remnant gesture from the long-ago age of chivalry, and those who perceive something wanton or abnormal in her addiction to handsome young men forget her loneliness, her extraordinary vanity, and her dread of growing old—common human frailties which usually serve to keep the fashion and entertainment industries thriving. That her favorites were ever more than ardent admirers is doubtful, besides being, at this point in time, unimportant. Apart from the possible exception of Lord High Admiral Thomas Seymour, who died during Mary's reign, Leicester seems to have been the only one who stirred her deeply. Even so, she rejected, on grounds of policy, the idea of marriage to her former playmate, whose domestic life was not above reproach. To Sir Christopher Hatton, who catered to her assiduously, she gave affection only. The same was true of Sir Thomas Heneage. Sir Philip Sidney, the Galahad of his day who was to die a hero's death in the Lowlands, touched her only because he resembled in some respects his uncle as a young man, the Earl of Leicester. The Earl of Essex, whose name was to be linked so closely with hers, was the Indian summer attachment of a spinster old enough to be his grandmother, an attachment in which feelings romantic struggled with feelings maternal. Through all her favorites she renewed her youth, bathed in their flattery, and discovered fresh interests.

But Elizabeth never forgot the Queen in being the woman. Though the common allegation that she distinguished between courtiers and ministers has been exaggerated, she did not confuse physical or even intellectual attraction with administrative ability. Burghley and Walsingham, Nicholas Bacon and Sir Thomas Smith were hardly courtiers to the manner born, but, if she saved her smiles for those who entertained her, she gave her trust to those who wore the harness of her service. Rarely, however, did she let even her ministers dominate her. Relying on their judgment, she made her own decisions, at least those of gravest import. Though sincerely liked by few around her, and liking fewer, standing outside the normal range of friendship by reason of position and perhaps even of personality and intelligence, she cherished no thought and contrived no policy that did not, in her opinion, tend to her country's welfare. Though her policies were not always wise, she generally knew what her people wanted. And her people, who saw her largely from afar, adored her.[7]

Raleigh appeared at Court at a time when Leicester, grown gross in chest and belly, was losing his attraction for Elizabeth. Thirty years old, a man of mature and handsome aspect made more glittering with grey silks and the large pearls he loved, Raleigh impressed both Court and Queen, the former with acute jealousy, the latter with as acute pleasure. Neither could help observing Raleigh's handsome presence, his brilliance in conversation, and his boldness in speech and manner. Aubrey mentioned him as "a tall, handsome, and bold man . . . damnable proud";[8] and one can be sure that the Court, where he soon had scarcely one real friend because of Elizabeth's favor, agreed that he was "damnable." But Raleigh ignored the pack that nipped at him and kept his eyes on the Queen. So long as he could retain her favor he was secure. Anything else mattered not at all. He was now her "Water," as she playfully called him, and "Water" he proposed to remain. Efforts of her old admirers, men like Hatton and Heneage, who, feeling Raleigh's competition, renewed their professions of love in the fall of 1582, Raleigh took in stride. It was a slippery path, this endeavor to retain a capricious woman's favor, with jealous courtiers eager to push him off into disgrace or oblivion, but Raleigh, the most versatile Englishman of his age, was not easily intimidated by persons or circumstances.

The marks of favor presently became evident. The Duke of

[7] *Ibid.*, 177-87, for an excellent analysis of Elizabeth as woman and queen. See also J. A. Froude, *History of England from the Fall of Wolsey to the Defeat of the Spanish Armada*, VII, 12-13; XI, 2-28.

[8] Aubrey, *Brief Lives*, II, 182.

Anjou was en route to Antwerp, where he was to be invested with the sovereignty of Brabant, and Raleigh was appointed a member of the party that saw him over to the Continent—men like Leicester, Lord Hunsdon, Sidney, and Fulke Greville. The Queen herself accompanied the group as far as Canterbury. When the others returned from the investiture, William the Silent, Prince of Orange and great antagonist of Philip II, gave Raleigh dispatches for the Queen and her Council and instructed him to convey to her the Latin message, *Sub umbra alarum tuarum protegimur* ("Under the shadow of thy wings are we protected").

Raleigh, however, became more than a private envoy, honorable as that was. In April 1582, he received a new commission as a captain of infantry in Ireland, but the Queen permitted him to absent himself in view of her need for his services at home. Though Burghley never warmed to him, he consulted Raleigh about Ireland and kept notes of a conference in October 1582 which bear the heading, "The opinion of Mr. Rawley upon the means of subduing the rebel in Munster."[9] Raleigh seems also to have submitted reports on the condition of the fortifications at Portsmouth, and sat on a commission with Sir Thomas Heneage to investigate a complaint against the lord mayor.

Obviously his advice, his cleverness, and his handsome presence, particularly the last, convinced the Queen that something more tangible should be done for him. The Crown had at its disposal, as a part of its prerogative, numerous offices, landholdings, monopolies, and other perquisites which the sovereign might dispense as she saw fit. In 1583, Elizabeth gave Raleigh a lease of part of Durham House in the Strand for his use, a residence of which Aubrey said, "I well remember his study, which was a little turret that looked into and over the Thames, and had the prospect which is pleasant perhaps as any in the world."[10] To maintain such an establishment was hardly an exercise in economy, so, in April of the same year, when the Queen acquired the lease of two estates from All Souls College, Oxford, she granted them to Raleigh.[11] In May, she also be-

---

[9] For Raleigh's commission, see *Cal. S.P. Ireland, 1574-1585*, 358; for the Burghley conference, see *ibid.*, 406.
[10] Aubrey, *Brief Lives*, II, 183.     [11] *Egerton Papers*, 94.

stowed on him the patent for wines, by which he acquired the right to one half of the fines imposed for infringement and an annual fee of £1 from every vintner for a license to sell his wines. Raleigh leased the patent to one Richard Browne for seven years at £700 per annum. An industrious man, Browne made so much money that Raleigh demanded an increase in the lease rate. When Browne refused, Raleigh managed to have his own patent revoked, then reissued for thirty-one years. His profits soon moved up to £1,200 annually, though he became involved in extensive litigation owing to the fact that his license conflicted in some places with established private interests. This type of patent created a kind of industrial feudalism and was bitterly resented.[12]

But this was not all of Raleigh's good fortune. In March 1584, he received a license to export woolen broadcloth, a license that was renewed for several years and increased in specification until Burghley protested that conditions were altogether too favorable for Raleigh. This license, like his wine license, was unpopular for it collided with vested merchant and shipping interests, and Raleigh's agents were so remorseless in enforcing the rights of his patent that in 1586 the Merchant Adventurers of Exeter succeeded in obtaining an investigation into the probity of the agents. The cloth license proved very profitable for Raleigh, netting him within a year of issue £3,500 in currency of that day. In view of the return from both the wine and woolen licenses, it is scarcely to be wondered that hatred and jealousy of him increased throughout England.[13]

Raleigh's rise was steady during most of that decade. Evidently in the early part of 1584—no one knows exactly when—he was raised to the knighthood. As "Sir Walter," he was appointed Lord Warden of the Stannaries upon the death of the incumbent, the Earl of Bedford.[14] The Lord Warden was

---

[12] For the wine patent given on May 4, 1583, see *Patent Roll*, 25 Elizabeth, pt. ix, and, for the reissue on Aug. 9, 1588, *ibid.*, 30 Elizabeth, pt. vi; see also W. H. Price, *The English Patents of Monopoly*, 146. The trouble with Browne and other private interests is related in Edwards, *Ralegh*, I, 63-66; II, 24-25, 26-29.

[13] Edwards, *Ralegh*, I, 62-63; Stebbing, *Ralegh*, 37; *Cal. S.P. Domestic* (hereafter *Dom.*), *1581-1590*, 641. The patent system is ably discussed by E. Lipson, *The Economic History of England*, III, 352-86.

[14] *Cal. S.P. Dom.*, *1581-1590*, 293.

responsible for regulating mining privileges in Devon and Cornwall, for holding the Stannary Parliament of miners on wild Crockern Tor above Dartmoor, and for adjudicating customs disputes. Hated as Raleigh was by the Court and by many business people, he was not only respected but beloved in the two western counties. Though the wardenship made him their superior, the miners saw in him no supercilious courtier speaking the elegant language of the Court, but a compatriot, who rendered sound judgments, who made their concerns his, and who spoke throughout his life in the broad accent of their neighborhood. Subsequent appointments as Lieutenant of Cornwall and Vice Admiral of the West, particularly the latter, made it possible for him to deal in privateering, which helped to defray his ever-increasing expenses, and to distribute a limited amount of patronage, which earned him both loyalty and friendship from those favored. He was so well thought of that he was elected a member of the Parliament of 1584, in which he and Sir William Courtenay represented Devon in the Commons.

Raleigh made a lot of money during his career and lost much of it, largely on colonizing projects. While America claimed most of his colonizing interest, Ireland accounted for some of it as well as for his losses. In 1586, he received another of those amazing rewards of Elizabeth's favor. The Desmonds of Munster had been pretty thoroughly subdued by that time and their lands confiscated. Their property, however, was practically a wasteland, and the government proposed to repopulate it by dividing it among Englishmen who should settle colonies of English people there. Raleigh and two men associated with him, Sir John Stowell and Sir John Clyston, acquired control of three and one half seigniories, each seigniory consisting of 12,000 acres. These were located along the Blackwater, mainly in Waterford and Cork. In addition, Raleigh acquired properties in Youghal and the rent of Lismore Castle from the Bishop of Lismore. On his lands Raleigh settled families from Devon and Cornwall, but the good relations he had enjoyed with people of these counties in England broke down when they became his tenants in an alien land. Though the acquisition of so much property appeared a reasonably reliable investment, in reality the reverse was nearer the truth. Raleigh employed the best methods of cultivation known at the time, but poor management by his stewards, governmental prohibition on the export of wood, trouble with his tenants over rents, and the dishonesty of his partners wrecked his chances of making a solid profit.[15]

If his investments in Irish lands came to an unhappy end, he acquired, in 1587, property in England that helped compensate for his losses. The year before, Anthony Babington of Derbyshire, formerly a page to Mary Queen of Scots, had conspired with fellow Catholics to assassinate Elizabeth and deliver Mary. The plot, as well as Mary's endorsement of it, was discovered by Walsingham, and Babington was executed in 1586. While his fate remained uncertain, Babington offered Raleigh, through intermediaries, £1,000 for his life, obviously considering Raleigh the logical person to intercede for him. Raleigh seems to have ignored the offer, but, even had he accepted it, contemporaries would have thought little of it since traffic in pardons was considered a legitimate business. Perhaps it was well for Raleigh that he did not try to help Babington, for, when that rash man had gone to his doom, the Crown, in 1587, granted Raleigh most of his landed property in the three counties of Lincoln, Nottingham, and Derby.[16] Raleigh was now a very wealthy man. He was not only enriched and knighted by reason of the Queen's fondness for him, he was also raised to a position where he was made responsible for her personal safety. The same year in which he acquired the Babington properties, Elizabeth appointed him Captain of the Guard, Sir Christopher Hatton, who had held the office, being raised to Lord Chancellor. The Captaincy of the Guard carried no salary but merely the issuance of a uniform consisting, according to the warrant, of "six yards of tawney medley at thirteen shillings and fourpence a yard; with a fur of black budge, rated at ten pounds."[17] In this orange-colored uniform while on duty, or in his brilliant silks and pearls when off duty, Raleigh was ever near the Queen. He had come up the ladder of her favor faster than either Leicester or Hatton, and he cherished hopes of climbing higher. As Captain of the

---

[15] *Cal. S.P. Ireland, 1586-1588*, 77, 78, 88, 168, 216; D. B. Quinn, *Raleigh and the British Empire*, 129-61.

[16] For grant, see *Additional MSS* (British Museum), 6,697, ff. 227, verso 235.

[17] Warrant Book, in *ibid.*, 5,750, ff. 114-15.

Guard, he was more courtier than soldier, and not a minister at all. Beyond his reach as yet lay the Privy Council and service as a statesman, in which his value might be measured by something other than his wit or the Queen's caprice. Might not this ultimate recognition of ability also be his? Raleigh certainly thought so, and with every visible justification.

# CHAPTER 4

# Virginia

RALEIGH, reported a seventeenth-century writer, slept but five hours of the twenty-four, gave four to reading, two to conversation, and the rest to business and whatever else was necessary.[1] How much of the daily time allocated to business was taken up during the 1580's with his projects for colonizing Virginia is impossible to determine, but it must have been considerable, especially when one considers the amount of money he invested in these enterprises. Colonization of the New World was like a fever in his blood which he could never shake off. Now it was Virginia, later it was Guiana, and in both his plans were doomed to failure. If Fortune at first smiled invitingly, then slammed the door in his face, he never lost hope that, one day, she would be less unkind. A man who could scarcely be accused of being a Pollyanna, Raleigh was grimly trustful and resolute that, in the end, he would succeed in establishing a permanent colony across the Western Ocean.

Initially he worked with his half-brother, Sir Humphrey Gilbert, in the latter's ventures. Gilbert had a patent of exploration and colonization that ran from 1578 to 1584.[2] Owing to his involvement in the Irish campaign, Gilbert had attempted little after the failure of the 1579 expedition with which Raleigh had been associated. If he was to try again, he must do so before the patent expired; it was questionable whether Elizabeth would issue him another, for she liked him at Court and thought him an unlucky man at sea. Interestingly enough, Gilbert's aims differed in part from that of his fellow explorers. Since the time of John and Sebastian Cabot, English captains had sought a northwest passage to Cathay and hoped to discover gold en route. Gilbert, in his *Discourse*, urged the dispatch of an expedition and in 1576 Martin Frobisher thought he had found such

[1] D. Floyd, *Observations on Statesmen and Favorites of England since the Reformation*, 489.

[2] R. Hakluyt, *The Principal Navigations, Voyages, Traffiques and Discoveries of the English Nation*, VIII, 17-23.

a passage when he entered Hudson Bay. Ore that he brought back was presumed to have gold in it and, before 1578 was gone, Frobisher, sponsored by a quickly formed Company of Cathay, made two more voyages for ore which assays eventually revealed to be worthless. Meanwhile, Sir Francis Walsingham, who developed a lively interest in a northwest passage, sent the renowned Portuguese pilot, Simon Fernandez, to America.[3] Fernandez returned with accounts that quickened men's imagination, as did voyages by two other English captains.

Gilbert, however, had another idea in addition to exploration, namely colonization. No doubt with Walsingham's approval, Gilbert made an agreement with two prominent spokesmen of the Catholics, Sir George Peckham and Sir Thomas Gerrard, to establish a Catholic colony in the New World.[4] In this way England might be saved from troubles with her own Catholics, while these same people would remain loyal subjects overseas. But as the plan began to formulate, the Spaniards took alarm. The Spanish ambassador, Bernardino de Mendoza, wrote anxiously to Philip of the agreement of July 1582 between Gilbert and the Catholics, and told of how he had tried to discourage the English Catholics from accepting. But by December 1582 a company was organized to develop the proposed colony, and Raleigh not only bought shares but built a ship of novel design, the *Bark-Raleigh* of 200 tons, to accompany the expedition.[5]

By winter of 1583, Gilbert and Raleigh, who was Gilbert's vice admiral, were restless to be off. Then the Queen intervened and forbade either to leave. Gilbert must have been crestfallen, for he had staked everything he possessed on this voyage. His importunities, as well as Raleigh's in his behalf, finally won a reluctant assent from the Queen, though her prohibition on Raleigh's going still held. In a gracefully worded letter on March 17, 1583, Raleigh informed his half-brother of Elizabeth's change of mind:

[3] C. Read, *Mr. Secretary Walsingham and the Policy of Queen Elizabeth*, III, 399 n. 5.
[4] *Ibid.*, 400-02.
[5] *Cal. S.P. Spanish, 1580-1586*, 384-85; Quinn, *Voyages and Colonizing Enterprises of Gilbert*, I, 76-81.

Brother,

I have sent you a token from Her Majesty, an anchor guided by a lady, as you see; and farther, Her Highness willed me to send you word that she wished you great good-hap, and safety to your ship, as if herself were there in person; desiring you to have care of yourself, as of that which she tendereth; and therefore, for her sake, you must provide for it accordingly.

Further, she commandeth that you leave your picture with me. For the rest, I leave till our meeting, or to the report of this bearer, who would needs be the messenger of this good news. So I commit you to the will and protection of God, Who send us such life or death, as He shall please, or hath appointed.

Richmond, this Friday morning.

Your true brother,<br>W. Raleigh[6]

Not until June 11 was the expedition of four ships able to put to sea. Almost at once it encountered the bad luck that dogged it throughout. After a night of great storm, the *Bark-Raleigh*, two days out, deserted the fleet and returned to England. Though the captain alleged sickness aboard as the reason for his flight, Gilbert was not convinced and hoped Raleigh would make an example of the "knaves" responsible. Reaching Newfoundland, Gilbert annexed it in the name of the Queen, then went exploring with his ships. In a dense fog, the *Delight*, second largest to the *Bark-Raleigh*, ran onto a sand bar, the seas rose, and more than one hundred men aboard the stricken vessel perished. Storms now chased the *Golden Hind*, forty tons, and the *Squirrel*, ten tons, back to Newfoundland. Still resolute, Gilbert explored the coast until lack of food, incessant storms, and heavy fogs impelled him at last to listen to the clamors of his men and start back for England by way of the Azores.

Even now, winds and mountainous seas harried the two tiny craft. Earlier, in order to encourage his men, Gilbert had deliberately chosen to make his flagship the frail *Squirrel*. When fears grew that the *Squirrel* might not make a safe harbor and

---

[6] Edwards, *Ralegh* (*Letters*), II, 19.

the men aboard the *Golden Hind* begged him to come aboard their larger craft, Gilbert refused, explaining that he would not desert the crew of the *Squirrel* with whom he had gone through so many perils. Later, when the two ships drew close on the afternoon of September 9, those aboard the *Golden Hind* saw Gilbert sitting in the stern of the *Squirrel* with a book in his hand. To calm the men of both ships, he called out, "We are as near to heaven by sea as by land." Then, hurried by the relentless wind, the *Squirrel* whirled into the lead. About midnight, the seas still turbulent, the men of the *Golden Hind* saw the lights of the *Squirrel* suddenly wink out. A heroic death for brave Sir Humphrey Gilbert—truly, as the Queen had said, a man of "no good hap at sea."[7]

Gilbert's death, though a cause of real grief to Raleigh, served to inspire him to greater efforts. He helped Adrian and John Gilbert in their unwearying search for the northwest passage. More important, on March 25, 1584 he acquired a charter that gave to him and his heirs the powers and privileges that Gilbert had possessed under his charter of 1578: in brief, "free liberty to discover barbarous countries, not actually possessed of any Christian prince and inhabited by Christian people, to occupy and enjoy the same for ever."[8] This was a significant moment in the history of both England and America. In the first place, though Raleigh had no idea how expensive colonization would be and though he lacked the means to see it through, the great English imperialist movement had begun. The New World was to be exploited for itself, and, a colony there being an extension of England, such a settlement stood as a counterpoise to the burgeoning Spanish Empire. Secondly, unlike contemporary colonists of other countries, the English colonists were to live as much under the protection of the Common Law as did their brethren at home. Gilbert's charter had contained a similar provision, but Raleigh's colonization projects, although ultimately unsuccessful, were the first in which the Common Law provision had real significance; after all, Raleigh was the first

---

[7] The contemporary report of Gilbert's last voyage is given by Hakluyt, *Voyages*, VIII, 34-77. The best work on Gilbert is Quinn's *Voyages and Colonizing Enterprises of Gilbert*. For what he accomplished, see Peckham's report in Quinn, *ibid.*, II, 435-82.

[8] Raleigh's charter is in Hakluyt, *Voyages*, VIII, 289-96, and D. B. Quinn, *The Roanoke Voyages*, I, 82.

to plant an English colony in the New World. Years later, undoubtedly drawing on his experience, the men responsible for founding the Jamestown settlement in Virginia insisted on the incorporation of essentially the same provision in their charter.

England had done little to develop the discoveries of John and Sebastian Cabot; in the meantime, the French had explored the St. Lawrence Valley and the Spanish had established themselves in Florida. At last alert to the possibilities of the New World, English explorers moved in three directions. Early explorers, including Gilbert, were chiefly interested in what is now the New England-Nova Scotia-Newfoundland area. Raleigh's interest at this time was mainly in the great coastal bow from Chesapeake Bay to Florida, and he invested heavily in three voyages made here in 1584, 1585, and 1587. Lastly, English explorers moved toward the unoccupied stretch of South American coast from the Orinoco to the Amazon delta. This last area, known as Guiana, was presumed to contain an infinite quantity of gold and silver rivaling the magnificent Spanish resources in Mexico and Peru. His North American ventures failing, Raleigh developed a lively interest in this area in 1595 and in the last tragic years of his life. The New World drew him irresistibly.[9]

In April 1584 he sent out two ships commanded by Philip Amadas, who came of a Plymouth family related to John Hawkins, and Arthur Barlow, who had been with Raleigh in Ireland. Accompanying the exploratory expedition was the famous pilot, Simon Fernandez. The ships sailed by way of the West Indies, the great buccaneering route and, after watering and provisioning in the Indies, reached what is now the Carolina coast in July. On the 13th, the men landed on the island of Wokoken and took possession of it for Raleigh in the Queen's name. Barlow described this land as "very sandy and low towards the water's side, but so full of grapes, as the very beating and surge of the sea overflowed them, of which we found such plenty, as well there as in all places else, both on the sand and on the green soil on the hills, as in the plains, as well on

---

[9] For competent analyses of English exploration, see C. M. Andrews, *The Colonial Period of American History*, I, 19-26; Quinn, *Raleigh and the British Empire*, 12-51; W. F. Craven, *The Southern Colonies in the Seventeenth Century, 1607-1689*, 27-39.

every little shrub, as also climbing towards the tops of high cedars, that I think in all the world the like abundance is not to be found."[10]

Contact with the inhabitants occurred on the third day when a curious Indian, venturing onto a sand bar near the ships, was given food, clothes, and trinkets in exchange for a canoe-load of fish. Word of the great ships quickly spread among the Indians, who eagerly traded skins and furs for kitchen utensils and weapons. From the Indians the English learned that their chief was named Wingina and the whole area Wingandacoa. Later the Indians entertained the visitors at a little village on Roanoke Island. Though the English failed to find a good harbor, they were pleased with the country and with the friendliness of the Indians, of whom two, Manteo and Wanchese, returned with them to England.

In the meantime, Raleigh had not been idly waiting for the reports of Amadas and Barlow. Soon after the two captains had sailed for America, Raleigh summoned from Paris Richard Hakluyt, who was about his own age. Besides being chaplain to the English embassy, Hakluyt, who had studied at Christ Church, Oxford, was a passionate and profound geographer and one of the greatest collectors of voyage accounts and maritime journals that ever lived. Actually there were two Richard Hakluyts, cousins, both geographers and men deeply interested in the commercial and colonial expansion of England. The younger was the chaplain, while the elder was a lawyer who had studied at the Middle Temple, who had often advised Frobisher and Gilbert, and who was to work almost as closely with Raleigh as his younger cousin. For the moment, however, it was the younger Hakluyt on whom Raleigh called for assistance. In London by July, Hakluyt spent long hours with Raleigh and wrote his *Discourse of Western Planting*, which was frankly designed to persuade the Queen that the state, rather than individuals, should assume the responsibility for developing colonies in the New World.[11]

Raleigh and the Hakluyts shared so many of their ideas on

[10] Hakluyt, *Voyages*, VIII, 298.
[11] For the Hakluyts, see G. B. Parks, *Richard Hakluyt and the English Voyages* and E. G. R. Taylor, *The Original Writings and Correspondence of the Two Richard Hakluyts*.

colonization that it is difficult to be sure where Raleigh's leave off and the Hakluyts' begin. It is reasonably safe to assume that in this propaganda pamphlet Hakluyt's ideas fairly represent those Raleigh held at this time. Basing England's prior claim on the Cabots' work, Hakluyt argued that it was England's duty to bring the glories of civilization and Christianity to North America. Strategically, English settlements would be of great value as bases of operation against Spanish and Portuguese fishing fleets on the Newfoundland banks and especially against the treasure fleets of Spain in the West Indies. By hitting at Spain in the New World and at the source of her wealth, the English could overthrow her empire and relieve England and Europe of Spanish intimidation. Furthermore, England would acquire from her settlements products which she could not herself produce and which she had at present to import from the Continent; her trade could thus be free from many tariffs and taxes. In addition, the colonists and Indians would furnish a lively market for manufactured commodities. This was good mercantilist reasoning, and the pamphlet followed through by listing the kind of emigrants most useful to both England and the colonies. The list included carpenters, millwrights, builders, gardeners, craftsmen. But the list does not end here. Penniless vagrants, debtors languishing in prison, unemployed soldiers, and Puritan clergymen were also mentioned as desirable colonists since their dispatch overseas would relieve the home country of the burden of unemployment and a source of social disorder. The *Discourse* was a model of close reasoning, persuasive eloquence, and enlightened thinking for its day.[12]

But neither the literary feats of Hakluyt and Raleigh nor the glowing reports of Amadas and Barlow could induce the Queen to throw the resources of the nation behind the colonization project. True, she graciously accepted the name Raleigh suggested for the new territory, "Virginia," which was a tribute to her spinsterhood and, at the same time, resembled the name of the Indian ruler. She also furnished Raleigh a ship for the expedition he was preparing and possibly subscribed in a small way to the funds being raised. More than this she would not do. Perhaps, however, the lands, patents, and honors she gave him

---

[12] It is printed in Taylor, *The Original Writings* . . . , II, 211-326.

were her way not only of rewarding him as a favorite courtier but of supporting his colonization schemes as well.

Throughout the fall and winter of 1584-1585, Raleigh busied himself with the project. In the event that the government would not give financial assistance, he had the elder Hakluyt draw up a program by which the land could be cultivated on so profitable a basis that the colony would not require aid.[13] Raleigh inscribed the title "Lord and Governor of Virginia" on his seal, and had a bill introduced into the House of Commons confirming the title. Though the bill passed the House, it seems to have died in the Lords. The Commons attached certain restrictions to his freedom of action. They forbade his taking along imprisoned debtors, wives, wards, and apprentices. In their prohibition of wives, they prevented the establishment of a true colony.[14]

Meanwhile the Spanish ambassador, who, though expelled for political activities, kept in touch from Paris with developments in England, wrote Madrid that Raleigh was fitting out "no fewer than 16 vessels, in which he intended to convey 400 men. The Queen has assured him that if he do not sail himself she will defray all the costs of the preparations."[15] Also from Paris, Hakluyt, in a letter to Walsingham, confirmed that plans for Raleigh's colony as well as for one of Sir Francis Drake's buccaneering raids "doth much vex the Spaniard."[16]

On April 9, two days after Hakluyt wrote, Raleigh's expedition sailed from Plymouth. If Raleigh originally intended, or even hoped, to lead it, he never had a chance; the Queen saw that her favorite courtier remained at home, and Mendoza grossly exaggerated when he reported to his king that Elizabeth agreed, in return, to assume the expenses of the preparations. In Raleigh's stead went his cousin, Sir Richard Grenville, who had served on the committee for Raleigh's bill and knew of his plans.[17] Grenville sailed with ten, not sixteen, ships as the Spaniards had feared. With him went a distinguished company,

---

[13] See *ibid.*, 327-38.

[14] *Cal. S.P. Colonial, America and West Indies, 1675-1676, Addenda 1574-1674*, 26.

[15] *Cal. S.P. Spanish, 1580-1586*, 532.

[16] *Cal. S.P. Colonial, America and West Indies, 1675-1676, Addenda 1574-1674*, 27.

[17] A. L. Rowse, *Sir Richard Grenville*, 203.

including Ralph Lane, one of the Queen's equerries, a veteran of the Irish service, and the governor of the colony; Philip Amadas; John Arundel, Grenville's half-brother; John Stukely, Grenville's brother-in-law; Thomas Cavendish, soon to become one of England's great navigators; Thomas Hariot, destined to be the outstanding English scientist and mathematician of his day, whom Raleigh had attached to his staff as early as 1580 when Hariot was fresh out of St. Mary's Hall, Oxford; and John White, a skillful painter as well as cartographer.

Grenville, a proud, stern man, was as aware as Raleigh that the chief way in which the investors in an expedition could be paid off was by looting Spanish ships. He set his course for Virginia by way of the West Indies. Before he reached the North American continent, he seized two Spanish vessels, freed a number of well-fixed passengers for substantial ransoms, and, at San Domingo, sold part of the captured cargoes for supplies he needed. Then he sailed for the Florida coast, sighting it on June 20, and reached the Cape Fear area a few days later. Here, on June 29, ones of the vessels, the *Tyger*, nearly capsized when she struck bottom in an attempt to slip through the great sand bar along the Carolina coast. Large quantities of wheat and other provisions were spoiled when water burst through the ship. For the near-wreck of the *Tyger* Grenville blamed Fernandez, the Portuguese pilot.

Soon after reaching Wokoken Island, their original objective, the English informed Chief Wingina on Roanoke Island of their arrival. A party of the leaders then went exploring in a pinnace. Invariably the Indians received them with open-handed hospitality, and they responded with a wary kindness. The harmony, however, was spoiled when the English, noticing a silver cup stolen, burned a town in retaliation for the theft. Such treatment of the Indians became typical, and the savages began, in consequence, to feel the animosity which eventually helped ruin Raleigh's colonies.

With houses under construction on Wokoken, Grenville sailed for England on August 25, leaving Lane and 107 settlers behind and assuring them of his return before Easter. Six days later, near the Bermudas, he captured the *Santa Maria*, a Spanish ship with a quantity of gold, silver, and pearls worth 40,000 ducats, and a cargo of cochineal, sugar, ivory, and hides worth 120,000 ducats; the total, in values of our day, amounted to more than $1,500,000. Sending half the Spaniards aboard the *Tyger*, Grenville shifted his flag to the *Santa Maria*. He brought the sluggish Don into Plymouth on October 18, nearly a fortnight after the rest of the fleet reached Falmouth and but a month after Drake left on the great raid to the West Indies that practically spelled an end to the cold war that had gone on for so many years.[18] Feeling more confident of England now, and disturbed at Spanish war preparations, Elizabeth was not averse to giving Philip II an exhibition of England's strength.

Raleigh was visiting in Plymouth when Grenville arrived, no doubt having hurried down from London on learning that the *Tyger* was standing off the coast. In the wrangling over the division of the spoils his decision was necessary. Naturally the Queen came in for her share, and Sir Lewis Stukely, John Stukely's son and the man who was later to become Raleigh's Judas Iscariot, said that Raleigh bemoaned the Queen's lifting a rich string of pearls without so much as giving him one. Elizabeth was capable of doing this, but Raleigh would have been far more rash than he really was to have made such a complaint in public. As it was, Grenville's capture of the *Santa Maria* enabled Raleigh to pay off the investors, to replenish his own depleted funds, and to purchase supplies and equip a ship to send out to Lane.

Meanwhile Lane and most of his colonists in Port Ferdinando, as they called their settlement, were finding Virginia anything but a Promised Land. The difficulty lay mainly in the shortage of provisions. The colonists had arrived too late to clear and plant the land, and quantities of the provisions and seed they had brought from England had been ruined when the *Tyger* went aground. Though Grenville had spared what supplies he could, Lane was worried about the future of the colony from the time Grenville had left—he hoped that, in event of dire necessity, God would instruct even the ravens to feed them.[19] For-

[18] The tale of the capture may be found in *ibid.*, 216-20; *Cal. S.P. Colonial, 1574-1660*, 4; Hakluyt, *Voyages*, VIII, 317.

[19] *Cal. S.P. Colonial America and West Indies, 1574-1660*, 3.

tunately the Indians remained friendly until the spring of 1586, not only keeping the colonists supplied with maize but showing them how to plant it after the winter had gone. Fortunately, too, Lane was a disciplinarian and kept strict control of his men.

Finally the Indians turned menacing as the English demands for food increased. Informed by a friendly savage of the Indians' plan to wipe out the colony, Lane attacked first, killing several of them in a brisk skirmish on June 1, 1586. Although this action thoroughly intimidated the Indians, the English thereafter kept reasonably close to the confines of their settlement and anxiously scanned the horizon for Raleigh's relief ship. Such a ship was on the way, though it had not sailed from England until after Easter. Raleigh also sent out Grenville with the *Tyger* and two other vessels, but, since one of the latter ran aground while leaving the harbor, the spring season was well advanced before the little squadron put to sea.

In the end, the destiny of Raleigh's colony was determined neither by him nor by the Indians. On June 8, a lookout on Croatoan Island sighted a fleet of sails. These proved to be Drake's squadron up from its raid through the West Indies and its destruction of St. Augustine in Florida. Drake offered Lane supplies, men, and a ship, the *Francis*. A number of Lane's own men were actually on board the *Francis* to take possession when a violent storm sent all ships to sea. Later, while other ships put back to the anchorage off Port Ferdinando, the *Francis* headed for England, her crew determined not to spend any more time in America. At a hurried conference, Drake offered Lane another ship but by this time the colonists entreated their leaders to take them all back to England. Lane finally consented, and Drake offered them passage. The colonists and Drake's sailors then evacuated the settlement on June 18 or 19 with a haste barely short of panic, leaving valuable equipment behind, as well as two of their number who were exploring the interior.

Hardly had Drake left when Raleigh's relief ship arrived. After spending some time searching for the colonists, she headed back to England. About a fortnight following her departure, Grenville also appeared with his squadron. As mystified as those on the relief ship by the colony's disappearance, he left fifteen men on Roanoke Island—a rash half-measure—with stores for two years, then returned home. He sailed by way of the Azores, and the spoil he acquired helped compensate for the failure of the colony.

For certainly the colony had failed, and Raleigh's efforts had been almost wasted. The waste was not complete, for Raleigh realized that, to succeed, a colony must be a true colony. These colonists of 1585-1586, who had included so many former soldiers, were paid regular wages and were fed from a commissariat. It was more a military venture than a true colony, with Lane more interested in its military than in its agricultural and commercial value. Lane hungered for a gold mine or a passage to the South Sea. Hariot, who was impressed with the value of tobacco and potatoes, disagreed. He thought that, with the cultivation of native and West Indian plants and the raising of cattle and swine, the colony could be made profitable.[20]

Raleigh agreed with Hariot, whose ideas were shared by the Hakluyts. Any new colony, Raleigh resolved, must have a different economic basis—agriculture, not the ephemeral hope of discovering gold. It must have a different composition—trained farmers who truly wanted to make permanent homes in Virginia. All this, however, would cost money, with no chance of a speedy return on his investment. Though he sighed at the drain on his resources, Raleigh continued to persevere in his dream. He would yet plant an English settlement in the New World that would endure against hazards from Philip's admirals, the craft of the savages, and the dreadful loneliness of a wilderness land.

[20] The three main contemporary records of this attempt at settlement are Lane's "An Account of the Particularities of the Employments of the Englishmen left in Virginia, etc.," in Hakluyt, *Voyages*, VIII, 320-45; Hariot's "A Brief and True Report of the New Found Land of Virginia," in *ibid.*, VIII, 348-86—the "Report" being a publication so perfectly printed that the quarto edition of 1588 has become a well-nigh priceless collector's item; and the magnificent collection of paintings by John White now in the British Museum. The accounts by Lane and Hariot, an annotated list of White's drawings, and many valuable documents pertaining to Raleigh's Virginia ventures at this time may be found in the superb compilation by Quinn, *The Roanoke Voyages*, I and II. Good secondary accounts may be found in Craven, *Southern Colonies in the Seventeenth Century*, 49-52; J. A. Williamson, *The Age of Drake*, 240-47; and especially Quinn, *Raleigh and the British Empire*, 65-106.

# CHAPTER 5

# Shadows of the Future

DURING the years 1586 to 1588 a number of events occurred that cast long shadows across Raleigh's life. One was the development of an alleged link with Spain growing out of his capture of Don Pedro Sarmiento de Gamboa, Governor of the Straits of Magellan. Another was his popularization of the use of tobacco. The third was the appearance of a young and handsome rival for the Queen's favor, the Earl of Essex. The fourth was the fateful Virginia expedition that was to end so mysteriously. Of the four, the first cast by far the longest shadow, though the faintest at the time.

The long undeclared war with Spain furnished Elizabethan gentlemen with an unparalleled opportunity to enrich themselves by preying on Spanish and Portuguese commerce, even on that of France until Henry of Navarre, leader of the Huguenots, was accepted as Henry IV, the legitimate king. This privateering was not only good business, it was also patriotic, and few men were more inspired by these two motives than Raleigh. With the Queen's issuance of many letters of marque following Philip's embargo on English ships in Spain's Atlantic ports, Raleigh sent privateers to sea. Within a few days of his hurrying Grenville off to Virginia on the vain relief mission, he dispatched two swift pinnaces, the *Mary Spark* and the *Serpent*, on a raid to the Azores. The prize-taking and Spanish-taunting career of these cockleshells, the first of only fifty tons, the second of thirty-five, was nothing short of spectacular, and among the prisoners taken and held for ransom, in the custom of the day, was Sarmiento.[1]

Brought to England, Sarmiento was met by Raleigh at Plymouth and entertained with all courtesy. The Queen and Burghley were delighted with Raleigh's prisoner since Sarmiento could be useful to them. Although many of their lieutenants had been eager for years to bring the issue between

---

[1] An account of the voyage of the pinnaces is in Hakluyt, *Voyages*, VI, 434-37.

England and Spain to one of open warfare, both Elizabeth and Philip tried to the last to find a less hazardous and expensive solution. Elizabeth wondered now if Philip could be dissuaded from continuing his embargo on English shipping perhaps in return for a curb on English privateering. She and Burghley held conversations with Sarmiento; so did Raleigh. The result was that Sarmiento was freed without ransom payment to convey to his royal master the wishes of the English government. Raleigh clearly lost money on the arrangement.

On the other hand, Raleigh may have been looking for reward in other ways. He was an attentive host to Sarmiento in England and his Good Samaritan abroad. On his way back through France to Spain, Sarmiento was captured by Huguenots. Although Elizabeth and Philip were annoyed that the Spaniard, now in the role of diplomatic agent, should have been taken, it remained for Raleigh to secure his release. Notified of the capture by Mendoza, the Spanish ambassador to England now residing in Paris, Raleigh sent over two of his staff, who successfully entreated Henry of Navarre, in Elizabeth's name, to release Sarmiento.

Reports by both Sarmiento and Mendoza indicate that Raleigh was looking to Spain for profit. Sarmiento described Raleigh as considering it wise to offer his services to Philip since the Queen's favor could not last for long. "If," added Sarmiento, through Mendoza, "he would really look after Your Majesty's interests in that country [England], apart from the direct reward he would receive, Your Majesty's support, when occasion arose, might prevent him from falling." What Raleigh was ready to do, according to Sarmiento, was to sell to Spain at least one of his fighting ships for 5,000 crowns, and perhaps two ships as well, and to thwart English efforts to establish Don Antonio on the throne of Portugal.[2] The Portuguese Pretender had gained support from Walsingham, Leicester, and Lord Admiral Howard. The Queen oscillated between, on the one hand, continuing her current policy of trying to keep the peace, and, on the other, turning Drake and others loose to assist Don Antonio and to scourge Spanish shipping. Perhaps her indecision was aided by Raleigh's opposition to the expedi-

[2] *Cal. S.P. Spanish, 1587-1603*, 2.

tions; Mendoza reported that Raleigh was "very cold" to them, and was "secretly trying to dissuade the Queen from them."[3] Perhaps, too, the fact that Drake found it difficult to obtain seamen because of wholesale desertions can also be laid to Raleigh's opposition to the expeditions, though Drake in a complaining letter to the government named no one.[4]

On the face of it, Raleigh's conduct seems questionable, but this is probably seeing only the obvious. Raleigh, who had acknowledged to Leicester only the year before that he had "consumed the best part of my fortune, hating the tyrannical prosperity" of Spain,[5] was no traitor, certainly not in the conventional sense. Prominent Elizabethan gentlemen maintained their own intelligence agents abroad, their own important "contacts." Raleigh kept his lines open to France as well as to Spain, and even to Denmark. If these connections could bring him profit, excellent. In any event, they brought him intelligence, and this might be of great value not only to himself but to England; his intercession with Henry of Navarre in Sarmiento's behalf is a case in point. Indeed it is possible that the Queen and Burghley knew of all his transactions with Sarmiento and approved of his being considered an ally by Philip, for in this way the latter might disclose useful information.

Philip, himself, was wary about the sudden friendliness of this man who was acquiring a status in Spanish hatred second only to Drake. To Mendoza, Philip wrote: ". . . as for his sending for sale at Lisbon the two ships he mentions, that is out of the question; in the first place, to avoid his being looked upon with suspicion in his own country, in consequence of his being well treated whilst all his countrymen are persecuted; and secondly, to guard ourselves against the coming of the ships under this pretext being a feint or trick upon us—which is far from improbable."[6]

Philip seems to have read his man well on this score; at any rate, he was not taken in like Sarmiento and Mendoza. Raleigh was undoubtedly endeavoring to ingratiate himself with Philip for reasons of patriotism and personal gain. In this second

[3] *Ibid.*, 24.     [4] Read, *Walsingham*, III, 231 n. 4.
[5] *Correspondence of Robert Dudley, Earl of Leycester*, 193.
[6] *Cal. S.P. Spanish, 1587-1603*, 56.

course, he was but following the example of that scourge of the Spaniards, Sir John Hawkins. The latter had told Philip that he had served Elizabeth long enough, that he would be a partner to Spanish efforts to get rid of her, and that he would welcome Philip's trust. Accepted as a valuable Spanish connection in England, he received good Spanish gold for his employment, and, at the same time, kept the English government informed of intelligence he received. What Hawkins did, Raleigh could also do. It is almost as ridiculous to suppose that Raleigh had become Philip's tool as to believe Mendoza's report of September 1586 that Raleigh was a partner to the plot to assassinate the Queen.[7] That Raleigh knew of Babington's design is likely, but so did others, particularly Walsingham, and Raleigh may have learned about it from him or from the Queen herself. Babington's plea to Raleigh to secure a pardon for him presumably originated not simply because of Raleigh's favor with the Queen but also because of Babington's awareness of Spanish hopes of making a friend of Raleigh. Neither such hopes nor English accusations of a Spanish connection were to end here; the charge of treason was to be thoroughly exploited with tragic effects in 1603 and 1618. By an odd quirk, the individual most responsible for Raleigh's ultimate downfall was another Sarmiento, the Spanish ambassador to England during the middle years of the reign of James I.

Even as privateering and the Sarmientos figured prominently in Raleigh's life, so in a lesser way did tobacco. Since its introduction into Europe, tobacco had claimed devoted adherents and fanatical enemies. Though Raleigh is sometimes considered its European sponsor, the Spaniards actually introduced the leaf from America, and the drug nicotine was named after the French ambassador at Madrid, Jean Nicot, who sent samples of tobacco to Catherine de Medici in Paris. This formidable contemporary of Elizabeth professed to like it, as did many people in England, who picked up the custom of smoking from Raleigh's returned colonists and Drake's seamen. Thomas Hariot, who published in 1588 his *Brief and True Report of the New Found Land of Virginia*, praised the medicinal virtues of tobacco. For savages, smoking "purgeth" all "gross humours" from the head

---

[7] *Ibid., 1580-1586*, 623.

and stomach, "openeth all the pores and passages of the body; by which means the use thereof not only preserveth the body from obstructions, but also (if any be . . .) in short time breaketh them: whereby their bodies are notably preserved in health, and know not many grievous diseases, wherewith all we in England are often times afflicted."[8] However, tobacco was probably popular less for its curative qualities than for the pleasure it afforded. Paul Hentzler, a German traveler to England in 1598, said that he and other onlookers at a bear-baiting could scarcely see what was going on because of the haze of tobacco smoke.

The individual most responsible for the popularity of tobacco was Raleigh, who tried to grow the plant in Ireland and who introduced smoking to Elizabeth's Court. Many stories are told of his association with tobacco, particularly the tale of his servant, who, coming into a room to find his master smoking and thinking him on fire, dashed a bucket of water over his head. It was also reported that once, while in a stand at Sir Robert Poyntz's park at Acton, he smoked a pipe of tobacco, "which made the ladies quit it until he had done."[9] Raleigh was never one to let the amenities stand in the way of his pleasure.

More interesting than these was the Queen's wager with him. In conversing with her one day, he remarked facetiously that he knew tobacco so well that he could even weigh the smoke. This was too much for Elizabeth, who wagered him an unnamed sum of money that he could not make good his boast. The amount must have been small, for Elizabeth, whose whole reign was an exercise in economy, was chary with her bets. Raleigh must have delighted in the opportunity to see his Queen lose. Drawing pinches of Virginia leaf from his gilded leather tobacco pouch, he weighed the tobacco on a scales. Then, filling his long-stemmed silver pipe, he smoked the quantity to ashes. Afterward, he weighed the ashes, subtracted their weight from the weight of the tobacco, and came up triumphantly with the answer. As she paid the wager, Elizabeth jested that she had heard of men "who turned gold into smoke, but Raleigh was the first who had turned smoke into gold."[10]

[8] Hakluyt, *Voyages*, VIII, 363.
[9] Aubrey, *Brief Lives*, II, 181.
[10] J. Howell, *Epistolae Ho-Elianae*, 552.

It was Raleigh's misfortune that, unlike Elizabeth, her successor from Scotland conceived so violent a dislike of tobacco that he wrote a diatribe against it. To King James, smoking was "A custom loathsome to the eye, hateful to the nose, harmful to the brain, dangerous to the lungs, and in the black stinking fume thereof, nearest resembling the horrible Stygian smoke of the pit that is bottomless."[11] It may well be that James never forgave Raleigh for making smoking the fashion in England.

Raleigh did not have the Queen all to himself in these months while he was popularizing tobacco and preparing another colonization project. A rival of formidable stature had appeared, young Robert Devereux, Earl of Essex. His mother was the beautiful Lettice Knollys, whose grandmother was sister to Anne Boleyn, the Queen's own mother. Born in 1567, he was but nine years old when his father died. Two years later, to the Queen's indignation, Leicester married Lettice. Essex was thus not only related to the Queen but was also the stepson of her chief favorite until Raleigh came onto the stage. He received an education at Trinity College, Cambridge, and never lost the love of reading and meditation he acquired there. Hunting was also a passion with him, as were most sports. When Elizabeth sent Leicester with an expeditionary force to aid the Dutch against the Spaniards in 1585, he took Essex along. To his other loves Essex soon added that of arms. Tall, auburn-haired, high-spirited, and graceful, he seemed the very embodiment of chivalry. In the victory at Zutphen, where the gallant Sidney received a mortal wound and declined a drink of water in favor of a less badly injured soldier, Essex covered himself with such glory that Leicester knighted him on the battlefield.

The idol of the expeditionary force, Essex returned to England to a different kind of glory. Elizabeth looked upon him and found him, in the bloom of his young manhood, exciting to behold. She kept him near her almost exclusively, playing at cards or some other game till cockcrow. It mattered not at all at this time that he was moody, impulsive, and spoiled; he was a novelty. He must have been something more, too, else so many of his contemporaries might not have supported him with such enthusiasm in his new role as a rival to Raleigh. That they

11 "A Counterblast to Tobacco," in R. S. Rait, *A Royal Rhetorician*, 54.

hated Raleigh and desired to see him supplanted was certainly true, but Essex seems also to have stood in their eyes as a symbol of the gallantry and youthfulness and vigor of their own era. Furthermore, though he never quite grew up, he could exercise, when not in his moods, a real charm of personality: he could be generous, enthusiastic, lovable. By contrast, Raleigh's aura of man-of-the-world was familiar to the Queen and suspected by those who hated him.

Although Essex rose with extraordinary celerity to the position of prime favorite, Elizabeth refused to let him malign the Captain of the Guard. Essex came to suspect that the Queen's preoccupation with him did not necessarily signify that she had utterly renounced Raleigh any more than the latter's ascendancy had signified that she no longer appreciated Leicester or Hatton. In the summer of 1587, Essex received startling evidence that she still valued Raleigh. Essex's sister Dorothy was married to Sir Thomas Perrot, Raleigh's old antagonist; she had married him secretly and thereby called down upon herself the Queen's wrath. Banished from the royal presence, she was invited by Lady Warwick, a friend of hers, to a party in honor of the Queen. When Elizabeth discovered her as one of the guests, the royal anger was dreadful, perhaps stimulated by Raleigh, as Essex, who was also present, believed. Actually Elizabeth did not need any reminder by Raleigh, if indeed he said anything at all, to perceive an insult in Dorothy Perrot's being at the Warwicks'.

Elizabeth's treatment of Dorothy angered Essex. Writing to a friend later, he said that he accused the Queen of being rude to his sister "only to please that knave Raleigh, for whose sake I saw she would grieve me in the eye of the world. From there she came to speak of Raleigh, and it seemed she could not well endure anything to be spoken against him." Fully aware that Raleigh, at his post as Captain of the Guard, was within earshot, Essex deliberately described to the Queen "what he had been, and what he was." At this, Elizabeth grew furious, and with bitter words she worked over the reputation of Essex's mother, Lettice, whom she detested. Distraught, Essex considered Raleigh responsible for it all. Life held no pleasure for him, he said, when he observed "such a wretch as Raleigh highly esteemed of her." If she should "drive me to be friends with Raleigh," she would merely "drive me to many other extremities." "What comfort can I have," he asked in despair, "to give myself over to the service of a mistress that is in awe of such a man?"[12]

To Raleigh, who was meant to overhear Essex's attack the scene must have been infuriating and humiliating almost beyond endurance. While the Queen's defense was reassuring, he was under no illusions that Essex had mortally affronted her. To be sure, almost at once Essex fled to the seacoast to seek a heroic death in the Lowlands when Robert Carey, courier of the Queen, caught up with him and remanded him to the Court. Once he was back, however, Elizabeth forgave all, and before the summer was over, she had made him Master of the Horse and a Knight of the Garter. Raleigh could not compete with Essex's youthful appeal.

Fortunately, during part of this year which inaugurated a rivalry with Essex that was to last, off and on, until the latter's death, Raleigh had his colonization project to divert him. By this time, Virginia was no longer a synonym for easy wealth. Lane's men had little that was good to say of it, while Drake's sailors compared it unfavorably with the West Indies. Although Raleigh encouraged Hariot to publish his account of the year in Virginia, it won few friends at Court; Raleigh's enemies wasted few opportunities to ridicule his plans for a colony.

Notwithstanding criticism and apathy, Raleigh pursued his plans vigorously through the winter of 1586-1587. He realized that henceforth he must induce men with families to migrate to Virginia, men who were interested not in buccaneering but in establishing permanent homes there. They should comprise the bulk of the shareholders in the venture. Each man was to receive five hundred acres, and the amount of his investment in the company was to determine how many additional acres he should receive. The one hundred and fifty settlers who volunteered to go were to have their own government, for which Raleigh chose John White as governor, with twelve assistants.

[12] See Essex's letter to Edward Dyer in the *Tanner MSS* (Bodleian Library, Oxford); G. B. Harrison, *The Life and Death of Robert Devereux, Earl of Essex*, 30-32.

Sir Walter Raleigh. Painted in 1588 and attributed to Zuccaro.

Queen Elizabeth I. Attributed to Marcus Gheeraerts the Younger.

The Virginia and Carolina coast as depicted in *La Virgenia Pars*,
by John White, one of his watercolor charts and drawings
made between 1585 and 1587.

Robert Devereux, Second Earl of Essex. Painted in 1597 by an unknown artist.

SERO SED SERIO

Robert Cecil, First Earl of Salisbury. Painted in 1602
and attributed to J. De Critz.

King James I of England and VI of Scotland.
Painted in 1621 by Daniel Myrtens.

# THE
# HISTORIE OF
## THE WORLD.
### IN FIVE BOOKES.

1  Ntreating of the Beginning and first Ages of the same, from the Creation unto Abraham.

2  Of the Times from the Birth of Abraham to the destruction of the Temple of Salomon.

3  From the destruction of Jerusalem, to the time of Philip of Macedon.

4  From the Raigne of Philip of Macedon, to the establishing of that Kingdome in the Race of Antigonus.

5  From the settled rule of Alexanders Successors in the East, untill the Romans (prevailing over all) made Conquest of Asia and Macedon.

#### By Sir WALTER RALEGH, Knight.

The true and lively portraiture of the honourable and learned Knight Sr Walter Ralegh

Title-page to the third edition of Raleigh's *History of the World*, 1617.
The portrait is by Simon Passe.

Sir Walter Raleigh. By an unknown artist. Although bearing the date 1598, this portrait is usually attributed to the latter period of Raleigh's life, probably after his release from the Tower in 1616. The sash on his left arm may indicate a symbol of authority in view of his former services or of his forthcoming Guiana expedition. His right hand rests on a cane often used after his wound at Cadiz.

On January 7, 1587, he incorporated them under a charter as the "Governour and Assistants of the Citie of Ralegh in Virginia." This colony, therefore, was a real one, exercising certain powers of self-government and consisting of householders, not of men being paid wages by a company that proposed to support the project by privateering.[13]

The colonists sailed from Plymouth on May 8, 1587, with Simon Fernandez going along as pilot of the squadron of three vessels. This squadron, consisting of one ship, a flyboat, and a pinnace, was a far cry from the fleet of eleven lavishly equipped ships that had sailed with Lane. Possibly Raleigh, with so many ventures requiring funds, was unable to do more. Possibly he felt himself caught in the flood-tide of Essex's rise to favor and found it necessary to conserve his resources as his own tide ebbed. In any event, he was keenly interested in the enterprise for which those three small craft sailed bravely for the New World.

Raleigh's instructions to White and the others were very explicit. They were to sail by way of the West Indies, where they were to take on water, provisions, and plants. Once they reached Roanoke, they were to establish Manteo, an Indian who had returned with Grenville, as lord of that area. Then, picking up the fifteen men Grenville had left, they were to proceed to the Chesapeake Bay area and found the city of Raleigh; Roanoke had proved inadequate in good harbors for seagoing vessels.

The colonists encountered trouble from the very first, and Fernandez seems to have been responsible for much of it. In the Bay of Portugal, the ships ran into heavy weather, and Fernandez "lewdly forsooke our Fly-boate."[14] In the West Indies he prevented them from loading salt and from taking aboard oranges and "pines" (pineapples?) for planting in Virginia. By mid-July, they sighted land that Fernandez assured them must be Croatan. He was mistaken by one hundred and sixty miles, and he nearly lost the ship and the pinnace in the breakers off Cape Fear. Later he refused to lead the colonists on to the Chesapeake; since his authority over the crews exceeded even that of the captains, the sailors obeyed him.

[13] Quinn, *Raleigh and the British Empire*, 106-08; Hakluyt, *Voyages*, VIII, 386.
[14] Hakluyt, *Voyages*, VIII, 387.

On the face of it, the behavior of Fernandez seems to have been downright treacherous, as if he wished the colony to fail despite the fact that he had invested heavily in it. Rumor had it that he was in the pay of Spain. On the other hand, Fernandez's reputation may have been greater than his ability. It is likely that he was sorely disappointed at White's refusal to go privateering in the West Indies in order to help pay for the expedition and that he vented his spleen by preventing the colony from gathering provisions in the islands. He may also have suspected that the Indians were more warlike in the Chesapeake area and that, regardless of Lane's harsh treatment, those in the Roanoke region would be more tractable. Whatever the explanation, his conduct was certainly mysterious, and John White, on whose account we are dependent, disliked him and questioned his loyalty. Still, White did not oppose him in the decision to remain at Roanoke. White was familiar with Roanoke from having been there with Lane and liked it. Besides, his daughter Eleanor, wife of Ananias Dare, was pregnant, and further travel at this time might be hazardous to her.

The settlers now began to unload, and their spirits rose when, on July 25, the flyboat arrived safely. Their spirits needed cheering, for at Roanoke there was no trace of the fifteen Englishmen left by Grenville. Lane's fort had been burned to the ground, and grass was growing inside the first floors of the houses that remained. Five days after the arrival of the flyboat, a party went to Croatoan. Through Manteo, who accompanied the group, the English learned from friendly Croatoan Indians then and later that other Indians whom Lane had antagonized had killed several of Grenville's holding force and compelled the rest to flee in a boat to an island near Port Ferdinando; after that, they disappeared. The same hostile tribe killed one of White's group while he was catching crabs.

Notwithstanding the evidence of Indian hostility and the cheerless prospect of Lane's village, the colonists began to rebuild the houses. In the first recorded English Protestant service in the New World, Manteo was christened on August 13 and declared Lord of Roanoke and Dasemunkepenc. It was indeed a season of "firsts," for, on August 18, Eleanor Dare gave birth to a daughter who was soon christened "Virginia." Had White been able to remain with his daughter and his new granddaughter, his cup of pride would have been full. As it was, he had to make the difficult decision of leaving them and returning to England.

The decision was forced upon him by the assistants. The colony was short of provisions, livestock, and salt; doubt was spreading of the wisdom of remaining at Roanoke; and the whole future of the colony seemed in jeopardy. The assistants therefore wanted to send representatives back to England to present the situation to Raleigh and to ship out the needed supplies as soon as possible. When none volunteered to go, the assistants entreated White to make the voyage. Vainly he declared that going back would ruin him in the eyes of Raleigh and all Englishmen. He also said that his property in Roanoke would be neglected and his goods stolen. To these protests the colonists retorted that they would look after his possessions and would give him a certificate, which they dated August 25, stating the necessity of his returning to England. Eventually, and with great reluctance, he consented. Before he departed, the assistants announced their intention of presently moving fifty miles farther up into the mainland. Whether this was in the direction of Chesapeake Bay or Albemarle Sound is not known. In any event, White let them keep the pinnace and sailed on the rickety flyboat, leaving behind eighty-nine men, seventeen women, and eleven children.[15]

Once back in England, White found the fate of the colony involved in the great struggle between England and Spain that was approaching its climax. Philip II had at last declared his objective to be the conquest of England, and the English government was energetically gathering ships and men to meet the Spanish onslaught. Though busy with developments in Ireland and defense assignments at home, Raleigh listened to White and prepared a relief expedition at Bideford under Grenville. But when about ready in late March 1588, Grenville was forbidden by the Privy Council to leave port. Raleigh, however, managed to induce the government to let White sail with two pinnaces to Virginia. Unfortunately, to White's anguish, priva-

[15] For the story of the settlement until White's departure, his own account is the best source. *Ibid.*, 386-403.

teering off Madeira proved more attractive to those aboard than a voyage to Virginia, with the result that, after a season of plundering, the pinnaces were badly mauled by French pirates and, by late May, barely escaped to England and safety.[16]

By this time, the threat from the Armada was so imminent that there were no ships to spare for Virginia. In fact, defeating the Spaniards during the summer and following up the defeat occupied the rest of 1588, so that not until early in 1589 were men and financial resources again available for Virginia. Raleigh now felt that he could no longer sustain by himself the burden of colonization. He had invested over £40,000 in Virginia colonization, a sum which, in current values, amounted to perhaps $1,000,000. Not all of it had been lost, thanks to some successful privateering, but he could not afford to bear what he believed should be carried by the government or by a syndicate. Since the government evinced no interest, he turned to businessmen, particularly to William Sanderson, a rich London merchant who had already invested in his projects. Among the nineteen men who now agreed to sponsor the colony were White, the younger Hakluyt, and Thomas Smythe, active now in the Levant Company, soon in the great East India Company, and eventually in the London Company that settled Jamestown. On March 7, 1589, a deed was drawn up by which Raleigh transferred to the new syndicate the right to plant a colony and to trade without special taxes or customs in the area covered by his patent. He kept for himself and his heirs only one fifth of all the precious metals that might be found. He surrendered neither the patent nor the right to establish other colonies, but he had managed to rid himself of the enormous expense of continuing the Virginia settlement by placing it in the hands of a wealthy corporation. He assured these men, moreover, that he would endeavor to secure them a royal charter. If he was unsuccessful in this, it was not for lack of good intentions or effort. Nor did he ever lose

[16] *Ibid.*, 404-22; Quinn, *The Roanoke Voyages*, II, 561-69. As A. L. Rowse indicates (*The Expansion of Elizabethan England*, 218), it was undoubtedly evident that someone of the "force and authority of a Grenville" was needed, but though both Raleigh and Grenville tried hard to assist the colony, their efforts were sorely hampered by the great crisis with Spain. White's little effort was all that materialized.

interest in that little group of settlers living between the forest and the sea.[17]

The fate of that group, the famous "Lost Colony," has been recounted many times but ends only in speculation. The known facts are comparatively few. Perhaps because of the difficulty of obtaining shipping owing to the national emergency and the lure of privateering, the new syndicate was not able to send White with three ships to Virginia until 1591. Even then, it was largely owing to the energy and investment of Raleigh rather than the syndicate that White got his expedition together. The squadron spent weeks privateering in the West Indies before turning northward. Not until August did the expedition sight the coast near Roanoke. On the night of August 12-13, the ships anchored off the northeastern tip of Croatoan Island, then proceeded with painful slowness, making constant soundings, to Roanoke. Smoke rising from Roanoke as if in signal raised White's hopes. Two boats set out for the town through the reef, but one capsized, drowning a half dozen men and a ship's captain. At White's urging, the others continued towards Roanoke. By the time they reached the northern tip of the island, darkness had fallen. Sighting a fire through the trees, the craft hung offshore, the men blowing trumpets and singing familiar songs. No sound came to their ears except that of the waves breaking against the rocks and sand.

Next morning, August 18, they went ashore. The fire they discovered to have come from smouldering logs, rotten and dry, and perhaps ignited by lightning. Reaching the settlement, the men saw that the houses had been removed but that the palisade was still standing. Though the lighter cannon had disappeared, several of the heavier pieces with cannon balls were lying about

[17] Parks, *Hakluyt and the English Voyages*, 134-36; Quinn, *Raleigh and the British Empire*, 120-21, 126-28; E. Hazard, *Historical Collections*, I, 42, and Quinn, *The Roanoke Voyages*, II, 569-76, for assignment of the patent benefit. For Raleigh's financial association with the remarkable Sanderson in this and other ventures and their legal controversies, see Quinn, II, 576-78, text and footnotes, and J. W. Shirley, "Sir Walter Raleigh's Guiana Finances," in *Huntington Library Quarterly*, XIII (1949), 55-69. Shirley argues with considerable plausibility that to raise money when he needed it, Raleigh resorted to some pretty sharp measures, including using his friends and relatives, asking friends to stand bond for him when he had no credit, even suing relatives. On the other hand, contrary to the Sanderson allegations, Mr. Shirley declares "That Raleigh stooped to forgery and had his agents destroy court interrogatories would be difficult to prove." (Shirley, XIII, 68).

in the tall grass. Sailors searching through the ruins found five chests evidently buried by the colonists and later looted by the Indians. White recognized a number of his papers, books, and maps half ruined by the rains.

Where had the colonists gone? Before White had left for England, they had agreed to leave a sign indicating the place to which they might move and a maltese cross if they were in distress. White now found carved in Roman letters on one of the posts of the stockade the word CROATOAN and, on a tree near the shore, the letters CRO. In neither place was the carving of a cross to be seen. Manifestly the Croatoan Indians or Croatoan Island had some connection with the mystery, and White was eager to go to the island, off which, by a stroke of irony, the ships had anchored that first night. Unfortunately a violent storm now drove the ships to sea, and no plea White made could induce the captains to spend more time near such unfriendly shores.

The end of Raleigh's colony has remained an unsolved mystery. Did the colonists go to live with the Croatoans, or were they captured and then killed? Though there was no cross indicating distress, the unfinished word on the tree suggests haste. So, too, does a discovery made in 1947 by the National Park Survey. Near the fort archaeologists came upon a pit for making charcoal with a number of well-fired sticks still remaining in their horizontal layers. When the colonists left the settlement is also a problem. In June 1588, practically a year after White had sailed for England to get provisions, a Spanish patrol boat, dispatched by the Governor of Florida, explored the coast as far north as Chesapeake Bay. On its way back, its crew located the English colony, identifying a shipyard, a sloop, and other evidence of activity. Though the Governor contemplated attacking the settlement, there is no indication that he did so. Thus, by mid-1588, the colony was still extant.

Raleigh never completely gave up hope of finding his people. He sent out several expeditions, the last of which was made in 1602, under Samuel Mace, who returned after King James had restricted Raleigh's freedom. Trading with the Indians in the vicinity of Croatoan Island, Mace learned little about the colony. Very likely, had the settlers still been on Croatoan and alive, they would have signalled Mace as they would have signalled White on August 12-13, 1591.

The answer probably lies with the Indians. The Jamestown settlers were very curious about the Roanoke people, but expeditions they sent there found no trace of the colony. On the other hand, they heard conflicting tales from the Indians: that the colony had been massacred; that people were living inland in stone houses with tame turkeys; that at least seven people were still alive in the interior—four men, two boys, and a young girl. But all this was vague and insubstantial. All of which one can be reasonably sure is that, by 1607, when Jamestown was settled, Raleigh's settlers were not on Croatoan. The entire colony may have been massacred or succumbed to disease. Or, the settlers may have moved voluntarily into the interior or have been taken there as captives. In either case, had there been adult male survivors, it is unlikely that they would not have made an effort to get in touch with the Jamestown settlement twenty years later. What may well have happened is that the Indians killed the men soon after the colony moved to Croatoan or inland and assimilated the women and children. Possibly the existence of English features and names among Indians of Robeson County, North Carolina, can be accounted for thus early. There is, too, another possibility, namely, that, despairing of ever being succored by White and Raleigh, those colonists who did not choose to remain in Virginia may have boarded the pinnace in the hope of returning to England and have been lost at sea. In the end, the answer is speculation—fascinating speculation, to be sure, but from this point on, the historian must give way to the imagination of the historical novelist.[18]

Raleigh's interest in Virginia was a lively one, but he was no

[18] For accounts of the "Lost Colony," see White's reports (still the main source), in Hakluyt, *Voyages*, VIII, 386-422, and Quinn, *The Roanoke Voyages*, II, 598-622. Very valuable, too, is the narrative by Quinn (*Ibid.*, II, 579-98), and his Appendix III on "The Archaeology of the Roanoke Settlements" (pp. 901-10). See also A. Brown, *The Genesis of the United States*, I, 189; E. Channing, *A History of the United States*, I, 124-30; F. L. Hawks, *History of North Carolina*, I; American Historical Association, *Papers*, V, pt. 4; T. Williams, "The Surroundings of Ralegh's Colony," in *ibid.* (1895), 17; H. McMillan, *Sir Walter Ralegh's Lost Colony* (Raleigh, N.C., 1907); Rowse, *Grenville*, 205-43; Quinn, *Raleigh and the British Empire*, 47-128; Craven, *Southern Colonies in the Seventeenth Century*, 52-57; C. W. Porter, III, "What Became of the Lost Colonists?" in *American Heritage*, IV, No. 2 (Winter, 1953), 53.

dedicated idealist about it. He looked upon its colonization as part of England's stake in the great struggle with Spain. The problems of colonization intrigued him for their own sake, to be sure, and had they been solved, he might have won prestige that would have led him to a seat in the Privy Council, a goal to which he always aspired and which he never attained. But Raleigh was a businessman, financially interested in many ventures, and colonization must be made profitable or transferred to some agency better prepared to sustain its expense. Perhaps, if he had been more tenacious, prepared to risk his all, which he decidedly was not, he might have succeeded in establishing a settlement that would have endured. On the other hand, his was the trail-blazing effort, and he continued confident that Virginia would be subdued. "I will yet live to see it an English nation," he wrote during the years when misfortune had overtaken him at the hands of Elizabeth's successor.[19] It was one of the ironies of history that, when Virginia was finally settled on a permanent basis, the man who had made the greatest effort to achieve that objective in earlier years had no part in the venture; he was a prisoner in the Tower.

[19] Quoted by Edwards, *Ralegh* (*Life*), I, 91.

# CHAPTER 6

# The Armada and England's Counterattack

THE greatest single event during Elizabeth's reign was the defeat of the so-called Invincible Armada of Philip II of Spain. This was but the climax of a policy that began in 1585 when Elizabeth sent Leicester with an expeditionary force to aid the Dutch and Drake to ravage the West Indies; it was on Drake's return that he stopped at Roanoke to bring Lane and his men back to England. Within England itself, the government ordered the Jesuits out of the country, Walsingham closed in on the Babington conspirators, and Elizabeth signed the death warrant for Mary Queen of Scots. In the weaving of the web by which Elizabeth was induced to send the romantic but devious Mary to the block in February 1587, Raleigh had no part. He was not a Privy Councillor nor even the chief favorite since, by then, Essex had returned from the Lowlands and was already impressing the Court. Philip came out into the open, with Mary's death, and sought the English crown for his own line. Had Drake not struck hard at Cadiz in 1587, destroying Spanish shipping, the Armada would probably have sailed that year. If this had occurred, Raleigh would not have had the ships available to send White and his settlers to Roanoke, and there would have been no "Lost Colony." But in the summer of 1588, after a winter and spring of prodigious activity in Spanish shipyards, gun foundries, and recruiting centers, the Armada put to sea on its mission of destruction under the Duke of Medina-Sidonia, a grandee who loved his orange groves more than his galleons.

Raleigh's part in preparing defenses against the Armada was by no means inconsiderable. As a member of the council of war that met in November 1587 to consider defense measures,[1] he pressed strongly for heavy cannon for Portland and Weymouth. In December, acting as Lieutenant General of Cornwall, he

[1] M. Oppenheim (ed.), *The Naval Tracts of Sir William Monson*, II, 267.

worked with Sir John Gilbert and Lord Bath to raise a force of infantry and cavalry in Devon and Cornwall. As fear of an immediate Spanish attack subsided, he sent John White off to Roanoke with the two relief ships that went on a career of privateering rather than on a mission of rescue. Raleigh also slipped over to Ireland to check on his estates and catch up on his duties as Mayor of Youghal. He was there when news reached him of the sailing of the Armada. Rushing back to England, he raised fresh levies of troops and further strengthened coastal defenses.

But Raleigh was more than a soldier; he appreciated the value of seapower and considered that England's safety depended primarily upon her fleet. Writing years after the Armada, he pointed out that ships have a mobility that armies do not possess. Ships can land a heavy concentration of troops at a point of their own choosing and thereby place at a disadvantage defending troops racing alongshore trying to keep up with them.[2] Spanish veterans might have had some difficulty with the nation's best troops at Tilbury, but little or no trouble at all with the poorer forces scattered along the coast. Furthermore, showing evidence of his knowledge of ship design, Raleigh thoroughly approved of fighting ships that were built comparatively low in the water and could sail close to the wind. Such ships, provided they did not attempt to close and board the huge, heavily manned galleons, could easily defeat the enemy.[3] At the same time, these swift, maneuverable ships should not be over-gunned, as the English were wont to do. Too many guns endangered a ship in heavy weather, required too many men to handle them, and necessitated a larger supply of powder and shot than most ships carried.[4] Nothing must impede the effectiveness of the ships on which England must rely for her preservation.

England's task was formidable. The Armada consisted of 130 ships of assorted sizes, mounted 2,500 pieces of ordnance, and carried 19,000 soldiers and 8,000 sailors. Its mission was to seize a port on the Isle of Wight, avoiding a sea battle if possible, and convoy from the Lowlands the savagely fighting

[2] *History of the World*, bk. v, ch. i, sec. 9 (*Works*, VI, 102).
[3] *Ibid.*, sec. 6 (*Works*, 81-82).
[4] *Observations on the Navy and Sea-Service*, in *Works*, VIII, 342-43.

veterans of the Duke of Parma's army. Once loose in England, Parma's troops might well have conquered the country. On the other hand, these minions of Philip II, coming, it was said in the propaganda of the day, with whips strengthened with brazen tags filed thin to scourge the naked backs of Englishwomen, were bound to meet rough treatment at sea.[5] The English ships outnumbered those of the Spaniards, mounted heavier guns, and could outsail the enemy. Furthermore, leaders like Drake, Hawkins, Frobisher, and Lord Admiral Howard of Effingham were confident of their ability to beat the Spaniards; after all, English seadogs had been humiliating the Spaniards with almost monotonous regularity for twenty years.

The fourth week of July 1588 merely confirmed the beliefs of the English captains. At first, there were anxious moments, possibly not fully shared by Drake, when the Spaniards were sighted off the Lizard on July 19th, reportedly in crescent formation. For days, the wind on which the Spaniards had sailed toward their destination had bound the English to their ports. Even now, numbers of the ships were got to sea only by oared boats pulling them. Once at sea, however, they engaged the enemy in a nine-day running fight up the Channel, the English preferring not to fight at close quarters on the Spaniards' terms but standing off and hammering at long range the high-sided galleons crowded with troops. Unable to land on the English coast, the Spaniards put into Calais Roads, where they were routed out by fireships. Then the English guns again opened up, and the enemy fled away to the north. Had not the wind shifted, the galleons would have perished in the shoals off Zealand. The English pursued until their powder ran out, thanks in good part to Elizabeth's parsimony. But the wind took over where the English guns left off. In a wild passage around the tip of Scotland and down the Irish Sea, more than fifty-six vessels were wrecked. The ferocious Irish, disregarding the bonds they enjoyed with the Spaniards—bonds of Catholicism and hatred of the English—looted, stripped, and killed with the utmost zeal the helpless Dons cast up on their shores. Barely one half the splendid Armada survived to reach Spain.

[5] See the ballad by T. Deloney, in A. F. Pollard, *Tudor Tracts, 1532-1588*, 498-502.

With the dead were numbered the great Spanish admiral, Oquendo, and Philip's own son, the Prince of Ascoli.

Some doubt surrounds Raleigh's contribution to the glorious victory. He was certainly not with Leicester's forces at Tilbury when the Queen, wearing a breastplate, appeared on a white horse and made the most dramatic speech of her life to the kneeling troops. Most of Raleigh's biographers have asserted that when the Armada hove in sight, Raleigh dashed aboard one of the ships with a body of gentlemen volunteers and put to sea to join the English fleet.[6] Perhaps he did; he would surely have liked to do so. Unfortunately for this dramatic view of him, his name does not appear in any of the English official correspondence dealing directly with the battle. Nor did he ever mention having been engaged in the conflict, and Raleigh was hardly so modest as to neglect such an opportunity for favorable publicity.

But all this does not necessarily signify that his role was entirely passive, that he had no active part in the great running fight in which the English plucked the Spaniards feather by feather. It must have been a real satisfaction for him to know that the Admiral's flagship, the *Ark*, launched the year before and sold to the government, had been personally designed by him; it was the crack vessel of the fleet. In addition, the *Roebuck*, another of his ships, performed so notably as to win especial praise. Still, was his participation confined to contributing ships? After the enemy passed up the Channel, Raleigh rode to London, eager to get into the fight in some way. According to a Spanish correspondent's report to Philip, he finally won his reward, for when word reached Elizabeth that Drake had cornered the enemy off Gravelines, "the Queen thereupon sent Richard Drake and Ralegh with all speed to order the Admiral to attack the Armada in some way, or to engage it, if he could not burn it."[7] Though this report is not without error, it is accurate in a sufficient number of respects to lead one to suspect that it was based on pretty sound intelligence. If, as seems possible, the report is true in regard to Raleigh, his was a distinctly

---

[6] Martin Hume is an exception, as is Donald Barr Chidsey, while Milton Waldman remains on the fence.

[7] *Cal. S.P. Spanish, 1587-1603*, 392.

Johnnie-come-lately role and, in his opinion, hardly worth alluding to in after years.

Raleigh's work did not end with the northward flight of the Armada. If the Spaniards landed in Ireland, he and Grenville were to intercept them.[8] But presently it became evident, in view of the Spanish desire to get home and the lack of Irish hospitality to the shipwrecked, that their services were not needed. Accordingly, on orders from the Privy Council, they abandoned plans for embarking troops for Ireland, and Raleigh, who had gone to Ireland soon after the winds blew the Armada far up the North Sea, returned to London in time for Christmas.[9]

Hardly was he back in the capital when he tangled with Essex in a bitter quarrel. Though Essex had little to fear from any rival to Elizabeth's affection, his jealousy made him grossly suspicious. Once when the Queen was impressed by the tilting performance of Lord Mountjoy's son, young Charles Blount, she sent him a gold chessman, a queen, which he wore the next day tied by a ribbon to his arm. When he saw it, Essex scoffed, "Now I see every fool must have a favor." Blount challenged him, and in a duel at Marylebone Park wounded Essex in the thigh. Though probably delighted at being fought over by two young men, Elizabeth was nevertheless exasperated with the arrogant Essex. "By God's Death," she exclaimed, "it is fit that someone or other should take him down, and teach him better manners, otherwise there would be no rule with him."[10] But a quarrel between Essex and Raleigh was a very different sort of affair. Whereas Essex and Blount were not inimical to start with and became good friends afterward, probably because Blount was no real rival for Elizabeth's favor, Essex and Raleigh had already been enemies for at least two years. What the occasion was for their quarrel in December 1588 is obscure, but Essex appears to have provoked Raleigh into making some barbed rejoinder for which the Earl challenged him. Though ignorant of the duel to be fought, the Queen was so distressed by Essex's behavior that the Privy Council ordered the affair hushed up and forbade the two men to fight.[11] Anything serious

[8] *Cal. S.P. Foreign, 1588* (July-Dec.), 230.
[9] *Cal. S.P. Dom., 1581-1590*, 557.
[10] For incident, see Harrison, *Essex*, 32-33.
[11] *Cal. S.P. Dom., 1581-1590*, 566.

happening to Essex would have hurt her cruelly. It would seem that, with Leicester's death in early September, Elizabeth was drawn ever more closely to his stepson, notwithstanding his deficiencies.

Certainly Raleigh's day of favor had unmistakably waned, and his troubles were increasing. In January 1589 he interceded with the Queen in behalf of the Earl of Pembroke, who wished to acquire the rangership of New Forest. The Queen refused to consider Pembroke, who was deeply mortified.[12] Raleigh's only consolation was that she likewise rejected Essex's choice and gave it to Charles Blount. Rebuffed by the Queen, Raleigh soon found himself having vainly to defend his *Roebuck*'s seizure, in February, of a Flemish ship bound from Cadiz to the Lowlands. To the Council the seizure was not privateering but piracy. Raleigh, however, looked upon the war as a total war with nice legal distinctions as most unrealistic.[13] Later that winter, he succeeded in finding the group of London businessmen who agreed to take off his shoulders the principal financial responsibility for the Virginia Colony. For this transfer his enemies at Court accused him of deserting the colony. Raleigh was rarely free of attack from one quarter or another; within a year, it was rumored that Sir John Perrot, father of his old antagonist, Thomas, was plotting against him, but nothing came of the allegation.[14]

The spring of 1589 witnessed a great counteroffensive against the royal toiler in Madrid's grim Escorial Palace. It took the form of a combined operations task against Lisbon, the objectives being to plunder the enemy, to liberate Portugal from Philip's rule, and to install as king Don Antonio, the Portuguese Pretender. The operation was financed as a private enterprise, with investments by a number of individuals who included the Queen and Raleigh. Commanding the naval forces, which by April consisted of about two hundred ships, was Drake, while his counterpart in charge of the nearly 20,000 troops was Sir John Norris, the outstanding English general of his day. The expedition got away in mid-April, destroyed an enormous amount of shipping in Corunna, the first port attacked, and in the mouth of the Tagus leading to Lisbon. Drake wanted to force the

---

[12] *Ibid.*, 575-76.     [13] *Ibid.*, 578, 580.     [14] *Ibid.*, 674.

Tagus but was overruled in favor of the army's marching over-land and besieging Lisbon. Unfortunately for the English, they lacked heavy siege guns, and the Portuguese showed no en-thusiasm for rising in behalf of Antonio. Consequently the troops were finally withdrawn. The expedition returned to Eng-land in June far short of the success anticipated and with perhaps half of the men casualties of the enemy or of disease. At a heavy price England had demonstrated both her ability to carry the war to the enemy and her inability to knock him out of the con-flict.

Whether Raleigh accompanied the expedition is uncertain. He invested in it, and he may have gone along with it, though there is no direct, reliable contemporary evidence that he did so. While he had always opposed Don Antonio's claims, his opposition would not necessarily have deterred him from ac-companying the expedition. Essex went, and in dramatic fashion, too. Disguising himself, he dashed down to Plymouth and boarded the *Swiftsure,* the ship on which was Sir Roger Wil-liams, Norris' second-in-command. At once, without orders from Drake, the *Swiftsure* put to sea. In a fury when she discovered her favorite fled, Elizabeth vowed she would make Drake and Norris pay the costs of the expedition and would hang Williams. Essex remained with the army during the Lisbon incident. Pos-sibly he escaped from Court not simply because of the lure of action but because he could not tolerate Raleigh's having an opportunity to outshine him. Still, if Raleigh went along, it is surprising that he was not blamed for the expedition's failure at Lisbon. Certainly he was not with Essex, Norris, or Wil-liams.[15] He may have been with Drake, and Drake had wanted to force the Tagus, a maneuver to which Raleigh's action at Cadiz seven years later bore a resemblance. Furthermore, while Essex and Norris fumbled away the army's chances, Drake seized more than two hundred prizes; Raleigh would therefore have been associated with the victorious aspect of the expedition and would have gained little recognition from Norris and Essex.

There are two possible indications that Raleigh was with the expedition. On the way back to England, Raleigh's ships needed

[15] The editor of the *Cal. S.P. Spanish, 1587-1603* says flatly that Raleigh ac-companied the expedition to Lisbon in 1589 but took no part in the land opera-tions. *Ibid.,* 188 n.

personnel to help man one of his prizes, and his captains used a number of Williams' men. When the prize reached England, Williams claimed it entirely on the ground that without his help the ship could not have been brought in. Raleigh protested, and the Council supported him; the Queen was still furious with both Essex and Williams. The latter, a rugged individual more forthright than wise, would not be silent. When the Queen gave Raleigh a gold chain as a pledge of her esteem, Williams told the Council that he, himself, was as deserving of a chain as anyone. Perhaps he did not realize that the Queen's gesture was her way of showing her disapproval of Essex; or perhaps, realizing this, his loyalty to Essex was greater than his discretion. In any event, the incident of the prize and that of the chain would seem to indicate that Raleigh accompanied the expedition but, because of his connection with Drake, suffered none of the onus of defeat.[16]

However, the Queen could not long be deprived of her boyish, impulsive Earl. Her heart softened, and she again admitted Essex to her presence. His return to Court boded no good for Raleigh. Circumstances now afforded an excellent opportunity to snipe at the Captain of the Guard from the vantage point of the beloved favorite. It was probably sheer coincidence that, soon after Essex was restored with all the warmth accorded the Prodigal Son, Raleigh left in August for Ireland. There seems little doubt that he was under some sort of cloud, though it may have been one only of despondency at the fickleness of the Queen and at the endless quest for favor. Courtiers and hangers-on were quick to draw another conclusion. "My Lord of Essex hath chased Mr. Ralegh from Court, and hath confined him to Ireland," wrote Sir Francis Allen to Anthony Bacon, brother of the famous Francis.[17] Both Allen and Anthony Bacon, as members of the Essex faction, chose to believe this the reason for Raleigh's departure. Back in London in December, Raleigh was annoyed to learn of the rumor. To his cousin, Sir George Carew, he explained, "For my retreat from the Court it was upon good cause to take order for my prize," perhaps

[16] Hume, *Ralegh*, 72. An acute analysis of this expedition is made by R. B. Wernham, "Queen Elizabeth and the Portugal Expedition of 1589," in *English Historical Review*, LXVI (1951), 1-26, 194-218.

[17] T. Birch, *Memoirs of the Reign of Queen Elizabeth*, I, 56.

alluding to his trouble with Williams.[18] The Essex supporters, however, were exultant while he was away. Ireland, land of discontent and half-savage peoples, was a suitable exile, even if temporary, for a man so contumacious as not to bow out forever from Court and leave the royal favor undisputed. How little they knew of Raleigh!

[18] Edwards, *Ralegh* (*Letters*), II, 41.

# CHAPTER 7

# Poet, Patron, and "Atheist"

RALEIGH's sojourn in Ireland during the late summer and autumn of 1589 is commemorated by his meeting and exchange of poetical compliments with Edmund Spenser. He may have met the author of *The Faerie Queene* earlier at Smerwick when both were in the command of Lord Grey. Spenser had but recently taken up residence on his 3,000-acre estate at Kilcolman in Munster. Raleigh's estate, four times as large, lay about thirty miles southeast of the poet's. Both seigniories had been carved from the forfeited lands of the Earl of Desmond, which had amounted to over a half-million acres. The two men had Irish experience and problems in common and shared a vital interest in poetry. In his delightful *Colin Clout's Come Home Again*, Spenser tells the story of their meeting:

> One day . . . I sat (as was my trade)
> Under the foot of Mole, that mountain hoar,
> Keeping my sheep amongst the cooly shade
> Of the green alders by the Mulla's shore.
> There a strange shepherd chanced to find me out,
> Whether allured with my pipe's delight,
> Whose pleasing sound yshrilled far about,
> Or thither led by chance, I know not right:
> Whom when I asked from what place he came
> And how he hight, himself he did yclepe
> The Shepherd of the Ocean by name,
> And said he came far from the main-sea deep.
> He, sitting me beside in that same shade,
> Provoked me to play some pleasant fit;
> And when he heard the music which I made,
> He found himself full greatly pleased at it.
> Yet, aemuling my pipe, he took in hond
> My pipe (before that aemuled of many),
> And played thereon (for well that skill he conned),
> Himself as skilful in that art as any.

He piped, I sung; and when he sung, I piped;
By change of turns, each making other merry,
Neither envying other nor envied—
So piped we, until we both were weary.

Raleigh was much impressed by Spenser and by what the poet had written thus far in *The Faerie Queene*. Sir Philip Sidney had been Spenser's patron until Sidney's death in the Lowlands, then Leicester, who had died after the Armada. Now Raleigh promised to do what he could for Spenser; later, Essex would assume responsibility. When Raleigh finally returned to London in December, he took his friend with him, introduced him to the Queen, and won for him a pension of £50, a sum to which Burghley objected as being excessive. Though disappointed at the small recognition accorded him at Court, Spenser was grateful even for small favors and dedicated *Colin Clout* to Raleigh, acknowledging, he said, "myself bounden unto you, for your singular favours and sundry good turns showed to me at my late being in England, and with your good countenance protect against the malice of evil mouths, which are always wide open to carp at and misconstrue my simple meaning."[1]

Raleigh was well acquainted with "the malice of evil mouths" and kept most of his own poetry unpublished and circulating largely within the Court. Writing poetry was by no means unusual among prominent Elizabethans, but since publication smacked of professionalism, few of the poems by gentleman amateurs found their way into contemporary print. Raleigh was so scornful of public opinion that it is doubtful if the label of "professional" would have troubled him. The truth was probably that he wrote poetry as a solace, an outlet for intense emotion, and cared nothing thereafter for what happened to it. This is as likely an explanation as any for much of his poetry subsequently being ascribed to others and much of it evidently being lost.

His greatest effort was *Cynthia*, most of which either was never completed or has disappeared. This poem was by no means finished when Raleigh read it to Spenser in 1589. In fact, Raleigh was at the task of composition for years, and in this

[1] Dedication of *Colin Clout's Come Home Again*.

69

poem of his Queen and his courtship of her it is difficult to be sure how much applies to the cloud over their relationship in 1589 and how much to the stormy break between them in 1592. *Colin Clout*, however, was dedicated to Raleigh in 1591, and, though not published until 1595, obviously alludes to the situation in 1589 in the following description of Raleigh's *Cynthia*:

> His song was all a lamentable lay
> Of great unkindness and of usage hard,
> Of Cynthia, the Lady of the Sea,
> Which from her presence faultless him debarred,
> And ever and anon, with singulets [sighs] rife,
> He cried out, to make his undersong,
> "Ah, my love's queen and goddess of my life!
> Who shall me pity, where thou dost me wrong?"

It is clear that eventually Cynthia was appeased, for she was

> . . . moved to take him to her grace again.

It is by no means so clear what happened to most of Raleigh's poem.

Though one should make allowance for his gratitude to Raleigh and for poetic hyperbole, Spenser had a high opinion of Raleigh as a poet. In *Colin Clout*, he observed:

> Full sweetly tempered is that Muse of his,
> That can empierce a Princes mighty heart

Not only could Raleigh appeal to the Queen's sentiments through poetry, he could also inscribe a lovely and stately sonnet as an introduction to Spenser's masterpiece:

> Methought I saw the grave, where Laura lay
> Within that Temple, where the vestal flame
> Was wont to burn; and passing by that way,
> To see that buried dust of living fame,
> Whose tomb fair love, and fairer virtue kept,
> All suddenly I saw the Faery Queen:
> At whose approach the soul of Petrarch wept,
> And from thenceforth those graces were not seen.
> For they this Queen attended, in whose stead

Oblivion laid him down on Laura's hearse:
Hereat the hardest stones were seen to bleed,
And groans of buried ghosts the heavens did pierce.
    Where Homer's spright did tremble all for grief
    And cursed the access of that celestial thief.

Spenser replied in graceful acknowledgment, deprecating his own superb effort and extravagantly lauding Raleigh's muse:

To thee that art the summer's Nightingale,
Thy sovereign Goddess's most dear delight,
Why do I send this rustic madrigal
That may thy tuneful ear unseason quite?
Thou only fit this argument to write,
In whose high thoughts Pleasure hath built her bower
And dainty Love learned sweetly to indite.
My rhymes I know unsavoury and sour
To taste the streams that like a golden shower
Flow from the fruitful head of thy Love's praise;
Filter perhaps to thunder martial stower,
Whenso thee list thy lofty Muse to raise;
    Yet, till that thou thy Poem wilt make known,
    Let thy fair Cynthia's praises be thus rudely shown.

Raleigh's lavish eulogizing of Spenser, by showing Homer shaken by Spenser's entrance into Heaven, and Spenser's equally extravagant praise of Raleigh, were, in the picturesque description of one of Raleigh's ablest biographers, but "an interchange of Chinese compliments, in number delighting in their own grace and turns of phrase and emphasis."[2]

Sweetness and light, however, are rarely associated with Raleigh. Unlike most Elizabethan poets, he was intensely personal, and the contemporary preoccupation with aesthetics found him deliberately remaining outside the cult. Perhaps it is the dark, melancholy, personal note so alien to the exuberance of his own era that makes his poetry seem surprisingly modern. For here was a man of vast and bitter experience, loving life and craving wealth and power, but a man who could stop on occasion and, perceiving the sham and loathing it, could wonder why he con-

---

[2] E. Thompson, *Sir Walter Ralegh, Last of the Elizabethans*, 71.

tinued to struggle against odds impossible to overcome. True, he wrote deftly, delicately, of nymphs and shepherds, of "Coral clasps and Amber studs," but generally he left such subjects to others of his contemporaries. More likely was he to speak of the "weary soul and heavy thought," of the uncertainty of love, and of the mystery of life. As the distinguished editor of the latest edition of his verse, Miss Agnes Latham, has written, Raleigh from his experience "knew how beauty is never more keenly apprehended than in the moment that emphasizes its inevitable decay, that light shows never brighter than between the two darknesses. He begins a love-song, and the last verse is an epitaph."[3] What remains of *Cynthia* is a noble poem in imagery, thought, and passion; it is too little known. But in it, as in so many of his other poems, are the acerbic allusions, freighted with experience, to human frailty and the tragic transience of life.

Raleigh could examine with a clinical eye and express an opinion astringent in its accents. For example, in his *A Poesie to prove affection is not love*, he declares:

> Affection follows Fortune's wheels
> And soon is shaken from her heels;
> For following beauty or estate
> Her liking still is turned to hate.
> For all affections have their change
> And fancy only loves to range.

> Desire himself runs out of breath
> And getting, doth but gain his death:
> Desire, nor reason hath, nor rest,
> And blind doth seldom choose the best,
> Desire attained is not desire,
> But as the cinders of the fire.

> As ships in port desired are drowned,
> As fruit once ripe, then falls to ground,
> As flies that seek for flames, are brought
> To cinders by the flames they sought:
> So fond Desire when it attains,
> The life expires, the woe remains.

[3] Latham, *Ralegh's Poems*, xxvii.

72

And yet some Poets fain would prove
Affection to be perfect love,
And that Desire is of that kind,
No less a passion of the mind.
As if wild beasts and men did seek,
To like, to love, to choose alike.

A similar emphasis, somberly ironical, appears in the solemn epitaph written on Sir Philip Sidney's death in the Lowlands:

There didst thou vanquish shame and tedious age,
Grief, sorrow, sickness, and base fortune's might:
Thy praising day saw never woeful night,
But passed with praise from off this worldly stage.

. . . . . . . . . . . . . . . . .

What hath he lost that such great grace hath won?
Young years for endless years, and hope unsure
Of fortune's gifts, for wealth that still shall dure:
Oh happy race with so great praises run.

Probably nothing Raleigh ever wrote revealed so brilliantly his mastery of the savage thrust as *The Lie*. In those years when Essex supplanted him and when his own mischance brought him to a parting of the ways with the Queen after 1592, he brooded upon his experience of the world and penned a denunciation in which anger, bitterness, and disgust combined to form a ruthless, unsparing attack:

Go, Soul, the body's guest,
    Upon a thankless arrant;
Fear not to touch the best,
    The truth shall be thy warrant:
Go, since I needs must die,
    And give the world the lie.

Say to the Court it glows
    And shines like rotten wood:
Say to the Church it shows
    What's good, and doth no good.
If Church and Court reply,
    Then give them both the lie.

73

Tell Potentates they live
   Acting by others action,
Not loved unless they give,
   Not strong but by a faction.
If Potentates reply,
   Give Potentates the lie.

Tell men of high condition,
   That manage the Estate,
Their purpose is ambition,
   Their practise only hate:
And if they once reply,
   Then give them all the lie.

. . . . . . . . . . . .

Tell zeal it wants devotion;
   Tell love it is but lust;
Tell time it meets [measures] but motion;
   Tell flesh it is but dust:
And wish them not reply
   For thou must give the lie.

. . . . . . . . . . . .

Tell wit how much it wrangles
   In tickle points of niceness;
Tell wisdom she entangles
   Herself in over wiseness:
And when they do reply,
   Straight give them both the lie.

Tell physic of her boldness;
   Tell skill it is pretension;
Tell charity of coldness;
   Tell law it is contention:
And as they do reply,
   So give them still the lie.

. . . . . . . . . . . .

Tell Arts they have no soundness,
   But vary by esteeming;

74

Tell schools they want profoundness,
   And stand too much on seeming.
If Arts and schools reply,
   Give Arts and schools the lie.

.   .   .   .   .   .   .   .

So when thou hast, as I
   Commanded thee, done blabbing,
Although to give the lie
   Deserves no less than stabbing,
Stab at thee he that will,
   No stab thy soul can kill.

It is hardly surprising that a poem so critical in its spirit and content should provoke offended interests into replying. The answers to *The Lie* were numerous and biting. One starts:

Go, echo of the mind,
A careless truth protest;
Make answer that rude Rawly
No stomach can digest.[4]

Another reply, after enumerating the points challenged by Raleigh, ends:

Such is the song, such is the author
Worthy to be rewarded with a halter.[5]

Still another, somewhat more sophisticated, contains counter-charges:

The Court hath settled sureness
   In banishing such boldness;
The Church retains her pureness,
   Though Atheists show their coldness:
The Court and Church, though base,
   Turn lies into thy face.

The potentates rely,
   Thou base, by them advanced,

[4] J. Hannah, *The Poems of Sir Walter Raleigh . . . and Other Courtly Poets,* xxvi.
[5] Latham, *Ralegh's Poems,* 137.

75

> Sinisterly soarest high,
>     And at their actions glanced:
> They for this thankless part
>     Turn lies into thy heart.[6]

Men were always finding something sinister in Raleigh, and by many he was believed an atheist. The charge was given wide currency by Father Robert Parsons in a polemical counterattack to the Queen's proclamation of October 18, 1591 against the Jesuits. If Raleigh was admitted to the Privy Council, Parsons contended, one might expect at any time a royal edict denying the basic principles of Christianity. Parsons spoke of "Sir Walter Ralegh's school of atheism by the way, and of the conjurer that is M[aster] thereof, and of the diligence used to get young gentlemen to this school, wherein both Moses and our Savior, the Old Testament and New Testament are jested at, and the scholars taught among other things to spell God backward."[7]

Raleigh's tolerance has been exaggerated, particularly his tolerance towards Catholics, but it was ironical that he should have been singled out by a Catholic for an attack that found favor with his enemies, many of whom were bitterly anti-Catholic. But Parsons also called Lord Burghley an atheist, so Raleigh was in respectable company at the very least.

The appellation "atheist" has an unpleasant connotation for most people even today, but in the sixteenth century it could be utterly damning: men were burned for atheism. That it lacked precise definition made it a convenient tag to apply to one's enemies, much as, today, it is possible to ruin a man's reputation by calling him a communist; whether he is or not is beside the point. Elizabethans considered as atheists people who would now be generally classified as atheists proper—skeptics, agnostics, deists, unitarians, persons seemingly acting without regard to ethical considerations—or, as the ablest analyst of Raleigh's thought has declared in a recent study, simply "a dubious character or an intractable opponent."[8]

[6] Quoted by Hannah, *The Poems of Raleigh . . . and Other Courtly Poets*, xxvii-xxviii.

[7] *An Advertisement Written to a Secretary of My L. Treasurers of England, by an English Intelligencer as He Passed through Germany towards Italy* (1592), 18, quoted by E. A. Strathmann, *Sir Walter Ralegh, A Study in Elizabethan Skepticism*, 25; see also pp. 26-30.

[8] *Ibid.*, 96.

Raleigh's beliefs are not easy to categorize, for his was not a mind that saw things in blacks and whites or that accepted dogma without examination. He had read his Machiavelli, he cited him in his writings, and his behavior occasionally comported with the advice of the great Italian. But that Raleigh accepted Machiavellian principles without qualification is as much a misapprehension as that he believed without reservation in the theology of the day. Raleigh did not disbelieve in a God; rather, he was uncertain of the precise nature of God. One summer evening in 1593, Sir George Trenchard, Deputy Lieutenant of Dorset, gave a dinner party to which he invited, among others, Raleigh and his brother Carew; Sir Ralph Horsey, also Deputy Lieutenant; Ralph Ironside, a clergyman of Winterborne; and Vicar Whittle of Forthington. Carew Raleigh made a number of remarks to which Horsey objected as "loose" and dangerous. When Carew asked Ironside why this should be so, Ironside replied that "the wages of sin is death." To Carew's jesting rejoinder that death came to saint and sinner alike, the clergyman declared that "death which is properly the wages of sin, is death eternal, both of the body and of the soul also."

"Soul, what is that?" asked Carew, greatly daring.

When Ironside expressed a disinclination to inquire closely into what constituted the soul, and then fell silent altogether, Raleigh took over from his brother and entreated Ironside to answer Carew's question. "I have been a scholar some time in Oxford," Raleigh added; "I have answered under a bachelor of art, and had talk with diverse; yet hitherunto in this point (to wit what the reasonable soul of man is) have I not by any been resolved."

The conversation that followed satisfied Raleigh neither on the nature of the soul nor the nature of God. "Marry, these two be like," he said impatiently, "for neither could I learn hitherto what God is." Finally, he requested that grace be said, "for that . . . is better than this disputation."

The dinner party became, in 1594, the subject of an investigation conducted under authorization of the Queen's "High Commissioners in Causes Ecclesiastical." The investigating commission met at Cerne Abbas and included Viscount Howard of Bindon, Thomas Howard, Chancellor Francis James, John Williams, Francis Hawley, and Sir Ralph Horsey. The last had been present at the party. The written testimony submitted by Ironside contained a reasonably full account of the dinner conversation. Although no formal action was taken against Raleigh as a result of the investigation, there can be little doubt that his intellectual interests, Renaissance-natured in their number and diversity and in his desire to preserve an open mind, made him liable to suspicion.[9]

What Raleigh actually believed shows evidence of a penetrating and sophisticated mind, if not one of great originality. In his opinion, God is known by His works or His words—"either by the observing and conferring of things . . . or else by the word of God Himself."[10] Furthermore, God "hath not any bodily shape or composition, for it is both against His nature and His word."[11] Nor should God and Nature be confused, for "it is God that only disposeth of all things according to His own will . . . it is nature that can dispose of nothing, but according to the will of the matter wherein it worketh."[12] Though men know by means of their reason the existence of God, they cannot know His essence: "such a nature cannot be said to be God, that can be in all conceived by man."[13] God, therefore, is mystery, real in the evidence of His presence but inconceivable in image and essence. By comparison, the anthropomorphic conception of many of Raleigh's contemporaries was something less than crude.

Raleigh on man's soul was reasonably conventional.[14] He speaks of three kinds of souls: the "feeding" soul, the "feeling" soul, and the soul "endowed with reason." Animals have only the first two types and are mortal, whereas man's soul is immortal and possesses "an heavenly beginning." The substance of the soul, "with its appetite and affection and desire," he admits, is hardly known (a view he acknowledges St. Augustine as sharing), but it comes from God and returns to God. Sin, however,

[9] For a full report of the Cerne Abbas inquiry, see G. B. Harrison, *Willobie His Avisa*, App. III. For comment, see Strathmann, *Ralegh, A Study in Elizabethan Skepticism*, 46-52.

[10] *History of the World*, bk. v, ch. i, sec. 1 (*Works*, II, 4).

[11] *Ibid.*, bk. I, ch. ii, sec. 1 (*Works*, II, 46-47).

[12] Preface to *ibid.* (*Works*, II, lvii).

[13] Preface to *ibid.* (*Works*, II, lx).

[14] The quotations that follow are from Raleigh's *A Treatise of the Soul*, in *Works*, VIII, 571-91.

comes not from God. Rather, "the body doth communicate it to the soul, as the soul doth impart many things to the body; for they both make one person, and the soul in the body is straightway subject to the state of sin with the body. . . ." He considered the soul of man to be immortal, a belief, he points out, which ancient thinkers, including Plato, shared and the Sadducees denied. The soul "hath no cause of death within it or without it . . . but liveth and abideth for ever after the body is dissolved."

Raleigh's thought is well within the traditional frame. His conceptions of God and the soul were foreshadowed by the great Christian fathers, Jerome and Augustine. His argument that the desires of the soul constitute evidence of immortality was used by Plato. His insistence that the soul furnished form to the body, giving life and motion to the whole, was straight out of Aristotle. If he leans more strongly toward Plato in preference to any other thinker, ancient or modern, his writing is studded with scriptural allusions with which he buttresses argument after argument. Certain modern writers have seen in Raleigh's writings and associations with liberal thinkers evidence of greater modernity in religious thinking than he may have deserved. As Edward Strathmann has pointed out in his masterly analysis of Raleigh's intellectual interests, Raleigh's emphasis on reason did not prevent him from yielding to scripture as the ultimate authority, and the skepticism evident in his arguments was not a device to attack Christianity but to support it.[15]

The more closely one examines his writings, both prose and poetry, the more one sees a profound respect for religion. In his remark,

> Say to the Church it shows
> What's good, and doth no good,

he criticized the Church as an institution falling down in its mission, but that did not prevent him from telling the Dean of Westminster that he meant to die in the faith professed by the Church of England.[16] In his argument with Ironside, the latter's reasoning, rather than his convictions, annoyed him—"you

---

[15] Strathmann, *Ralegh, A Study in Elizabethan Skepticism*, 126-32. See also R. W. Battenhouse, *Marlowe's "Tamburlaine,"* 50-68; V. T. Harlow (ed.), *The Discoverie of Guiana*, xxxii-xxxviii; U. M. Ellis-Fermor, *Christopher Marlowe*, 163; M. C. Bradbrook, *The School of Night*, 61.

[16] D. Jardine, *Criminal Trials*, I, 508.

answer not like a scholar," Raleigh told the clergyman. To his son, in later days, Raleigh wrote, "Serve God; let Him be the Author of all thy actions,"[117] and there is little reason to conclude that this paternal advice was mere lip-service to a convention. His *The Passionate Man's Pilgrimage* is one of the truly great religious poems of his time. That Raleigh did not wholly convince some people, even to the day of his death, that he was not an atheist was owing less to what he actually believed, or professed to believe, than to what men preferred to think he believed. For Raleigh's enemies were legion.

Part of the reason for the reputation of "atheist" that he acquired was undoubtedly the attraction that he felt for any man with a different sort of mind or interest. One brilliant, devil-may-care Elizabethan with whom his name is linked was Christopher Marlowe. Another, held in almost equal disrepute, was Thomas Hariot. Much has been written of the relationship between Marlowe and Raleigh, who may have been introduced by their mutual friend, Hariot. Most of the evidence of direct contact between Raleigh and the author of *Tamburlaine* and *Dr. Faustus* is based on inference. According to Mr. Strathmann, the sole bit of evidence that the two had ever conversed is the testimony of a spy, Richard Cholmeley, himself accused of atheism, that "Marlowe is able to show more sound reasons for atheism than any divine in England is able to give to prove divinity, and that Marlowe told him that he hath read the atheist lecture to Sir Walter Raleigh and others."[18] All this aside, each was acquainted with the other's works, and a bond of intellectual understanding may have existed between them. Raleigh was the more serious, the more realistic, as his reply to Marlowe's *Passionate Shepherd to His Love* indicates.[19] Marlowe's song is joyous and carefree:

> Come, live with me and be my love
> And we will all the pleasures prove

[17] *Works*, VIII, 570.

[18] Strathmann, *Ralegh, A Study in Elizabethan Skepticism*, 40 and n. 51; the quotation is from *Harleian MSS* (British Museum), 6848, fol. 190.

[19] For suggestions concerning the mental affinity of Raleigh and Marlowe, see Thompson, *Ralegh*, 78; Ellis-Fermor, *Marlowe*, 163, 165; Harlow (ed.), *Discoverie of Guiana*, xxxiv-xxxv.

That valleys, groves, hills and fields,
Woods or steepy mountain yields:

And we will sit upon the rocks,
Seeing the Shepherds feed their flocks
By shallow rivers, to whose falls
Melodious birds sing madrigals:

. . . . . . . . . . . . .

The Shepherd swains shall dance and sing
For thy delight, each May-morning!
If these delights thy mind may move,
Then live with me, and be my love!

But Raleigh has the Nymph reply in a tone that manages to be
both teasing and serious:

If all the world and love were young,
And truth in every Shepherd's tongue,
These pretty pleasures might me move,
To live with thee, and be thy love.

Time drives the flocks from field to fold,
Where Rivers rage, and Rocks grow cold,
And Philomel becometh dumb,
The rest complains of cares to come.

. . . . . . . . . . . . .

But could youth last, and love still breed,
Had joys no date, nor age no need,
Then these delights my mind might move,
To live with thee, and be thy love.

Like Raleigh, Marlowe was hounded by the rumors of atheism. His former tutor, Francis Ket, was sent to the stake in
1589 on the charge. Less cautious than Raleigh, Marlowe was
finally brought to a near-reckoning when, in 1593, a warrant
was issued for his arrest on the charges of atheism and blas-
phemy. But it was only a near-reckoning after all, since, before
the law closed in, he died on May 30 from a knife wound received in a tavern brawl at Deptford. It is as absurd to conclude,
as has been done, that Raleigh contrived to have Marlowe

assassinated as it is to contend, as has also been done, that Raleigh was the real William Shakespeare![20]

Raleigh's association with Hariot likewise caused talk. Marlowe was rumored to have boasted that, beside his friend Hariot, "Moses was but a juggler," and that Hariot "being Sir W. Ralegh's man can do more than he." At least, this was the report of an informer.[21] Hariot, of course, was Raleigh's friend and protégé, the scientist and mathematician who had gone with Lane to Virginia. After 1593, Hariot became a member of the retinue of Henry Percy, Earl of Northumberland, but he and Raleigh remained close friends. Hariot's scientific interests led people to suspect his orthodoxy, and he had to clear himself before the Council. Aubrey, the seventeenth-century biographer, reported that Hariot taught the doctrine of deism to both Raleigh and Northumberland and that the divines looked upon his death from cancer of the lip or tongue as "a judgment upon him for nullifying the Scripture."[22]

Also suspicious company for Raleigh was Dr. John Dee, a strange person who has left a revealing diary. He knew astronomy, geography (this alone would have interested Raleigh), and mathematics, and wrote a treatise on the Gregorian calendar which formed the basis for government acceptance of the change from the old Julian calendar until the English ecclesiastics, their fear of anything Catholic extending even to a time calculation, persuaded the government to cling to the old, if less accurate, method. But Dee's curious mind also led him into astrology and into delving into the occult. He heard mysterious noises in the night, dreamed weird dreams, spoke of evil spirits. How he escaped the stake was nothing short of a miracle, but Elizabeth seems to have liked him and Raleigh became his good friend. On April 18, 1583, Dee wrote, ". . . the Queen went from Richmond toward Greenwich, and at her going on horseback, being new up, she called for me by Mr. Rawly his putting her in mind, and . . . gave me her right hand to kiss."[23] Raleigh

[20] For the assassination theory, see S. A. Tannenbaum, *The Assassination of Christopher Marlowe*; for the Shakespeare claim, see H. Pemberton, Jr., *Shakspere and Sir Walter Ralegh*.

[21] See *Harleian MSS* (British Museum), 6848, fols., 185-86; C. F. Tucker Brook, *The Life of Marlowe*, 98-100.

[22] Aubrey, *Brief Lives*, I, 287.

[23] *The Private Diary of Dr. John Dee*, 20.

wrote to him, over two months later, of the Queen's good will to him.[24] As late as October 9, 1595, Raleigh invited Dee to dine with him at Durham House.[25] Many people thought Hariot was the master conjurer alluded to by the Jesuit Parsons in his attack on Raleigh's "school of atheism," but Dee was certain he himself was the one Parsons had in mind. In any event, the fact that Raleigh and Dee enjoyed any kind of association was probably equally damning to each.

Raleigh's abilities and interests, as well as the patronage he gave, are reflected in the attention scholars accorded him. Richard Hakluyt expressed his indebtedness to him. Martin Bassaniere of Paris dedicated to him his edition of an original narrative of the French attempt to settle Florida. The publisher of John Case's *Praise of Music* dedicated this outstanding musical publication of its day to Raleigh as a skilled musician. Thomas Churchyard, the poet, inscribed his *Spark of Friendship* to him. Undoubtedly in response to his lively interest in chemistry and drugs, a medical treatise was also dedicated to him. An antiquarian's continuation of an ancient Irish history contained a warm tribute to Raleigh in the introduction as "rather a servant than a commander to his own fortune." And so it went, by no means concluded with this list, an impressive catalogue of interests by this amazing man.[26]

Raleigh was generous with his time and money, and careless of his reputation, where his interests and sympathies were involved. Anyone at all intellectually unusual could be sure of a hearing and possibly of support; he preserved an open and inquiring mind. It was his misfortune, from the point of view of contemporary popularity, that he took no pains to disguise his superiority but, rather, gloried in it in a manner so boldly insolent that it graveled men. They rejoiced at every misfortune that overtook him, and would have felt that he had received his just deserts had he been executed for atheism. No wonder they believed that his trip to Ireland in 1589, when he visited with Spenser, was a flight or an exile from Court; this was what they wanted to believe, for surely, in their eyes, he merited some kind of reduction in standing. And soon, if not in 1589, they were to have an opportunity to applaud more vigorously.

[24] *Ibid.*, 21.     [25] *Ibid.*, 54.     [26] Stebbing, *Ralegh*, 53-54.

# CHAPTER 8

# Marriage, Imprisonment, and Release

RALEIGH returned to Court with Spenser in December 1589, disappointed his enemies by being received in kindly fashion by Elizabeth, perhaps because of her glorification in *The Faerie Queene*, and then turned sharply upon one of those enemies. This was the Lord Deputy of Ireland, Sir William Fitzwilliam, a faithful but irascible servant of the Crown who hated courtiers in general and the arrogant Raleigh in particular. They had recently tangled over the lease of Lismore which Raleigh had acquired from a man named Parker. Another lease, however, had also been obtained by Sir William Stanley, who had sublet to John Egerton and then joined the Spaniards in 1587. His wife appealed to the Privy Council for Lismore's return to Egerton, and the Council referred the matter to the Lord Deputy at the time, Sir John Perrot, whose own loyalty was soon to be questioned. Raleigh fought to keep Lismore, and no action had been taken either by Perrot or by his successor, Fitzwilliam, when Raleigh appeared in Ireland in the summer of 1589. Then, perhaps taking advantage of his lapse from favor, Fitzwilliam began to look with a kind eye on Lady Stanley's suit.

This action was clearly in Raleigh's mind when he wrote in December to Sir George Carew, whom he had charged with the financial arrangements for the restoration of Lismore. It is a remarkable letter, revealing so patently both the angry property-holder, challenged in his possession, and the haughty courtier. But one can also discern in the superficially confident assumptions a man who, however great his wealth and power, did not feel quite secure and who was therefore deeply disturbed:

"If in Ireland they think that I am not worth . . . respecting, they shall much deceive themselves. I am in place to be believed not inferior to any man, to pleasure or displeasure the greatest; and my opinion is so received and believed as I can anger the best of them. And, therefore, if the Deputy be not as ready to stead me as I have been to defend him, be it as it may.

"When Sir William Fitzwilliam shall be in England, I take myself for his better by the honorable offices I hold, as also by that nearness to Her Majesty which still I enjoy, and never more. I am willing to continue towards him all friendly offices, and I doubt not of the like from him, as well towards me as my friends. This much I desire he should understand. . . .

"For the suit of Lismore, I will shortly send over order from the Queen for a dismiss of their cavillations."[1]

Raleigh's confidence in the Queen's favor was justified. In April 1590, Elizabeth instructed Fitzwilliam to quash Lady Stanley's lawsuit. Lismore was henceforth to be Raleigh's without question, though he was presently to have difficulty with Fitzwilliam over other problems.

Conditions were ripening for an enlargement of the Queen's favor. Early in 1590, Essex secretly married Frances Walsingham, widow of Sir Philip Sidney and daughter of Elizabeth's great minister, who died in April. When, by fall, Frances' pregnancy impelled Essex to announce the marriage, Elizabeth was furious. Not only did she consider it a loss of dignity to the Essex house because of the difference in rank, she also raged at the affront to herself. That either the clergy or her courtiers should marry invariably shocked and disgusted her. Her feeling was pathological, springing largely from psychological causes that had their origin in her youth. Essex, however, comported himself with considerable discretion; while proud of his wife, he neither talked of his marriage as a triumph over the jealous Queen nor brought Frances to Court. As a result of this judicious behavior, the Queen again felt kindly disposed to him by November.

While Essex's lapse made Elizabeth more appreciative of Raleigh, foreign affairs were developing an aspect that opened up possibilities of action for the restless Captain of the Guard. With the assassination of Henry III of France in 1589, Henry

[1] Edwards, *Ralegh (Letters)*, II, 41-42; *Cal. S.P. Carew, 1589-1600*, 15; Quinn, *Raleigh and the British Empire*, 146-49, for discussion of the situation in Ireland.

of Navarre, the Huguenot leader, became king. Refusing to accept a Protestant ruler, French Catholic nobles formed a Catholic League and called on Philip II of Spain for assistance. Philip eagerly complied and sent troops, one column entering Picardy, another Brittany. Desperate for aid, Henry and his generals appealed to Elizabeth. Eventually, but with no great enthusiasm, she acknowledged the appeals. Expeditionary forces crossed the Channel under Sir John Norris and Sir Roger Williams, with Essex going over early in August 1591 as Lord General.

Raleigh was now very close to the Queen again and, in the resurgence of hostilities, opportunity seemed at the very door. It was decided to dispatch a squadron under Lord Thomas Howard to the Azores to cut off the Spanish Plate Fleet en route from Central America with the gold and silver of Mexico and Peru, and in January 1591 Raleigh was appointed Vice Admiral under Howard.[2] This was his first naval command of significance, one from which he might well obtain glory and profit, and he busied himself through the winter rounding up ships and men.

Then came the intervention of fate—perhaps a kindly fate, as it turned out—in the form of a command from the Queen forbidding him to sail. Possibly Howard complained that he could not sail in Raleigh's company (Raleigh and the Howards rarely agreed),[3] but it is more likely that the Queen was simply continuing her old policy of keeping him, a devoted and respected courtier, at home. As has been so aptly said, "Raleigh had found his path to the top, but he always hated it and hankered after the life of action that was . . . for many of his best years denied him."[4] Though his vigorous cousin, Sir Richard Grenville, took his place, Raleigh contributed his ship, the *Bark-Raleigh*, and paid for victualing two of the dozen assorted vessels in the squadron. One of the two was the *Revenge*, now Grenville's flagship.

The squadron could have had better luck. Wretched weather prevented it from getting to sea, disease decimated crews when it finally broke out of harbor, and the Plate Fleet was so slow

---

[2] *Cal. S.P. Dom., 1591-1594,* 6.
[3] The suggestion is by Rowse, *Grenville,* 292.
[4] Williamson, *Age of Drake,* 235.

in arriving from the West Indies that word reached Spain of the English ships hovering off the Azores. A myth that refuses to die is that, with the Armada, Spanish seapower went the way of Nineveh and Tyre. While Philip II did not again assemble so massive a fleet as the Armada, his shipyards turned out scores of vessels fashioned more on the English model than were the Armada galleons and more skillfully armed. His new squadrons kept England more or less in a state of constant anxiety throughout the 1590's, particularly as England's great captains died off. Now he sent fifty-three men-of-war to convoy the Plate Fleet and deal with Howard's ships.

Raleigh's intelligence notified him of Philip's intention, and he hurried off a pinnace to warn Howard and Grenville; unfortunately the pinnace arrived too late. The Spaniards caught the English on September 10 when many men were lying ashore recovering from scurvy or filling the water casks. At Howard's order, the ships put to sea, several of them having to slip their cables to reach open water. Grenville, who had stood by to pick up the men ashore, now found himself cut off by the leading vessels of the huge enemy fleet. Though he might still have had a chance of picking his way through the heavy ships opposing him, he seems to have disdained to flee. Rather, he evidently made up his mind to cover the retreat of his countrymen, show the Dons whom he had fought a good part of his life what an Englishman thought of them, and still smash his way to the open sea.

The result was one of those epics of heroism, of men fighting against fearful odds, which have become something of a hallmark of the British Navy. Three times as small as a number of her opponents, the *Revenge* had ninety of her crew below decks with illness and only about one hundred available for active duty. Even so, surrounded by five massive galleons, raked by thousands of musket balls from the marines lining the Spanish bulwarks, hammered by Spanish cannon, and repeatedly boarded by cursing masses of steel-helmeted Dons, the *Revenge* fought on, undaunted and apparently invincible. After fifteen hours, there was little left of her. She had received eight hundred heavy shot, many below the waterline. Her masts had been shorn off, while her maindeck was a tangle of spars and rigging.

Her decks looked like a charnel house, with nearly half her effectives dead or dying. But the doughty Grenville, dripping from several wounds, had inflicted severe blows. Two galleons had gone to the bottom, and a thousand Spaniards had lost their lives.

Finally, with his crew so reduced and their pikes broken, Grenville wanted to blow up his ship rather than accept the Spanish admiral's terms of surrender. Those terms were that the survivors who were commoners should be sent to England and the gentlemen kept in honorable captivity for ransom. To Grenville's disgust, his men voted to accept the terms, and prevented him from falling on his own sword. After the surrender, Grenville lingered on the Spanish flagship for three days, a much-admired prisoner. Then, according to a Dutch resident in the Azores, one Linschoten, the dying Grenville showed his contempt of death by crushing a wineglass in his mouth and swallowing the fragments, while the blood trickled down the corners of his mouth. No doubt the Spaniards were properly horrified by the terrible seadog's act, if indeed it is not simply a fictitious part of the Grenville legend. Presently death claimed him, but not before he is said to have given voice to a stirring declaration of patriotism, "Here die I, Richard Grenville, with a joyful and quiet mind, having ended my life like a true soldier that has fought for his country, Queen, religion and honor."[5]

Within a few weeks of the news of the *Revenge* reaching England, the only English warship captured by the Spaniards during the many years of the war, an anonymous pamphlet appeared containing an account of Grenville's heroism that rang through England like a trumpet call. This was Raleigh's *Report of the Truth of the Fight about the Isles of Azores*, based on interviews with *Revenge* survivors conducted by himself and others.[6] The pamphlet is written in superb English prose, vivid, muscular, and grand. It was an effective counterblast to critics of the English defeat and of Howard's flight. Toward Spanish efforts to magnify their victory Raleigh was contemptuous. He

[5] Rowse, *Grenville*, 300-20, for an excellent account of the fight. See also Williamson, *Age of Drake*, 380-83, and, of course, Raleigh's account in Hakluyt, *Voyages*, VII, 38-53, and Linschoten's in *ibid.*, VII, 62-87.
[6] Hakluyt, *Voyages*, VII, 38-53.

held up Spain to the view of the world as a "ravenous" country,[7] ambitious with "bloody and injurious designs, purposed and practised against all Christian princes, over whom they seek unlawful and ungodly rule and empire."[8] The scorn fairly drips from his pen: ". . . how irreligiously they cover their greedy and ambitious pretences with that veil of piety. But sure I am, that there is no kingdom or commonwealth in all Europe, but if they be reformed, they then invade it for religion's sake; and if it be, as they term Catholic, they pretend title; as if the Kings of Castile were the natural heirs of the world."[9] He was especially eloquent in his condemnation of their treatment of the natives in Hispaniola and elsewhere, whose rescue from the tyranny of Spain may have furnished a popular incentive for his future expedition to Guiana.

Despite the bigotry in the pamphlet, Raleigh could be generous. He conceded that the Spaniards treated the captured Grenville with magnanimity. He had lofty praise of Grenville, though privately he thought him a fool, albeit magnificent, to have fought an unnecessary battle of extermination. Raleigh even admitted publicly that ". . . the other course had been the better, and might right well have been answered in so great an impossibility of prevailing."[10] Gossip that he had challenged Howard to a duel for deserting his kinsman was pretty well dispelled by his defense of the Admiral's decision not to return to help the *Revenge*. To have turned about would have meant the sacrifice of the entire squadron; besides, Grenville, "out of the greatness of his mind," could not have been persuaded to any other course.[11]

It was hard for Raleigh to reconcile glory with financial disaster. All twelve investors in the expedition had sustained heavy loss. Though a few prizes were taken, so little was realized that, as Raleigh admitted to Burghley, "We might have gotten more to have sent them a-fishing."[12] Plunder was a means of supporting these patriotic ventures, as well as an inducement to undertake them. Unless they proved profitable, an outcome which depended on both good luck and good management, the seas might well return to Spanish control.

[7] *Ibid.*, 53.    [8] *Ibid.*, 50.    [9] *Ibid.*, 51.
[10] *Ibid.*, 42.    [11] *Ibid.*    [12] Edwards, *Ralegh (Letters)*, II, 43.

The latter part of 1591 and early 1592 must have been an exciting and gratifying period in Raleigh's life. His pamphlet was being read and eagerly agreed with throughout England, in the stately manor houses as well as in the smoky waterfront taverns. For once, he probably felt a real pride of authorship: the pamphlet was good, and there were few who did not know who wrote it. Furthermore, in addition to writing the pamphlet, he participated in a humane cause when, in October, he joined with Essex in saving from execution the brilliant Puritan clergyman, John Udall. The latter had criticized the bishops sharply and, in consequence, had been adjudged a traitor. Raleigh was but one of several prominent laymen who believed a grave injustice had been done, but it was he, above all others, who was responsible for saving Udall's life by his intercession with the Queen.[13] He had the further gratification of seeing Udall pardoned in June 1592.

The month of January 1592 brought Raleigh vivid manifestation of the Queen's favor, one of the evidences of which he was most appreciative, a gift of real estate. Elizabeth persuaded the Bishop and Chapter of Salisbury to lease to her the manor of Sherborne in Dorset, which she gave to Raleigh for an annual rent of £360. This holding was further extended by a lease of Wilscombe Manor from the Bishop of Bath and Wells, whose marriage at an elderly age so disgusted the Queen that she practically forced the lease from him on condition of his retaining office. Raleigh loved Sherborne and made it his country home. He seemed not at all perturbed at the curse reputedly laid on the estate by St. Osmund, Bishop of Sarum, at any transference of title.[14]

The final manifestation of his mounting good fortune came in his appointment to chief command of an attack on the Isthmus of Panama and the Plate Fleet. His second-in-command was Sir John Burrough. This was to be an expedition after the manner of Drake. Raleigh provided one ship; his brother Carew, another; the Queen, two; London citizens, two; while George Clifford, Earl of Cumberland, joined with six. Raleigh

---

[13] Birch, *Memoirs of the Reign of Queen Elizabeth*, I, 62; Thompson, *Ralegh*, 81-82.
[14] For Sherborne gift, see *ibid.*, 88; *Cal. S.P. Dom.*, *1591-1594*, 173.

invested heavily in the expedition, borrowing extensively to meet his obligations. In February, he hurried to the West Country to raise additional supplies, but even when finally ready the fleet was held in the Thames by contrary winds.

Meanwhile, the Queen had exercised her sex's prerogative and changed her mind. Raleigh was to accompany the expedition for but fifty or sixty leagues and then return in a ship to be loaned him for the purpose by the Lord Admiral, Charles Howard. His place in command was to be assumed by Sir Martin Frobisher. Once again Elizabeth had frustrated Raleigh in his opportunity for action, depriving him of participation in an expedition on which he had set his heart. If her decision was hard to take, Frobisher's appointment in his stead was even harder, for the harsh Frobisher was profoundly unpopular with sailors. "I have promised Her Majesty," Raleigh wrote on March 10 from Chatham to Sir Robert Cecil, the hunchbacked son of Lord Burghley, whom the old man was preparing to take his place, "that if I can persuade the companies to follow Sir Martin Frobisher, I will without fail return . . . though I dare not be known thereof to any creature."[15]

Eventually Raleigh reconciled himself to the changes, though Court gossip was hot that at long last he had lost his heart to Elizabeth Throgmorton in a secret marriage or an affair and that, if he once put to sea, he would not dare come back until the Queen's anger had subsided. Cecil had evidently apprised him of what was being whispered, for, in the same letter in which he spoke of Frobisher, Raleigh said, "I mean not to come away, as they say I will, for fear of a marriage, and I know not what. If any such thing were, I would have imparted it unto yourself before any man living; and, therefore, I pray believe it not, and I beseech you to suppress, what you can, any such malicious report."[16] But Raleigh was hedging against disaster with the lawyer's device of denying everything and affirming nothing. The weeks until the fleet sailed on May 6 were anxious ones indeed. Finally he put to sea and, secure for the moment, he must have seriously wondered whether he should return as directed. The next day, he received another reminder when Frobisher overtook him in a fast ship with orders to turn back

<hr>

[15] Edwards, *Ralegh* (*Letters*), II, 45-46.          [16] *Ibid.*, 46.

and let the fleet continue. Though he made up his mind to return, he decided to do so at his own discretion; he would see the fleet at least as far as Cape Finisterre.

He now ran into a whole covey of misfortunes. He halted a ship from Spain belonging to the Governor of Calais, and from an Englishman escaped from Spain he learned that Philip II had ordered the Plate Fleet not to sail from America this year. Though this was staggering news, Raleigh kept on for Finisterre. Near the Cape, a violent storm swooped down and badly mauled the fleet. Once the blow was over, he met with his commanders and made new dispositions in view of the Plate Fleet's not sailing and the lateness of the season for an attack on Panama. Dividing his fleet into two squadrons, he sent one under Burrough to the Azores to intercept any ships from the West or East Indies that might be en route to Spain, while he ordered Frobisher with the other squadron to the coast of Spain to keep Spanish attention off Burrough. Then he headed back to England, arriving in Plymouth on May 18.

If Raleigh expected to be arrested when he went ashore, he was mistaken. In fact, it was not until six weeks later, long after he had returned to Durham House in London, that Elizabeth suddenly sent him to the Tower. The reason for his incarceration was never stated. It could have been for his refusal to comply immediately with her order to return. Actually it was for his involvement with Elizabeth Throgmorton, and everyone knew it.

This young woman was the daughter of Nicholas Throgmorton, dead since 1571, who had been a courtier, an ambassador to France, and a member of Parliament. An energetic man possessed of a perceptive, rather devious mind, Throgmorton, like Raleigh later, made a brilliant defense of himself when charged with treason during Mary Tudor's reign. His daughter, a maid of honor to Queen Elizabeth, was tall and graceful, with blue eyes and blond hair, a charming, thoughtful person whose correspondence is as delightful as it is difficult to decipher because of the spelling. To her, a woman mature and in her late twenties, no real beauty or substantial heiress, belonged the laurels for winning the attention of the forty-year-old Raleigh. And to her, as to him, came punishment: imprisonment in the Tower but in a suite apart from her alleged seducer.

Was Raleigh really guilty of seducing Elizabeth Throgmorton, as most people believed? Tongues wagged furiously on that point, and at least one anonymous letter, the authenticity of which is not completely established by any means, contains a writer's scurrilous observations that Raleigh had been "too inward with one of her Majesty's maids," and that "All is alarm and confusion at this discovery of the discoverer, and not indeed of a new continent, but of a new incontinent."[17] The main evidence is scanty and not very satisfactory. One source was the Latin statement by William Camden in his *Annals*, published in 1615, that Raleigh had violated one of the Queen's maids whom he later married.[18] Neither Raleigh nor his lady, in the Tower at the time, denied what Camden wrote, which, however, proves nothing. Another source was an allusion by Robert Cecil to Raleigh's "brutish offence,"[19] which also proves nothing. Cecil was but picking up the Court line, for Raleigh's marrying any woman, let alone seducing her, would have been a "brutish offence" in the Queen's eyes. Nor did any child come of the "seduction," as alleged in some quarters. That Raleigh married Elizabeth Throgmorton there is little doubt, though no record of the time of marriage exists. Their names were linked romantically at least two months before the expedition sailed, and Raleigh's denial to Cecil of any marriage may have been the truth or a stalwart lie given in the hope that he could sail before the truth was discovered and that the wealth with which he expected to return would soften the Queen's anger. Or he may have married Elizabeth in the interval between his return and his imprisonment, or even after his imprisonment.

The answer about the marriage, if not to its precise time, may well lie with Elizabeth Throgmorton herself. As Lady Raleigh, she was a devoted, honorable wife, whose life was filled with sadness which she bore steadfastly. Her pride in her husband and her high heart were never more evident than in the succession of disasters that befell her. It is extraordinarily difficult to

---

[17] J. Collier, "Continuation of New Materials for a Life of Sir Walter Raleigh," in *Archaeologia*, XXXIV (1852), 161.

[18] ". . . honoraria Reginae virgine vitiata, quam postea in uxorem duxit."

[19] *Cal. S.P. Dom., 1591-1594*, 273.

imagine a woman of such maturity and spirit and character, one, furthermore, who knew the Court and its royal mistress, letting herself be seduced. It is doubtful that the "brutish offence" was quite what Raleigh's enemies preferred to think. In a letter written from the Tower to Sir Moyle Finch and signed "E.R.," rather than "E.T.," and composed in spelling even more weird and phonetic than Raleigh himself sometimes employed, she indicates that they were secretly married: "I asur you treuly I never desiared nor never wolde desiar my lebbarti with out the good likeking ne advising of Sur W: R: hit is not this inprisonment if I bought hit with my life that shuld make me thinke hit long if hit should doo him harme to speke of my delivery [from the Tower]: but Sur R.S. [Cecil] was somwhat deseved in his Jugment in that and hit may be hee findeth his eror."[20]

Raleigh had committed the crime never entirely forgiven of any of the Queen's favorites: the crime of becoming romantically involved with another woman. He was certainly not ignorant of the Queen's aversion to such entanglement: she hated Leicester's wife with unbounded passion, and she denied Lady Essex a place at Court. That Raleigh was willing to risk her wrath speaks well of his love for Elizabeth Throgmorton, whatever it may indicate of his judgment and of his gratitude to the royal spinster who had raised him from a gentleman adventurer and on whose continued favor depended the success of his many enterprises and the achievement of his aspirations. Of all her favorites Raleigh seemed the best choice to remain single. No doubt his loyalty in this respect accounted, at least in part, for Elizabeth's renewed favor to him after Essex's marriage. Now even her "dear Water" had fallen, and her fury at his defection, which she construed as a violation of her trust, her love, her very honor, was worse than that visited on any favorite. Let him and his inamorata cool their ardors in lonely separation in the Tower.

Raleigh could not believe that he was forever ruined so far as restoration to the Queen's favor was concerned. After all, his confinement was hardly severe. Lodged in the Brick Tower

---

[20] Historical Manuscripts Commission Report (hereafter HMC), *Allen George Finch MSS*, I, 33-34. For marriage discussion, see also Harlow (ed.), *Discoverie of Guiana*, xxi; F. Sorenson, "Sir Walter Raleigh's Marriage," in *Studies in Philology*, XXXIII (1936), 182-202.

with almost the comforts of home, he transacted business with his agents, lost none of his estates, retained his position and title as Captain of the Guard, and had as his keeper his own well-liked cousin, Sir George Carew. At the same time, he chafed at the loss of liberty. Learning one day, when Carew and another cousin, Sir Arthur Gorges, were present, that the Queen was being rowed past the Tower, he demanded that he be rowed out to look upon her face again. When Carew refused, Raleigh seems to have staged an absurd fight with him. At first enjoying the spectacle hugely, Gorges intervened when it began to grow rough, and received a sharp cut across his knuckles for his pains. This comedy, reported by Carew to Cecil, did nothing to enhance Raleigh's reputation or chances of release, nor did a letter he sent to Cecil in late July, ostensibly about expenses for Guardsmen's coats but actually to declare his love for the Queen. The letter is in the pattern of courtly behavior and romantic hyperbole that the Queen, despite her nearly sixty years, usually adored. But, even for a veteran courtier like Raleigh, the letter was a little fantastic:

"My heart was never broken till this day that I hear the Queen goes so far off, whom I have followed so many years with so great love and desire in so many journeys, and am now left behind her in a dark prison all alone. While she was yet near at hand, that I might hear of her once in two or three days, my sorrows were the less, but even now my heart is cast into the depth of all misery. I that was wont to behold her riding like Alexander, hunting like Diana, walking like Venus, the gentle wind blowing her fair hair about her pure cheeks like a nymph, sometimes sitting in the shade like a goddess, sometimes singing like an angel, sometimes playing like Orpheus, behold the sorrow of this world once amiss hath bereaved me of all. Oh! love that only shineth in misfortune, what is become of thy assurance! All wounds have scars but that of phantasy: all affections their relenting but that of womankind. Who is the judge of friendship but adversity, or when is grace witnessed but in offences? There were no divinity but by reason of compassion, for revenges are brutish and mortal. All those times past—the loves, the sighs, the sorrows, the desires, can they not weigh down our frail misfortune? Cannot one drop of gall be hidden in so great heaps of sweetness? I may then conclude, *spes et fortuna, valete* [hope and fortune, farewell]. She is gone, in whom I trusted, and of me hath not one thought of mercy, nor any respect of that that was. Do with me therefore what you list. I am more weary of life than they are desirous I should perish, which if it had been for her, as it is by her, I had been too happily borne. Yours not worthy any name or title—W.R."[21]

The letter, though sent to Cecil, was written for the Queen, to whom Raleigh could not address it directly. Absurd as it was, it represented the best effort Raleigh could make to secure his release. Denial of guilt would have been folly, hence his allusion to his marriage as "our frail misfortune." But whether Cecil showed the missive to the Queen, as Raleigh certainly expected him to do, is not known. Possibly not; Cecil was never quite the friend that Raleigh thought him. Even if the Queen saw the letter, it is unlikely that so obvious an artifice, however susceptible she was to gross flattery, would have won him a respite from punishment that she considered well merited. Hence Raleigh remained in the Tower, furious that Sir William Fitzwilliam had ordered cattle on his Irish estates sold for cash to pay an alleged debt of £400 to the Queen and alarmed that the Irish were again contemplating revolt.[22] He also felt frustrated at having to deal with sea matters not directly but through correspondence with Lord Admiral Howard, whom he thanked for looking after certain of his interests during "this unfortunate accident."[23]

Ironically the Queen let Raleigh out of prison, at least temporarily, because she needed him. His fleet returned to Dartmouth with complete vindication of the plans he had issued Frobisher and Burrough. Thanks to Frobisher's diversion off the Spanish coast, Burrough captured a number of prizes, of which the choicest was a great Crown of Portugal carrack, the *Madre de Dios*, a seven-decker of 1,600 tons, huge for its day. She mounted 32 brass cannon and had nearly 700 people aboard. But what astounded and delighted her captors was the cargo of 537 tons of spices alone and an exotic miscellany of jewels,

[21] HMC, *Salisbury MSS*, IV, 220.     [22] *Ibid.*, 221.
[23] Edwards, *Ralegh* (*Letters*), II, 53-54.

drugs, silks, calicoes, carpets, costly scents, ebony, ivory, and the like. Various wild estimates of the carrack's worth were made, but when the final assay was effected, the figure was placed at £141,000, or from five to ten times that in modern values.[24]

No such prize had ever been seen in the West Country, and there was a burst of pillaging and pilfering when the carrack reached Dartmouth on September 8. None could control either officers or men, many of whom were shocked and angered to learn that Raleigh was a prisoner. To restore order, wrote Sir John Hawkins in frantic haste to Burghley, "Sir Walter Raleigh is the especial man." Hawkins pointed out that Raleigh could do nothing effective where he was, but, if he were released, "it might very much set forward Her Majesty's service, and might benefit her portion."[25] The implication in Hawkins's letter that she might lose money was horrifying to Elizabeth. She released Raleigh from the Tower and sent him off without delay but as a state prisoner with a keeper. Meanwhile Burghley hurried Cecil to the west to do what he could and perhaps to keep an eye on Raleigh when he arrived.

It is not difficult to imagine the eagerness, even the zeal, with which Raleigh hastened to his task. Threatening to strip suspected plunderers to the skin, he could not reach the West Country fast enough, for not only would the Queen's portion be affected by the pillage but his own investment as well. It was in a role deeply humiliating to him that he appeared in his beloved west, the Warden of the Stannaries and the Lieutenant General of Cornwall, a prisoner.

Both he and Cecil found the rumors of the richness of the prize and of its plundering hardly exaggerated. "There never was such spoil," Cecil wrote Burghley. Everyone he met within seven miles of Exeter who had anything in a cloak, a bag, or a mail collection that smelled of spices he brought back to Exeter. He committed two innkeepers to prison, discovered a bag of seed pearls and musk in a shop, feared that "the birds be flown

---

[24] See Burrough's report of the taking of the *Madre de Dios* in Hakluyt, *Voyages*, VII, 105-18. As G. R. Elton so aptly observes (*England under the Tudors*, 380), "The *Madre de Dios* played the part for a new generation which the *Cacafuego* had played for their elders: hopes of another such capture kept the ships at sea."

[25] Quoted by Edwards, *Ralegh* (*Life*), I, 151-52.

for jewels, pearls, and amber," and promised to try to suppress the two thousand buyers converging on the ports. He was particularly pleased that his arrival made people "stagger." Something else also pleased him. "Her Majesty's captive comes after me, but"—and here Cecil was positively gleeful—"I have out-rid him, and will be in Dartmouth before him."[26]

Four days later, September 23, Cecil wrote to Sir Thomas Heneage, the Vice Chamberlain, a fascinating account of Raleigh's arrival. Within a half hour of Cecil's boarding the carrack, Raleigh appeared with his keeper. "I assure you, Sir," said Cecil, amazed, "his poor servants, to the number of a hundred and forty goodly men, and all the mariners, came to him with such shouts and joy, as I never saw a man more troubled to quiet them in my life. But his heart is broken; for he is very extreme pensive longer than he is busied, in which he can toil terribly." Raleigh's capacity for work astonished many contemporaries, and Cecil was evidently just discovering that "Her Majesty's captive" was something more than a courtier. He laughed to see Raleigh rage at the spoils stolen, but he quickly sobered when Sir John Gilbert greeted Raleigh with tears. He even became concerned that, whenever congratulated on his liberty, Raleigh would reply, "No, I am still the Queen of England's poor captive." "I wished him to conceal it," said Cecil, "because here it doth diminish his credit, which I do vow to you before God, is greater amongst the mariners than I thought for. I do grace him as much as I may, for I find him marvelous greedy to recover the conceit of his brutish offence."[27]

Raleigh served as joint commissioner with Cecil and William Killigrew. The principle on which the distribution of the spoils taken by privateering operated was comparatively simple: one-third went to the Queen, one-third to the victualer, and one-third to the officers and crew. The Queen had contributed about one-fifth of the tonnage and one-tenth of the original joint-stock of £18,000, and thus was entitled to a tenth of the spoils, or approximately £14,000. Raleigh actually offered her £80,000, writing Burghley, "Fourscore thousand pounds is more than ever a man presented Her Majesty as yet. If God have sent it

---

[26] *Ibid.*, 153-54; *Cal. S.P. Dom., 1591-1594*, 272-73.
[27] Edwards, *Ralegh (Life)*, I, 154; *Cal. S.P. Dom., 1591-1594*, 273.

for my ransom, I hope Her Majesty of her abundant goodness will accept it."[28] It was a princely offer made in a lofty manner typical of Raleigh. In the final division, Elizabeth was given the bulk of the spoils. Raleigh and Hawkins, who had invested £34,000, received £36,000. Cumberland, whose expenses had amounted to only £19,000, received as much as Raleigh and Hawkins together. The City of London, which had spent £6,000, was awarded £12,000. Raleigh, who had been paying interest right along on £11,000 he had borrowed to finance the voyage, was understandably bitter about the awards to Cumberland and London. "I that adventured all my estate," he told Burghley angrily, "lose of my principal, and they have double. I took all the care and pains; carried the ships from hence to Falmouth, and from thence to the north cape of Spain; and they only sat still."[29] Even the Chancellor of the Exchequer, Sir John Fortescue, was moved to speak to Burghley in Raleigh's behalf since he feared that Raleigh might not be induced to plan another expedition if not properly rewarded. *86250*

But the Queen was not impressed by Raleigh's generosity, the financial drubbing he received, or the service he had rendered. He had preferred Elizabeth Throgmorton to Elizabeth Tudor, and for this crime she never really forgave him. Back he went to the Tower, the proper resort for such a miscreant, and remained there during the fall. By an exercise of extraordinary grace, however, the Queen condescended to free him and his lady in December. Raleigh then retired to Sherborne, still in disgrace but relieved beyond measure that at last he had his liberty.

[28] Edwards, *Ralegh* (*Letters*), II, 68.
[29] *Ibid.*, 76-78.

# CHAPTER 9
# Years of Disgrace

RALEIGH's enforced retirement and his banishment from the Court, the center of his frenzied efforts to secure the recognition on which he staked so much, was a chastening experience but by no means an idle period in his life. At Sherborne, which both he and "Bess" Raleigh, as he called his lady, loved and came to regard as their real home, he proved himself an industrious gentleman farmer. He took a reasonably active part in the Parliament of 1592-1593. Ireland continued to interest him. He still liked to converse with any man of unusual mind. And always on the periphery of his thinking hung the vision, entrancing in its allurement, of the New World, not Virginia any longer but a tropical land of magical promise farther south.

Sherborne, which was missed almost as much by the bishop who formerly enjoyed it as it was loved by Raleigh, was a blessed place of refuge for the harassed courtier. It was "my fortune's field," he told Cecil in May 1593.[1] At Sherborne, he built, he planted, he bred and raced horses. He became especially fond of a great medieval sport, falconry, and in August he wrote Cecil, who also raised falcons, "The Indian falcon is sick of the buck worm, and, therefore, if you will be so bountiful to give another falcon, I will provide you a winter gelding."[2] He wrote a little poetry and he read many books. However, he did not remain at Sherborne following these beloved pursuits all the time. He continued as Lieutenant of Cornwall, Deputy Lieutenant of Devon, and Warden of the Stannaries; these duties often called him to the West Country. Though occasionally he went up to London, he was never invited to attend the royal presence. Unless the Queen's wrath could eventually be appeased, his day was over; none knew this better than he. Man of action that he was, he also knew that he could not continue indefinitely in the bucolic life of Sherborne.

He was therefore not disappointed that Parliamentary duties

[1] HMC, *Salisbury MSS*, IV, 311.     [2] *Ibid.*, 364.

kept him close to London through the winter and spring of
1593. His first seat had been as junior knight for Devon in the
Parliament of 1584, followed by standing as the senior Devon
member in the Parliament of 1586. Irish service for the Crown
prevented him from standing for the Parliament of 1588, in
which so many of the Armada heroes sat, but he was elected to
the Parliament of 1593 for the Cornish borough of St. Michaels.
His inability to secure a seat representing one of the counties of
Cornwall, Devon, or Dorset, where Sherborne was located,
must have cut him sorely, for more prestige adhered to county
seats than to borough seats. Perhaps, as has been suggested by
one Parliamentary scholar, his disgrace gave the gentry an
opportunity to show their true feelings toward the fallen
favorite; perhaps, moreover, Raleigh had neither the votes nor
the influence over the gentry necessary to give him an assured
seat of stature.[3] On the other hand, the fact that he sat for a
borough rather than a county in no way diminished the importance of his role in this Parliament.

The Parliament of 1592-1593 was called primarily "for con-
sultation and preparation of aid" (meaning money) in the undeclared war against Spain.[4] In a speech that seems delightfully
naïve and refreshing, the Lord Keeper of the Great Seal, Sir
John Puckering, urged that the Commons address themselves
strictly to the problem and not make any new laws since there
were already many good laws in force, more, indeed, than were
well executed! Speaker of the House was Sir Edward Coke,
destined to become the greatest legal figure in English history
but a man who was to disgrace the Common Law which he
revered by his conduct in Raleigh's treason trial. Also present
was Coke's greatest opponent for the offices of Solicitor General and Attorney General, Francis Bacon, presently to be known
as the author of a collection of brilliant essays and already
cherishing hopes of becoming Lord Chancellor. Other members
included Sir Francis Drake, whose feeling toward Spain was no
secret; Fulke Greville, the poet; and, of course, Sir Robert
Cecil, skilled in the numerous ways of keeping the House from

---

[3] J. E. Neale, *The Elizabethan House of Commons*, 54-55.
[4] S. D'Ewes, *The Journal of All the Parliaments During the Reign of Queen
Elizabeth, Both of the House of Lords and House of Commons*, 469.

getting out of bounds and shrewdly reminding the members of his thorough Parliamentary experience by prefacing his speeches with, "As I remember. . . ."

Cecil's control, however, did not prevent certain members from speaking on forbidden subjects; freedom of speech did not exist without important qualification under Elizabeth.[5] For expressing their concern about the succession to the throne, Peter Wentworth, a member, like Raleigh, for a Cornish borough, and Sir Henry Bromley were imprisoned, the former dying while in the Tower.[6] Two days after they went to prison, James Morrice, Attorney of the Court of Wards, dared offer two bills against the strong measures of bishops and the ecclesiastical courts toward Puritan ministers.[7] This Parliament was a strongly Puritan assemblage, and many members favored Morrice's proposals. But the Queen refused to tolerate further discussion of the subject. As a consequence of his boldness, Morrice lost his position and his right to practice, and spent several years a prisoner in Tutbury Castle. By punishing such violation of her "no trespassing" signs, clearly posted years before, Elizabeth prevented straying onto the forbidden field of the royal prerogative.

Raleigh's part in this Parliament was decidedly impressive. He served on most of the important committees and spoke in favor of several bills, notably the subsidy bill and a bill to prevent Germans and Dutchmen from retailing foreign wares in England, while he vigorously opposed a bill against a group of Puritan sectaries, the Brownists. In both the bill for the subsidy and that against the retailing of foreign wares in England, Raleigh pointed out the need of clarifying policy toward Spain and those who assisted her directly or indirectly. He came out strongly for an open declaration of war and for spelling it out in the subsidy bill. He knew, he said, that as yet many people thought it not unlawful to take prizes from the Spaniards. He knew too that if war became "open" and there-

[5] J. E. Neale, "The Commons' Privilege of Free Speech in Parliament," in R. W. Seton-Watson, *Tudor Studies.*

[6] J. E. Neale, "Peter Wentworth," in *English Historical Review*, XXXIX (1924), 36-54, 175-205; Neale, *Elizabeth I and Her Parliaments, 1584-1601*, 251-66; Elton, *England under the Tudors*, 460-61.

[7] D'Ewes, 474-76; Neale, *Elizabeth I and Her Parliaments, 1584-1601*, 267-79.

fore unquestionably lawful, the Queen would have more volunteers than she could use. But no one should think that he spoke simply to please the Queen, "to whom he was infinitely bound above his deserts." He spoke of necessity from what he saw and knew, and what he perceived was the growing strength of Spain and the "malice and ill purpose" of her rule. Philip II had shown his power and influence in Denmark and Norway, in France and Brittany, in the Low Countries, and even in Scotland. He was building ships at a rapid rate and had still not given up his hopes of invading England. To counter this threat, England must prepare her navy and send troops to Brittany. Again and again in this session, Raleigh warned of Spain's growing might.[8]

Spanish power was one of the reasons he opposed letting the Dutch retail wares in England. Expressing a view that many shared in England in the seventeenth century, and one that is not entirely dead in certain quarters of the world even today, Raleigh growled, "The nature of the Dutchman is to fly to no man but for his profit." The Dutch refused to obey for long any injunction not to trade, and, because of their avarice, they actually "maintained the King of Spain in his greatness," providing the sinews by which he kept up his formidable fleets and armies. Furthermore, the Dutch, by their policy, had succeeded in capturing "the trade of the world." Thus spoke both the English entrepreneur, jealous of Dutch commercial supremacy, and the hater of Spain and all who trafficked with her.[9]

But it was in his position on the Separatist Bill that Raleigh spoke with a voice that reached far into the future. Ever since the revival of Protestantism in England with the accession of Elizabeth, Puritanism had been steadily growing, a movement based, for the most part, on the austere tenets of Calvinism and cherishing as a form of organization either the Presbyterian system that John Knox had established in Scotland or the Congregational model of Robert Browne. Most of the Presbyterian advocates were willing to remain nominally within the Church of England but planned to subvert it, overthrowing the hierarchy of bishops and establishing their own system, which ap-

[8] For the quotations above and other speeches against Spain, see D'Ewes, 478, 484, 492; Neale, *Elizabeth I and Her Parliaments, 1584-1601*, 298-312 *passim*.
[9] D'Ewes, 509.

peared to subordinate state to church. Unlike the Puritans of Presbyterian persuasion, the followers of men like Browne and George Barrow chose to separate at once from the Church of England, hence the term "Brownists," "Barrowists," or "Separatists." Though she mistrusted all Puritans, even those whose concern was only to remove from the Church all taint of Romanism, Elizabeth was particularly antagonized by the Separatists. She regarded religious dissent that expressed itself in violating the law of the land not simply as an act of civil disobedience but one of political deviation tantamount to treason. The capital penalty had only recently been demanded for several Separatist leaders, as well as for three Puritans who plotted the assassination of Elizabeth in order to establish a Presbyterian system. Now, in this Parliament, a severe bill was framed against all Separatists, threatening them with exile if they did not conform.

Raleigh was only one of a number of men who spoke against the bill, but he saw more clearly than anyone the implications of such persecution. He admitted that he had no regard for Brownists, who, in his opinion, deserved to be rooted out of the realm. At the same time, the danger to the state if the law was passed should also be considered: "For it is to be feared that men not guilty will be included in it, and that law is hard which taketh life, or sendeth into banishment, where men's intentions shall be judged by a jury, and they shall be judges what other men meant; but that law is against a fact, that is just; and punish the fact as severely as you will."[10]

As Raleigh looked at the situation, he felt that law cannot properly judge conscience, for conscience is beyond its jurisdiction. An action resulting from conscience or an idea may be subject to prosecution and penalty, but the idea itself cannot be banished or killed—there is a foreshadowing of Milton in this. On the other hand, if law is to be admitted as a judge of conscience, despite the impossibility of its truly becoming one, the door would be opened to gross injustice visited upon the innocent as well as upon the guilty. Raleigh's is an eloquent argument against thought control.

But there was another aspect to the argument of which no

[10] H. Townshend, *Historical Collections, An Exact Account of the Last Four Parliaments of Elizabeth,* 76; D'Ewes, 517.

one appeared to have thought. One can almost hear the sharp, scornful voice of the practical man of affairs, but one not without humaneness: "If two or three thousand Brownists meet at the sea side, at whose charge shall they be transported? Or whither will you send them? I am sorry for it; I am afraid there is near twenty thousand of them in England; and when they are gone, who shall maintain their wives and children?"[11] Thanks largely to Raleigh's intervention, the bill was revised, with his name listed first after the Privy Councillors in the large committee to which it was recommitted.

While Raleigh was engaged in Parliament, he was also trying to clear up difficulties rising from his Irish possessions. Years earlier he had formed a partnership with three men, one of whom was Henry Pyne, and secured a license to ship from Munster all articles of export regardless of whether they appeared on the list of prohibited items. He then started to cut timber, which, for the most part, was shaped into staves for wine casks for the Canary Islands and Madeira, with which England traded despite the war. Some of the timber, however, went into naval construction. When everything appeared to be going nicely in 1592, the Deputy, Fitzwilliam, halted the business and arrested Pyne, Raleigh's agent, on the grounds that he was exporting timber to Spain proper and acting as a go-between for Catholics who had fled to the Continent and those still in England and Ireland. These were serious charges; Pyne was accordingly brought to London and questioned in July. He cleared himself of any taint of treason and in August Raleigh wrote Cecil, entreating his support of Pyne's request for an end to the restraint on the wine-stave trade.[12] In January 1594 Raleigh was formally granted permission to export staves to Madeira, the Canaries, Bordeaux, and La Rochelle.[13] One can almost see the sardonic smile of triumph as he thought of Fitzwilliam.

Quite apart from his timber enterprises in Ireland and his

[11] *Ibid.*, 517; Townshend, 76; Neale, *Elizabeth I and Her Parliaments, 1584-1601*, 288-89. See the excellent discussion in W. K. Jordan, *The Development of Religious Toleration in England*, I, 214-45. The best general study of the issues raised by the Puritan movement of the age is by M. Knappen, *Tudor Puritanism.*

[12] HMC, *Salisbury MSS*, IV, 363.

[13] For this controversy, see *ibid.*, IV, 278, 332, 464; Quinn, *Raleigh and the British Empire*, 152-55.

efforts there in 1594 and 1595 to mine iron ore and build smelters, Raleigh's interest involved a concern for the defense of Ireland. He feared that preoccupation with what was happening on the Continent in 1593 was making the government neglect that defense. Writing Cecil in May, he pointed out that only recently a million had been spent in Ireland—"a better kingdom might have been purchased at a less price, and that same defended with as many pence, if good order had been taken." Now he wondered if Ireland was not less secure than ever. The Queen should find it "no small dishonor to be vexed with so beggarly a nation, that have neither arms nor fortification." Part of the difficulty lay with the King of Spain, who, in Raleigh's graphic language, "seeketh not Ireland for Ireland, but having raised up troops of beggars at our backs, shall be able to enforce us to cast our eyes over our shoulders, while those before us strike us on the brains." On the other hand, the English administration was also at fault, for "good advice either neglected or weakly executed hath taught our enemies to arm those parts, which lay bare to the sword."[14] He consistently favored a strong policy toward the Irish. He believed that they would construe a policy that was now conciliatory, now severe, as evidence of weakness and as an invitation to revolt. Whatever one may think of his humanitarianism, or lack of it, so far as the Irish were concerned, he understood them. They were neither a submissive people nor, in view of their sufferings and humiliation, a reasonable people. Give them a chance to revolt, and they would seize it. Had Raleigh's warning been heeded at this time, the dreadful experiences of 1598 to 1601 might have been avoided and the treason and execution of Essex might never have occurred.

After Parliament went home, Raleigh became ill. What the nature of his affliction was is not clear but he started regularly to go to Weymouth for sea bathing and to Bath for the waters. At first, he thought himself worse for such a cure. Possibly, highstrung as he was, he suffered from a nervous reaction to his misfortune and time was all that was needed to restore his health. In any event, the birth of a son, eleven months after he and Bess were released from the Tower, seems to have cheered

[14] HMC, *Salisbury MSS*, IV, 310-11.

him greatly. From the start, the boy, also named Walter, was a vigorous, spirited youngster whom Raleigh did not hesitate to belabor for his rudeness but of whom he was enormously proud.

For all that he busied himself as a country gentleman, entertained astrologers, mathematicians, theologians, and poets, fled the plague in 1594, and caught a Jesuit "with his capes and chalice . . . a notable stout villain,"[15] Raleigh was restless. There were those who thought he was contriving a return. Wrote Walsingham's former secretary, Nicholas Faint, to Anthony Bacon, ". . . it is now feared of all honest men that he shall presently come to the court; yet it is well withstood. God grant him some further resistance."[16] The fearful Faint need not have been so fearful. Gloriana continued unappeased, and Raleigh was compelled to witness from afar the growing rivalry between Essex and Cecil, behind whom naturally stood his sick old father, the great Burghley, who had earlier advised his son to avoid being a man like Raleigh. Utterly frustrated, Raleigh cast about for some way by which he could capture the Queen's attention, some bold, magnificent stroke that would bring her such pleasure she would invite him to renew the ties of friendship, perhaps even of courtship. And, at last, he was certain he had the solution.

[15] *Ibid.*, 510-11.
[16] Birch, *Memoirs of the Reign of Queen Elizabeth*, I, 151.

# CHAPTER 10

# The First Expedition to Guiana

EVERY man has his El Dorado, that sought-for turning where Fortune joins him at last and, taking him by the hand, leads him to his heart's desire. Raleigh's El Dorado was not simply the figurative aspiration but the literal objective as well. This was the original city of gold, called Manoa by the natives and reported to be hidden somewhere back in the valley of the Orinoco in the mysterious land of Guiana. This land, lying between the Amazon and Orinoco Rivers and including the entire valley of the latter, was a jungle infested with wild beasts, crocodiles, and poisonous snakes. In the sixteenth century its hazards to the white man were magnified owing to the resentment of the savages at the treatment they had received from those Spaniards who had attempted to penetrate the area.

Spaniards had been trying for years to solve the mystery of Guiana. They believed that another branch of the fabulously wealthy Inca civilization that Francisco Pizarro had conquered in Peru existed in the interior, the Incas having fled to escape Pizarro. They based their belief on tales told by Indians and on an even stranger tale related by a Spaniard named Martinez, who died in Puerto Rico swearing he had been in a city of gold which he said was El Dorado. He had been led there, blindfolded, by natives who introduced him to the Emperor. This personage often bathed in turpentine, then had gold dust blown on his body. In the Emperor's residence all the kitchen- and table-ware was of gold and silver. He had ropes, chests, and troughs of gold and silver. More magnificent still was a garden in which he had a life-size copy in gold and silver of every herb, flower, and tree that grew in his kingdom. Martinez was permitted to leave with many precious gifts from the Emperor, but, harassed by hostile Indians, he lost them in his struggle to reach the coast.

Though Martinez may have been babbling only of feverish visions, the Spaniards had discovered much the same concentration of wealth in Mexico and Peru, so they saw little reason to doubt that they might find a third civilization. Furthermore, in Peru, where they found so many golden objects, they discovered little gold to be mined; the source might therefore lie in El Dorado. For decades the Spaniards had pressed the search, the most zealous explorer being Don Antonio de Berrio. This indefatigable man, a veteran of the wars of Charles V and Philip II, had come out to New Grenada in 1580 at sixty years of age to look after property left to his wife. He had been on the hunt for fifteen years, had made three expeditions into the interior, and, after comparing notes with three competitive explorers, placed the location of El Dorado back in the steep Guiana Highlands. Though he wanted to continue the search, the hostility of Spaniards living along the Guiana coast made it impossible for him to raise a sufficient force. All he could do for the moment, therefore, was to base himself at San Josef on Trinidad, place a small outpost near the mouth of the Orinoco, and send his principal lieutenant, Domingo de Vera, to Spain for reinforcements. Though a few of these arrived in 1594, more were being assembled in Spain to be sent out in 1595.[1]

Raleigh knew a great deal about Berrio's work; in fact, he was well acquainted with Spanish efforts to penetrate the Orinoco Valley. He read what the Spanish explorers had written, and he talked with seamen who had sailed on those coasts. Nor was his interest transient, for he admitted that Guiana had fascinated him for years, as it had Richard Hakluyt. Raleigh may have first learned about Guiana in detail from Don Pedro Sarmiento de Gamboa, whom his privateering captain, Jacob Whiddon, had captured at sea in 1586 and brought to England. Raleigh's interest in the mysterious land was not exclusively a desire to find gold. He wanted gold, to be sure, wanted quantities of it in order to be relieved of the burden of disgrace and secure reinstatement to the Queen's favor; money was one of the surest ways to the penurious Elizabeth's good graces. But he was even more eager for England to acquire Guiana and

[1] Williamson, *Age of Drake*, 316-64; Harlow (ed.), *Discoverie of Guiana*, Introduction.

thereby break the monopoly that Spain exercised in the colonization of South America. Few men have shown more zeal for building an empire or spent more money to that end than Raleigh; few have failed more consistently.

When, precisely, Raleigh began to plan an expedition to Guiana is uncertain, probably in 1593. He was talking about it to influential people by the end of the year in an effort to find investors, for his spirited but anxious lady wrote to Cecil on February 8, 1594, a letter that one can be sure she never showed her husband: "I hope you will rather draw Sir Walter towards the East, than help him forward toward the sunset, if any respect to me, or love to him, be not forgotten. But every month hath his flower, and every season his contentment, and you great counsellors are so full of new counsels as you are steady in nothing; but we poor souls that hath bought sorrow at a high price desire and can be pleased with the same misfortune we hold, fearing alterations will but multiply misery, of which we have already felt sufficient. I know only your persuasions are of effect with him, and held as 'orrekeles,' tied to them by love; therefore I humbly beseech you, stay him rather than further him, by the which you shall bind me for ever. . . ."[2]

Bess Raleigh might as well have spared herself the effort of writing. Short of a command from Cecil or the Queen, Raleigh could not be diverted from an expedition that had captured his imagination. He sent out Whiddon on a reconnaissance to the Orinoco in 1594. Whiddon found the native chiefs unfriendly to Berrio, who traitorously invited a number of Whiddon's crew ashore and ambushed them. Raleigh seems also to have learned more news of Guiana, thanks to Captain George Popham's capture of Spanish documents on the high seas.[3]

In late 1594 and 1595, Raleigh prepared for his expedition. He obtained a patent that was made out simply to "our servant Sir Walter Raleigh," a bald address indeed compared with the Virginia charter of years before when he had been both "trusty" and "well beloved." In his new patent he was commissioned not only to discover and conquer lands unpossessed by any Christian prince but also to "offend and enfeeble the King of

[2] HMC, *Salisbury MSS*, IV, 485.
[3] Quinn, *Raleigh and the British Empire*, 178-79.

Spain." Naturally Raleigh would be delighted to accommodate on both counts.

His expedition attracted considerable attention. Though the Queen ignored it, Lord Admiral Howard contributed a ship, *The Lion's Whelp*, and Cecil is generally believed to have invested money in the enterprise (Guiana always attracted Cecil). Aboard the four ships, apart from the crews, were about one hundred and fifty officers, soldiers, and gentleman volunteers. Among the last, perhaps as contributors too, were Raleigh's nephew, John Gilbert; Sir Richard Grenville's son, John; and a cousin of Raleigh, Butshead Gorges. Also with the expedition in command of a small galley was a man devoted to Raleigh to the day he died, Lawrence Keymis, Oxford Fellow, geographer, mathematician, and mariner.

The expedition sailed from Plymouth on February 6, 1595. Two ships that were expected to join it under Captains Amyas Preston and George Somers missed it. Two others under George Popham and Sir Robert Dudley had agreed to meet Raleigh later at Trinidad. On the trip across the Atlantic, Raleigh and Captain Cross, who commanded a small bark, lost touch with Keymis and *The Lion's Whelp* under Captain George Gifford. Reaching the Canary Islands, Raleigh and Cross waited a week for both them and the privateers under Preston and Somers. When no ship showed up, Raleigh weighed anchor for Trinidad, arriving on March 22, where he was disappointed to meet neither Popham nor Dudley. Actually they had already been there, talked with Berrio, and explored the Orinoco estuary. After waiting in vain for Raleigh, they went off privateering only ten days before Raleigh finally reached the rendezvous.

What to do now? John Aubrey mentioned in his account of Raleigh that when the latter went to sea, he took along a trunkful of books. Now he was no doubt glad to put aside his reading and the contemplative life and become the man of action. Ordering his barge equipped, he explored the coast of Trinidad. He noted the coves and rivers, the oysters growing on mangrove trees, and the great pitch lake; the pitch he considered a great source of profit.[4] Finally returning to the Spanish settlement at Port of Spain, he decided to attack the Spaniards. Nightly,

[4] *Works,* VIII, 392.

Indians came to him to complain of Spanish cruelty. But the determining factor was his fear of leaving an armed garrison at his back when he was over four hundred miles from his ships. He explained that, had he left the garrison alone when it was daily expecting supplies and reinforcements, "I should have savored very much of the ass."[5] Hence, though the Spaniards had not been hostile up to this point. Raleigh threw his forces at them, captured Berrio, and burned San Josef. He also released five native chiefs whom Berrio had bound with one long chain, tortured, and staked out to starve.

Raleigh was relieved to discover, on returning from burning San Josef, that Gifford and Keymis had arrived with their ships. Now he could consider getting on with his expedition into the interior. To this end, he entertained Berrio as an honored guest. As a matter of fact, the Spaniard, cruel as he was, was neither better nor worse than most Spanish administrators of his day. Raleigh liked his demeanor—"a gentleman of great assuredness"—and his courage.[6] Ignoring the man's cruelty to the Indians, for whom Raleigh felt more sympathy than for the Irish, Raleigh talked with him as gentleman to gentleman. Berrio chatted freely but became melancholy and sad when he saw that Raleigh meant to seize the land. Turning guileful, he tried to dissuade the Englishman by pointing up the difficulties: Manoa, the capital of El Dorado, he said, was much farther from the coast than Whiddon had been led to believe. This disclosure Raleigh thought it wise to conceal from his men lest they lose heart.

He now prepared for the up-river trip. He had the galley cut down for river travel and took in addition a barge, two wherries, and a ship's boat from *The Lion's Whelp*. Over one hundred men accompanied him, carrying provisions for a month. But though eager to be off, and willing to endure hardship up to a point, Raleigh was no lover of the kind of life he and his men were forced to lead on the boats, "being all driven to lie in the rain and weather, in the open air, in the burning sun, and upon the hard boards, and to dress our meat, and to carry all manner of furniture in them, wherewith they were so pestered and unsavoury, that what with victuals, being mostly fish, with

[5] *Ibid.*, 395.　　　　　　　　[6] *Ibid.*, 396.

the wet clothes of so many men thrust together, and the heat of the sun, I will undertake there was never any prison in England that could be found more unsavoury and loathsome, especially to myself, who had for many years before been dieted and cared for in a sort far differing."[7] The twenty years and more between, on the one hand, the hardened Huguenot irregular and the tough conqueror of Irish rebels and, on the other, the disgraced courtier were taking their toll. When one thinks of what many of the Spanish conquistadors—even Berrio—had endured, Raleigh seems hardly of heroic mold. As one able scholar of the great Elizabethan age has observed, "In any short and sharp affair with sword in hand he was as brave as the best, but he lacked endurance."[8]

Notwithstanding his present physical softness and his fastidious repugnance at rough-and-ready living, Raleigh headed for "that labyrinth of rivers," the Orinoco: "all the earth does not yield the like confluence of streams and branches, the one crossing the other, so many times, and also fair and large, and so like one to another, as no man can tell which to take. . . ."[9] Few who have seen the delta would venture to say he was exaggerating. The Indian guide, Ferdinando, and his brother were soon as bewildered as Raleigh. Then, as if to make matters worse, Indians ashore captured Ferdinando. Instantly Raleigh seized an old native and threatened to kill him if his people did not at once release the guide. Actually, Ferdinando escaped, but Raleigh persuaded the captive to guide them through the river maze. Without the old man's knowledge—for Ferdinando was useless here—Raleigh said they would never have found their way to Guiana or back to their ship.[10]

Their troubles were not over. Not only did the numerous tributaries occasionally confuse their new guide, the sun also burned down in tropical fury, the thick jungles cut off any movement of air, and bread supplies ran short. Raleigh had to keep assuring his men that in but one more day they would find enough food; actually they did catch a few fish. Despite their hardships, which, after all, were not so dire, Raleigh observed with pleasure "birds of all colours, some carnation, some crim-

[7] *Ibid.,* 397.       [8] Williamson, *Age of Drake,* 367.
[9] *Works,* VIII, 420-21.       [10] *Ibid.,* 422.

son, orange tawney, purple, green."[11] A number of the creatures
flew within range of the men's fowling pieces, and thus helped
relieve the food shortage.

Finally, leaving the galley behind, Raleigh followed the
guide's direction up a stream so narrow that the branches of
trees on both sides met in the middle and the men had to slash
a passage through with their swords. Raleigh admitted that,
but for their need, they would have hanged the guide for leading them into such a place.[12] The guide, however, presently
brought them to a native village, where they procured an ample
supply of fish, fowl, bread, and Indian liquor.

The morning view was exciting to Raleigh, for now he saw
for the first time the savannah country of the Orinoco Valley.
It was "the most beautiful country that ever mine eyes beheld;
and whereas all that we had seen before was nothing but
woods, prickles, bushes, and thorns, here we beheld plains of
twenty miles in length, the grass short and green, and in divers
parts groves of trees by themselves, as if they had been by all
the art and labour in the world so made of purpose." He noticed
as he was rowed along that "the deer came down feeding by the
water's side, as if they had been used to a keeper's call."[13] But
in this paradise there was something sinister. He had a young
Negro who took it into his head to go swimming. To the horror
of the watchers, no sooner had he dived into the water than a
crocodile seized and devoured him. The river, said Raleigh in
disgust, teemed with "thousands of those ugly serpents."[14] His
boat now laden with supplies, he rejoined the galley and continued up the broad river.

Not long afterward, Captain Gifford in the galley spied four
canoes speeding downriver. Instantly he gave chase. Two of the
canoes escaped, but the other two, in one of which were three
Spaniards, were run ashore, the occupants fleeing for the woods.
To the delight of the English, they found in the captured canoes
a large store of excellent bread, of which Raleigh said, "nothing
on the earth could have been more welcome to us, next unto
gold."[15] Their hopes of discovering even gold were raised by
finding in one of the canoes a quantity of ore and in the bushes

[11] *Ibid.*, 425.   [12] *Ibid.*, 426.   [13] *Ibid.*, 427.   [14] *Ibid.*
[15] *Ibid.*, 428.

nearby a refiner's basket with quicksilver, saltpeter, and "divers things" for trying metal. They pursued the Spaniards but could not catch them. Instead they stumbled onto three Indians, one of whom they kept as a guide. All the Indians were amazed that Raleigh spared their lives. They had feared that the English would eat them, "for the Spaniards, to the end that none of the people in the passage toward Guiana, or in Guiana itself, might come to speech with us, persuaded all the nations that we were men-eaters and cannibals."[16]

The Indians were due for even greater surprises when the expedition continued up the Orinoco and made contact with the native tribes along the banks, for Raleigh's policy was friendliness itself. Though he admitted that it was difficult to prevent "the meaner sort" among his men from stealing, he exercised a firm control over them in other ways. When the natives saw that the Englishmen shared their food with them and did not attempt to molest their women, "they began to conceive the deceit and purpose of the Spaniards, who indeed (as they confessed), took from them both their wives and daughters daily, and used them for the satisfying of their own lusts, especially such as they took in this manner by strength." Raleigh was insistent that his men leave the native women alone, and the Queen, with her hatred of anything sexual, must have been pleased when he said, "I protest before the majesty of the living God, that I neither know nor believe that any of our company one or other, by violence or otherwise, ever knew any of their women; and yet we saw many hundreds, and had many in our power, and of those very young and excellently favoured, which came among us without deceit stark naked." But perhaps Elizabeth scoffed at the very possibility of such restraint, despite Raleigh's compliment in telling the Indians that his men's good behavior was by his Queen's command, and thereby "drew them to admire Her Majesty."[17]

Raleigh now pressed on, cheered by a distant view of the mountains of Guiana, feasting in friendship with the chief, Toparimaca, and staring in astonishment at the wife of a visiting cacique who resembled an unnamed lady in England in all but color. Raleigh's friendship induced the Indians to reveal to him

[16] *Ibid.*, 430.     [17] *Ibid.*

the remedies for the poisoned arrows they used, poison so dreadful that its victims sometimes died "stark mad, sometimes their bowels breaking out of their bellies, and are presently discoloured as black as pitch, and so unsavoury, as no man can endure to cure or attend them."[18] The Spaniards knew nothing of the remedies, compounded mainly of the tupera root. In addition to this gift of knowledge, the Indians presented Raleigh, when he arrived at the town of Morequito, with abundant supplies of venison, fowl, fish, pineapples—"the princess of fruits"—parakeets, and an armadillo. Raleigh, in turn, informed the one-hundred-and-ten-year-old chief of this land, Topiawari, that it had been the Queen's pleasure that he undertake this voyage for the natives' defense and to deliver them from the tyranny of the Spaniards.[19] Topiawari, whose nephew had been murdered by Berrio, was impressed.

The next day, while old Topiawari, a man of "gravity and judgment, and . . . good discourse,"[20] walked back to his home, Raleigh continued up-river. This time he steered for a tributary, the Caroni, in order to see the famous falls there. The current, however, proved so swift when they neared the falls that his eight-oared barge barely made a stone's throw in distance despite the river's being as wide as the Thames at Woolwich. Accordingly, Raleigh, though admittedly "a very ill footman," walked to see the falls. Again his poet's eye caught color and movement, and in a vivid passage he said that he had never seen "a more beautiful country, nor more lively prospects, hills so raised here and there over the valleys, the river winding into divers branches, the plains adjoining without bush or stubble, all fair green grass, the ground of hard sand, easy to march on either for horse or foot, the deer crossing in every path, the birds towards the evening singing on every tree with a thousand several tunes, cranes and herons of white, crimson, and carnation, perching on the river's side, the air fresh, with a gentle easterly wind; and every stone that we stopped to take up promised either gold or silver by his complexion." The river itself at this point consisted of "ten or twelve overfalls . . . every one as high over the other as a church tower, which fell with that fury, that the rebound of waters made it seem as if

[18] *Ibid.*, 436.     [19] *Ibid.*, 437-38.     [20] *Ibid.*, 440.

it had been all covered over with a great shower of rain: and in some places we took it at the first for a smoke that had risen over some great town."[21]

This Guiana of his was a strange and fascinating land. From Topiawari's son, Caworako, he heard of a race of men called Ewaipanoma, with eyes in their shoulders, mouths in the middle of their breasts, and hair growing backward through their shoulders. When Raleigh expressed doubt, Caworako swore they were the mightiest men around and wielded gigantic clubs; one of them had been captured only the year before and taken to his father's country.[22] Raleigh heard, too, of a tribe of Amazons living between the river of that name and the Orinoco. Remembering the stories of Amazons in ancient myth and story, Raleigh tried to find out all he could of these warlike women. The natives told him they were bloodthirsty and cruel to those who invaded their territory. They lived by themselves for eleven months of the year. Then in April came the great holiday. The kings and warriors of the neighboring tribes assembled on the borders. Up sauntered the Amazons, mindful of the need of perpetuating their kind. The Amazon queens made their selections with a discriminating eye, after which the rest of the women "cast lots for their valentines." For a month, the holiday-makers feasted and danced and drank and caroused. Finally, with the going down of the moon, the party broke up. Any male offspring of this Saturnalia were returned to the fathers, while females were kept and the begetters were sent presents.[23]

Intrigued as Raleigh was by such a land, and eager to continue his quest, he was forced to retreat by the arrival of the rainy season. The river now rose so dangerously that, with real reluctance, he ordered the expedition to return to Morequito. Again Raleigh talked with Topiawari. Was it possible, he asked him, to go on to Guiana after the rainy season? Topiawari replied that it was not, since Raleigh had too few men; the Spaniards had failed with a larger force. Topiawari thought Raleigh should go to England and return with an army. A number of the tribes would then gladly join him, for they hated the Guianans, who raided them for their women and children. Perhaps, if Raleigh had been of true explorer fiber, he would

---

[21] *Ibid.,* 442.    [22] *Ibid.,* 444.    [23] *Ibid.,* 408-09.

have pressed on toward the mountains of Guiana and solved the mystery, but he was no Cortez, who chose to burn his own ships. Instead, he told the old chief that he would indeed go back to England and would endeavor to return the next year. By their own wish, he left two Englishmen with Topiawari. They were Francis Sparrow, who stayed to sketch the topography, and a young lad, Hugh Goodwin, who was to learn the language. Sparrow was eventually captured by Spaniards and taken to Spain, from which he escaped to England in 1602. Raleigh found Goodwin still in Guiana when he appeared there again in 1617. Meanwhile, he agreed to take Topiawari's son with him to England, where he was christened "Gualtero."

Raleigh now started down-river for the squadron, after having penetrated over three hundred miles into the interior. On the way he learned from a cacique of a gold mine near Mount Iconuri. He sent Lawrence Keymis with a small detachment to see if such a mine existed, while he continued down with the expedition.[24] Keymis learned enough about the mine to believe it of value, though he did not see it, and rejoined his leader at the Cumaca farther down. Eventually, following a bout with high winds and rough waters, Raleigh reached the ships. He had not lost a single man except the Negro who fell a victim to the crocodile. Despite their hazards and exposure, the men were remarkably healthy; not even malaria had touched them. This was not only a result of good luck and—as Sir Robert Schomburgk, the great Guiana explorer of the mid-nineteenth century attests[25]—of the salutary climate of the interior, it was also a tribute to Raleigh's fine leadership.

After destroying three Spanish settlements, Raleigh sailed for England. On July 13 he met Captains Preston and Somers off Cuba and prowled in company with them for a while. Then he sailed northward, hoping to look for his "Lost Colony" in Virginia, but, the winds proving contrary, he headed for England, where he arrived in August.

Raleigh's return, while cheering to his wife, who dashed off

[24] *Ibid.*, 454.
[25] See Sir R. H. Schomburgk (ed.), *Discoverie of Guiana*, Introduction.

the joyful news to Cecil,[26] meant little to England. Cecil himself appears to have been something less than enthusiastic; after all, he had invested in the expedition and, though reliable gold assays of the ore brought back were promising, Raleigh had returned only with samples. Furthermore, a London alderman induced one of the officers of the mint to declare the ore worthless, a slander that infuriated Raleigh. Calumniators who had said on his departure that he intended to go over to the Spanish king's service now declared that he had never left England at all but had hidden all the while in the remote regions of Cornwall. Others contended that the ore must have been brought originally from Barbary to Guiana and thence to England.[27]

The slanders and calumnies sent Raleigh rushing to pen and ink. Hot with outrage, he dashed off one of the magnificent travel classics of all time, *The Discovery of the Large, Rich, and Beautiful Empire of Guiana, with a Relation of the Great and Golden City of Manoa.*[28] Published in 1596, the volume was dedicated to Cecil and the Lord Admiral. Eagerly Raleigh pointed out the advantages of Guiana in a brilliant conclusion to his narrative: "Guiana is a country that hath yet her maidenhead, never sacked, turned, nor wrought; the face of the earth hath not been torn, nor the virtue and salt of the soil spent by manurance, the graves have not been opened for gold, the mines not broken with sledges nor the images pulled down out of their temples. It hath never been entered by any army of strength, and never conquered or possessed by any Christian prince."[29]

But this was not simply a travel classic, it was also a treatise of empire. England should take possession of this land. It was easily defensible, if forts were strategically placed at the mouth of the river, while the land approach of an enemy was almost out of the question. The country offered excellent opportunities for agricultural development and trading possibilities. Furthermore, with the conquest of Manoa, not an insuperable task, a rich additional source of wealth could be added. As if to titillate

[26] HMC, *Salisbury MSS*, V, 396.
[27] See *Works*, VIII, 379-81, 385-88.
[28] *Ibid.*, 379-476. Two fine English editions are those by Schomburgk and Harlow.
[29] *Works*, VIII, 464.

his countrymen's pride, Raleigh mentioned that among the Inca legends was one that from England would come the means of delivering the Indians from their Spanish conquerors. But, Raleigh pointed out, England must waste no time in taking Guiana, "for whatsoever prince shall possess it shall be greatest; and if the king of Spain enjoy it, he will become unresistible."[30]

Perhaps Raleigh's account was a little too glowing, too profuse with the splendors and promise of Guiana, to impress the Queen, if indeed she read it at all. It is likely, however, that the problem was more fundamental. Raleigh was ahead of his era. Neither his efforts and those of Hakluyt in 1585 with regard to Virginia nor his efforts now, a decade later, in respect to Guiana could persuade Elizabeth of the strategic, political, economic, or social value of a colonial empire. To the Queen and her government Virginia or Guiana was merely an area for private enterprise, for individual merchants and others with venture capital to risk in exploiting. The time had not yet arrived for colonization to be viewed as an English national policy.[31]

Besides, Raleigh's was a strange tale by any reckoning. People might be excused if they looked incredulous or smiled pityingly as they read of oysters growing on mangrove trees, of real, live Amazons, of a weird race of men without heads, of savages bathing in turpentine and gold dust! Although subsequent explorers have confirmed many of the geographical observations in his narrative, as well as the reported facts that oysters do grow on mangrove trees and that gold is to be found in Guiana (now Venezuela), his contemporaries would not take him seriously. They refused to distinguish between what he said he saw and what he said he merely heard about. To most of them, his *Discovery* was simply a fantastic potpourri of well-told fabrications, a verdict agreed to as late as the eighteenth century by the historian David Hume; in their opinion, this was Raleigh up to his old tricks of deceiving people. Though the Queen's opinion is not known, her silence and her persistent refusal to restore him to favor may be eloquent testimony of her own lack

[30] *Ibid.*, 467.
[31] See A. D. Innes, *The Maritime and Colonial Expansion of England*, 33-35.

of trust in his veracity. Even more damning was her utter dis-
interest in doing anything about Guiana. Raleigh became so
concerned that early in 1596 he sent out Keymis and, later,
Captain Leonard Berry to explore and map the Guiana coast and
the Orinoco estuary.[32]

If Raleigh's narrative of Guiana fell short of its purpose of
vindicating the man himself and awakening national interest in
colonial empire, it achieved success in other ways. Excited by his
reading of the *Discovery*, George Chapman, the poet and
classicist, wrote a poem in praise of Guiana.[33] Though no record
exists of a meeting between Raleigh and Shakespeare, the *Discovery* was certainly not unknown to the Bard. In both *Othello*
and *The Tempest* he alludes to Raleigh's headless men, while it
is possible that the dreadful Caliban may have been inspired
by the narrative.[34] Milton has passages in his *Paradise Lost*
that appear to indicate his debt to the rich imagery and sonorous
prose rhythms of the *Discovery*.[35]

The work caught on with readers. Between 1599 and 1602,
four German editions were published, two Latin versions in
1599, one Dutch version as early as 1598 and successive Dutch
editions in 1605, 1617, 1707, 1727, and 1747. French editions
also appeared, as have at least a half-dozen English editions, the
latest as recently as 1928. Among travel accounts, it has consistently been one of the best-sellers, and deservedly so.

On the other hand, his literary success was a hollow victory
for Raleigh. The Queen's opinion was all that mattered, and
his prayer for Guiana that the "King of all kings and Lord of
lords will put it into her heart which is lady of ladies to possess

---

[32] For Keymis, see Hakluyt, *Voyages*, X, 441-50; for Berry, *ibid.*, XI, 5.

[33] G. Chapman, *Poetical Works*, III, 50.

[34] *Othello*, act I, scene iii, lines 143-45; *The Tempest*, act III, scene iii, lines
44-48; Harlow (ed.) *Discoverie of Guiana*, xcix.

[35] See, for example, Book XI, the lines:

> Rich Mexico, the seat of Montezuma,
> And Cusco in Peru, the richer seat
> Of Atabalipa, and yet unspoiled
> Guiana,* whose great city Geryon's sons
> Call Eldorado.

\* "Guiana . . . hath yet her maidenhead."
One of the best brief analyses of Raleigh's influence on Milton is by Thompson,
*Ralegh*, 115.

it"[36] went unheeded. He had, therefore, to consider other means of regaining her favor. Fortunately rumors and plans were afoot to do something at last to thwart the resurgence of Spanish power. Grasping with haste that was close to despair this new opportunity, Raleigh blew out the candle that lighted his literary efforts and turned to more active courses.

[36] *Works,* VIII, 467.

# CHAPTER 11

# Action at Cadiz

CAUGHT up in the agitation for a revival of the war with Spain, Raleigh bent furious efforts to make his contribution effective. This did not prevent him, however, from taking an interest in his wife's suit to recover her portion from Lord Huntingdon, her former guardian, or from continuing to meet with his old intellectual acquaintances, including Dr. John Dee, whom he invited to dine with him on October 9 at Durham House. At the same time, the Spanish war claimed most of his attention. He acknowledged that, having set out for Guiana "in the winter of of my life" (he had been forty-three at the time!), he had returned "a beggar and withered."[1] A renewal of hostilities could well present opportunities for recouping his losses. Even more important, he might be able to take a role in the conflict that would restore him at long last to the good graces of his sovereign.

The English zeal for reviving the half-moribund struggle with Spain had its basis not in a mere desire for economic gain, though that motive certainly existed, but in a fear that Spain was again contemplating invasion. Not a century has passed from Philip II to the present that England has not had to face the specter of invasion. The point from which enemy forces might operate has been the French coast or the Lowlands, but no invasion has been possible to contemplate without control of the sea lanes to England. In 1595 and 1596, although popular apprehension was not so great as in 1588, the government and many prominent citizens were fully as alarmed. True, the Spanish position in the Netherlands was not so strong as in the Armada year and Henry IV of France, having reconciled himself with the Pope and won over the Guise party to his side, was able to face the Spaniards with a nominally united France. On the other hand, his resources were exhausted, his people likewise, and his dissatisfaction with Elizabeth's lack of consistent

[1] *Works*, VIII, 380, 381.

support was so acute that there was a chance of his accepting the Pope's offer to mediate between France and Spain. Meanwhile, active fighting continued only in Picardy, while the Spaniards maintained themselves strongly in Brittany and sent to the Netherlands reinforcements and a new leader, the Archduke Albert, who had repulsed the English expedition at Lisbon in 1589. Though Prince Maurice of Nassau was winning a few victories in the Lowlands, assisted by a small English force under Sir Francis Vere, Spain's power still appeared menacing.

Raleigh was seriously disturbed by the situation. Though Drake and Hawkins had sailed on a plundering expedition to the West Indies and were presumed to be returning victorious, he feared that Spain would take advantage of their absence to mount an invasion. In letters to Cecil and the Privy Council during November 1595 he warned of intelligence he had received that the Spaniards were assembling a fleet of sixty ships for Ireland. He himself favored an offensive to forestall the Spaniards, and offered to procure a pinnace for a small price to send to the Spanish coast for further intelligence. What he dreaded most of all was a landing in the dangerously exposed West Country. He was also disturbed about Guiana. England must not wait for "this dolt and that gull" to be satisfied before doing anything. Unless measures were taken to secure it in the coming winter, "farewell Guiana for ever!" A smashing blow against Spain proper might succeed in preventing the Dons from reinforcing Berrio and conquering the native chiefs.[2]

At last, with Essex and others joining their pleas for action to those of Raleigh, the Queen decided to send an expedition to Spain. Philip II's dickering with the Earl of Tyrone in Ireland was truly as important in helping her make up her mind as was the menace of Spanish power on the Continent. Already, had the English but known it, the thrust into the West Indies by Drake and Hawkins had forced the Spaniards to call off an offensive against England in 1595, but now, in early 1596, the English intended to give them no opportunity to prepare another offensive. That Philip would have dispatched ships and troops for a landing in either England or Ireland can scarcely be doubted; he was greatly encouraged by news of the new Irish revolt led

[2] For letters, see HMC, *Salisbury MSS*, v, 444-45, 457-58, 466-69, 472-73.

by Tyrone and by the fabulously good news that both Drake and Hawkins had died on the abortive West Indies voyage. The death of the two great seadogs, who, as Raleigh told his wife years later, "died heartbroken when they failed of their enterprise,"[3] depressed the English as much as it elated the Spanish. But in no way did it deter the English from developing their plans for an assault upon Spain.

For once, Elizabeth let her captains prepare a truly formidable expedition. A fleet of ninety-six ships were equipped, to which the Dutch, eagerly accepting an invitation to collaborate, added twenty-four of their own. A landing force of roughly 10,000 was organized under Sir Francis Vere, who was recalled from the Continent. A council of war of five was appointed to advise the joint commanders, Lord Admiral Charles Howard and Essex. These five were Raleigh and Lord Thomas Howard, representing the sea forces; Vere and Sir Conyers Clifford, speaking for the land elements; and Raleigh's cousin, Sir George Carew, acting as a kind of representative-at-large. The English fleet was divided into four squadrons under Lord Admiral Howard, Essex, Lord Thomas Howard, and Raleigh. With Raleigh, in the capacity of his second-in-command, went Drake's favorite captain, Robert Crosse in the *Swiftsure*. Raleigh's flagship was a new two-decker, the *Warspite*, mounting forty guns at this time. The Dutch ships formed a fifth squadron under Admiral Jan van Duyvenvoord.

Throughout the early spring, trouble of various kinds harassed the expedition. Foul weather hindered the mobilization of ships. Word arrived that Spanish warships were assembling in force at Cadiz and Ferrol, intelligence that spurred Essex to urge the Lord Admiral to sail with what ships were available and let Raleigh bring on the rest. By this time, too, more information of the extent of Drake's disaster, news of a Spanish threat to Brest, and the fall of Calais to the Dons caused the Queen to become uncertain about dispatching the expedition at all. Henry IV of France, of course, would have much preferred English reinforcements in France to an attack on the Spanish coast, and he did not hesitate to say so.

Added difficulty was caused by Raleigh's delay in the Thames.

[3] *Works*, VIII, 639.

He was charged with the task of getting the victualers and transports to sea, but his ships remained scattered, pinned down by contrary winds, while the crews deserted as fast as they were impressed into service. Wildly impatient at Plymouth, Essex turned from forbearance of Raleigh to criticism: "he hath had . . . all the wished winds he could desire," he told Cecil.[4] His suspicions were fed by that gossipy toady, Anthony Bacon, who wrote his brother, the elegant Francis, that "Sir Walter Ralegh's slackness and stay by the way is not thought to be upon sloth, but upon pregnant design."[5] As if in reply to these criticisms, which he probably knew about anyway, Raleigh burst out to Cecil that "as fast as we press men one day they run away another and say they will not serve. . . . I cannot write to our generals at this time, for the pursuivant found me in a country village a mile from Gravesend, hunting after runaway mariners and dragging in the mire from ale house to ale house. . . . Sir, by the living God there is no king nor queen nor general nor any else can take more care than I do to be gone. . . ."[6] But at last he got his men aboard their ships and, with a favoring wind, put to sea and joined the fleet on May 21.

He found, on his arrival, an unusually edgy group of officers, who were scarcely prepared to welcome him despite their eagerness to be off. There were those who believed that he had tried to have both Essex and the Lord Admiral relieved of their commands in favor of himself. Very soon a fierce quarrel broke out at the dinner table between Raleigh and Vere over their respective spheres of authority, with the haughty Clifford supporting Vere, and Arthur Throgmorton, Bess Raleigh's brother, upholding Raleigh with such spirit and high words that he was cashiered and only restored after Essex's intervention. Essex settled the Raleigh-Vere altercation by giving the former seniority at sea and Vere seniority on land. Essex himself had an unpleasant run-in with Charles Howard, when the Lord Admiral in a fit of jealous temper whipped out his penknife and cut out Essex's signature, which had been appended above his own on a joint letter to Elizabeth. Few campaigns have begun

[4] HMC, *Salisbury MSS*, VI, 174.
[5] Quoted by Edwards, *Ralegh (Life)*, I, 206.
[6] HMC, *Salisbury MSS*, VI, 169.

with such sharp quarreling among the leaders and their supporters.[7]

Fortunately, relations between Raleigh and Essex were surprisingly amicable. This was an expedition in which both strongly believed and from which both expected much in terms of glory; Raleigh also hoped for pecuniary gain and, of course, for what had been for three years an elusive will-o'-the-wisp, a restoration to royal favor. Usually an extraordinarily difficult colleague, he seems to have made a determined effort to get along with Essex. It is scarcely surprising, however, that his new attitude excited as much suspicion as appreciation. Sir Anthony Standen, Walsingham's former Catholic spy whose protector was now Essex, observed to Bacon that Raleigh's "carriage to my Lord of Essex is with the cunningest respect and deepest humility that I ever saw or have trowed."[8]

At length, by June 3, the massive fleet sailed out of harbor and on June 18 stood off Cadiz, the largest port and wealthiest city of Spain. The destination was such a well-kept secret that few in the fleet knew of it outside the high command. Furthermore, Philip's intelligence, usually good, fell down completely. To make his lot more difficult, the English spread such a net of ships over the sea that they swept up coasters and other craft that might have given the alarm. Then, on June 15, Spanish officers sighted the burgeoning white sails of the fleet off Cape St. Vincent, and messengers on muleback started up the rocky mountain trails to warn the gentleman responsible for the defense of Cadiz, none other than the Duke of Medina-Sidonia, cultivator of orange trees and commander of the unfortunate Armada. He had left his reputation in the wild northern seas, and when, on returning to Spain, he fled for sanctuary to his orange groves at San Lucar, even the ragamuffins of the streets refused to let him forget the terrible English captain whose guns had wrought such dreadful havoc among his galleons. "Viene el Draque! Drake is coming!" they jeered. Drake might now be dead, but his countrymen were at hand under Lord Admiral Howard, who had commanded the English fleet in 1588. The news of their approach shocked the Spanish grandee, sick of

[7] *Ibid.*, 195; Harrison, *Essex*, 106; J. S. Corbett, *The Successors of Drake*, 53.
[8] Quoted by *ibid.*, 53.

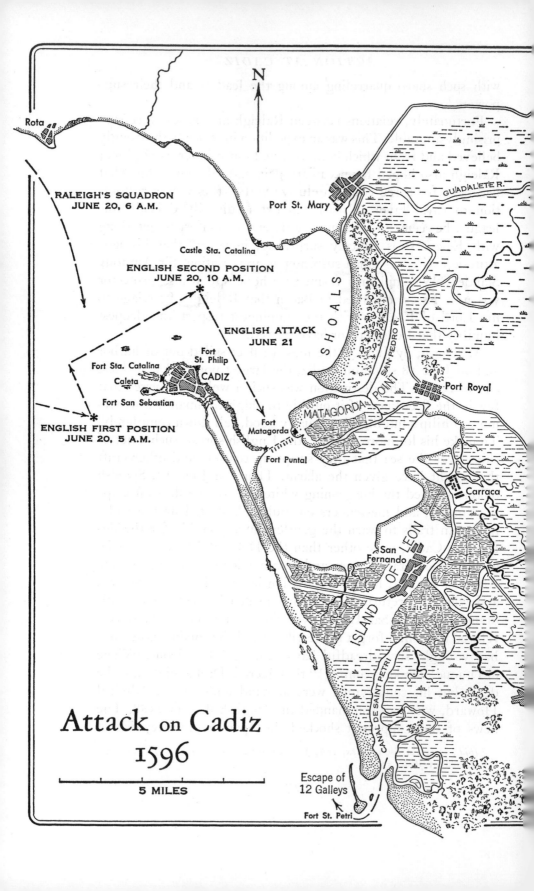

N

Rota

RALEIGH'S SQUADRON
JUNE 20, 6 A.M.

Port St. Mary

GUADALETE R.

Castle Sta. Catalina

ENGLISH SECOND POSITION
JUNE 20, 10 A.M.

S H O A L S

SAN PEDRO R.

ENGLISH ATTACK
JUNE 21

Fort
St. Philip

Fort Sta. Catalina

CADIZ

Caleta

SAN PEDRO POINT

Port Royal

Fort San Sebastian

MATAGORDA

ENGLISH FIRST POSITION
JUNE 20, 5 A.M.

Fort
Matagorda

Fort Puntal

Carraca

ISLAND OF LEON

San
Fernando

Salt Pans

CANAL DE SAINT PETRI

Attack on Cadiz
1596

5 MILES

Escape of
12 Galleys

Fort St. Petri

fever near Cape Trafalgar. He roused himself, wrote a flurry of orders, and had himself carried in a litter to the foot of Cadiz Bay.

But before his orders reached their recipients in Cadiz, the officers in the port had been forced to make their own dispositions to meet the English attack. A glance at the map will reveal that if the right forefinger and thumb are held parallel, the forefinger slightly crooked, that was roughly the formation of the Cadiz area in 1596. Along the finger lay Point Rota and the castle of Santa Catalina guarding the entrance to Port St. Mary. Three thousand yards across to the tip of the thumb was Cadiz at the end of a long peninsula; the battery of St. Philip defended it on the bay side. Cadiz, however, could be approached on the sea side through a creek called the Caleta, which was guarded by forts known as St. Sebastian and Santa Catalina (not to be confused with the castle of the same name). Facing inward lay Fort Puntal protecting both the inner bay and the entrance to Port Royal. For naval support to these land defenses the Spaniards could muster six large galleons, three new frigates that had recently handled Drake so roughly at Puerto Rico,[9] three strong Levant ships, and twenty powerful galleys. There were also about forty merchantmen, most of them armed, loading cargoes for New Spain. The Spaniards planned to have the larger warships take station in line abreast between the St. Philip battery and the castle of Santa Catalina, with galleys advanced into the outer bay and the rest of the ships defending the Puntal channel to the inner harbor.

The English plan of attack was basically simple. Initially it was proposed that Essex with his squadron and the transports was to take Cadiz, developing his assault from the inside. The squadrons of the two Howards and that of the Dutch were to attack the Spanish fleet. While Sir Alexander Clifford with a small squadron was deputed to dispose of the galleys, Raleigh with another small squadron was to sail close inshore and prevent any merchant ships escaping. This planning took up most of June 19 and, except for Raleigh's departure to his station, nothing further was done. Then, as if aware that they had paid too much attention to the enemy's escaping fleet, something

[9] *Ibid.*, 66-67.

obviously impossible in the face of the English superiority in numbers, Essex and the two Howards held a rump meeting at which they decided to change the plans and attack Cadiz from the sea side. Essex was to land in the Caleta and storm St. Sebastian, while the Lord Admiral was to throw troops across the peninsula just below the city. Although Clifford was to carry out his original assignment, Raleigh was directed to ignore the merchant ships and prevent the escape of enemy warships.

All did not go as anticipated. With the attack due to open at dawn on Sunday, June 20, the leaders learned before daybreak that their sailing masters had misjudged the distance, that Cadiz was farther away than they thought. In the confusion of milling ships, of lights showing, and of signal guns going off, the Spaniards readied their own vessels and shore batteries. Daybreak found the English still confused. At a council of war held without Raleigh, who was still away on his original mission, Essex was all for taking advantage of wind and tide and moving right in to destroy the Spanish fleet. When the Lord Admiral objected that the combined enemy fire from ship and shore would be too severe, Essex then decided to carry out the second plan previously agreed to, namely, to land in the Caleta—and this despite the fact that in clear view of the English the Spaniards had moved four galleys into position to dispute such a landing. To make life a little more miserable and hazardous for any landing force, the freshening wind had rolled up so nasty a swell that two boatloads of troops capsized almost as soon as they put off from the *Due Repulse*, Essex's flagship, and fifteen men drowned in their armor.

Fortunately for all concerned, Raleigh returned at this moment and persuaded Essex to put a stop to such tragic nonsense. Absent on his original assignment since early the previous day, Raleigh had intercepted five big merchantmen, which only the sudden descent of fog prevented him from capturing. When the fog lifted, four had made their escape to San Lucar, but one he drove ashore under the guns of the castle near Rota. Now, at six in the morning, he arrived in time to prevent disaster. His practiced soldier's eye saw at once that however promising an amphibious attack would have been had the English been ready at an earlier hour, it was out of the question at this time. Never known for tact, he told Essex in front of the latter's officers that to attempt a landing now would ruin the expedition and jeopardize the Queen's very safety. Essex retorted that it was all the fault of the Lord Admiral, who had insisted that they take Cadiz before entering the bay with the fleet. When Raleigh continued to expostulate, Essex, finally impressed, declared that if Raleigh could convince the Lord Admiral of the madness of the present venture, he would hold back his troops. Raleigh now climbed down into his boat and rowed to Howard's flagship. Ultimately Raleigh's lucid arguments convinced the Lord Admiral that Essex's attempt to land in the Caleta would end in disaster. Reluctantly he consented to try forcing the bay without a troop landing.

Overjoyed, Raleigh now dashed back to the *Due Repulse*, her decks thick with men who stared, grim-eyed, at the flashing oars of Raleigh's boat. For truly on Raleigh's message hung life or death for many of them. When he came within hailing distance, after picking his way through the cluster of heavily loaded landing craft, he shouted to Essex, "Entramos! Entramos! We're going in!"[10] From the crowded bulwarks of the *Due Repulse* a storm of cheering broke out. Essex, in a burst of boyish enthusiasm, tossed his plumed hat into the air, and the wind, catching it in mid-flight, blew it into the sea.

It was now noon, the troops to be brought back aboard the ships, and the next tide to wait for. So many preparations were necessary that it was night before all was at last ready. Once again, though Essex was eager to go in, Raleigh raised a voice of caution, entreating Essex and the Lord Admiral to wait until morning. Raleigh had clearly saved the expedition from disaster earlier in the day, and now he may have done so a second time. True, the rash ones, eager to emulate Drake's dash, criticized him, but Raleigh's was the wiser course. The English had agreed, as he pointed out, "neither . . . in what manner to fight, nor appointed who should lead, and who should second; whether by boarding or otherwise."[11] Cadiz harbor, moreover, was new territory to most of the officers, certainly to both Raleigh and Essex.

[10] Edwards, *Ralegh* (*Letters*), II, 148.
[11] *Ibid.*

The situation was a strange one. Raleigh, definitely a subordinate, seems virtually to have assumed command. Not only did Essex and Howard acquiesce to his suggestion of anchoring at the harbor entrance until daylight, June 21; they also accepted a battle plan he submitted about ten o'clock the night before. Briefly he purposed to batter the galleons and then assign the large fly-boats to board each galleon. When the leaders concurred with the plan, the order of battle was drawn up. Raleigh received the post of honor, as well as that of the greatest danger, namely, leadership of the van. Supporting his *Warspite* were Sir George Carew in the *Mary Rose*, Sir Robert Southwell in the *Lion*, Sir Francis Vere in the *Rainbow*, Sir Conyers Clifford in the *Dreadnaught*, Captain Crosse in the *Swiftsure*, Lord Thomas Howard in the *Nonpareill*, and a dozen or so other ships with a number of fly-boats. Lord Thomas Howard claimed the command, in which he was supported by the Lord Admiral, by virtue of his rank as Vice Admiral, but Raleigh declared, "I was resolved to give and not take example for this service; holding mine own reputation dearest, and remembering my great duty to Her Majesty."[12] No doubt Essex would have received the post—he certainly wanted it—had not the Lord Admiral obeyed the Queen's injunction not to let the Earl hazard himself unnecessarily. Raleigh, on the other hand, was more expendable.

Determined not to be headed by Lord Thomas Howard, Raleigh launched the attack shortly after dawn. While most of the merchant shipping took refuge in Port Royal and Port St. Mary, the big Spanish men-of-war fell back to the channel between Fort Puntal and Matagorda Point at the entrance to Port Royal. Raleigh made straight for the four great ships that constituted the Spanish main line of resistance. These were four of Spain's famed Apostolic galleons, the *St. Philip*, *St. Andrew*, *St. Matthew*, and *St. Thomas*. The first two had boarded Grenville's *Revenge*, and now Raleigh steered straight for the *St. Philip*, "being resolved," as he said, "to be revenged for the *Revenge*, or to second her with mine own life."[13]

Raleigh's bold maneuver did not pass unchallenged. From

[12] *Ibid.*, 149.     [13] *Ibid.*, 151.

the batteries of the bay side of Cadiz and from the galleys flew a hail of shot. The range was so long that Raleigh showed his scorn by answering each enemy discharge with a blare of trumpets. Soon the ships following him made life so uncomfortable for the galleys that these swift craft spun about and sped to join the Apostles. As they swept up abreast of the *Warspite*, her gunners went to work on these "wasps," or, as Raleigh described his part with a typical euphemism, "I bestowed a benediction amongst them."[14]

Eager as Raleigh was to close with the galleons, he had been ordered not to board them; he was not to risk a Queen's ship but to leave the boarding to the fly-boats. Hence he dropped anchor and exchanged shots with the Apostles at long range. For this he was roundly criticized, particularly by Essex, who thrust up through the ships and anchored next to him. It was not that Raleigh lacked courage or venturesomeness. Admiral Sir Julian Corbett, an Essex admirer, has explained that Raleigh had had little experience in naval action or of the effect of gunfire at sea and he may have thought he was close enough or else was persuaded by his sailing master to anchor now lest he go aground;[15] the latter reason sounds more plausible. In any event, the *Warspite* took such a heavy pounding in its new position that Raleigh hurried to Essex and told him that if the fly-boats did not come up, "I would board with the Queen's ship; for it was the same loss to burn or sink, for I must endure the one."[16] Gallantly Essex assured him that he would second him in whatever he did, and Raleigh, immensely relieved, returned to his battered flagship.

What ensued now came close to being comical. Elizabethan captains possessed an invincible—one might almost say incorrigible—individualism and a thirst for glory that set at odds the military discipline often needed to accomplish a task. Raleigh had been absent between a quarter- and a half-hour. During that time, Vere, previously engaged with the galleys, had pushed ahead of the *Warspite* in the *Rainbow*, while Lord Thomas Howard, joined on the *Nonpareill's* deck by the Lord Admiral, squeezed ahead of the *Rainbow*. Not to be thus maneuvered

[14] *Ibid.*    [15] Corbett, *The Successors of Drake*, 81.
[16] Edwards, *Ralegh (Letters)*, II, 152.

out of first place, Raleigh weighed anchor and slipped past Vere to lie athwart the channel. Vere could not let Raleigh's maneuver pass without trying to counter it. With Raleigh's attention again engaged by the enemy, Vere secretly got a hawser aboard the *Warspite* and sought to draw the *Rainbow* closer. When Raleigh's men discovered this neat little trick and reported it, Raleigh ordered the hawser hacked off at once.[17] Meanwhile, Essex plunged a ship's length ahead of Raleigh and to port, thus joining Raleigh and Vere in opposing the four Apostles, the three frigates, the galleys, and Fort Puntal.

It is doubtful how long the three English ships could have sustained the unequal contest had not Raleigh decided the issue by literally coming to grips with the enemy. If it is true that Raleigh's inexperience as a naval commander prevented him from seeing any other course than playing at long bowls (too long to do any real damage) or boarding, and had therefore slowed down the battle by his caution, his critics could only commend his next move. In his opinion, the contest had lasted long enough and could be settled only by laying the *Warspite* alongside the *St. Philip* and boarding her. To this end he succeeded in getting a warp out to draw the *Warspite* alongside the huge Apostle. Seeing this maneuver, Essex and Lord Thomas Howard were quick to imitate it, and the Spaniards, having suffered severely from the English gunnery, decided to end the battle.

What followed was a scene of horror that appalled even the unsentimental Raleigh. The Apostles cut their cables and ran aground, this action, said Raleigh, "tumbling into the sea heaps of soldiers, so thick as if coals had been poured out of a sack in many ports at once; some drowned and some sticking in the mud." The *St. Matthew* and the *St. Andrew* were captured before their captains could destroy them, but the *St. Philip* and the *St. Thomas* burst into flame and blew up. For the enemy, as Raleigh wrote in his terse, vital prose, "The spectacle was very lamentable . . . for many drowned themselves; many, half burnt, leapt into the water; very many hanging by the ropes' ends by the ships' sides, under the water even to the lips; many swimming with grievous wounds, stricken under water, and put

[17] *Ibid.*

out of their pain; and withal so huge a fire, and such tearing of the ordnance in the great *Philip*, and the rest, when the fire came to them. . . ." Truly, he observed, "if any man had a desire to see Hell itself, it was there most lively figured."[18] He did his best to spare them further suffering. He took no more lives, and both he and the Lord Admiral beat off the Dutch fly-boats which, having taken no part in the battle up to this point, now darted forward and started to finish off the poor wretches struggling in the water. Raleigh's consideration for the helpless Spaniards, a people he usually hated, was as real as his contempt for the Dutch. On the other hand, he was in the position of having an uncomfortable appreciation of the Spaniards' agony; toward the end of the fight with the Apostles, he received a painful wound in his leg, which was "interlaced and deformed with splinters."[19] To the end of his days he walked with a limp as a result of this wound.

The suddenness of the disaster seemed to paralyze the Spaniards, for they offered little resistance to an English landing force under Essex and Vere. Within a few hours, Cadiz fell, even before Medina-Sidonia could reach it to organize its defenses. The English now sacked the city, and between those eager to get at the Spaniards and those interested in loot, the fleet was left without a commander. Worse still, no one gave orders to seize the Spanish mechantmen. Raleigh's men bore him ashore, but, suffering acutely and fearful of being shouldered in the press of wild-eyed looters, he returned to the *Warspite* that night. His pain was probably not allayed by the suspicion that he would miss out on the spoils despite the promise of a full share.

In truth, the spoils were great and might have been greater. Ransom for the citizens of Cadiz totaled 120,000 ducats, while there was enormous property to be confiscated, not to mention ransom for the city itself, consisting of 40,000 ducats. Raleigh pointed to the merchantmen and their cargoes as the greatest prize of all, perhaps 8,000,000 ducats. In the morning of June 22 he sent Sir John Gilbert, his stepbrother, and Arthur Throg-

[18] For preceding descriptive quotations, see *ibid.*, 153. See also Hakluyt, *Voyages*, IV, 248-49.
[19] Edwards, *Ralegh (Letters)*, II, 154.

morton, his brother-in-law, to Essex, Vere, and the Lord Admiral for permission to enter Port Royal and capture the ships. Unfortunately for the expedition, these leaders were so preoccupied with bringing some order out of the tumult and confusion that his request went unattended. Then, in the afternoon, the Spanish merchants of Cadiz and Seville offered a ransom of 2,000,000 ducats for the merchant fleet. Evidently the leaders, except for the Lord Admiral and Raleigh, were willing to negotiate; Raleigh still wanted to seize the ships and ransom them afterward; Howard scorned any effort to treat with the enemy. The Spanish commander, however, decided the fate of the great West Indian fleet: great columns of smoke were soon billowing skyward as the entire fleet was destroyed by fire. Medina-Sidonia could now return in sorrow to San Lucar and nurse himself back to health amid his orange groves, but he had at least the satisfaction of knowing that, however great his countrymen's loss, he had deprived the hated English of what they wanted most from the taking of Cadiz.[20]

What to do now was the question. Though Essex and Vere wanted to stay and fortify Cadiz (Drake's old idea), the others, knowing Elizabeth would disapprove, insisted on leaving. Hence, on July 3 and 4, the expedition embarked. Slowly the ships sailed northward. They stopped in at Faro, sacked the town, and departed with the library of Bishop Osorius, which was subsequently presented to Oxford for its new Bodleian Library. Off Lisbon, the leaders debated the next move. Essex was anxious to go to the Azores in hopes of capturing the Plate Fleet from America or to remain in the Lisbon area until the

---

[20] Accounts of the taking of Cadiz are numerous. Raleigh's (*Ibid.*, II, 146-56) is outstanding in many ways, particularly in literary style, but needs supplementing in fact. The account Cecil prepared, which was probably based on the Lord Admiral's, is in PRO, *S.P. Dom.* (Elizabeth I), 259/114. Monson's is in *Naval Tracts*, I, 344-57, and is by no means friendly to Raleigh. No student of this voyage should overlook the valuable historical commentary in Monson, I, 358-95; II, 1-20. Another account not overly friendly to Raleigh is that by Sir Francis Vere, in his *Commentaries*, which is included in C. H. Firth, *Stuart Tracts*, 106-19. The *Sloane MSS* (British Museum), 1303, 1, is less critical of Raleigh than laudatory of Essex. The most impartial and complete account is that in the *Lambeth Palace MSS*, No. 250. By far the best secondary history of the expedition is Corbett, *The Successors of Drake*, chs. II, III, IV, V; but see also E. P. Cheyney, *A History of England from the Defeat of the Armada to the Death of Elizabeth*, II, 53-91; Rowse, *The Expansion of Elizabethan England*, 304-11.

Fleet arrived. Again he was voted down, largely because food supplies were short. Raleigh was especially anxious to get home. He was running short of stores, and sickness had broken out among his men. The expedition thereafter returned to England, straggling into port in helter-skelter fashion.

The Cadiz triumph had a mixed reception in England. Though the people at large rejoiced, the Queen was furious that more spoil was not taken, and she suspected, with good reason, that officers and men in both services had stolen much that rightfully belonged to her. Raleigh could appreciate her anger, for his own spoil was valued at only £1769, whereas Vere received £3628. So wrathful was the Queen that she canceled the victory celebrations throughout the country except in London, and stormed at the Lord Admiral for turning down Essex's suggestion for cruising to the Azores to intercept the Plate Fleet or to wait for it at Lisbon. And indeed news arriving in September that the Plate Fleet reached Lisbon only two days after the English left the coast seemed to confirm the wisdom of Essex even as it pointed up the reckless eagerness on the part of Howard and Raleigh to get home. Though Raleigh came in for his share of condemnation from many quarters, considerable ridicule was cast upon the activity of both Howard and Essex, particularly the latter, in creating sixty-six knights (Howard had knighted but five following the Armada). Elizabeth not only delivered herself of some caustic comments on this prolific knighting; she also entered into an acrimonious controversy with Essex over the spoils and forced him to surrender much of them to her.

For the country generally, however, Essex was the hero of the hour, eulogized in pulpit and tavern alike. His fame continued to increase as the significance of what has been called the Elizabethan Trafalgar spread throughout Europe. Spain's power had been assailed at its source, its finest port sacked and occupied for a fortnight without harassment by any Spanish relieving army, an enormous ransom exacted, forty merchantmen and eleven warships destroyed, and two of Spain's largest warships captured. Spanish power was revealed as impotent to halt the bold resurgent strength of England. "Great is the Queen of England!" exclaimed the Venetians, who scrambled for copies of her picture. "O! what a woman, if she were but a Christian!"[21] The people of England were almost as forthright in their praise of the Earl of Essex, who, they were sure, was responsible for giving them the victory.

If amidst the recriminations and acclaim for others, Raleigh seemed all but forgotten, such was not the case. A discriminating correspondent had early informed Cecil, who had been promoted to Principal Secretary of State during Essex's absence over Essex's candidate, Thomas Bodley, "I do assure your honour his [Raleigh's] service was inferior to no man's, and so much praiseworthy as those which formerly were his enemies do now hold him in great estimation; for that which he did in the sea service at Cadiz could not be bettered."[22] Sir Anthony Standen, whose opinion of Raleigh was usually as disparaging as his adulation of Essex was unbounded, told Burghley after Cadiz, "Sir Walter did (in my judgment) no man better; and his artillery [had] most effect. I never knew the gentleman till this time: and I am sorry for it, for there are in him excellent things besides his valour. And the observation he hath in this voyage used with my Lord of Essex hath made me love him."[23] Standen's comment on Raleigh's attitude toward Essex was confirmed by Raleigh's handsome praise of the Earl at Cadiz,[24] and Essex appears to have acknowledged the former favorite's good intentions by a show of friendliness through the winter and spring of 1597, a display motivated by a recognition of Raleigh's value to him in another contemplated voyage for the coming summer. As for Cecil, both he and Burghley, after much weighing of the evidence, could hardly fail to perceive that the individual most responsible for the Cadiz triumph was not the lionized Essex, but the sardonic, unpopular Raleigh.

Soon after the taking of Cadiz, Raleigh had expressed to Cecil his hope that the Queen would "take my labors and endeavors in good part."[25] The longed-for restoration, however, could not be realized so long as the Queen remained angry over

---

[21] Quoted by J. E. Neale, *Queen Elizabeth*, 341.
[22] HMC, *Salisbury MSS*, VI, 229.
[23] *Harleian MSS* (British Museum), 6845, fol. 101. Quoted by Edwards, *Ralegh (Life)*, I, 221.
[24] See Raleigh to Cecil, July 7, 1956. *Ralegh (Life)*, II, 135.
[25] *Ibid.*, 135.

the results of the expedition. When restoration finally came, it was thanks in part to both Cecil and Essex. The Earl wanted Raleigh with him on his new expedition to Ferrol and the Azores. As for Cecil, Raleigh remained constantly friendly with him. But, as has been so aptly observed before, the real English Machiavelli was not Raleigh but Cecil,[26] who found Essex's popularity and Raleigh's courage and ability desirable attributes in strengthening his own position in power. With cold calculation Cecil used friendship for personal gain; Raleigh did not perceive the disingenuousness of Cecil until it was too late. Now, in late 1596 and early 1597, with a great power rivalry developing between Cecil and Essex, Cecil looked with a warily friendly eye upon Raleigh. It is possible that he may have been really touched by the beautiful letter of commiseration that Raleigh sent him in January on the death of his wife.[27] In any event, the two men now drew close, while Raleigh seems to have helped smooth over some of the friction between Cecil and Essex. Raleigh saw Essex often in February and March and Cecil probably more frequently, while the three dined together at Essex House on April 18. Out of this meeting evidently came an understanding to help one another achieve what each wanted: Raleigh, his restoration at Court; Cecil, the Chancellorship of Lancaster Duchy; Essex, assistance in his expedition. In further-ance of the last, Raleigh agreed to raise 6,000 men.[28]

The climax to this era of good feeling from Raleigh's point of view arrived just before summer. The Queen, who had quarreled with the willful Essex and then had become reconciled to him, was overjoyed to see the three men working amicably together; it appeared as if oil and water had at last mixed. For this agreeable condition Raleigh had been mainly responsible. She therefore turned a not unfriendly ear to Cecil when he spoke in behalf of Raleigh, while she could not help noticing that Essex did not oppose the suggested restoration of his former rival to his full duties as Captain of the Guard. Accordingly, on June 1, 1597, Raleigh at last achieved the objective for which he had been working since his marriage was discovered in 1592.

[26] A recent observation to this effect was made in 1951 by H. R. Williamson, *Sir Walter Raleigh*, 104-05. See also Sir P. Magnus, *Sir Walter Raleigh*, 81-82.
[27] HMC, *Salisbury MSS*, VII, 35-36.
[28] *Cal. S.P. Dom.*, *1595-1597*, 391; Harrison, *Essex*, 140.

To be sure, Essex could not bear to be a witness and hence went off to Chatham on the day when Cecil presented Raleigh to the Queen. According to the courtier, Rowland Whyte, Elizabeth received Raleigh "very graciously, and gave him full authority to execute his place as Captain of the Guard, which immediately he undertook, and swore many men into the places void. In the evening he rid abroad with the Queen, and had private conference with her; and now he comes boldly to the privy-chamber, as he was wont."[29]

It had been long in coming, this day when once again he could walk with Gloriana, five years since his disgrace and almost one year since he had elevated her in prestige throughout Europe by his bold action at Cadiz. That he had now resumed his place in her affections was out of the question. He never was able to recoup his losses in this contest of the heart, and Essex must have known it was impossible, else he could not have consented to Raleigh's restoration. But, for Raleigh, the great fact was that he was back at Court, near his Queen, and for the moment that was all that mattered. This incredible June day was probably one of the happiest and least troubled of his life. Well it was, if so, for dark and worrisome times lay ahead that were to make his years of disgrace seem, by comparison, like a pleasant interlude of sunshine.

[29] A. Collins, *Letters and Memorials of State in the Reigns of Queen Mary, Queen Elizabeth, and King James*, II, 64-65. A slightly different version is given in HMC, *Lord De L'Isle and Dudley MSS*, II, 285-86.

# CHAPTER 12

# The Islands Voyage

THE campaign of 1597 had its origin in two sources of inspiration: the passionate desire of Philip II to avenge the Cadiz disaster and the determination of Raleigh, Essex, and Cecil to make it impossible for him to accomplish his revenge. Humiliated beyond measure by the Cadiz debacle, Philip called upon his seemingly inexhaustible resources to build and outfit an expedition for the invasion of England. There appeared to be no end to the armadas he was able to hurl against that hated land.

We know now that the situation was quite different from its appearance. Despite the bullion he received from America, Philip was practically bankrupt, and was able to preserve his armies and maintain his fleets only by keeping his men's pay permanently in arrears; their investment in time was thus of such consequence that they could not afford to desert. The need for ship timber stripped Spain's forests, eroding the land, while the draining away of the sturdy Spanish peasants into the forces left many a family impoverished; eventually the survivors, lacking the means to pay their rents, drifted to the cities, where they swelled the masses living on alms. Taxes and controls on the middle-class merchants and shopkeepers discouraged expansion of this potentially productive group, while the devotion of Spaniards to their religion found at least one of every four adults serving the Church in some capacity. Spain was having increasing difficulty in maintaining her commitments in Italy, France, the Lowlands, the New World, and on the high seas. Her weakness, however, was known only to a few. To the European multitude she was still the dreaded colossus that held half the known world in fee. Her able Adelantado of Castile knew better. Charged in late 1596 with forming an expedition at Ferrol and Corunna to assist the Irish, he dared tell his royal master that an expedition at this time was impossible owing to the shortage of ships, men, money, guns, ammunition, and supplies. Though disappointed at the report, and deeply grieved that he might not live to consummate his revenge, the ailing Philip planned to strike for sure in 1597, and a mighty blow it should be.[1]

The second point of inspiration for the campaign of 1597— the English desire to prevent Philip from dispatching his expedition—originated as much in the ambition of Robert Cecil for power as in the desire of Essex for glory or that of Raleigh for fame and financial reward. Actually, contrary to his feeling in 1595, Raleigh had had no fear of a Spanish expedition in 1596, and wrote a brief pamphlet at the time in which he expressed his doubts, his *Opinion upon the Spanish Alarum*;[2] at the same time, he urged a strengthening of the coastal defenses in the event that the Spaniards actually did come. In 1597, he veered to the Cecil-Essex view that the Spanish menace was growing and must be nipped at its source. Essex, of course, was wildly enthusiastic. After all, this was to be his expedition, and his instructions as commander were signed on June 15.

The role of Cecil is less easy to appraise. One of the last important acts of the great Burghley had been to secure the office of Principal Secretary for his second son. This thin, little, sickly hunchback, called her "pygmy" by Elizabeth and the "archback" by some of his enemies, became an exceedingly able minister and the first of the Earls of Salisbury with their eminent tradition of service to their country. But Robert Cecil consolidated his position by methods that reckoned not of friendship or morality or any emotion except a sense of dedication to his office. Though but a shadow of his father in ability, he possessed in high degree the capacity to dissimulate, to make men his tools while letting them think themselves his colleagues or even his masters. This was, of course, an age in which the slippery principles of Machiavelli were scorned in public by princes and ministers who then proceeded to apply them. Cecil was such a person.

There has persisted about Cecil an aura of morality and gen-

[1] For a summary of economic conditions in Spain, see R. T. Davies, *The Golden Century of Spain*, 263-75. For statement on portion of population engaged in clerical occupations, see *ibid.*, 289; J. P. de Oliveira Martins, *A History of Iberian Civilization*, 241.

[2] *Works*, VIII, 676-81.

tleness and a kind of quiet warmth; it was the work of careful design. Trained by his father, he knew the secrets of statecraft and the management of men when yet a very young man. His humiliating physical condition undoubtedly magnified his efforts to master his profession and achieve a superiority over the magnificent creatures of the Court who strutted and preened their feathers and talked in grandiose fashion. Though only thirty-four years old, he was already grey and drawn with overwork. But, if one is inclined to pity the little man, so gentle-seeming and ill and now wifeless, one is repelled by the ruthlessness, the lust for power, the determination to eliminate all obstacles to his dominance. Most of his contemporaries were deceived by him, none more so than Raleigh, though Essex too was taken in. These two were in his way, or, at least, Essex was at this time. Raleigh, on whose friendship Cecil could count, might be useful in any future trial of strength with Essex. As for Essex, one had only to give him enough rope; already his quarrels with the Queen were becoming more serious and occurring more frequently. In the meantime, why not let Raleigh appear to bring the two of them together in an apparent feast of love, a move for which Raleigh could be rewarded by restoration to favor? And why not encourage both Raleigh and Essex, particularly Essex, in a venture against Spain where the hazards of personal differences were as great as those of shipwreck or Spanish guns? He himself would, of course, improve his position at home while these two glory-seekers were at sea. Some such thoughts as these may well have passed through the mind of Robert Cecil as he deliberately broke with the cautious policy of his father in trying to avoid warlike measures where possible, a policy which was also to become a hallmark of his own career after the Islands Voyage. True, Elizabeth still gave the commands, but her disgust at the Cadiz expedition was so great that it must have required a great deal of concrete data from Cecil and eloquence from Essex to persuade her to consent to another venture.

The good feeling in which the triumvirate worked through the early summer days before the sailing of the expedition persisted through at least one challenge. Henry Brooke, Lord Cobham, was a good friend of Raleigh and brother-in-law of

Cecil, and, the Wardenship of the Cinque Ports falling vacant, Raleigh sought it for Cobham. Essex, who disliked Cobham, supported Sir Robert Disney for the post. The Queen, however, gave it to Cobham, a move which made Essex furious with Raleigh. On the other hand, Cecil's assistance in helping the Earl obtain for himself the appointment as Master of Ordnance, the principal military post, probably went far to soothe Essex's resentment. Certainly his indignation appeared to vanish in a conspicuous display of good fellowship and entertainment.

On July 6, after he and Essex had been entertained by Cecil, evidently attending a theater performance, Raleigh wrote Cecil a curious letter for which it is hard to find an adequate explanation. Alluding to Essex, Raleigh told Cecil that "he was wonderful merry at your conceit of *Richard the Second*. I hope it shall never alter, and there of I shall be most glad of, as the true way to all our good, quiet, and advancement, and most of all for Her sake whose affairs shall thereby find better progression."[3] It is going too far even to suggest that Cecil was putting thoughts into Essex's mind by his display of mimicry. But one cannot help noting that this was the very play, with its drama about the unseating of a sovereign, that the conspirators in the Essex revolt hired to be performed on February 8, 1601. It is an odd circumstance that the first showing involving Essex afforded so much pleasure and the second was attended with such tragedy.

The expedition resembled that of the previous year. Ferrol, which sheltered the growing fleet of Spain, was to be treated like Cadiz, the Spanish navy was to be destroyed, and the yearly Plate Fleet from America was to be captured either there or in the Azores. Plans were evolved to seize and garrison the island of Terceira in the Azores and others as well, if desirable. The fleet, consisting of about one hundred and twenty sail of all types, including supply ships, was divided into four squadrons. Chief in command, now that the Lord Admiral had retired, was Essex, who took over one squadron himself. The Vice Admiral was Lord Thomas Howard, in charge of another squadron. Raleigh was Rear Admiral, commanding the third squadron, and he flew his white pennant again from the *Warspite*. The

<hr/>

[3] Edwards, *Ralegh* (*Letters*), II, 169-70.

fourth squadron consisted of the Dutch contingent under the sturdy, reliable Jan van Duyvenvoord. The second in command was expected to be Vere, but that able veteran discovered on reporting that he was displaced as Lieutenant General by young Charles Blount, now Lord Mountjoy, who had never actually commanded in the field. Though Vere went along as Marshal, he suffered from acute embarrassment and humiliation.[4] When the fleet sailed from Sandwich to Weymouth to take more troops aboard, he and Raleigh actually shook hands at Essex's request, burying the hard feelings of the previous campaign.

The expedition had an inauspicious beginning. Putting to sea on July 10, it encountered heavy winds, during which the squadrons broke away from one another. Raleigh pressed on for Finisterre. By the end of the week, a gale had begun to blow that flung the *Warspite* almost on her beam ends, rent her bulkheads, and crumbled her brick cookroom. Fearing for his ships, Raleigh came about and fled back to Plymouth, arriving there on the 18th. Quickly he dashed off an account of the storm to Cecil which, however vivid, fell short of the description by the poet John Donne, whom it thoroughly terrified. Essex arrived at Falmouth, his flagship barely afloat, and the Dutch soon followed him into harbor. Raleigh at once wrote again, informing Cecil that the fears he had felt that Essex had been lost were fortunately unfounded. The Earl had arrived "in great extremity and imminent peril of sinking in the sea, which I knew would betide him ere he would yield to either sea or winds. . . . Sir, I beseech you to work from Her Majesty some comfort to my Lord General, who, I know, is dismayed by these mischances, even to death, although there could not be more done by any man upon the earth, God having turned the heavens with that fury against us, a matter beyond the power, or valor, or will of man to resist. . . ."[5]

It was an open, manly letter expressing relief that a fellow creature had been saved from disaster. Lamed for life by the wound at Cadiz, and seasick almost every time he left port, Raleigh probably suffered agonies in the storm. Both he and Essex, however, may have been abashed to learn subsequently

[4] Vere, *Commentaries*, in Firth, *Stuart Tracts*, 121.
[5] Edwards, *Ralegh* (*Letters*), II, 171-75.

that that salty veteran, Lord Thomas Howard, had ridden out the storm and shown the flag off Corunna before returning. On the other hand, Lord Thomas was a far more skillful sailor than either Raleigh or Essex. Meanwhile, the latter two worked hard with Cecil to get the ships refitted and resupplied and sail to join Howard.

During this period of frenzied refitting, Cecil began to act strangely, almost ominously. The Lord Admiral told Essex that he never saw a person receive more comfort than the Queen when she learned by Raleigh's letter that the Earl was safe; she wept tears of relief and joy.[6] But if she liked the letter, Cecil did not; he thought it extravagantly phrased for the Queen, and he told Essex that "if I could have forborne to show it for other things, by Jesus I would not have showed it."[7] Essex's dissatisfaction at Cecil's tardiness in answering his communications[8] was believed by Cecil to have originated with Raleigh. In an enclosure with his letter to the Earl, Cecil therefore jibed at "good Mr. Raleigh, who wonders at his own diligence, because diligence and he are not familiars." Cecil could not "bear to be accused of dullness, especially by your rear admiral, who making haste but once in a year to write a letter by post, has dated his last dispatch from Weymouth, which I know was written from Plymouth."[9]

The little man was angry and disturbed. No one was more diligent than Raleigh in writing letters; in fact, at times he fairly snowed the Secretary under with correspondence. But Cecil was obviously worried that Raleigh and Essex were drawing closely together—he suspected at his expense. He countered with expressions of esteem so fulsome that Raleigh's words of praise for Essex seem quite anemic by comparison. "The Queen," he assured Essex in one letter, "is so disposed now to have us all love you, that she and I do every night talk like angels of you."[10] Writing a few days later, Cecil remarked that a dispatch from Essex and his "appendents was written more like angels than men; so much wisdom, so much caution, so much humility, and such providence, nay so great good-husbandry, as I will keep it for a monument of your virtues. A man

[6] HMC, *Salisbury MSS*, VII, 306.  [7] *Cal. S.P. Dom.*, *1595-1597*, 473.
[8] *Ibid.*, 470.  [9] *Ibid.*, 473.  [10] *Ibid.*

may see what persecution doth, and what storms; the next that catches you at sea will not be appeased with praying, till Jonas be thrown into the sea, which will be the captain of the *Warspite*. I am a little saucy, but I love to prattle with you whilst I may. . . ."[11]

Mild though he appeared, Cecil was not one to indulge in such persiflage simply to pass the time. The stakes were high, and he never took his eye off his objective: to consolidate his power as, next to Elizabeth, chief in the land. Raleigh's friendship, genuine on Raleigh's part, he treated almost contemptuously. Was he trying to drive a wedge between the reigning and the former favorite? Did he really wish the expedition to be shattered on the rock of their conflicting personalities? It is impossible to be sure. One can only surmise, and that surmise would be that he hardly wished them well in anything. Actually Raleigh and Essex had far more in common, including their enthusiasm for the expedition and their views on its conduct, than did Essex and Cecil. The courtiers, however, were temperamentally most unlike and were natural rivals for glory and for the Queen's favor. Fully aware of all this, Cecil seems to have contrived to fan the hot coals of their rivalry by disparaging the one in laudatory letters to the other. Though Essex, who loved flattery, may have been unsuspecting, the same could not be said of his uncle, Sir William Knollys. "If we lived not in a cunning world," he told Essex, "I should assure myself that Mr. Secretary were wholly yours. I pray God it have a good foundation and then he is very worthy to be embraced. I will hope for the best, yet will I observe him as narrowly as I can. But your lordship knows best the humour both of the time and the person."[12] As it turned out, neither Essex nor Raleigh appraised with accuracy at this time the inscrutable Cecil.

The fleet was about to make a second attempt to sail when Howard returned on July 31, and not until August 17 were all the squadrons again at sea bound for Spain. Disease among the troops, many of whom were put ashore, resulted in the expedition's becoming more of a naval project. While the lateness of the season and Howard's report of the incomplete state

[11] *Ibid.*, 479.
[12] Birch, *Memoirs of the Reign of Queen Elizabeth*, II, 351.

of Spanish preparations made Essex and Raleigh think of a cruise to the West Indies on the Drake-Hawkins pattern to intercept the Plate Fleet near its source, the Queen directed them to carry out their original objective, with the amendment that they attempt to destroy the Adelantado's fleet at Ferrol with fireships. The Queen also expressly forbade Essex to lead the perilous maneuver to set fire to the enemy;[13] it was understood that Raleigh should assume the duty. Essex fretted at this restriction on his activity, and fretted even more when the wind turned favorable and the transports were still not ready. Hence he left all his troops behind except a thousand veterans. He also left behind an annoyed Cecil, who suspected, with considerable reason, that neither Essex nor Raleigh was as keen on destroying the immobilized Spaniards at Ferrol as on making a run to the West Indies;[14] Cecil's opinion was shared by Raleigh's cousin, Sir Arthur Gorges.[15]

The fleet headed straight for its objective until, off Cape Ortegal, another storm caught it and mauled it badly. Raleigh's mainyard snapped, Essex's ship sprang a leak, while the galleon captured at Cadiz, the *St. Matthew*, lost bowsprit and foremast and survived only because Sir George Carew took her into Rochelle. The wind veered easterly, making an attack on Ferrol out of the question, much to Essex's satisfaction. Separated by the storm, the squadrons now converged on the Azores to intercept the Plate Fleet. Raleigh arrived on September 15, ten days after Essex reached the island of Flores. Accompanied by Gorges, his captain, he went aboard Essex's ship to report. According to Gorges, Essex "seemed to be the joyfullest man living for our arrival."[16] Though certain of his followers had tried to persuade him that Raleigh had deserted him, he protested that he never believed it. There was fundamentally no reason why he should, for both men understood this was exactly what they preferred to an assault on Ferrol—the capture of the Plate Fleet they considered far more valuable to England than the destruction of the Adelantado's armada at Ferrol, most of

---

[13] HMC, *Salisbury MSS*, VII, 349.
[14] *Ibid.*, 361.
[15] A. Gorges, *A Larger Relation of the Said Island Voyage*, in S. Purchas, *Purchas His Pilgrimes*, XX, 48-49.
[16] *Purchas*, XX, 67.

which they were sure would not be ready to sail this late in the season. Besides, an erroneous report had reached them that the part of that armada ready for action was now headed for the Azores to convoy the treasure ships to Spain; Essex and Raleigh were therefore where they could do the most good, or so they chose to think.

The council of war, held soon after Raleigh arrived, decided that the English should spread out and cover the central group of the Azores by squadrons, Mountjoy and Blount to the east off St. Michael, Howard and Vere watching the powerfully fortified island of Terceira in the north, Raleigh and Essex cruising off fortified Fayal on the west, with the Dutch south of Fayal. Essex was so eager to take his station that he wanted to leave at once. Raleigh, however, requested permission to water, which Essex granted and sent his own barge to assist. Then at midnight Raleigh received an order from the Earl to suspend the watering operation and follow him immediately to Fayal, where he could complete watering. Though he got to sea as quickly as possible, Raleigh neither found nor overtook Essex. In fact, when he entered the roads at Fayal the next morning, he still saw no sign of Essex and became seriously disturbed. As Gorges explained, ". . . we could not but greatly marvel, because when he sent for us, he was six leagues nearer it [Fayal] than we were, and, besides, set sail toward it six or eight hours before us."[17]

Raleigh was in a spot. The forts opened fire on him; the inhabitants, fearing a battle, started fleeing to the interior; and Raleigh's men begged him to attack. Knowing the high-spirited Earl, whose honor was easily offended, he declined. Besides, some of Essex's followers, particularly the notorious sycophant, Sir Gelly Meyrick, who commanded one of the transports, insisted that no one should land until Essex arrived. Finally, on the fourth day, when Raleigh sent boats at some distance from the anchorage to obtain water, the enemy fired on them. At this point, Raleigh lost patience. Loading into boats one hundred and sixty sailors and one hundred soldiers from his own ships, he made for the rocky beach, where more than double that

[17] *Ibid.*, 75.

number of Spaniards opened such a heavy fire that his advance elements hung back.

No one could ever justly accuse Raleigh of lacking courage in battle. With a scornful shout to his men that those who were not afraid should follow him, he drove his barge into the hottest area of fire, leaped into the surf, and, accompanied by a little knot of officers, charged the trenches on the rocky beach. Surprised at the assault, the enemy ran for the woods and hills. But though he had established a beachhead, this was not enough for Raleigh. He intended to attack the town, Villa Dorta, lying four miles away and defended by two strong forts. One of these defended the town, while the other, on a rocky hill, covered the approach he intended to use in attacking the first. With Meyrick and a half-dozen of Essex's transport commanders refusing to move, Raleigh drew on his own ships to raise his force to nearly five hundred, many of them Dutch troops. Then, still wearing no armor except his gorget, he led his little force toward the Town Fort. A group of about forty gentlemen remained close to him as, staff in hand, he limped unconcernedly across the field of fire from the High Fort to the shelter of some rocks and deserted trenches. The moment the officers reached cover, the men, who had kept good order up to this point, broke ranks and dashed for the same rocks to escape the storm of musket balls and round shot. Though this might now seem like a very sensible procedure, then it was considered craven. Disdainfully Raleigh turned on the men and wondered aloud if this was "the manner of . . . Low Country troops, to show such base cowardice at the first sight of the enemy."[18]

Meanwhile his forward movement having caused the Spaniards to withdraw from their advanced positions, Raleigh called for volunteers to reconnoiter a way past the High Fort, whose cannon were seeking out the concealed English. When no one offered to go, he declared that, though it was hardly the duty of the commanding officer to be a scout, he would ask no one to do what he himself was not willing to do. Indignant that none still came forward, he prepared to reconnoiter the way himself. Over the protests of his officers, he insisted on going, and put on his breastplate and helmet. Gorges, seeing Raleigh was deadly

[18] *Ibid.*, 85.

serious about making his own reconnaissance, offered to accompany him; and the two men, with a handful of followers, picked their way up the hill.

It was hot, dangerous work. Round shot lopped off the heads of two of the band, a musket ball burned into the flesh of Gorges' leg, and bullets tore Raleigh's clothing in several places. So deadly grew the fire that Raleigh, concerned for Gorges, suggested that he pocket the large red scarf he was wearing since it appeared to draw the enemy's fire toward him. Gorges replied that Raleigh's white scarf was just as prominent as his red one. Later Gorges acknowledged that he wished he had not been wearing the scarf, but neither he nor Raleigh thought it fitting to honor the Spanish marksmen by removing their colors. So the two officers gallantly continued their reconnaissance, their scarfs flying like bright banners. Their mission completed, they returned to lead their men to an attack on the Town Fort. To their surprise, they presently discovered that the enemy had hastily evacuated both fort and town and had fled to the hills. Raleigh now decided to wait until morning before assaulting the High Fort.[19]

By morning the arrival of Essex and Howard forced a change in plans. These two had gone off on a wild-goose chase after a carrack without notifying Raleigh, and now found, to their surprise, the Rear Admiral already engaged in operations ashore. Sir Gelly Meyrick, Sir Christopher Blount, Sir Anthony Shirley, and other Essex men gleefully exhorted the Earl to court-martial Raleigh, who, they contended, deserved to die for having disobeyed fleet orders expressly forbidding any captain to land without permission from the Earl on penalty of death. Even Vere, less rancorous than the others, alluded to Raleigh's act as a "crime."[20] Acutely aware of his honor, Essex summoned Raleigh to come aboard the flagship at once and announced the displacement of all land captains who had assisted the Rear Admiral. Before the messenger arrived, Raleigh had gaily left in his barge, in no way suspecting what awaited him but anticipating, rather, congratulations on his achievements and support for his attack on the High Fort.

[19] *Ibid.*, 84-91; *History of the World*, bk. v, ch. i, sec. 9 (*Works*, VI, 103-05).
[20] Vere, *Commentaries*, in Firth, *Stuart Tracts*, 125.

He soon discovered his mistake. Black looks met him as he stepped aboard the flagship and walked to Essex's cabin. After a feeble attempt to welcome him, Essex challenged him with a breach of orders. The situation was dangerous, and Raleigh quickly sensed it. Fortunately his nimble wit stood by him. He declared that he had not committed any error at all. He insisted that, though there was an article that no captain should land without direction from Essex or some other "principal commander" on pain of death, he was not a captain as such but a principal commander under the Earl, and therefore not subject to the article nor under the power of martial law since he was "a successive commander of the whole fleet in Her Majesty's letters patent, your Lordship and my Lord Thomas Howard failing." Furthermore, he pointed out that Essex himself had agreed he should leave Flores and water at Fayal. Raleigh's position was sound, and Essex realized it; for years, "successive" commanders had not been subject to court-martial, and that Raleigh as Rear Admiral was such a commander admitted of no doubt.[21]

The dispute was over in a half-hour. Essex was so impressed with Raleigh's reasoning that he accompanied him ashore. He was even on the point of accepting his Rear Admiral's invitation to dine when Blount intervened and induced him to return to the *Due Repulse*. With Essex back aboard his ship, Raleigh began to suspect that the Earl's sycophants might still persuade him to adopt a tough attitude. Accordingly, Raleigh made plans that if the Earl tried to seize him, he would take his squadron into action against Essex rather than submit.

Fortunately for all concerned, and for the honor of England, Lord Thomas Howard, who was respected by both Essex and Raleigh, came forward as a peacemaker. He persuaded Essex to accept an apology from Raleigh if the latter would make one. Then he went to Raleigh, who could not see that he had done wrong and who was wary of again boarding Essex's flagship. Howard, however, promised him that if Essex offered him violence, he could count on Howard's coming to his assistance. Reassured, Raleigh went aboard the *Due Repulse*, where Essex and his council censured him, and Raleigh, for the good of the

---

[21] For Raleigh's defense, see *Purchas*, xx, 94-95.

service and to save Essex's face, apologized for an offense that was not really an offense. He demanded in return that Essex reinstate his displaced officers since he and he alone, he declared, was responsible for their actions. This was granted him. Perhaps the most absurd part of the whole altercation was that Essex did not even mention the capture of Fayal in his official report.[22]

From now on, the expedition became a depressing—or perhaps hilarious, at this distance—catalogue of mistakes and frustration. When the English finally remembered the Spaniards in the High Fort and mounted an assault, they found the place abandoned and one dead Englishman and one dead Dutchman, both with their throats cut. Hot were the recriminations: from Essex's men that Raleigh's troops had let the Spaniards escape, with lost ransom money; from Raleigh's supporters that Essex had not joined his troops to Raleigh's to take the Fort at once instead of spending the time "disciplining and correcting our own pretended faults for landing," as Gorges explained with justifiable heat.[23] In revenge for the two atrocities, the English burned Horta, then sailed away. Essex was determined to throw such a net of ships across the approaches to the strong port of Angra on Terceira that the Plate Fleet could not possibly slip through unseen. But suddenly timid about his anchorage, he changed his mind and, near midnight on September 25, took the entire fleet to St. Michael's Island. This was a most unfortunate decision from the English point of view and the Spaniards should have blessed the Earl, for, about three hours after his ships left for their new station, the Plate Fleet, deep-laden and fabulously rich in treasure, sailed at a stately pace into the very area that Essex had vacated. Though four English ships sought to check the enemy, their efforts were futile; the Spaniards sailed without loss into the harbor of Angra, which was protected by forts too powerful to be assailed successfully by men-of-war.[24]

Though beside himself when he discovered what had happened, Essex had no one to blame but himself. He had been

[22] *Ibid.*, 24-33; HMC, *Salisbury MSS*, VII, 439-40.
[23] *Purchas*, XX, 97.
[24] Vere, *Commentaries*, in Firth, *Stuart Tracts*, 126-28; Oppenheim, *Monson's Naval Tracts*, II, 26-30, 66-67, 81; Corbett, *The Successors of Drake*, 201-07; *History of the World*, bk. v, ch. i, sec. 10 (*Works*, VI, 102).

unable to adhere to a single plan. He was like a weathercock; the most influential voice was the last one to speak to him. Certainly for this egregious error he could not blame Raleigh. The latter, meanwhile, almost captured a huge East Indian carrack but for a little Dutch ship's springing too soon the trap that Raleigh had set and causing the carrack to run ashore on St. Michael where its crew set it ablaze. Loss of the carrack, which would have been a fine consolation prize for losing the Plate Fleet, was a disappointment too acute to be borne. Thoroughly embittered at the failure of the cruise, the English headed for home, straggling northward in a kind of every-ship-for-itself manner.

When they arrived, the English learned that they had just missed disaster. The Adelantado, whose ships they had neglected to destroy at Ferrol, had sailed with a fleet about as large as the Armada of 1588. He intended to stop at Brittany for troops and galleys, then, seizing Falmouth and garrisoning it, to lie off the Scilly Islands and await the return of Essex, Howard, and Raleigh. With the English fleet off the Azores, the coast was wide open, and the Spaniards might have succeeded in taking Falmouth and laying their trap for Essex. In the disordered fashion in which they were sailing homeward—Raleigh even having stowed his heaviest guns away in the hold of the *Warspite*—the English ships would have been easy targets for the Adelantado. It was a near thing for the English, for though the Adelantado was delayed in sailing, he went north in formation on the same gale that filled the English canvas; the two fleets were thus sailing on roughly parallel courses.[25]

England echoed with alarm guns, the beating of muster drums, and the clashing hoofs of couriers' horses as intelligence reached London on October 23 that the Spaniards were off the coast. Though panic flashed in certain quarters, most of southern England rallied sturdily to meet the crisis. Luckily the arrival of the fleet relieved apprehensions of its safety but, now that it

[25] The best account of the Adelantado's plans and voyage is in Corbett, *The Successors of Drake*, 212-27, but see also the excellent historical note in Oppenheim, *Monson's Naval Tracts*, II, 72-83. Good secondary accounts of the Islands Voyage are by Corbett, *The Successors of Drake*, chs. VII and VIII; Cheyney, *History of England*, II, 421-43; Rowse, *The Expansion of Elizabethan England*, 314-18.

was secure in Plymouth, it could not beat to sea in the teeth of the wind to meet the Spaniards. While Essex raced to London to hasten defense measures, Raleigh, who had landed at St. Ives, sent the *Warspite* on Essex's orders around to Plymouth and rode overland to take general command of the area as Lieutenant General. This was the part of England that he loved the best, and he was determined that the enemy should not be permitted to burn and ravage as they had done but a few years before on the Cornish coast in the vicinity of Penzance. For a few days, tension ran high, then further intelligence began to come in during the last days in October and early in November that the gale that had blown the English ships home and had become very nasty had also scattered and shattered part of the Spanish fleet. Though a few Spanish squadrons appeared off the English coast, all were back in their home ports again before the English could put to sea in mid-November.[26]

With this surprise ending was concluded the Islands Voyage, about as futile an expedition as England ever launched. Also with it came to an end the sea career of Raleigh as a regular naval commander. Though his judgment was open to question on several counts, particularly in the understanding he shared with Essex not to attack the Spanish fleet at Ferrol, generally his reputation stood up far better than Essex's. The fault for the failure of the expedition was largely the Earl's, and the Queen recognized it. At the same time, it was unlikely that the supporters of Essex would let him assume the blame that was properly his; Raleigh was the villain of the piece. Hence, notwithstanding the good feeling that appeared to prevail between Essex and Raleigh when they returned, an end to it was not long delayed.

[26] For Raleigh's part in the defense arrangements, see HMC, *Salisbury MSS*, VII, 447, 450, 455-56, 461, 466-67, 472; *Cal. S.P. Dom.*, *1595-1597*, 528-29.

# CHAPTER 13

# The Final Rivalry
## with Essex

AFTER the Islands Voyage, Raleigh was soon involved in developments in which he had to exercise the utmost delicacy and discretion. If he failed to secure the seat in the Privy Council on which he had set his heart, and if he never completely recovered the confidence of the Queen, he concealed his bitterness. Time was beginning to run swiftly now—he was forty-five when he returned from Fayal, the Queen was sixty-four and visibly aging despite the skill of coiffeurs and make-up artists—and Essex still appeared unshakeable in the position of favorite.

But Essex was building up a store of trouble for himself. Expressing the attitude of many of the Court, which in turn usually reflected that of the Queen, the courtier Rowland Whyte observed, concerning Essex, that the Queen "is not pleased with his service at sea, and that his proceedings towards Sir Walter Raleigh in calling his [Raleigh's] actions to question before a Council of War is misliked here."[1] The omission of Raleigh's exploit at Fayal was damning for its evidence of jealousy and childishness. Then, too, Essex annoyed the Queen by objecting to the elevation of Lord Admiral Howard as Earl of Nottingham. Raleigh entered the scene not as a protagonist but as a peacemaker. As Lord High Admiral and Earl of Nottingham, Charles Howard now had precedence over all Earls, including Essex, who sullenly quit the Court and the Privy Council, complaining that the cold and the long speeches he heard gave him a headache. Raleigh tried to ease the situation by ingeniously suggesting that the Queen might make Essex Earl-Marshal.[2] If this move appeased Essex, it infuriated Howard, who saw himself superseded and who retired from Court in a huff. Ra-

---

[1] Collins, *Letters and Memorials of State*, II, 74; HMC, *Lord De L'Isle and Dudley MSS*, II, 302.
[2] Birch, *Memoirs of the Reign of Queen Elizabeth*, II, 365.

leigh now tried, by Elizabeth's direction, to soothe the Lord Admiral, but Howard nursed his hurt and, never very friendly to Raleigh, counted him henceforth an enemy. The lot of the peacemaker is proverbial.

That winter of 1597-1598, Raleigh sat in Parliament as senior knight for Dorset. He was late for the early days of the session because of his defense duties and his health. Though he possessed a strong constitution, the strain of the last few years had worn him down, and he and Bess went to Bath for the waters. The Privy Council sent him its good wishes for a quick recovery, while the Speaker of the House gave Raleigh's step-brother, Sir Adrian Gilbert, special permission on November 21 to go down to visit him. The illness was probably physical exhaustion, from which he had recovered by December 20, when his name first appears as a member of the committee for a bill against persons pretending to be soldiers or sailors.[3] Raleigh spoke judiciously to both this bill and one related to it that was sent down by the Lords.[4] In a conference with the Lords over these bills Raleigh and the Commons' committee were offended that, instead of meeting with them on an informal basis, the Lords compelled the committee to stand uncovered while they remained seated and kept their hats on. Even the Lord Keeper, who delivered the Lords' reply in this meeting that could hardly be called a conference, disdained the courtesy of either standing up when he spoke or removing his hat.[5] Raleigh reported this "indignity" to a House that listened in anger and demanded an explanation. The Lords ultimately vindicated themselves by stating that, when bills were brought from the Commons, they would indeed meet with the members of the Lower House, but that, when the Commons arrived for an answer from the Lords, they should receive it in the manner given.[6] This explanation of procedure was accepted without further dispute. In addition to these bills, Raleigh served in connection with measures for the maintenance of the navy, for increasing the number of men in the service, and for the discharge of the Queen's debts.[7] All of these were measures in which his experience made him a valuable participant.

[3] D'Ewes, 575.    [4] *Ibid.*, 579.    [5] *Ibid.*, 580.
[6] *Ibid.*, 585.    [7] *Ibid.*, 582, 578, 591.

When Parliament was over in the winter of 1598, Raleigh busied himself in many ways. With the great Burghley's death in August, he again sought admission to the Privy Council, but the position went to Lord Shrewsbury; in this denial was to be seen the hand of Cecil, who retained the real executive power after Elizabeth despite the elevation of Thomas Sackville to Lord Treasurer. Nor did Raleigh win the position of Vice Chamberlain that he wanted. These blows were bitter, and rumor was rampant that Raleigh was planning another voyage to Guiana, this time with Sir John Gilbert. It could have been a consolation activity, or, possibly, the death of Philip II of Spain in September revived old Guiana dreams. He sent out at least one small vessel to remind the natives there of his friendship. Perhaps more important to him for the time being, however, were the lavish building additions which he planned and carried out with a loving hand at Sherborne into 1601. This enterprise he attacked with special vigor after fire partially burned out Durham House in October 1600. He continued active with his Wardenship of the Stannaries, adjusting numerous disputes that rose, particularly between the tin miners and Plymouth. In his capacity as commander in the west, he was often consulted about naval and defense matters. He began to take steps to get rid of his Irish holdings as troubles in that unhappy island mounted. He found time, too, to devote considerable attention to the island of Jersey, of which he was appointed governor in September 1600. Though his appointment proved expensive, both for itself and for his having to remunerate his unsuccessful rival, Lord Henry Seymour, he reconstructed its defenses, relieved one district of compulsory military service, registered the island's real estate, and developed new trading and fishing connections. Raleigh's name still evokes a pleasant association in Jersey.

Of all his activities and involvements during the years from 1597 to 1601, those concerning Ireland and the Earl of Essex were the most important. English policy in Ireland, rarely consistent, now severe, now conciliatory, reaped its due harvest beginning in 1598 with the revolt of Hugh O'Neill, the Irish Earl of Tyrone, and his defeat of an English army on the Blackwater in August. Munster was ravaged, and many of Raleigh's English tenants fled for their lives to the coast towns. Though it is doubtful that Raleigh visited Ireland during this crisis, he was evidently consulted as to the most effective way of quashing the threat to English rule offered by Tyrone. He replied to Cecil in October that it could be "no disgrace if it were known that the killing of a rebel were practised, for we see that the lives of anointed princes are daily sought, and we have always given head money for the killing of rebels, who are evermore proclaimed for a price. So was the Earl of Desmond, and so have all rebels been practised against. . . ."[8]

Whatever its morality, this was a forthright statement of opinion. Why fool around with the expense and effort of attempting to crush a rebellion by the use of armies when a musket shot or a knife thrust would eliminate the inciter? Assassination is a thoroughly detestable policy in any age notwithstanding its use during Raleigh's era by the English in Ireland, by Philip II of Spain to rid himself of his great Dutch protagonist, William the Silent, or by its elevation to a doctrine by certain Jesuits as justification for liquidating princes whom they considered tyrants. On the other hand, to deplore its acceptance by Raleigh is to judge the morality of one age by that of another. He was contemptuous of the Irish, thinking them worse than savages, and would smash them with no more qualms of conscience than one would step on the head of a snake. Like many highly cultivated Englishmen then and afterward—men who did not hesitate to consider themselves Christian—he had a blind spot where Ireland was concerned. At the same time, despise the Irish as he did, he had too much respect for their capabilities and too little regard for the extent and consistency of English support to want the task of pacifying the island for himself or his friends. He was quite content to see that dubious award go to Essex.

Relations between the two men had grown steadily worse. At first, on returning from Fayal and during early 1598, Raleigh and Cecil saw a great deal of Essex; Rowland Whyte observed in January that "none but they enjoy him."[9] For this apparent

[8] *Cal. S.P. Dom, 1598-1601*, 112-13.
[9] Collins, *Letters and Memorials of State*, II, 79; HMC, *Lord De L'Isle and Dudley MSS*, 308.

good feeling Raleigh's role in helping restore the Earl's precedence over Nottingham was partially responsible. Then, when the Queen's scorn for Essex's conduct and ill success in the Islands Voyage began to manifest itself, the Earl cooled rapidly toward Raleigh. No doubt men like Meyrick and Blount contributed to the undermining of Essex's confidence in Raleigh.

The question of the Irish appointment further aggravated the situation. As early as March, Raleigh, Sir Robert Sydney and Sir William Russell were rumored to be in line for the appointment; later Blount, who was Essex's stepfather, was also mentioned.[10] It seems highly improbable that if Raleigh had actually been offered the post, he would have dared refuse it or that, in such an event, Essex would have deigned to accept it. But that Raleigh was not eager for the job is likely. On July 1, the Queen, Essex, the Lord Admiral, and Cecil discussed the selection. The Queen proposed Sir William Knollys, but the Earl brushed the suggestion aside and said that Sir George Carew was the man for the job. Carew, of course, was Raleigh's cousin and Cecil's friend; let him assume the responsibility, not Knollys, who was Essex's uncle. The discussion grew warm, and Essex lost control of himself. Giving Elizabeth an ugly look, he turned his back on her. At this display of boorishness, the outraged Queen boxed his ears and told him to go and be hanged. Instantly Essex reached for his sword, swearing he would not tolerate such an insult even from Henry VIII had he been living. Fortunately the Lord Admiral intervened, and Essex left in a huff.[11] Despite this incredible insolence, the Queen continued to put up with Essex.

From his sulking at Wansted, Essex emerged from time to time to brood with wrath and melancholy upon the worldly scene. Warned by men like Francis Bacon and Lord Keeper Egerton to be circumspect in his conduct toward the Queen, he considered the Queen had erred in her conduct toward him. Raleigh's eminence, moreover, provoked him so acutely that he resolved to undermine him again. The Queen's birthday falling on November 17, a great tournament was held in the tiltyard with Elizabeth as the honored guest. Raleigh as Captain

[10] HMC, *Lord De L'Isle and Dudley MSS*, 329, 332; Stebbing, *Ralegh*, 146.
[11] Harrison, *Essex*, 194-95; Neale, *Queen Elizabeth*, 348.

of the Guard had equipped his company with orange tawney plumes, and a gay effect it made. Suddenly Essex burst into view with a private army of knights and retainers amounting to 2,000 men—all clad in the same magnificence of orange-colored feathers and spoiling the splash of color made by Raleigh's little group. If the Earl was delighted at the success of his childish vanity, he soon lost his good humor. In the tilts he did very poorly, while the Queen was so annoyed at the contempt he had shown her that presently she called off the ceremonies.[12]

The Irish appointment went eventually to Essex notwithstanding his father's unfortunate experience there. As early as November 8, 1598, that inveterate letter-writer, John Chamberlain, wrote that Essex would probably go to Ireland in the spring with Mountjoy as his deputy. Essex, he reported, was to be accompanied by most of the men on whom he had conferred knighthood, "for it is thought fit they should not come too easily by their honor. . . ."[13] Essex's habit of making so many knights clearly annoyed those whom it did not amuse. He varied between considering his appointment a sacrifice to his country's need and regarding it as an unparalleled opportunity to vindicate his name. He went over to Ireland at the end of March 1599, after first riding with his followers through the streets of London like a conquering hero. The people cheered him wildly, for he was as adored as Raleigh was hated, and they trooped after him for several miles. Even Shakespeare caught the enthusiasm in his historical play of the hour, *Henry V*:

> Were now the general of our gracious empress
> (As in good time he may) from Ireland coming,
> Bringing rebellion broached on his sword,
> How many would the peaceful city quit
> To welcome him![14]

Essex's behavior in Ireland was extraordinary. With the largest expeditionary force—16,000 infantry and 1,300 cavalry —that had left England during Elizabeth's time, he let himself

---

[12] Sir H. Wotton, *Reliquiae Wottoniae*, 190.
[13] *The Letters of John Chamberlain*, I, 51.
[14] *Henry V*, Prologue, act v. The best account of Essex's expedition as well as of other Elizabethan expeditions to Ireland is by C. Falls, *Elizabeth's Irish Wars*.

be persuaded by the Irish Council to defer the campaigning season until summer when the crops were in full growth and the horses had fattened. Meanwhile, he dubbed knights by the score, thereby eliciting caustic comments from observers and provoking the Queen to the point where she forbade him to make any more knights. In addition, he paraded about the country with so little attention to the realities of his task that the Queen angrily remarked that it was costing her a thousand pounds a day for him simply to go on progress. Worse still, he became conciliatory toward the Irish at a time when the Queen wanted them subdued. Furious, she lashed his policy with bitter scorn and sent him new instructions. Her criticism threw him into a rage, and in a letter to her he said he knew who was responsible for the official disapproval in London: "Is it not known that from England I receive nothing but discomforts and soul's wounds? . . . Is it not lamented of your Majesty's faithfullest subjects, both there and here, that a Cobham and Raleigh—I will forbear others, for their places' sakes—should have such credit and favour with your Majesty when they wish the ill success of your Majesty's most important action, the decay of your greatest strength, and the destruction of your faithfullest servants?"[15]

Though little is known of Cobham's opinions of Ireland, Raleigh was becoming an obsession with Essex. It cannot be doubted that Raleigh opposed the Earl's policy of doing nothing but make a truce with Tyrone. But that Raleigh, with vested interests still in Ireland, would desire an English defeat indicates a misjudgment not only of his patriotism but of his business sense as well. Toward Irish rebels Raleigh was insistent that no reconciliation should precede their submission: any other course was appeasement, a confession of weakness, and would lead to a further strengthening of the insurgents. While Raleigh was disposed always to be harsh with the Irish, Essex's softer policy originated less in humanitarianism than in ignorance of what to do about the situation and in a desire to cut free from Ireland and hurry to London to defend his reputation. Ironically, had Essex pursued the Raleigh policy, he might have crushed the

[15] Quoted by Edwards, *Ralegh* (*Life*), I, 253-54.

rebels, as Mountjoy did eventually, and returned in triumph with a reputation needing no defense.

Essex's conduct grew so peculiar that almost anything came to be expected of him. On August 9 the English fleet was mobilized and troops were called into the old Armada camp at Tilbury when word arrived that the Adelantado was at sea, again bound for the Isle of Wight. Panic swept over London at rumors of his having made a landing, women wailing publicly in fear, chains being strung across the streets, and citizens barricading themselves in their houses. In this crisis Raleigh went down to the fleet as Vice Admiral under Lord Thomas Howard and helped get the ships in readiness for whatever might happen. Ostensibly these preparations were against the Adelantado, but, when his turned out to be the "Invisible Armada" and the alarm subsided, men began to find something mysterious in the sudden assembling of forces. Many came to believe it was directed against a descent upon the coast by Essex or as a warning to him that England was not defenseless. Two years later, Sir Christopher Blount acknowledged in his confession that Essex had contemplated, about this time, landing at Milford Haven and marching on London. On the other hand, one has to be a little wary of confessions extracted by, or by the threat of, torture.[16]

Presently, however, Essex really appeared, not with an army but with a small group of followers on September 28. He surprised the aging but still vain Queen dressing in her bedroom, her hair sprawled untidily over her face. Though at first received by her with more kindness than he deserved, he was soon placed in arrest. She and Cecil saw eye to eye on his breach of orders to remain in Ireland and to make no truce with Tyrone. Meanwhile, he suffered from the stone and was literally ill from humiliation. Though the Queen ultimately canceled plans for a Star Chamber trial and let him go to his own house with a keeper, he was still not free by any means, and men grew angry and active in his behalf.

It was probably during the winter of 1600, the early period of Essex's imprisonment, that Raleigh wrote Cecil a letter that has been both damned for its cold-blooded Machiavellism

[16] *Chamberlain Letters*, I, 80-85, for crisis, especially p. 83 for the warning to Essex. For Blount's confession, see Howell, *State Trials*, I, 1434.

and praised for its sagacity. Evidently in response to a request from Cecil, who had examined Essex, Raleigh gave his opinion on the policy that should be followed toward the Earl:

"I am not wise enough to give you advice; but if you take it for a good counsel to relent towards this tyrant, you will repent it when it shall be too late. His malice is fixed, and will not evaporate by any [of] your mild courses. For he will ascribe the alteration to Her Majesty's pusillanimity, and not to your good nature; knowing that you work but upon her humour, and not out of any love towards him. The less you make him, the less he shall be able to harm you and yours. And if Her Majesty's favour fail him, he will again decline to a common person."

Citing a number of instances in which revenge was not taken upon the instrument of a great man's fall, Raleigh entreated Cecil not to fear reprisal. Of further instances, Raleigh observed:

"I could name you a thousand . . . and therefore after-fears are but prophecies—or rather conjectures—from causes remote. Look to the present, and you do wisely. His son shall be the youngest Earl of England but one, and, if his father be now kept down, Will Cecil [Cecil's son] shall be able to keep as many men at his heels as he, and more too. He may also match in a better house than his; and so that fear is not worth the fearing. But if the father continue, he will be able to break the branches, and pull up the tree, root and all. Lose not your advantage; if you do, I read your destiny."

As a postscript, Raleigh added: "Let the Q[ueen]. hold Bothwell [Essex] while she hath him. He will ever be the canker of her estate and safety. Princes are lost by security; and preserved by prevention. I have seen the last of her good days, and all ours, after his liberty."[17]

It is a shocking letter. The philosophy of "now that you have caught him, step on him" seems repellent to our own carefully cultivated sense of fair play. It is Machiavellian and, as realistic policy, strong medicine for one to take with equanimity. But, contrary to the surmise of a number of historians, Raleigh was not urging execution; if the Queen removed her favor from Essex, "he will again decline to a common person." Raleigh knew what it was like to be out of favor. At the same time, while

[17] Edwards, *Ralegh* (*Letters*), II, 222-23; HMC, *Salisbury MSS*, x, 439-40.

he had retained many of his honors and privileges during his own exile from Court, Essex should be deprived of his—"kept down." Furthermore, Essex should be held in prison or, if that was too severe, on some estate under surveillance. Perhaps Raleigh thought this might not be long in view of the Earl's illness. Chamberlain wrote Dudley Carleton on February 29 that Essex "hath been somewhat crazy this week" and, on March 5, that, in addition to bodily afflictions, he was "quite out of mind."[18] Perhaps indeed Essex was breaking up from his treatment. Confined, he was harmless; once freed, he would spare no adversary in his raging vengeance.

But for all that Raleigh played up to Cecil's self-interest, Cecil saw farther than Raleigh. Essex's offenses, however grave, scarcely merited the penalty of confinement for life, and no just provocation must be given for his becoming a rallying point for the disaffected in the realm. Far better to let him have rope enough to weave his own halter. In the Machiavellian game Raleigh was a tyro compared to Cecil; the future Viscount Cranborne and Earl of Salisbury played with a finesse that was the more deadly for its apparent ingenuousness. Summoned before part of the Privy Council in June, Essex was properly admonished but not released from his keeper until July and not given complete freedom until August. The one curb on his liberty was that he might not attend Court.

The days that Raleigh had dreaded now came to pass. Even as Raleigh, once banished from the Queen's presence, let no opportunity go by to win back her favor, so Essex tried unremittingly. He sent her delightfully phrased letters of suppliance and affection. This was all very well, in Elizabeth's opinion, and no more than he ought to do. At the same time, Essex was not content with letters of supplication; for quite some time he had been planning measures that stopped not short of revolution. Cecil and the Queen knew something of those plans—how much is not certain. Essex tried to persuade Mountjoy, his successor in Ireland, to cooperate with him and send troops to England. For a while, Mountjoy seemed half-inclined to join in the plans until fright at the implications of such a commitment and a growing interest in his own task in Ireland impelled

[18] *Chamberlain Letters*, I, 90, 92.

him to refuse. Essex, however, was not discouraged. Seeing in James VI of Scotland the successor of Elizabeth, he sought to obtain his good will. He warned James that he must assert his right to the throne since a plot was afoot to make the Spanish Infanta Queen of England. First mentioned in the conspiracy was Raleigh, who commanded in the west where he could assure the Spaniards a landing; since he was also Governor of Jersey, he could harbor them there on any occasion. Likewise mentioned in the plot were Cobham, as commander in the Cinque Ports and Kent; the Lord Treasurer; the Lord Admiral; Thomas, Cecil's brother, as President of the north; Carew, President of Munster; and Cecil himself.[19] These were, as Cecil later described them to Carew, "hyperbolical inventions."[20] Had either Mountjoy or James, who was sympathetic with Essex, supported the Earl, and had Essex been able to seize the Court by force, both Raleigh and Cecil would have been "removed" and Raleigh's post as Captain of the Guard given to Sir William Russell.[21]

A reconciliation with the Queen would have halted these conspirings, which were involving an increasing number of distinguished people. But the Queen, awaking at last to Essex's deficiencies, refused to heed his blandishments, and her official birthday, November 17, saw the final known letter from Essex to her. Now he became wildly reckless. Sir John Harington, who saw him about this time, said that "his speeches of the Queen becometh no man who hath *mens sana in corpore sano.*"[22] Perhaps it was one of these speeches that reached her by the grapevine, or possibly it was at a last interview with the Queen that Essex committed an irreparable error. Years later, Raleigh wrote that "Undutiful words of a subject do often take deeper root than the memory of ill deeds . . . the late Earl of Essex told Queen Elizabeth that her conditions were as crooked as her carcass; but it cost him his head, which his insurrection had not cost him but for that speech."[23] Few knew the vanity of his

[19] *Correspondence of King James VI of Scotland with Sir Robert Cecil*, 81-84.
[20] *Letters from Sir Robert Cecil to Sir George Carew*, 68.
[21] *Corr. of King James with Cecil*, 90.
[22] Birch, *Memoirs of the Reign of Queen Elizabeth*, II, 473.
[23] *Works*, VIII, 199.

sovereign so well as Raleigh, a vanity that seemed to wax rather than wane with the years.

Whatever the truth of Raleigh's observation, Essex's conspiracy, swelling rapidly through the late fall of 1600 and the early winter of 1601, came to a head on Sunday, February 8. For days, Essex House had drawn together scores of malcontents—nobles and commoners, and Puritan ministers, who, seeing in Essex the hope of their party, preached sermons little short of treasonous to hundreds of followers. The chief conspirators, Essex alone being absent, met at the Earl of Southampton's house on February 3 to go over final plans. It was hoped, of course, that James VI would cooperate. On Saturday evening, the 7th, after the conspirators had hired Shakespeare's group to put on *Richard II* for them, the Council ordered Essex to appear. This he would not do, and Cecil at once readied the government for action, one of the first steps being an order for Raleigh to double the Guard.

When morning came, February 8, it was Raleigh who accidentally touched off the explosion. With Essex was Sir Ferdinando Gorges, a kinsman of Raleigh and his subordinate in charge of Plymouth Fort. As Gorges' commanding officer, Raleigh sent for him to come by water to Durham House. Essex consented to Gorges' meeting Raleigh but only in the middle of the Thames and with two attendants present for safety's sake. Though Sir Christopher Blount wanted Gorges to capture or kill Raleigh, Gorges refused. Raleigh agreed to the conditions of meeting and, rowing out alone to see Gorges, ordered him back to Plymouth else he might soon find himself in Fleet Prison.

"Tush, Sir Walter," Gorges retorted, "this is not a time to talk of going to the Fleet. Get you back to the Court, and that with speed, for my Lord of Essex hath put himself into a strong guard at Essex House, and you are like to have a bloody day of it."

Though Raleigh sought to reason with Gorges, the latter refused to leave Essex.

Meanwhile, someone, allegedly Blount, fired four times at Raleigh from the river bank and missed, no tribute to his marksmanship. Then four armed men climbed into a boat at Essex

House stairs and rowed toward Raleigh. At this, Gorges pushed his kinsman's boat away with his own hands and bade him hurry to the other bank. And so they parted, Gorges to Essex House, Raleigh to the Court.[24]

At once, Cecil sent Lord Keeper Egerton, the Earl of Worcester, Sir William Knollys, and Chief Justice Popham to inquire of Essex the cause for this tumultuous assemblage. Their appearance provoked wild cries of "Away, my lord, they abuse you, they betray you, they undo you, you lose time!" There were even more menacing shouts: "Let us shop them up!" "Kill them! Kill them!" Essex spared the visitors but put them under guard.

From now on, Essex's revolt moved rapidly to a climax. Informing his gentlemen that Raleigh, Cobham, and Cecil had plotted to take his life, he galloped for the city.[25] "For the Queen! For the Queen! A plot is laid for my life!" he shouted on the way up Ludgate Hill. But, instead of grabbing their weapons and following him, the citizens gathered in their doorways and cheered him, then slunk inside as a herald sent by Cecil proclaimed him a traitor. Sheriff Smith of London, on whom Essex had counted for arms and men, gave him no aid. His situation hazardous in the extreme, he tried to retreat. Though he soon found Ludgate barred by chains and troops, and thus impassable despite repeated charges, he managed to find a way down to the riverside, where he crossed by boat to Essex House. Once inside, he discovered that the hostages had been released during his absence and that the residence was besieged on the land side and, within a short time of his arrival, from the riverside as well. He held out until the evening, when the Lord Admiral threatened to blow up the house, something Cecil said Howard would have done before but for the presence of Lady Essex and Lady Rich inside. Essex then surrendered. Perhaps he was relieved to learn that Raleigh was not on hand to witness the capitulation; at least Raleigh's name does not appear on Cecil's list of the commanders of the little army that put down the revolt. It is more likely that he was at his post

[24] For incident, see Jardine, *Criminal Trials,* I, 327, 328, 330-31, 346; Howell, *State Trials,* I, 1342-43, 1344-45, 1424.
[25] Jardine, *Criminal Trials,* I, 321, 344, 346, 349.

guarding the Queen on one of the most dangerous days of her long reign.[26]

The scotching of the Essex revolt—or riot, as some chose to call it—was Cecil's work, and the trial of Essex and his fellow conspirators saw the completion of this phase of the Secretary's labors. The trials were marked by a strange accent on painfully full confessions and acknowledgments of guilt. Among those executed were Raleigh's old antagonists, Sir Gelly Meyrick and Sir Christopher Blount. The latter, whose conduct at his trial was less confessional than that of the others, acknowledged, in answer to a question from Cecil, that neither he nor Essex really believed that Raleigh and Cobham intended to harm the Earl; the report to that effect was merely "a word cast out to colour other matters."[27] On the scaffold, when the sheriff interrupted Blount's prayers and confessions, Lord Grey and Raleigh, whose duties as Captain of the Guard required his presence, told the sheriff to let him finish in peace.

"Is Sir Walter there?" asked Blount.

When those standing on the scaffold said that he was, Blount called out, "Sir Walter Raleigh, I thank God that you are present. I had an infinite desire to speak with you, to ask your forgiveness ere I died, both for wrong done you, and for my particular ill intent towards you. I beseech you forgive me."

From this man who had cruelly wronged him on several occasions, especially at Fayal, but who was now so soon to meet his Maker, Raleigh could not spurn such an entreaty. "I most willingly forgive you," he said gravely, "and I beseech God to forgive you and to give you His divine comfort."[28]

Though Southampton was spared the death penalty, Essex did not experience the same mercy. At his trial he bore himself with the condescending arrogance of a man of lofty rank and position who could do no wrong but who was simply misunderstood. He smiled disdainfully, looked heavenward, made inso-

---

[26] For the Essex rising, see *ibid.*, I, 310-88; Howell, *State Trials*, I, 1334-59; *Cal. S.P. Dom.*, *1598-1601*, 547-50, 557-62, 573-75, 579-81, 585-87; *ibid.*, *1601-1603*, 3-5, 8-11, 13, 16, 22, 24-25, 26-27, 38-39, 50; *Cal. S.P. Ireland*, *1600-1601*, 198-200; *Letters from Cecil to Carew*, 65-75; *Salisbury MSS*, XI, 29-131 *passim*; Harrison, *Essex*, 276-93; Cheyney, *History of England*, II, 520-48.

[27] Howell, *State Trials*, I, 1424.

[28] *Ibid.*, 1414-15.

lent remarks, and indulged in wit that never quite came off. When Raleigh was called as a witness, he cried out, "What booteth it to swear the fox?"[29] He scornfully refused to acknowledge any truth in the argument of Francis Bacon, who had turned against him, that, to cover up his treason, he was blaming his enemies for his defection. He pointed a finger at Cecil as having good words to say of the Infanta's succession, an allegation that prompted a spirited reply from the little Secretary. And to the terrible sentence passed upon him of being hanged, drawn, and quartered—later mitigated to beheading— he made a flippant reply. Perhaps he believed that his once beloved and loving sovereign would not let this really happen.

But Essex was to die after all; both the Queen and Cecil were agreed on that. When Essex, back in the Tower, realized his fate, he fell under the spell of his devout chaplain and wrote out a detailed confession, naming his fellow conspirators and blaming in particular his own secretary, Henry Cuffe, as his chief instigator. He acquitted Cecil of upholding the Infanta and professed to bear no malice toward Raleigh and Cobham, whom he acknowledged to be true servants of the state.[30] In addition to this written confession, when he was brought to the scaffold in the Tower courtyard on the morning of February 25, 1601, he made an oral confession so abject and emotional as to be incredible to one who did not know the impulsive nature of the Earl.

Raleigh, as Captain of the Guard, was present at the execution. He had conducted himself with dignity and restraint during the trials under the most trying circumstances. It is likely that Essex's oral confession appalled him, and he may indeed have considered the Earl a boy who had never grown up. But that he gloated over his rival's few moments before the ax descended, as enemies contended, and that he stood in a window overlooking the scaffold where he blew out tobacco smoke in disdain and made objectionable comments does not ring true. He was in the courtyard in his official capacity, as he would be at the execution of the other conspirators. In the be-

---

[29] Jardine, *Criminal Trials*, I, 329.
[30] *Ibid.*, 368-69; Birch, *Memoirs of the Reign of Queen Elizabeth*, II, 477; Sir R. Winwood, *Memorials of Affairs of State in the Reigns of Q. Elizabeth and K. James I*, I, 300-01.

ginning, he stood close to the scaffold, in the event that Essex should want to speak to him. Many victims in that era sought, as did Blount, consolation in their final moments by asking the forgiveness of both their friends and their enemies. But, hearing angry comments from onlookers at his presence, Raleigh thought it only fitting to leave and walk to the distant Armory where he could observe without being seen by others. This move he literally regretted to his dying day since he did not hear the doomed man's expressed desire to be reconciled with him.[31]

People who saw Raleigh as he returned to Durham House after the execution noticed that his face looked sad and gloomy. Did he have a presentiment of uncertain days ahead? Essex had died at thirty-four; he was already forty-nine; and the mistress whom both had served was a tired old lady not long for this world. After her, what course would England take? What place would there be for him in a land where James of Scotland would sit at Whitehall and Robert Cecil, whose skill and power he had just seen so evident, would be the King's right hand? If Raleigh asked himself such questions, what indeed were his answers? Whatever their nature, he was soon to know the shape of things to come, and the melancholy on his countenance as Essex's remains were being disposed of was like a mirror of his own fate.

[31] Jardine, *Criminal Trials*, I, 507-08.

CHAPTER 14

# The Twilight Years
# of Power

THE period from the execution of Essex to the accession of
James was for Raleigh an interval of many diverse activities
and of such happiness as was possible for a man of his brilliant,
restless mind and somber nature. His Court rivals—Leicester,
Hatton, and Essex—were no more, and if Elizabeth no longer
regarded him with affection, she continued to take a certain
pleasure in his conversation and presence. He realized that her
chief reliance was on Cecil, now indeed more than ever secure
since the death of the once beloved favorite. But Cecil was his
friend, or so Raleigh thought, a man on whose loyalty he
counted and who would certainly interpose no obstacles to
further distinctions provided they did not clash with the Secretary's own designs. Unfortunately for Raleigh, his judgment
of men was often lamentably deficient: Cecil deceived him
utterly.

Though Raleigh contemptuously ignored the fact, his unpopularity became abysmal during these two years, largely
because of Essex's death. Essex had been a hero to the public,
and the taint of treason scarcely intimidated men from speaking,
if obliquely, in his behalf. "Sweet England's pride is gone,"
they lamented; and sadly they acknowledged that

> Though Law strict course of justice kept,
> The most and best of all sorts wept.[1]

The Earl had had a magical appeal. As arrogant in his way as
Raleigh, he was a far more kindly person, and men of every
rank and station regarded him with affection. With him departed the glorious, youthful exuberance of the Elizabethans.
Well indeed might people mourn the passing of the age as
well as of the young nobleman when they wailed:

[1] From Honor's Fame in Triumph Riding, quoted by Cheyney, History of
England, II, 545.

> All ye that cry O hone O hone
> Come now and sing O Lord with me.
> For why? Our Jewell is from us gone,
> The valiant knight of chivalry.[2]

Something bright and cherished had fled with Essex's life, perhaps their own youthfulness.

Men's bitterness fell heavily upon Raleigh and Cecil. Scornfully they spoke of

> Little Cecil tripping up and downe,
> He rules both court and crown.[3]

And surely they were right. Few could doubt that the clever little hunchback, wise in the ways of intrigue, incredibly circumspect, was the real power at last. Not even Raleigh could challenge his authority. It was on Raleigh rather than Cecil, however, that they loosed their real anger:

> Raleigh doth time bestride:
> He sits 'twixt wind and tide.
> Yet uphill he cannot ride,
> For all his bloody pride.
> He seeks taxes in the tin:
> He polls the poor to the skin:
> Yet he swears 'tis no sin.
> Lord, for thy pity![4]

Others used more pointed words as they contemplated the haughty worldling whom they held responsible for their idol's fall:

> Essex for vengeance cries
> His blood upon thee lies,
> Mounting above the skies,
> Damnable fiend of hell,
> Mischievous Matchivel![5]

---

[2] From *A Lamentable new Ballad upon the Earle of Essex his death. To the Tune of Essex's Last Good Night,* quoted in *Roxburghe Ballads,* I, 571.

[3] Quoted by Cheyney, II, 535.

[4] Thompson, *Ralegh,* 164. Quoted here by kind permission of Yale University Press.

[5] Quoted by J. O. Halliwell, *Poetical Miscellanies,* 13-14.

Through all this furor Raleigh remained unperturbed, and presently he found himself in the role of receptionist for foreign dignitaries. He looked after a Spanish envoy in March 1601, showing him the sights of London. During the summer, the Duke of Sully, the great minister of Henry IV of France, arrived in England incognito. Early apprised of his arrival, Raleigh rode to Dover to welcome him. Sully had just entered his room at Dover when Raleigh tiptoed in and playfully announced, "I arrest you as my prisoner, in the Queen's name." Startled, Sully spun about, then relaxed in laughter as he recognized his mischievous captor. As Sully observed, "It was the Captain of her Guard. I returned his embrace, telling him I should consider such an imprisonment as a great honour."[6]

The Queen was as little amused by the manner of Sully's entrance into England as she was prepared in September for the appearance of his distinguished compatriot, the Duke de Biron, Constable of France, who came to notify Elizabeth of his master's marriage to Marie de Medici. Within a year Biron was to die a traitor's death, his treason and execution shocking France almost as greatly as the Essex disaster had shocked England. Biron arrived in England with an enormous train of noble companions and less elevated followers, and though plans had been made for his entertainment, the Queen was at Basing and the government unready. Although Raleigh had not been assigned a part in Biron's reception, he was in London at the time and stepped into the breach, never having seen "so great a person so neglected." He took the party to Westminster, entertained them at the Bear Garden, and generally "labored like a mule," he informed Cecil.[7] Once he had conducted the visitors to Basing, he turned back to London, although it was midnight on Saturday, to supply a grave lack in his wardrobe. "The French," he told Cobham, "wear all black and no kind of bravery at all." Accustomed to the gay, colorful attire of Elizabeth's Court, he now rode to the capital in the sleepy hours of the night "to provide me with a plain taffeta suit and a plain black saddle."[8] Fashion has its martyrs, and the courtier in

[6] For incident, see *Memoires de Sully*, III, 29.
[7] Edwards, *Ralegh (Letters)*, II, 233.
[8] *Ibid.*, 234-35.

174

Raleigh counted few sacrifices too great to be sartorially correct and impressive, whether in grey silks and pearls or in simple black velvet. The Queen was so pleased with his efforts on this occasion of Biron's visit that she knighted his brother Carew.

Raleigh did not confine his entertaining to distinguished foreigners. Two Englishmen in particular claimed his and his wife's attention, one a man, the other a boy. The man, Lord Cobham, was a wealthy landowner, a loquacious and sometimes brilliant conversationalist, and a lover of travel. He was also a vain person whose conversation often degenerated to mere gossip, who fretted over trifles, and who, in the end, turned out to be a flabby-willed moral coward. At the same time, many people were sincerely drawn to him, including the Queen and Bess Raleigh. Many of Raleigh's letters to Cobham contain messages from Bess, to wit: "My wife will despair ever to see you in these parts if your Lordship come not now";[9] or again, "Bess remembers herself to your Lordship, and says your breach of promise [his failure to visit] shall make you fare accordingly."[10] Intimate, almost affectionate—this was Cobham's relationship with the Raleighs. He was a frequent visitor at Sherborne, and occasionally he and Raleigh went off on a tour, including one to France to see a last battle before the long war should end.

It seems incredible that one so wise in many ways as Raleigh should not have perceived his friend's fatal flaws and thereby have been more cautious about confiding in him. But Raleigh was notoriously undiscerning in his judgment of character. The fallacy of continuing on so unreserved a footing is even more evident when one considers that, in 1602, Cobham took a new wife, Frances Howard, the Lord Admiral's daughter and Countess Dowager of Kildare. She was not likely to forget that by Raleigh's intervention her father's precedence over Essex had been lost. Furthermore, between the new Lady Cobham and Bess Raleigh lay a deep animosity that went back many years. Lady Cobham neglected no opportunity to speak unfavorably of Bess in the Queen's hearing, an activity that prompted Bess to comment to Cecil, "I wish she would be as ambitious to do good as she is apt to the contrary."[11] Lady Cobham was cer-

---

[9] *Ibid.*, 206.    [10] *Ibid.*, 228.    [11] HMC, *Salisbury MSS*, XII, 84.

tainly not one to view with equanimity her new husband's friendship with the Raleighs.

The other visitor, the boy, whom the Raleighs entertained—and for months at a time—was Cecil's young son, Will. Along with Lord and Lady Lumley, with whom Will also stayed, the Raleighs became almost like foster parents to the motherless boy. They took him hunting and bathing, Bess nursed him when he was ill, while Raleigh saw that he kept to his books, in preparation for entrance to St. John's College, Cambridge.[12] Will Cecil grew dependent on Raleigh and wrote a pathetic letter of protest to him in 1600 that he did not come to visit more often: "Sir Walter, we must all exclaim and cry out because you will not come down. Your being absent, we are like soldiers that when their Captain [is] absent they know not what to do. . . . I pray you leave all idle matters and come down to us."[13] That Cecil, so busy with the affairs of state, appreciated this attention to his son and heir may be assumed, but that he weighed it in Raleigh's favor when the great crisis in Raleigh's life arrived is doubtful. Cecil kept his ambitions and his friendships in separate compartments.

Among Raleigh's pleasures in these months was his association with wits and poets, playwrights and scholars. He is believed by many to have been the founder, or one of the founders, of the Mermaid Tavern, that celebrated literary club in Bread Street, Cheapside. Rare evenings were passed over the wine with Ben Jonson, Francis Beaumont, John Fletcher, John Selden, and John Donne. As Beaumont wrote in his *Lines to Ben Jonson*:

> What things have we seen
> Done at the Mermaid! heard words that have been
> So nimble and so full of subtle flame,
> As if that every one from whence they came
> Had meant to put his whole wit in a jest. . . .

But if Raleigh loved in such company to polish the gem of his wit until it glowed, he must have been aware of sore hearts in the group, men whose hopes of a new day had been built on

[12] *Ibid.*, X, 84, 370; Edwards, *Ralegh (Letters)*, II, 404.
[13] HMC, *Salisbury MSS*, X, 459.

Essex. Very likely one Mermaid visitor, Shakespeare, whose patron was Essex's friend, Southampton (luckily spared execution but wasting in prison), chose not to enter the Mermaid until Raleigh came there no more—and that would be when Raleigh's own days of freedom were ended.

That October of 1601, Raleigh went up to Parliament. He was not very well. In fact, he had been too ill of an unnamed affliction to go to Bath in September. Even so, he was still strong enough to warn Cecil of a Spanish expedition preparing either for the Lowlands or for Ireland—he suspected the latter —and, in mid-October, he informed Cecil that the Spaniards had actually landed in force near Kinsale, where they were soon engaged by the English.[14] It was in the shadow of this Spanish invasion of Ireland and of the Essex affair that Parliament assembled on October 27 and continued until December 19. Raleigh sat as senior knight for Cornwall and played an exceedingly active part, serving on a score of committees and speaking frequently in both committee and formal session.

This Parliament of 1601 was no meek and mild assemblage; on the contrary, it was aggressive, Puritan-minded, and at times difficult to control. It had grievances to air, particularly against monopolies, which were granted by the Crown. It resented clergymen holding more than one benefice. It wanted a strong bill passed against Catholics. It was willing to grant a subsidy but a limited one only, and when one member objected on the ground that the Crown could take all private property if it wished, the House, said a contemporary, "hemmed and laughed and talked."[15] Time and again, the House had to be called to order for shouting, hawking, and coughing its disapproval of speakers. Cecil, who said that he had never observed such levity and disorder, scolded the House for conduct "more fit for a grammar school than a court of Parliament."[16] The members were indeed in a touchy mood, and though they agreed to take off their jingling spurs when they entered the House, a motion that they also put aside their boots and rapiers got nowhere.

Raleigh's work in this Parliament was especially significant

[14] See letters of Sept. 19 and 26, and Oct. 13 to Cecil. Edwards, *Ralegh* (*Letters*), II, 235-36, 240-41, 243-44.
[15] D'Ewes, 633.　　[16] *Ibid.*, 651.

for his position in relation to monopolies, to the subsidy, to the exportation of ordnance, to farming, and to the bill against Catholics. The bill against monopolies, which wished the charters and patents of monopoly to be tested in the Common Law courts, found over twenty speakers involved in the great debate. The list of monopolies, which included Raleigh's patent for tin, was so long, when read, a member growled his surprise that bread was not on the list, while Raleigh—called "the most hubristic of persons"—actually blushed at mention of the monopoly of playing cards.[17] Raleigh vigorously defended his tin patent, basing his argument on the ground that since he had acquired the patent, the miner, whatever the price of tin per hundredweight, received an assured rate of four shillings a week, which was twice what the workmen had received before. Even so, said Raleigh, if the other patents were to be repealed, he would freely consent to the cancellation of his.[18] As this greatest and most hated monopolist of all finished, a silence of amazement fell over the House. Other monopolists present, however, were disinclined to be so generous, possibly because they felt that, unlike Raleigh, they could not afford to be. The debate thus touched off became very bitter indeed. Fortunately the Queen, in one of the great addresses of her life, promised to review the whole question of monopolies.

In the matter of the subsidy, Raleigh urged the House to rally to the Queen, who was even putting up her jewels and apparel for sale.[19] When a member suggested that even those men with an annual income in land of £3 value should be liable, Raleigh warmly seconded him over the protests of those who would exempt both them and the "four pound men." If all should pay alike, said Raleigh, none would feel aggrieved since only by taxing the "three pound men" could the necessary subsidy be raised.[20] But when Cecil, who supported him, remarked that, in view of the Spanish danger, men should not hesitate to

[17] *Ibid.*, 648, 650, 645; Price, *English Patents of Monopoly*, 152-53; A. L. Rowse, *The England of Elizabeth, the Structure of Society*, 309.

[18] D'Ewes, 646. For the objections to Raleigh's tin patent, see W. R. Scott, *The Constitution and Finance of English, Scottish and Irish Joint-Stock Companies to 1720*, I, 111-13; G. R. Lewis, *The Stannaries*, 146.

[19] Neale, *Elizabeth I and Her Parliaments, 1584-1601*, 412-13; D'Ewes, 629.

[20] D'Ewes, 630.

sell even their pots and pans, Raleigh rounded on him in all seriousness, saying, "I like it not that the Spaniards our enemies should know of our selling our pots and pans to pay subsidies; well may you call it policy . . . but I am sure it argues poverty in the State."[21] And when Francis Bacon, who also agreed with Raleigh that the poor should not be exempted but who observed unctuously, *"Dulcis tractus pari jugo"* (freely, "It is pleasant to be drawn under equal yoke"), Raleigh grew angry. "Call you this *par jugum*," he said scornfully, "when a poor man pays as much as a rich, and peradventure his estate is no better than he is set at, or but little better; while our estates that be thirty pound or forty pound in the Queen's books, are not the hundred part of our wealth? Therefore it is not *dulcis* nor *pari*."[22] In Raleigh's opinion, the need was great and should be met by all in an act of patriotic sacrifice that should be recognized as a sacrifice.

His efforts in this Parliament were illuminated by two emphases: his anxiety about Spain and his concern over the intervention of government in private lives. The first was evident in his support of the subsidy and in a vigorous speech against the exportation of iron ordnance. Because of the exportation of such ordnance from England, the Spaniards were now virtually able to match the English ship for ship, whereas, in the old days, he added with a flare of exaggerated if pardonable Elizabethan pride, "one ship of Her Majesty's was able to beat ten Spaniards."[23]

The second emphasis was to be seen in his stand on farming and on the Catholic legislation. On the farming issue, he was instrumental in getting rejected a bill to compel the sowing of hemp for cables and cordage. He disliked "this constraining of men to manure or use their ground at our wills; but rather let every man use his ground to that which it is most fit for, and therein use his own discretion." With the same idea that what was good for the private interest was also good for the public interest, he took a strong stand against the Tillage Act, which required a farmer to plough under a third of his land. The land,

---

[21] *Ibid.*, 632-33.
[22] *Ibid.*, 633; Neale, *Elizabeth I and Her Parliaments, 1584-1601*, 415.
[23] D'Ewes, 671; Neale, *Elizabeth I and Her Parliaments, 1584-1601*, 420.

if unploughed, he said, "would have been good pasture for beasts." Later he explained that many poor men were unable to find seed enough to sow, which they were required to do under penalty of the law. The best course was to "leave every man free, which is the desire of a true Englishman."[24]

Equally consistent with his individualism and his sense of practicality was his objection to the bill against Catholics, or "recusants." Intended to enforce church attendance on Sunday by further increasing the penalties for absence, the bill tore up the tempers of the House. Then Raleigh showed by use of example how the assizes would be so overrun by churchwardens and offenders up for judgment that authority would be disrupted; besides, mere attendance at church would confer a kind of toleration in itself, thus making it difficult to single out those Catholics who might have stayed at home if the existing laws were retained. It was a clever stroke, rationally conceived and coolly delivered, and, after his speech, the bill went down by one vote.[25]

The next year Raleigh busied himself in three interesting ventures, of which two were in the nature of disengagement operations. He equipped two ships for America, one under Captain Samuel Mace, who landed south of Cape Hatteras; the other under Bartholomew Gilbert, who was killed by Indians in the Chesapeake area. He even planned for Mace to make a voyage in 1603 to both Virginia and Guiana. Thus he was renewing his ties with America when his world crashed in ruins.

[24] D'Ewes, 674; Lipson, *Economic History of England*, II, 402; Stebbing, *Ralegh*, 158; Neale, *Elizabeth I and Her Parliaments, 1584-1601*, 343.

[25] Neale, *Elizabeth I and Her Parliaments, 1584-1601*, 404; D'Ewes, 683; Townshend, 321. The influencing of votes was becoming an important factor in this Parliament, and Raleigh, like others, was not above using means of persuasion other than speaking in session or committee or in the lobbies. This particular bill went down by a vote of 106 to 105. At once, several of the defeated side claimed that they could have had the Speaker vote. When it was declared that he had no vote, a member rose to speak of a "foul and great abuse" whereby "a gentleman that would willingly have gone forth—to vote Aye—according to his conscience, was pulled back." At this, Raleigh spoke out boldly, "Why, if it please you, it is a small matter to pull one by the sleeve, for so have I done many times." The "great stir" that ensued found several less frank members, including Cecil, rebuking him and the practice. But as the Parliamentary journalist reported, "there was another gentleman, a No, pulled out, as well as the other was kept in." *Ibid.*, 320-22; D'Ewes, 683-84; Neale, *The Elizabethan House of Commons*, 401; Neale, *Elizabeth I and Her Parliaments, 1584-1601*, 404-05.

The first of the withdrawals was from Ireland. He had started liquidating his holdings there some time before and by December 1602 he completed the task, retaining only Inchiquin Castle, which was rented to the ancient Dowager Countess of Desmond. The second of the withdrawals was a refusal to fight a duel with Sir Amyas Preston in the summer. The reason for Preston's challenge is obscure, but Preston was one of the captains whom he had expected to meet off Guiana in 1595 but who had gone privateering with George Somers instead. Possibly Raleigh, unable to forget what he considered a dereliction, now alluded to it in terms that offended Preston. Raleigh never believed, at least during his maturity, in duelling, a practice in which, in his opinion, the hangman usually bestowed the garland of victory. He felt no desire to sacrifice his family, his estate, or himself; hence, as Thomas Fuller remarked in the seventeenth century, Raleigh declined the challenge "without any abatement to his valour."[26]

But the challenge, which he seems for a while to have considered accepting, impelled him to set his estate in order, including a conveyance of his properties to his son, after the custom of the day,[27] with provision for his wife. While his papers lay spread out one day, a book weighting them down, his friend Cobham passed through the library, picked up the book, and riffled the pages. It was written by a man named Snagge, who questioned the title of the King of Scotland to the succession. Originally Raleigh had borrowed it from Burghley's library and never returned it. Cobham now took it home with him and proved as lax as Raleigh in bringing it back. Although Cobham's interest in the book and his failure to return it were matters of no great moment at the time, the day was to come when they were to assume an ominous significance.[28]

As the year 1602 moved along and the Queen seemed wrapped in melancholy for increasingly long spells, Robert Cecil began to spin more rapidly the web of intrigue that ultimately ensured the succession of James VI of Scotland to the

[26] Fuller, *Worthies*, 501-02. The two men were reported to have become reconciled later on.

[27] For this custom, see *Notes and Queries*, CLVIII (1930), 364-65.

[28] Jardine, *Criminal Trials*, I, 430-32; Howell, *State Trials*, II, 20-22.

English throne, and incidentally brought about the ruin of Sir Walter Raleigh. From 1598 through 1600, Essex, Southampton, and Mountjoy had been in secret negotiation with James and in February 1601 James sent the Earl of Mar and the lawyer, Edward Bruce, afterwards Lord Kinloss, to look after the Stuart interests and to communicate with Essex. By March, when Mar and Bruce reached London, Essex was already dead. The Scots, however, were well received, and Cecil seized the opportunity to hold a clandestine meeting with them. Mar and Bruce left in May for Edinburgh unfeignedly relieved, for Cecil had committed himself to the succession of their master. James was reluctant at first to traffic with Cecil because of the latter's presumed support for the Infanta. This presumption Cecil had exploded during Essex's trial. That James, once his doubts were removed, was pleased to find a real friend in Cecil goes without saying; he had difficulty restraining his delight and keeping the support secret. But on the last Cecil insisted. This was a desperately serious work in which he had engaged himself; the Queen's aversion to anyone's meddling with the succession question was well known. Cecil had at least one bad moment when the Queen wanted him to open a royal mail pouch in which he discovered a letter from James to himself. If he broke into a sweat at this point, he could well be excused. Still, Cecil was equal to the occasion. Playing upon the Queen's horror of ill scents, he took out the letter but told her it smelled so bad from the filthy pouch that he wished first to open the missive and air it for a while. Elizabeth then turned to other matters, and Cecil successfully skirted disaster.[29]

The correspondence between James and Cecil was often conducted through an intermediary, Lord Henry Howard. This nobleman came of a collateral and Catholic branch of the Lord Admiral's family. He had suffered much from the Tudors, his father, the Earl of Surrey, being executed by Henry VIII; his brother, the Duke of Norfolk, losing his head under Elizabeth for treason in behalf of Mary Queen of Scots; and his nephew, the Earl of Arundel, being thrown by Elizabeth into prison, where he died. With such tragedy in his background, it is hardly

[29] The incident is related in Wotton, *Reliquiae Wottoniae*, 169-70.

surprising that he was scarcely normal. Actually he would have been a fit subject for psychiatric attention had such treatment been available at the time. Like James and Cecil, Henry Howard enjoyed intrigue and secret negotiation. But he also indulged in hatred of pathological intensity, and Raleigh had become its chief object. Precisely why he fixed upon Raleigh for his abuse remains something of a mystery, other than that he was consumed by jealousy all his life and may also have associated him with the Queen, whom he abhorred and feared with good reason. As a seventeenth-century historian remarked, Howard possessed "so venomous and cankered a disposition, that indeed he hated all men of noble parts."[30] Still, though Henry Howard was dominated by his hatred, he was a man of considerable ability, even if it was devoted to flattering James with an obsequiousness that went beyond all due acknowledgment of the prerogative, to helping bring Raleigh down, and, a few years later, to involving himself in the Overbury murder case. Howard was a dangerous enemy, gravely unbalanced, who shrank from no device to remove enemies, whether they existed in fact or in his diseased imagination. It may be, as has been intimated, that his malignant hatred influenced Cecil, but it is more likely that Cecil regarded him as a useful tool in accomplishing the succession to the English throne of James of Scotland, whose chief minister Cecil was determined to be.

The conspiracy that developed in the spring of 1601 during the visit of Mar and Bruce to London was conducted in great secrecy that was jeopardized only when James talked out of turn or sent letters that got mixed up with the regular dispatches. It was agreed that every respect should be paid the Queen, with James even ceasing to try to procure any recognition of his right to the throne. It was also agreed that the correspondence must never reach the eyes or ears of the Queen. To make their negotiations less easy to penetrate, the conspirators hit upon a series of numbers for the principal persons who would likely figure in the correspondence. Thus James was 30, Elizabeth 24, Mar 20, Cecil 10, Bruce 8, Cobham 7, Howard 3,

[30] W. Sanderson, *The Lives and Reigns of Mary Queen of Scotland and James the Sixth, King of Scotland,* 22. D. H. Willson (*King James VI and I,* 178) aptly describes Howard as a man of "pompous learning and emetic flattery—a worthless, self-seeking and crafty courtier."

Raleigh 2, and Northumberland 0.[31] So well-kept a secret was the conspiracy that few knew or even suspected its existence until the very last days.

Meanwhile Cecil proceeded against Raleigh with great adroitness, undermining him in both England and Scotland. He took extraordinary care to remove himself from the popular onus for Essex's death, letting the responsibility fall upon Raleigh. He blocked Raleigh's elevation as Earl of Pembroke. He tried to break up the friendship Sir George Carew enjoyed with Raleigh, his cousin. Taking Carew, President of Munster, into his confidence, he sought to build up in Carew's mind the image of a Raleigh who had deserted himself, Cecil, in favor of Cobham and who would even sacrifice Cobham on the altar of his own ambition. No doubt Cecil honestly did feel hurt at the close tie that developed between Raleigh and Cobham; he considered that Raleigh, by seeing so much of Cobham, was guilty of gross ingratitude for his restoration to favor. Certainly as early as midsummer of 1600, Cecil resented Raleigh's and Cobham's having "stolen" over to the Continent to see action in a war that he wanted ended.[32] He refused to admit Raleigh to the Privy Council in mid-1601. "Believe me," Cecil told Carew, "he shall never have my consent to be a Councillor without he surrender to you the captainship of the guard."[33] But Raleigh refused to relinquish this post that he loved, the highest, in fact, that he ever attained. Cecil, who played his cards close to his chest so that none could see, begged Carew, in March, 1602, to be careful of what he wrote in his letters to Raleigh and Cobham, "for they show all men's letters to every man."[34] Feeling, or affecting to feel, more aggrieved than ever, he burst out in June, "George . . . believe me, two old friends use me unkindly, but I have covenanted with my heart not to know it, for in show

[31] *Corr. of King James with Cecil,* xxxv-vi.

[32] *Letters of Cecil to Carew,* 8; Winwood, *Memorials,* I, 215.

[33] *Letters of Cecil to Carew,* 86. Oddly enough, it was Cecil's father, according to the Spanish ambassador, who was instrumental in keeping Raleigh's father-in-law, Nicholas Throgmorton, from ever becoming a Privy Councillor. Conyers Read, however, in the first part of his distinguished biography of Cecil (*Mr. Secretary Cecil and Queen Elizabeth,* 303) suggests that Elizabeth "distrusted both his Protestant zeal and his belligerency."

[34] *Letters of Cecil to Carew,* 108.

we are great, and all my revenge shall be to heap coals on their heads."[35]

He was to succeed only too well in heaping such coals, and he helped fan the flames that heated them by his correspondence with James. The Scottish monarch seems for a time to have thought that he could win Raleigh's support, and accordingly sent the Duke of Lennox in late 1601 to confer with him and Cobham at Durham House. Anxiously Cecil demanded to know who had served as intermediary. James informed him through Howard that it had been Sir Arthur Savage, to whom no harm should fall. Cecil, however, need not have worried, for Raleigh came to him and told him that he had refused to negotiate with Lennox. He still felt too much respect for the Queen and too deep an obligation to her to consider looking elsewhere.

"You did well," said Cecil, who had already committed himself to the accession of James, months before, "and as I myself would have made answer, if the like offer had been made to me."

When Raleigh then bluntly suggested that Cecil let the Queen know the particulars, "what had been offered; what answered," Cecil dissuaded him. The Queen would think it a weakness on Raleigh's part that he had ever let Lennox speak with him in the first place, while to disclose the conversation to her now would make her think it an attempt at ingratiation.[36] Few more wily statesmen than Cecil have ever lived.

But Cecil continued to worry about a possible link between James and Raleigh. Northumberland, who may have known how Raleigh really felt, told James he must affirm Raleigh's willingness to admit James's right to the throne. Perhaps Cecil also realized this, for he hastened to warn James to be on his guard. In Cecil's opinion, he, and he alone, kept Raleigh and Cobham quiet:

"I do profess in the presence of Him that knoweth and searcheth all men's hearts, that if I did not some time cast a stone into the mouth of these gaping crabs, when they are in their prodigal humor of discourses, they would not stick to confess daily how contrary it is to their nature to be under your sovereignty; though they confess (Raleigh especially) that . . . natural

[35] *Ibid.*, 116.
[36] Lord Hailes, *Secret Correspondence of Sir Robert Cecil with James* VI, 44ff.

policy forceth them to keep on foot such a trade against the great day of mart. In all which light and sudden humors of his, though I do no way check him, because he shall not think I reject his freedom or his affection, but always (under the seal of confession) use contestation with him . . . yet, under pretext of extraordinary care of his well being, I have seemed to dissuade him from engaging himself too far, even for himself. . . ."[37]

This was guileful, to say the least, but Cecil left nothing to chance. He knew that Raleigh still thought of him as a real friend and was loyal and generous to him in the name of friendship. At some time, therefore, Raleigh might say kind things of him in James's presence. The very possibility horrified the Secretary—it might be a kiss of death. Hence the future sovereign of England must be warned not to take seriously any good words Raleigh might speak of the future sovereign's future minister, Robert Cecil: "Let me therefore presume thus far upon your Majesty's favour, that whatsoever he shall take upon him to say for me, upon any humor of kindness, whereof sometime he will be replete (upon the receipt of private benefit), you will no more believe it (if it come in other shape), be it never so much in my commendation. . . ."[38]

One would suppose that Cecil had said just about everything necessary in order to ruin Raleigh in James's eyes, but the Secretary again took no chances. He had two arrows left in his quiver. Although James had no end of trouble with the Scottish Kirk, he was a Calvinist of narrow persuasion who prided himself on his piety and his knowledge of theology. His later abhorrence of the English Puritans was grounded less upon his disagreement with their doctrine than upon the threat they constituted to the Church of England, one of the pillars of monarchy. But nothing on earth, not even a Puritan, was quite so dangerous to religion or monarchy as an atheist. In its impression on the pious mind, "atheist" was the most effective smear possible. Deliberately—Cecil was nothing if not deliberate in all his actions—the Secretary fitted one of the arrows to his bow and winged it northward toward Edinburgh: "Would God [he said of Raleigh], I were as free from offence towards God in seeking,

[37] *Corr. of King James with Cecil*, 18.
[38] *Ibid.*, 18.

for private affection, to support a person whom most religious men do hold anathema."[39]

Then, even before his first dark shaft hit its mark, he fired his second: "I will . . . leave the best and worst of him, and other things, to 3 [Lord Henry Howard]."[40] Cecil could now somewhat relax, for he knew that Howard's damnation of Raleigh would be endless, zealous, and effective.

And so it was. Howard did not necessarily desire or plan for Raleigh's death. He wished rather to humiliate him by taking away his privileges and power; perhaps, in his desperation, Raleigh might then become so rash as to jeopardize his own safety. For quite some time Howard had been at his dedicated task. Though he singled out Raleigh for most of his venom, he inveighed as well against Northumberland and Cobham. Heatedly he told James that "Hell cannot afford such a like triplicity that denies the Trinity." He railed at the efforts he believed Northumberland—"this fool"—was making to change James's opinion of Raleigh and Cobham, "that accursed duality." He spoke of Raleigh as a man who "in pride exceedeth all men alive" and as one who countenanced "a pride above the greatest Lucifer that hath lived in our age." He saw Raleigh as a stronger spirit than Cobham, more deft, more subtle, more evil, employing "the soft voice of Jacob in courtly hypocrisy." It was Raleigh who "inspireth Cobham with his own passions." Even Bess Raleigh came in for her share of calumny. She was "president" at Durham House, "and . . . how weakly Cobham is induced to commend the courses that are secretly inspired by . . . that fellowship." Bess was "as furious as Proserpina with failing of that restitution in Court which flattery had moved her to expect"; hence she bent "her whole wits and industry to the disturbance of all motions, by counsel and encouragement, that may disturb the possibility of others' hopes." Indeed he saw her as "a most dangerous woman."[41] He told Mar that the Lord Admiral wished with all his soul he might level his cannon at Durham House as he had, the previous year, at Essex House. And in an uncanny strain of prophecy, Henry Howard wrote in

[39] *Ibid.*, 19.   [40] *Ibid.*, 19.
[41] Howard's letter to James is printed in Edwards, *Ralegh* (*Letters*), II, 436-44. See also Hailes, *Secret Corr.*, 39, 68.

June 1602: "The glass of time being very far run, the day of the Queen's death may be the day of their doom, if they do not agree with their adversary upon the way, lest he deliver them to the judge, and the judge to prison. . . ."[42]

The combined efforts of Cecil and Howard—the one motivated primarily by statesmanship, the other by spleen—could not fail with James Stuart. "We are exceeding far inamorat of them," he said of Raleigh and Cobham. He could not doubt that in all this "faction and phantasy" these two were contriving nothing to his advantage.[43] Howard might not know the details of what Cecil was writing to him, nor Cecil the details of Howard's correspondence, but they were allies in his behalf, and neither had anything favorable to say of Raleigh and Cobham. Gravely James assured Cecil, "Your suspicion, and your disgracing, shall be mine."

Cecil's action in carefully nurturing James's distrust of Raleigh and in trying—unsuccessfully—to detach Sir George Carew from his cousin did not prevent him from showing a calculatedly friendly attitude toward Raleigh. Letting the world know he wanted peace with Spain, he yet invested in privateering expeditions with Raleigh to raid Spanish shipping. In 1602, with Sir John Gilbert as agent, Cecil paid for the victualing of half an expedition, while Raleigh and the Lord Admiral divided the other half between them. On January 12, 1603, Cecil commissioned Raleigh to prepare a privateer, for the victualing of which he stood half the expense. The other half, he wrote Raleigh, "may be borne between my Lord Cobham and you, or for such part as any of you will not receive, let it remain upon my head."[44]

Cecil, however, was anxious to cover his steps. None must know of his investing in such a type of enterprise, especially James, who was bent on peace with Spain and who knew that, unlike Essex, Cecil abhorred what he once described to the royal Scot as the Earl's "greediness of war."[45] It simply would not do for the Queen's successor to discover that the Secretary,

---

[42] Hailes, *Secret Corr.*, 127.

[43] *Ibid.*, 124.

[44] For Cecil's privateering investments, see HMC, *Salisbury MSS*, XI, 528; XII, 118-19.

[45] *Corr. of King James with Cecil*, 35.

on whom he counted to further his policies, was a partner with the detestable Raleigh in robbing the Spaniards. "I pray you, as much as may be," he entreated Raleigh, "conceal our adventure, at the least my name above any others. For though I thank God I have no other meaning than becometh an honest man in any of my actions, yet that which were another man's *pater noster* would be accounted in me a charm."[46] This was, to be charitable, an inordinate display of self-righteousness, but Raleigh, who knew not the extent of his friend's undermining of his reputation, kept his secret and preserved the Secretary's good name.

The end of the most glorious reign in English history was now at hand. On March 24, after an illness of about three weeks' duration, the Queen passed away "as the most resplendent sun setteth at last in a western cloud."[47] Less than a week before, Sir Robert Carey had ordered relays of horses placed along the road to Edinburgh. With Elizabeth at last dead and James having been named as her successor before she fell into a coma, Carey leaped to the saddle, while Cecil called the Privy Council together to announce James's accession, then went down into Whitehall and Cheapside and proclaimed him king to crowds torn between grief at their loss and curiosity about the new sovereign. Their curiosity was not long in being satisfied for on May 3 James arrived at Theobalds, one of Cecil's residences outside London, after a triumphant tour southward.

Raleigh's experience with the pot-bellied, drooling, pedantic James was unhappy from the beginning. In the West Country at the time of Elizabeth's death, he hastened to London to sign the letter of welcome to the new monarch, who probably snorted in derision to see his signature. It was rumored that, while at Whitehall, Raleigh declared it his opinion that the wisest course for the English would be for them "to keep the government in their own hands, and set up a commonwealth, and not be subject to a needy, beggarly nation." English opinion of the Scots of that day corresponded closely to Dr. Johnson's contemptuous view in the next century. Though it is unlikely that Raleigh made such a remark, since he was a convinced monarch-

[46] HMC, *Salisbury MSS*, XII, 599.
[47] Quoted by Neale, *Queen Elizabeth*, 392.

ist, the rumor, if it reached James's ears, did nothing to endear him to the new sovereign. Raleigh rushed to see him, along with hundreds of others; he paid little heed to a royal proclamation or an order from Cecil forbidding state officers to attend James while on progress from Edinburgh. Raleigh, however, contended that the King's warrant was necessary to continue legal process in Cornwall and to prevent the waste of royal woodland properties; this was undoubtedly only a pretext for hurrying to get in a good word in his own behalf with James.

There is a story that when Raleigh was introduced to him, James, who could never resist a pun, remarked, "On my soul, mon, I have heard *rawly* of thee."[48] So he had, and when he looked at the tall, formidable Captain of the Guard, he may have felt intimidated. As Aubrey said of Raleigh, "He had that awfulness and ascendancy in his aspect over other mortals, that the king. . . ."[49] Though the sentence is incomplete, one's imagination is not strained to fill it out. James was a timid little man, skinny-legged, peevish-mouthed, wearing over-stuffed breeches and a quilted, stiletto-proof doublet, a sad figure of a monarch but one not without learning, shrewdness, and occasional good judgment. He had only to compare himself and Raleigh in mere appearance to realize that Nature had been unfair.

Another story exists which may only be legend and yet it sounds like Raleigh of the bold tongue. James was profoundly impressed with the splendor of his reception by the nobility and gentry, but, notwithstanding this evidence of wealth and power, he is reported to have remarked that he could have taken the throne by force if need be.

"Would to God that had been put to the trial," said Raleigh.

"Why do you wish that?" James asked.

"Because then you would have known your friends from your foes," Raleigh replied.

The cryptic retort evidently weighed heavily on James's mind; it was of a piece with what Cecil and Howard had told him of Raleigh. Aubrey said that "that reason of Sir Walter was never forgotten nor forgiven."[50] Certainly James hurriedly

---

[48] Aubrey, *Brief Lives*, II, 186.
[49] *Ibid.*, 186.     [50] *Ibid.*, 187.

ordered the deliverance of the process authorization to speed the departure of his uninvited and unwelcome guest.

Unpleasant events now crowded in upon Raleigh. While at Theobalds, James recalled all of Elizabeth's monopolies. Though wine-licensing was eventually ruled not strictly a monopoly, the Council forbade the levy of all dues, thus eliminating a large source of Raleigh's income. A second blow soon fell after the King's arrival. In mid-May, Raleigh was abruptly told by the Lord President of the Council that he was immediately relieved of the post that had given him the greatest pleasure, Captain of the Guard: it was given to Sir Thomas Erskine, a Scot who had served in that capacity in Edinburgh. Raleigh bowed his head to the storm since resistance was out of the question. The only consolation was that he was compensated in part by remission of the annual payment of £300 which he had been forced to make from his salary as Governor of Jersey.[51]

These were severe blows, but Raleigh did not learn from them. He seemed strangely obtuse at times in his judgment of men and situations. Evidently thinking James eager for glory, he showed him a pamphlet when the King was visiting Bess Raleigh's uncle, Sir Nicholas Carew, in Surrey. Its title was *Discourse touching a War with Spain, and of the Protecting of the Netherlands.*[52] Actually the pamphlet was a well-reasoned, cogent argument, but James, as a pacifist and an exponent of absolute monarchy, liked neither war nor the Dutch rebels. Raleigh's martial spirit filled him with fear and aversion; James was not simply a man of peace from principle; he was also a craven.

The blows were now resumed. When James had crossed the border into England, the Bishop of Durham met him at Berwick and requested that Durham House in London be given back to him. James complied and on May 31 ordered Raleigh to evacuate the residence "within such time as you shall think good to limit."[53] This was giving him considerable latitude and,

[51] For the blows, see *Harleian MSS* (British Museum), 11402, fol. 88; PRO *S.P. Dom.* (James I), 1/93. See also *Diary of John Manningham, 1602-1603*, 160, for a rumor of a sharp altercation between Cobham and Cecil over Raleigh's removal as Captain of the Guard.

[52] *Works*, VIII, 299-316.

[53] *Egerton Papers*, 377.

fearing Raleigh intended to remain for many weeks, the Bishop applied pressure to get him out at once. The royal commissioners, moreover, came to the Bishop's assistance by setting June 25 as the time limit for Raleigh's moving. Raleigh protested not against being forced to move (after all, in giving Durham House to him the Queen had previously turned out the Bishop) but against the haste. After twenty years of residence, he had accumulated an enormous number of possessions. Besides, he had laid in provisions for forty people in the spring, and hay and oats for twenty horses. The commissioners were firm, and the Bishop was insistent. Accordingly Raleigh quickly moved everything to the already overcrowded Sherborne.[54]

One day between the 12th and 16th of July, he went to Windsor Castle to join the King and his courtiers for a hunting expedition. While he was waiting on the terrace, Cecil came up to him and told him it was the King's wish that he remain behind since the Council wanted to put some questions to him. At the meeting with the Council, he was asked if he knew about a plot to seize the King and about any communication between Cobham and Count Aremberg, the ambassador from the Spanish Netherlands. Though Raleigh denied knowledge of either, he was placed in house arrest when dismissed. By July 20 he was a prisoner in the Tower on the charge of high treason, presently to be indicted "That he did conspire, and go about to deprive the king of his government; to raise up sedition within the realm; to alter religion; to bring in the Roman Superstition and to procure foreign enemies to invade the kingdom."[55] The coals were now burning brightly on his head, and his enemies, particularly Howard, were exultant.

[54] *Ibid.*, 377-81; HMC, *Salisbury MSS*, xv, 111; Edwards, *Ralegh (Letters)*, II, 262-70.
[55] See Howell, *State Trials*, II, I, for indictment and p. 13 for terrace scene; Jardine, *Criminal Trials*, I, 416.

# CHAPTER 15

# Arraignment for Treason

RALEIGH's imprisonment occurred as a result of his being accused of involvement in one of the two treason plots that attended James's accession. Rare was the accession of a new sovereign in any country of that day that did not see at least one desperate group planning to assassinate him, to turn him off the throne, or to force him to adopt a favorable policy. The more one contemplates the explosive forces within Elizabethan England, the more marvelous appears the peaceful transference of power to the Stuart monarchy. For this, the astute planning of Robert Cecil was largely responsible, planning that included superb use of intelligence to inform him of every subversive movement.

The two plots that developed were the Bye (or "Surprising") Plot and the Main Plot.[1] Cecil early held all the strings in his hand which he suddenly tightened until they became a snare that entrapped the conspirators. The Bye Plot had a religious motive. William Watson and Francis Clarke were Catholic priests who conspired with fellow religionists, Sir Griffin Markham and Anthony Copley, to seize the King and compel him to adopt a policy kindly disposed to Catholicism. Among others drawn in were Lord Grey, a Puritan and the son of Raleigh's old commanding officer in Ireland, and George Brooke, brother of Lord Cobham. Grey hated James more than Catholicism, while Brooke was a ne'er-do-well who could not resist the attraction of such a scheme. Eventually, in order to win James's gratitude, Watson set out to expose to the King the plot he himself had contrived, while Cecil closed in before the plot proved menacing except to its own members.

During the Bye Plot's development, the Main Plot was also forming, and about this there is far less knowledge and certainty. It had its origin in the discontent of Cobham with the ascendancy

[1] S. R. Gardiner, *History of England from the Accession of James I to the Outbreak of the Civil War*, I, 108-45.

193

of Cecil and the accession of James. Cobham made no attempt to conceal his dislike for both men. He talked loudly and recklessly with little concern as to who heard him. This did little to excite serious suspicion until he began to meet with Count Aremberg, ambassador to England from the Archduke Albert of the Netherlands. That he and Aremberg conferred regarding peace between England and Spain was well known. It was believed that, in addition, the two were negotiating for the succession of another possible contender, Arabella Stuart, James's cousin, who, once she was placed on the throne, would be persuaded to make peace, remove the penalties against Catholics, and marry whom her advisers wished. Apparently, too, Cobham was prepared to put up an enormous sum of money, more than a half-million crowns to be obtained from Spanish sources, in order to gain the support of discontented persons.

Naturally, where Cobham was concerned, Raleigh was suspected because of their close companionship. In fact, Henry Howard took the credit for revealing to Cecil the meetings at Durham House between the two. Raleigh's own discontent was no secret; after all, it had been forced upon him by his being deprived of honors and emoluments after James came to the throne. The factor that decided the government to move against Raleigh was a statement by George Brooke. When the Bye conspirators were apprehended, they sought to confuse their inquisitors and win favor for themselves by accusing all and sundry. Brooke claimed, when questioned, that the Bye conspirators considered Raleigh a fit man to have with them. This was not true at all, for the plotters were as wary of Raleigh as of Cecil; but Brooke's allegation was all that Cecil needed. He therefore had the Council question Raleigh on the day that the latter was waiting to join the King's hunting party.

Although Raleigh denied knowledge of both plots, the Councillors could scarcely believe that he knew nothing of Cobham's conversations with Aremberg, and Raleigh must soon have suspected their disbelief. Furthermore he did know something; he later admitted that Cobham had offered him 10,000 crowns to help effect peace between England and Spain, an offer, he said, to which he paid little attention since he considered it simply another of Cobham's idle conceits.[2] This sounds plausible and may well have been true; certainly he knew—or thought he knew—his friend well enough to judge when to take him seriously and when not. Hence, after his examination, he wrote to Cecil hedging his denial with qualifications. He admitted having seen Cobham enter the residence of one La Renzi, a merchant follower of Aremberg, after Cobham had left Durham House; from this he suspected that Cobham had talked with Aremberg.[3] Cecil then went to Cobham and confronted him with Raleigh's note. Certain that Raleigh had said more than he actually had, the unhappy nobleman cried out in rage and terror, "O traitor! O villain! I will now tell you all the truth."[4] He then confessed that he had held conversations with Aremberg, and he blamed Raleigh as the instigator who kept urging him on. Though the unstable Cobham almost at once retracted what he had said, then retracted the retraction, and finally retracted the retraction to the retraction, his initial statement was enough to commit Raleigh to the Tower.

Raleigh was in desperate straits and he knew it. That he had some knowledge of Cobham's designs is evident; that he had no part in furthering them is certain, and Cobham's accusation was invalidated by his unreliability. In any event, it was absurd that Raleigh, who hated Spain all his life and was eager to see the war continue, should suddenly reverse his position, thus agreeing with that of James, whom Cobham was charged with wishing to replace with Arabella. Innocence, however, was not enough to clear him. James feared him, Howard hated him, and Cecil distrusted him. In their eyes, he was guilty by association with Cobham.

The criminal procedure of the age was far removed from that of today.[5] A state prisoner was usually examined in private with little opportunity to confront his accusers. If he did not succeed in convincing the Privy Council of his innocence, he was brought into court, where the depositions of himself and others were read and vehemently argued against by lawyers of the Crown,

---

[2] Jardine, *Criminal Trials*, I, 425.
[3] *Ibid.*, 412; Howell, *State Trials*, II, 11.
[4] Howell, *State Trials*, II, 14; Jardine, *Criminal Trials*, I, 411.
[5] W. S. Holdsworth, *A History of English Law*, IX, 222-45, for a brief description.

who often intimidated the jury by their knowledge, their eloquence, and their menacing manner. The fact that the accused was permitted no defense counsel but had to rely on his own mental and moral resources and was usually not allowed to reply until the total case had been set forth against him almost always made his case look worse than it really was. In fact, if not in theory, the accused was considered guilty until proved innocent, and proof of innocence was almost impossible under the circumstances. All these things Raleigh knew only too well.

His awareness that at last he was entrapped because of his relationship with the absurd Cobham and because of his own folly in initially denying any knowledge of Cobham's negotiations with Aremberg made him moody and disconsolate. Sir John Peyton, Lieutenant of the Tower, wrote Cecil on July 21 that Raleigh still maintained his innocence "but with a mind the most dejected that ever I saw."[6] Two days later, he again spoke of Raleigh's "so strange a dejected mind" and said that "his fortitude is [not] competent to support his grief."[7] Finally, on the 27th, while Cecil and others were in the Tower examining prisoners, Raleigh slashed himself with a knife below the right nipple, and when Cecil's group rushed in, they found him in agony and protesting innocence of any crime against the state.[8]

Was this an attempted suicide? Though it has often been so argued, one may comment that Raleigh was too familiar with the handling of weapons not to know how to deliver a fatal blow to himself. Nor, if he really made up his mind to kill himself, was he the kind to lose courage in such an exigency. Rather it is more likely that he was making a clear play for public support, even as, when previously imprisoned by Elizabeth's order, he had fought Carew with daggers to win her sympathy. If the public could realize that this was innocence driven desperate, its support might gain him his life and perhaps his release. Cecil, moreover, may have perceived his motive and the possibility of its last-chance effectiveness. In any event, the Secretary seems to have hushed up the incident so that little news of it escaped.[9]

[6] HMC, *Salisbury MSS*, xv, 204.    [7] *Ibid.*, 208.

[8] See Cecil's letter to Sir Thomas Parry, in R. F. Williams, *The Court and Times of James the First*, I, 13.

[9] But the ever-alert Venetian envoy learned of it. *Cal. S.P. Venetian, 1603-1607*, 82.

Nor did the Crown, during the treason trial to follow, capitalize on the incident in its case against the prisoner.[10]

Something of the same mystery pertaining to the mock suicide hangs about a letter of Raleigh's which is preserved at All Souls College, Oxford, as a manuscript copy made in 1679.[11] Raleigh wrote it to his wife allegedly after his "suicide," using language that differs noticeably at points from his accustomed style and referring to an unknown daughter. The genuineness of the letter has been seriously questioned. Though many admiring biographers have reluctantly conceded that he did write it and therefore must have had an illegitimate child, they have generally agreed that it was probably written before rather than after the "suicide," the time element being an acceptable conclusion. "That thou didst also love me living, witness it to others, to my poor daughter," Raleigh begged Bess. "Be charitable to her, and teach thy son to love her for his father's sake." The portion of the letter that seems to offend in style includes the following:

"I am now made an enemy and traitor by the word of an unworthy man [Lord Henry Howard]. . . . Woe, woe, woe, be unto him by whose false hand we are lost. He hath separated us asunder, he hath slain my honor, my fortune, he hath robbed thee of thy husband, thy child of his father, and me of you both. Oh God, thou dost know my wrongs, know then, thou my wife and child, know then, thou my Lord and King, that I ever thought them too honest to betray, and too good to conspire against."

The above has been called by one recent biographer, Milton Waldman, a "meaningless transport" and the whole letter "a palpable concoction which some one has inflicted on posterity in the name of a very great stylist in prose." Another biographer, Edward Thompson, agreed, calling the letter "one of the most nauseating compositions in the English language," and rejecting it altogether. On the other hand, a Raleigh scholar of the last century, Edward Edwards, considered it "affecting," and the

[10] The most plausible exposition of the "suicide" is by Miss Agnes Latham, "Sir Walter Raleigh's Farewell Letter to His Wife in 1603," in *Essays and Studies*, xxv (1940), 43-48.

[11] The letter is printed in—among other places—*ibid.*, xxv (1940), 39-42; G. Goodman, *The Court of King James the First*, ii, 93.

historian of the seventeenth century, S. R. Gardiner, labeled it "one of the most touching compositions in the English language."[12]

The problem reduces itself primarily to one of authenticity. If not authentic, then it raises no additional problems. If authentic, why did Raleigh write it, and who was the daughter? Miss Agnes Latham set forth a few years ago what seem reasonable grounds for considering the letter authentic. Like Raleigh's attempted suicide, it was a sham and designed to bring public opinion to his support. Unfortunately it probably never reached Bess, who would surely have given it wide publicity; many copies exist of other letters he wrote her but only one of this. The names of persons to whom Raleigh admitted he was under financial obligation include those of known friends and relatives; in at least one instance, the exact debt mentioned has been verified. Business matters alluded to are those he was known to be interested in at the time. All this points to the letter's authenticity. As for the differences in style, the letter, though shammed, was written under stress. If its tone is here and there hysterical, this was in part design—he was building up a case for himself before the public—and in part sincerity. But, as Miss Latham has indicated, the letter is replete with Raleighan echoes notwithstanding such rhetoric as "Woe, woe, woe. . . . Oh God. . . . Oh, what will my poor servants think. . . . Oh Death, destroy my memory." In both matter and manner, the letter becomes acceptable provided it is viewed in the same light as the attempted suicide—a desperation more feigned than real in order to elicit a sympathetic public response. As Miss Latham comments, the letter is "essentially a fake. But it was Raleigh who faked it."[13]

What, then, of the allusion to a daughter? Again, Miss Latham is persuasive. Elizabeth Bassett was the daughter and heir of William Bassett of Blore, Staffordshire, and, at the time of James's accession, the ward of Lord Cobham. In an age when children were not consulted on their marriage, she

---

[12] Waldman, *Raleigh*, 155-56; Thompson, *Ralegh*, 395; Edwards, *Ralegh* (*Life*), I, 373; Gardiner, *History of England*, I, 121.
[13] *Essays and Studies*, xxv (1940) 58.

was betrothed to young Walter Raleigh, aged ten. The Earl of Newcastle, whom she later married, is reported to have said that, had Walter lived, he, the Earl, could never have won her. What more natural move for Raleigh than to refer to her whom he already considered his future daughter-in-law as "my poor daughter?" His letters are filled with allusions to "my cousin" when such a person was in that relationship several times removed, while even his servants were "my family." Rarely, moreover, did he refer to Walter by name; usually it was "my son," "your son," "my poor boy," "my poor child." Thus he did not need to say more than "my poor daughter" for Bess to know whom he meant and the precise relationship.[14]

From the time of his mock suicide until his trial on November 17, Raleigh never wavered; at the same time, he did everything in his limited power to bolster Cobham's courage and to persuade him to retract what he had said. Though a prisoner, Raleigh managed to gain messengers who would carry missives back and forth between Cobham and himself. One was Edward Cottrell, a Tower employee who was his servant. Another was John Peyton, son of the Lieutenant of the Tower. After John's father was promoted to the governorship of Jersey in Raleigh's stead, Raleigh won over young George Harvey, son of the new Lieutenant, Sir George Harvey. In a burst of conscientiousness, Sir George suppressed a letter from Cobham on October 24 in which Cobham begged to speak to the Council in Raleigh's behalf. A few days later, Raleigh managed to get a note to Cobham entreating him to tell the truth. Cobham's reply, as Raleigh acknowledged at his trial, "was not to my contenting."[15] Hence Raleigh sent him another request by Cottrell, who tied the paper to a string wrapped around an apple, and tossed the apple through Cobham's window in the Wardrobe Tower at eight o'clock in the evening. In the letter, Raleigh advised Cobham, "Do not as my lord of Essex did, take heed of a preacher. For by his persuasion he confessed, and made himself guilty."[16] The next night, Cottrell picked up the reply which Cobham

[14] For discussion of the relationship, see *ibid.*, 51-53.
[15] Jardine, *Criminal Trials*, I, 447.
[16] Howell, *State Trials*, II, 27.

slid under the door and carried it to Raleigh. This reply Raleigh considered "a very good letter,"[17] and pocketed it, intending to make full use of it if possible.

Raleigh entertained few allusions about what awaited him. Early he had begged Cecil, the Lord Admiral, Lord Thomas Howard, and other examiners to weigh their measures carefully, "for to leave me to the cruelty of the law of England . . . before your understanding and consciences be thoroughly informed, were but carelessly to destroy the father and fatherless."[18] But the Lord Admiral, though a more honorable Howard than Henry, chose not to intervene to save the man who had cost him precedence over Essex; nor did Lord Thomas, either. Nor, one can add, did Cecil, to whom Raleigh protested just before his trial, "A heavy burden of God, to be in danger of perishing for a prince [the King of Spain] which I have so long hated! . . . Vouchsafe now so to use the power which God and the King hath given you as to defend me from undeserved cruelty."[19]

Unfortunately Raleigh did not know Cecil, whose hostility to him the historian Henry Hallam has characterized as "insidious and implacable."[20] Of Raleigh's case, the French ambassador, Beaumont, told Henry IV that Cecil "undertakes and conducts it with so much warmth, that it is said he acts more from interest and passion than for the good of the kingdom."[21] Beaumont was wrong. Cecil was acting for what he believed the good of the kingdom, though with hardly the considerate objectivity by which his apologist, Algernon Cecil, contended that he was motivated.[22] The good of the kingdom, in Cecil's opinion, demanded the downfall of Raleigh as it had previously of Essex. Though it is possible that Cecil was a moral coward, as the judicious Stebbing has declared, and dared not appear to condone an alleged enemy of the state by speaking in his behalf, it is likely that he wanted to take no chances of Raleigh's being proved innocent; the new dynasty, with which he had identified

---

[17] Jardine, *Criminal Trials*, I, 447.
[18] Edwards, *Ralegh (Letters)*, II, 271.
[19] HMC, *Salisbury MSS*, xv, 284.
[20] Quoted by Stebbing, *Ralegh*, 204.
[21] Quoted by Edwards, *Ralegh (Life)*, I, 377.
[22] A. Cecil, *A Life of Robert Cecil, First Earl of Salisbury*, 206-12.

his own fortunes, could not afford to be considered unjust. "Always he shall be left to the law, which is the right all men are born into," he wrote Sir Ralph Winwood.[23] He did not crave Raleigh's death—this was not necessary—but his utter ruination. Yet, knowing the way of law and the courts, Cecil could have been in little doubt of the judgment of the court in Raleigh's case.

[23] Winwood, *Memorials*, II, 8.

# CHAPTER 16

# The Trial

THE trial opened on November 17 before the Court of King's Bench at Winchester in Wolversey Castle. It would have been held in London but for the plague, which was counting 2,000 victims a week. Plague or no plague, thousands of people turned out to watch Raleigh being driven to trial in his own coach in the charge of Sir Robert Mansel and Sir William Waad, the latter an unprincipled man skilled in extracting confessions in the investigative stage and a tool Cecil did not hesitate to use.

Raleigh was lucky to reach his trial with his life. The crowd hurled tobacco pipes, stones, mud—anything they could lay their hands on—at him, and hissed and cursed him. Extra guards were hurried up, but, had the mob rushed him, observers believed no protection available could have kept him from being torn to pieces. In no way, however, did he betray fear of what might happen. He had only contempt for people at large and greater contempt for mobs. He smoked his pipe and ignored their insults.[1]

However he might disdain his judges at Winchester, he could not ignore them as he had the mob. They were a mixed assortment of professionals and laymen. The professionals were Lord Chief Justice Popham, Chief Justice Anderson, and Justices Gawdy and Warburton. Sir John Popham, a mountain of a man, had been kidnapped by gypsies when a child and seems to have acquired a taste for highway robbery that lingered on even after he became a barrister. He accumulated a huge fortune by fair means and foul, including an extensive estate belonging to a murderer whose bribe did not prevent his conviction. Rich and secure now, Popham possessed a reputation for dealing out ferocious sentences, particularly to members of his former profession, the gentlemen of the highway. Like Raleigh, he was interested in America and, four years hence, was to join with Sir Ferdinando Gorges, Raleigh's kinsman, in sending out

[1] An account of the conveyance to Winchester may be found in Waad's letter to Cecil, Nov. 13, 1603. PRO, *S.P. Dom.* (James I), 4/76.

colonists to Maine. Their mutual interest in colonization, however, had no mitigating effect upon his attitude toward the man accused of treason.

As for the laymen, James could scarcely have assembled a less friendly collection of Commissioners of Oyer and Terminer. These were Lord Thomas Howard, now Earl of Suffolk and Lord Chamberlain; Charles Blount, who was Lord Mountjoy and Earl of Devonshire; Lord Henry Howard, presently to become Earl of Northampton, an irreconcilable enemy; Sir John Stanhope, Vice Chamberlain and friend of Suffolk and Cecil; Lord Wotton of Morley, utterly loyal to Cecil; the impossible Sir William Waad, Raleigh's keeper; and Cecil himself. All these men owed their present eminence to James, and none was disposed to consider objectively the brilliant man accused of jeopardizing the monarch responsible for their elevation.

The Attorney General was Sir Edward Coke. This remarkable person, who became one of the great judges in English legal history and ultimately the judicial and Parliamentary opponent of the royal master he was now so abjectly serving, possessed an unrivaled knowledge of the law and a mastery of invective almost equally comprehensive. A sour, truculent, abusive man, he behaved during this trial in a manner that disgraced the law he reverenced.[2] The best that can be said for him is that he was sincere. His was no play-acting performance. The stakes were Raleigh's conviction, and he sought with every means at his command to convince the Middlesex jury that "guilty" was the only conceivable verdict.

The trial opened with the clerk reading the indictment, then with Sergeant Hele, a vain, ambitious man whom Raleigh had himself employed in lawsuits, elaborating upon it. There were four main charges: that Raleigh had sought to overthrow the King and his government, to raise up sedition within the realm, to bring in Roman Catholicism, and to procure foreign enemies to invade the kingdom. The overt acts alleged were that Raleigh and Cobham conferred at Durham House on June 9 on how to obtain the throne for Arabella Stuart and that they agreed

---

[2] "His conduct of Raleigh's trial is a permanent stain on his memory." Holdsworth, *History of English Law*, v, 427. For able accounts of Coke, see *ibid.*, v, 423 ff.; *Dictionary of National Biography*; C. D. Bowen, *The Lion and the Throne: The Life and Times of Sir Edward Coke.*

Cobham should negotiate with Aremberg to obtain 600,000 crowns to accomplish their treason. They further agreed, according to the allegations, on three other points: first, that since Cobham was unlikely to obtain the funds from the Archduke Albert, who was unable to pay his own army, he was to go to Spain; second, that Arabella should write letters to the King of Spain, the Archduke, and the Duke of Savoy, pledging herself to make peace with Spain, to tolerate Catholicism, and to be governed by the King of Spain in her marriage choice; third, that Cobham was to return by way of Jersey, where he and Raleigh were to consult on the distribution of the money. The Crown also contended that Cobham informed Brooke of the scheme and that the two agreed "there never would be a good world in England till the King and his cubs were taken away." Raleigh was further reported to have aided the conspiracy by giving a book questioning the King's title to the throne to Cobham, who passed it on to Brooke, his brother, thereby confirming the latter in his treason. Finally, the Crown insisted that Cobham had promised Raleigh 10,000 crowns on receipt of the total sum from Spain.

To the clerk's reading of the indictment Raleigh pleaded not guilty, and after Hele finished his elaboration, Coke moved up to the attack. In his circuitous way he recalled to the jurors the details of the plot of the priests, the Bye Plot. Raleigh put up with the discourse as long as he could and then interrupted Coke to remind the jury that he was not charged with any part in the Bye Plot. Coke accepted the interruption, but proceeded to lengthy definitions of evidence and treason. Expatiating on the goodness and wisdom of James, whose line traitors would have cut off, he suddenly asked, "But to whom, Sir Walter, did you bear malice? To the royal children?"

It is instructive to go to the records and let the interchange appear as it occurred:

*Raleigh*: "Mr. Attorney, I pray you to whom, or to what end speak you all this? I protest I do not understand what a word of this means, except to tell me news. What is the treason of Markham and the priests to me?"

*Coke*: "I will then come close to you; I will prove you to be the most notorious traitor that ever came to the bar; you are indeed upon the *main*, but you followed them of the *bye* in imitation; I will charge you with the words."

*Raleigh*: "Your words cannot condemn me; my innocency is my defence. I pray you go to your proofs. Prove against me any one thing of the many that you have broken, and I will confess all the indictment, and that I am the most horrible traitor that ever lived, and worthy to be crucified with a thousand torments."

*Coke*: "Nay I will prove all; thou art a monster; thou hast an English face, but a Spanish heart."

To Coke, who then went on to outline the Cobham plot, Raleigh merely replied that all this was news. But Coke, thinking Raleigh's dry words denoted anger, remarked in sly triumph, "Sir Walter, I cannot blame you, though you be moved."

"Nay, you fall out with yourself," said Raleigh, amused. "I have said nothing to you; I am in no case to be angry."

Coke's bullying manner increasing with his exasperation, he pointed out the unreliability of Cobham's behavior as a prisoner and the ghastliness of his plot, both of which were due to Raleigh's "devilish and Machiavellian policy."

In reply, Raleigh again hewed to the line. "I do not hear yet that you have spoken one word against me," he said bluntly; "here is no treason of mine done. If my Lord Cobham be a traitor, what is that to me?"

*Coke*: "All that he did was by thy instigation, thou viper, for I *thou* thee, thou traitor! I will prove thee the rankest traitor in all England."

*Raleigh*: "No, no, Mr. Attorney, I am no traitor. Whether I live or die, I shall stand as true a subject as any the King hath. You may call me traitor at your pleasure; yet it becomes not a man of quality and virtue to do so. But I take comfort in it, it is all that you can do, for I do not yet hear that you charge me with any treason."

Raleigh was so cool, self-possessed, and superior in his logic and manner that he was making Coke appear like the angry, confused man he was at the time and the Crown's case a jest, albeit a cruel one. Hastily the Lord Chief Justice intervened in Coke's behalf, bidding both participants be more patient. Afterwards, Coke produced the earliest of Cobham's confessions for the clerk to read. In his statement, Cobham declared that, but for Raleigh, he would never have entered upon "these courses."

Raleigh was now given permission to speak. He acknowledged to the jury that he had had his suspicions about Cobham's communications with Aremberg but knew no details, certainly none not already known to Cecil. Furthermore, Cobham had retracted the confession that Coke had just read. Turning to Coke, Raleigh scornfully rejected his making out Cobham to be a tractable tool: "Mr. Attorney, you said . . . he is a simple man, but whether to favour or disable my Lord Cobham you may speak as you will of him, yet he is not such a babe as you make of him, but hath disposition of his own, and passions of such violence that his best friends could never temper them." Would it not have been strange, he asked quietly, for him to plot with such a man, who had neither love nor following, when he himself had so much to lose?

Dropping the subject of Cobham for the moment, Raleigh called the attention of the court to the changed situation in the world. England was never stronger, with Scotland united with her, Ireland quieted, and the Netherlands allied. Moreover, "instead of a Lady, whom time had surprised, we had now an active King, a lawful successor to the Crown, who was able to attend to his own business." The allusion to the departed Queen undoubtedly reminded those present that this was the first November 17th in more than forty years that had not been celebrated with feasting and holiday ceremonies as Elizabeth's Accession Day; and, by a curious irony, the most versatile and the last of the great Elizabethans, permanently crippled in his country's service, was on trial for his life. Truly a new era had come. Yet did not remembered glories—of sea fights and glorious triumphs—pass momentarily before men's eyes as he ridiculed in superb prose the suggestion that, after fighting Spain all his life, he would take her gold to betray England:

"I was not such a madman as to make myself in this time a Robin Hood, a Wat Tyler, or a Jack Cade. I knew . . . the state of Spain well; his weakness, and poorness, and humbleness, at this time. I knew that he was discouraged and dishonored. I knew that six times we had repulsed his forces, thrice in Ireland, thrice at sea, and once at Cadiz on his own coast. Thrice had I served against him myself at sea, wherein for my country's sake I had expended of my own properties £4000. I knew that where before time he was wont to have forty great sails at the least in his ports, now he hath not past six or seven; and for sending to his Indies he was driven to hire strange vessels;—a thing contrary to the institutions of his proud ancestors. . . . I knew that of five-and-twenty millions he had from the Indies, he had scarce any left; nay, I knew his poorness at this time to be such that the Jesuits, his imps, were fain to beg at the church-doors; his pride so abated . . . he was glad to congratulate the King, my master, on his accession, and now cometh creeping unto him for peace . . . and whoso knows what great assurances the King of Spain stood upon with other States for smaller sums, will not think he would so freely disburse to my Lord Cobham 600,000 crowns. . . . And to show I was not Spanish, as you term me, I had written at this time a Treatise to the King's Majesty of the present state of Spain, and reasons against the peace."

Following this masterly statement, a discussion took place on the validity of Cobham's evidence. The situation was so confusing that the jury foreman, Sir Thomas Fowler, requested the time of Raleigh's first letter and of Cobham's accusation. At this simple request, Cecil got to his feet and delivered a long speech on his former esteem for Raleigh. The oration left Fowler unanswered and probably more confused than before. Nor was it likely that his confusion was removed by Coke's succeeding speech, which could well serve as a textbook example of how even a great lawyer, when his emotions are involved, may lose himself in muddled reasoning.

To bring the issue out of the wordy murk, Raleigh now made a request that seems but simple justice: "My Lords," he said in a voice probably more commanding than beseeching, " I claim to have my accuser brought here face to face to speak. . . . I have learned that by the law and statutes of this realm in case of treason, a man ought to be convicted by the testimony of two witnesses if they be living." While waiting during those anxious weeks for trial, Raleigh had studied the law of treason, of which the basis was the statute of 1351 passed during the reign of Edward III. According to this statute, treason entailed the "compassing or imagining the king's death, levying war against the king, and adhering to the king's enemies." Raleigh now cited various subsequent statutes and scriptural allusions to support his position. "If," he continued, "you proceed to condemn me by base inferences, without an oath, without a subscription, without witnesses, upon a paper accusation, you try me by the Spanish Inquisition."

Though, in reality, he was hardly fair to the Inquisition, there was little doubt that he had aptly described the manner by which the court intended to try him. Coke even considered his comparison of the court's procedure with the Inquisition to be treasonable in itself, while Popham, supported by Gawdy and Warburton, pointed out that the subsequent statutes alluded to had either been repealed or did not apply to his case,[3] that he was being tried under the Common Law by which only one witness was necessary, and that, legally, a man could be condemned upon presumption and circumstances without any witness to the main fact.

To these statements, Raleigh replied, "Yet by your favour, my Lord, the trial of fact at the common law is by jury and witnesses."

"No, the trial at the common law is by examination," said Popham emphatically; "if three conspire a treason, and they all confess it, here is never a witness, and yet they may all be condemned of treason."

Raleigh was getting in deep but could not forbear remarking, "I know not, my Lord, how you conceive the law; but if you affirm it, it must be a law to all posterity."

"Nay," Popham retorted professorially, in what has become a legal classic, "we do not conceive the law, we know the law."

Coke now bored in again, with the confessions of Copley, Watson, Brooke, and La Renzi being read as well as Raleigh's own admission on August 13 of Cobham's offer of 10,000 crowns to him for furthering peace between England and Spain. An examination made of Lawrence Keymis was also read, one in which Raleigh's loyal follower admitted a meeting between Raleigh and Cobham while Aremberg was in London, though

[3] 1 Edward VI, cap. 12, and 6 Edward VI, cap. 11 alluded to; repealed by 1 and 2 Philip and Mary, cap. 10. See also Holdsworth, *History of English Law*, IV, 499; IX, 217.

he confessed he did not know the subject discussed. Raleigh let the reading of the examination pass, merely stating that Cobham made his offer before Aremberg arrived in England and that he had not taken it seriously. Though he knew the reading of these examinations had little bearing on his case, his self-possession during the wrangling over the reading provoked the hot-tempered Coke into shouting, "Thou hast a Spanish heart, and thyself are a Spider of Hell."

The Attorney General was still angry when a portion of Cobham's examination was read in which Cobham mentioned having obtained from Raleigh a book that questioned the King's right to the throne. This was the volume by Robert Snagge which Cobham had removed from Raleigh's table when Raleigh was settling his estate before the proposed duel with Sir Amyas Preston. When Henry Howard pressed him as to how he acquired it originally, Raleigh said that he had got it from the library of Lord Burghley. At this, Cecil jumped to his feet in defense of his father and explained that Raleigh had wrongfully removed it without permission while searching for "cosmographical descriptions of the Indies." It seems that even as Raleigh had taken the book without permission, so had Cobham.

But the issue that Coke then insisted on making of the book impelled Sir Robert Wroth to mutter something to one of his fellow jurors. Instantly Coke wheeled on him and accused him of saying that all this evidence was immaterial to the case. If Wroth really said as much, he was only telling the truth, but he hastily denied it; Coke was a dangerous man to antagonize.

The Attorney General was in no way calmed when Raleigh declared, "Here is a book supposed to be treasonable; I never read it, commended it, or delivered it, nor urged it."

"Why, this is cunning," Coke commented, as if the remark were devious indeed.

Momentarily Raleigh's composure cracked, as he said curtly, "Everything that doth make for me is cunning, and everything that maketh against me is probable." Again he insisted that since the case against him rested on Cobham's accusations, he should be permitted to face his accuser.

"He is a party, and may not come," Coke replied; "the law is against it."

Raleigh grew impatient. "It is a toy to tell me of law; I defy such law, I stand on fact."

But Cecil supported Coke, and onward through irrelevancies both interesting and tedious (mostly tedious) went the trial. Raleigh denied a statement made by Keymis in his examination that he had written Cobham while in the Tower bidding him not to be dismayed since one witness could not condemn him. There seems little reason for Keymis, who was devoted to Raleigh, to have made such a statement were it not true. But, true or not, it had nothing to do with the original treason charge. Furthermore, a man may confess to many things to escape torture, and though Howard protested that no torture was used, Raleigh forced from Waad a sullen admission that he had told Keymis he deserved the rack. This, the embarrassed Commissioners acknowledged, was something they had not known. They were less surprised, however, when the prosecution staged an entrance by the Earl of Nottingham—the Lord Admiral—with Arabella Stuart leaning on his arm, the old veteran shouting from the rear of the room that Arabella had nothing to do with any of these matters. This was true, but irrelevant, too. The crowning absurdity was Coke's producing a pilot named Dyer, who gave the following testimony: "I came to a merchant's house in Lisbon, to see a boy that I had there; there came a gentleman into the house, and enquiring what countryman I was, I said, an Englishman, whereupon he asked me, if the king was crowned? And I answered, 'No, but that I hoped he should be shortly.' 'Nay,' saith he, 'he shall never be crowned; for Don Raleigh and Don Cobham will cut his throat ere that day come.' " This testimony, admissible as evidence of any kind, was grotesque, but when Raleigh, recognizing it as such, inquired of Coke, "What infer you upon this?" the Attorney General retorted almost gleefully, "That your treason hath wings."

The case against Raleigh was falling of its own flimsiness when the prosecution attached significance to such evidence. Raleigh entreated the jury to consider that "there is no cause so weak, no title so bad, but the King's learned Counsel, by wit and learning, can maintain it for good. . . ." Cobham was his accuser, and the Crown would not let Cobham appear. Raleigh asked the jury to put themselves in his place: "Now if you yourselves would like to be hazarded in your lives, disabled in your posterities,—your lands, goods, and all you have confiscated,—your wives, children, and servants left crying to the world; if you would be content all this should befall you upon a trial by suspicions and presumptions,—upon an accusation not subscribed by your accuser,—without the testimony of a single witness, then so judge me as you would yourselves be judged."

The Crown now summed up the case, and when all seemed ended, Raleigh asked, "Mr. Attorney, have you done?"

*Coke*: "Yes, if you have no more to say."

*Raleigh*: "If you have done, then I have somewhat more to say."

*Coke*: "Nay, I will have the last word for the King."

*Raleigh*: "Nay, I will have the last word for my life."

*Coke*: "Go to, I will lay thee upon thy back for the confidentest traitor that ever came to the bar."

But Cecil, knowing that Coke had in his possession the trump card, entreated the Attorney General to let Raleigh have his last word when the time came for it. This was a point of principle on which Coke hated to concede an inch. When his angry objections got nowhere, he sat down in a huff, and only after persistent coaxing by the Commissioners did he stand up again and, with endless circumlocutions and repetitions, recapitulate the evidence for the jury. Interrupted at one juncture by Raleigh, who told him he was mistaken, the exasperated Coke whirled on the prisoner: "Thou art the most vile and execrable traitor that ever lived."

*Raleigh*: "You speak indiscreetly, barbarously, and uncivilly."

*Coke*: "I want words sufficient to express thy viperous treasons."

*Raleigh*: "I think you want words indeed, for you have spoken one thing half a dozen times."

*Coke*: "Thou art an odious fellow; thy name is hateful to all the realm of England for thy pride."

*Raleigh*: "It will go near to prove a measuring cast between you and me, Mr. Attorney."

In the eyes of most of posterity, Raleigh was correct, but Coke, to do him justice, was less interested in appearing in a favorable comparison with Raleigh than in procuring the latter's conviction. Vowing to expose Raleigh "for the greatest traitor that ever was," he waved a paper. It was his ace, and he exclaimed, "And to discover you, Raleigh, and all your Machiavellian tricks, hear what the Lord Cobham hath written, under his own hand, which I will read with a loud voice, though I be not able to speak this s'nnight after." Coke then shouted the contents of a letter from Cobham to the Lords in which Cobham disavowed what he had written in response to the request from Raleigh that Cottrell had wrapped around an apple and tossed into his window. Asking the Commissioners' pardon for "my double dealing," Cobham revealed that, on Aremberg's arrival, Raleigh had asked him, Cobham, to procure him an annual pension of £1500 from Spain for disclosing intelligence. Cobham said that, but for this request from Raleigh, he would never have dealt with Aremberg.

"Now, Raleigh," cried Coke triumphantly, "if thou hast the grace, humble thyself to the King and confess thy treasons."

That Raleigh was startled was clear to all; so were others who were present. But in a few moments, he rallied and said, "I pray you hear me a word. You have heard a strange tale of a strange man; you shall see how many souls this Cobham hath. . . ."

To Popham's question concerning the pension of £1500, Raleigh replied, "I say that Cobham is a poor, silly, base, dishonorable soul." It was no answer, but he was playing desperately for time to prepare his defense. When both Coke and Popham accused him of baseness and deceit, he brought from his pocket the confession that Cobham had repudiated. Though Coke protested, Raleigh passed it to Cecil, who read it aloud: "Now that the arraignment draws near, not knowing which should be first, I or you, to clear my conscience, satisfy the world with truth, and free myself from the cry of blood, I protest upon my soul and before God and his angels, I never had conference with you in any treason, nor was ever moved by you to the things I heretofore accused you of; and for any thing I know, you are as innocent and as clear from any treason against the King as is any subject living. Therefore I wash my hands, and pronounce with Daniel, *Purus sum a sanguine hujus* [I am pure of this man's blood]; and God so deal with me and have mercy on my soul, as this is true!"

"Now I wonder how many souls this man hath!" Raleigh exclaimed. "He damns one in this letter and another in that."

Well might Raleigh wonder, for the letter in his pocket, which he had hoped would be conclusive evidence of his innocence, had been completely cancelled by the later confession that Coke had read. He had lost, and he knew it. Though he denied that he had ever intended to accept the pension, he acknowledged that it had been offered him. He acknowledged, too that his fault was in concealing the offer. At the same time, he denied conspiring at treason. The acknowledgments, however, made Cobham's accusations seem more credible, and, after only fifteen minutes of deliberation, the jury returned with a verdict of guilty.

It had been a strange trial. That Raleigh knew more than he divulged is evident. On the other hand, it is out of the question that he had any part in the scheme to put Arabella Stuart on the throne, to support a Spanish invasion of England, or to install Roman Catholicism. It is also unlikely that he was prepared to back a peace with Spain or to accept the 10,000 crowns allegedly offered him by Cobham to help effect that peace. But knowledge of Cobham's conversations with Aremberg and the question of the pension of £1500 are different matters. At his examination at Windsor he denied knowing anything about the conversations, but in the letter which had elicited Cobham's original accusation he said that Cobham's visit to La Renzi after leaving Durham House had led him to suspect Cobham of conversing with Aremberg. It is reasonable to suppose that Raleigh was not as ignorant of the existence of the conversations as he had pretended.

His admission that Cobham had offered him a pension of £1500 seems less damning when one considers the light in which such pensions were viewed. Many Englishmen had accepted Spanish pensions, including Sir John Hawkins and Sir James Crofts, as well as Lord Henry Howard himself, and the Earls of Northampton, Dorset, and Devonshire. Within a few months of the trial, Robert Cecil was to accept a pension of £1000 which was raised to £1 500 the year following; in fact, from 1604 to his death in 1612, he accepted Spanish gold.[4] A holder of a pension disclosed such information as he wished. Sometimes one could serve as a pensioner for patriotic reasons, discovering information valuable to England or giving Spain false leads. Cecil's biographer has said that Cecil was guilty of "indelicacy" rather than "corruption."[5] The same might be said of Raleigh, who, deprived as he was of his offices, certainly needed money. On the other hand, he said that he declined the offer of the pension, and if the jury entertained doubts that he was telling the truth, they had no proof that he was not.

One is on surer ground in appraising the trial itself—it was grossly unjust in spirit, though not from the point of view of the law as it operated at that time. Since then, fortunately, the conception of justice in law and in court procedure has changed. Raleigh based his hope of acquittal on the statutes of Edward VI, which, like a portion of the provision in the Constitution of the United States, required that two witnesses must be produced in all treason trials.[6] Still, judicial opinion of Raleigh's time considered that this provision had been repealed by a statute of Philip and Mary.[7] The Justices relied heavily on hearsay evidence. At a later time, Lord Blackburn was to declare that "In England, hearsay evidence, that is to say, the evidence of a man who is not produced in court and who therefore cannot be cross-examined, as a general rule is not admissible at all."[8] The rule excluding hearsay evidence has been considered "the most famous and characteristic of all the rules of the English law of evidence," but it did not appear until near the end of the seventeenth century.[9] Meanwhile the Justices accepted the reading of Cobham's deposition as sufficient in itself without his appearing in court. To condemn them for following precedent is wisdom after the event. The fault lay rather in the system. Neither Justices nor Commissioners, however, can entirely escape censure, for if all appear to have taken it for

---

[4] Gardiner, *History of England*, I, 214-16.
[5] Cecil, *Cecil*, 363.
[6] See note 3.
[7] See note 3.
[8] Quoted by Holdsworth, *History of English Law*, IX, 214.
[9] *Ibid.*, 214, 217.

granted that Raleigh must be guilty to be standing trial in the first place, among them were men who wanted him condemned—"he never had a chance of escape," is the opinion of one legal scholar.[10]

As for the jury, to suggest that it was rigged is probably unfair. It is more likely that the jurors were intimidated into declaring Raleigh guilty on what amounted to bare suspicion. They could hardly forget that in the treason trial of Nicholas Throgmorton, Raleigh's father-in-law, a jury had been severely punished for bringing in a verdict of "not guilty."[11] They knew full well the verdict the Crown wanted in Raleigh's case; hence, after only fifteen minutes, they delivered themselves of an opinion that would condemn one of the greatest men of his time to a barbarous death.

More reprehensible was Coke, whose behavior was extraordinary even for him. He bullied, threatened, and cursed beyond his customary performance in trials. Years later, when he was removed from his future great office of Lord Chief Justice, Francis Bacon reminded him of his deportment as Attorney General. "In your pleadings," said Bacon, "you were wont to insult over misery, and to inveigh bitterly at the persons; which bred you many enemies, whose poison yet swelleth, and the effects now appear."[12] The story scarcely rings true that Coke was walking in the garden when the verdict of the Raleigh jury was brought to him, whereupon he remarked in astonishment, "Surely thou art mistaken; I myself accused him but of misprision of treason."[13] A contemporary, however, reported that "some of the jury were afterwards so touched in conscience as to demand of Raleigh pardon on their knees."[14] Perhaps—but if not conscience-stricken, they should have been, for presently, on the strength of their verdict, Lord Chief Justice Popham delivered the sentence.

Before pronouncing judgment, Popham admonished Raleigh, who had received the verdict with calmness and dignity. Popham

[10] Sir H. S. Stephen, "The Trial of Sir Walter Raleigh," in *Transactions of the Royal Historical Society* (1919), 179.

[11] Holdsworth, *History of English Law*, V, 195; VI, 630-31; IX, 225.

[12] Jardine, *Criminal Trials*, I, 444 n.

[13] *Ibid.*, 449 n.

[14] F. Osborne, *Some Traditional Memorials on the Reign of King James*, in *Advice to a Son*, 428.

expressed regret at seeing a man of his reputed wisdom entangled with so many treasons. It would have been "a bad and a base practice" for anyone to have sold himself as a spy to the enemy for £1500, but, for a man like Raleigh to do so, it was "the vilest action in the world." He deplored the "heathenish, blasphemous, atheistical, and profane opinions" which Raleigh was reported to hold. Raleigh should renounce these opinions, and let not Hariot or any "doctor" persuade him that Heaven was not eternal. Raleigh was "irreligious and wicked" for not confessing his offenses to a minister and wrong to try to induce Cobham not to confess to a preacher as had the Earl of Essex. As one studies Popham's insulting reproofs, one wonders whether Raleigh was being sentenced for treason or for alleged atheism; but, in an age when, as James wrote, Kings were "God's vice-regents on earth," perhaps the two offenses were not so far apart. Finally Popham delivered the ghastly sentence reserved for those unfortunates convicted of high treason:

"That you shall be had from hence to the place whence you came, there to remain until the day of execution; and from thence you shall be drawn upon a hurdle through the open streets to the place of execution, there to be hanged and cut down alive, and your body shall be opened, your heart and bowels plucked out, and your privy members cut off, and thrown into the fire before your eyes; then your head to be stricken off from your body, and your body shall be divided into four quarters, to be disposed of at the king's pleasure: And God have mercy upon your soul."[15]

[15] For the trial I have depended largely on Howell, *State Trials*, II, 1-31, and Jardine, *Criminal Trials*, I, 389-452. Of the two, Jardine's account is by far the better, being based on a report in the *Harleian MSS*, Vol. 39, the report in the *State Trials*, and a report written by Sir Thomas Overbury, who was present at the trial. In general, I have followed Jardine, but with excursions into the *State Trials*, particularly for dialogue. An excellent account of the trial, and one of the best among secondary sources, is by Bowen, *The Lion and the Throne*, 190-217.

# CHAPTER 17

# The Wait for Execution

THE trial produced an astonishing effect. Its natural, if not legal, injustice was so patent that revulsion swept England. There were hisses and groans even in the courtroom for Coke's attacks and Popham's castigation. One who was present noted that Raleigh "behaved himself so worthily, so wisely, so temperately, that in half a day the mind of all the company was changed from the extremest hate to the greatest pity."[1] Sir Thomas Overbury spoke of him as "humble but not prostrate, . . . affable but not fawning, . . . persuading with reason, not distemperedly importuning with conjuration." Toward the relentless Coke, according to Overbury, Raleigh was "patient but not insensibly neglecting nor yielding to imputations laid against him by words; and it was wondered that a man of his heroic spirit could be so valiant in suffering that he was never once overtaken in passion."[2] Sir Dudley Carleton, courtier and indefatigable letter writer who observed the proceedings, wrote his friend John Chamberlain that, of the two courtiers who hastened to be the first to report on Raleigh's trial to the King, one declared that "never any man spake so well in times past, nor would do in the world to come," while the other, a Scot, said that "whereas, when he saw him first, he was so led with the common hatred, that he would have gone a hundred miles to have seen him hanged, he would, ere he parted, have gone a thousand to have saved his life." Carleton, himself, affirmed, "And so well he shifted all advantages that were taken against him, that were not . . . an ill name, half hanged, in the opinion of all men he had been acquitted." Carleton was convinced that "never was a man so hated and so popular, in so short a time."[3]

Carleton perceived something about Raleigh's behavior that may be a clue to what was going on in his mind. Said the courtier, "He answered with that temper, wit, learning, courage,

---

[1] Quoted by Jardine, *Criminal Trials*, I, 461.
[2] *Ibid.*, 452-53.
[3] Williams, *Court and Times of James the First*, I, 20-21.

and judgment, that, save that it went with the hazard of his life, it was the happiest day that ever he spent."[4] Like many men of action, Raleigh shone brightest, and was most cheerful in public, during times of stress, when danger threatened from every quarter, when adversity stood insistent and seemingly inevitable. It had been so when he thrust the *Warspite* into the van at Cadiz, when he led the ground attack at Fayal, when he faced the angry Essex and his henchmen in the Earl's cabin. But this was a more serious occasion than any of those—more was at stake than his life or an expedition: the justice of England was also on trial. It is scarcely too much to assert that, as the victim of a corrupt and timid officialdom, vengeful courtiers, and short-sighted, letter-of-the-law attorneys and judges, he represented in his case the need of a change in official attitude and in the letter and spirit of the law towards the accused, as well as a revised conception of the individual's dignity and value. It is likely that, with his histrionic instinct, he appreciated the significance of his role, that he realized he was fighting for something more important than himself. Certainly he comported himself magnificently. Before the seventeenth century was gone, lawyers and judges were rallying to his defense. They condemned Popham and Coke in the light of a reinterpretation of the treason law that had appeared during the century, in part as a consequence of the gross injustice in cases such as Raleigh's. Thus Raleigh did not contend with Coke and Popham in vain. While possibly apocryphal, it has even been said that, before dying, one of the Bench in Raleigh's case, Justice Gawdy, admitted that "the justice of England has never been so degraded and injured as by the condemnation of Sir Walter Raleigh."[5]

But however admirable his conduct at the trial, however dauntless and dignified, he lost his composure when back in prison awaiting execution. The execution of Cobham, who, according to Carleton, behaved at his trial with "fear and trembling," displaying throughout a "poor and abject" spirit,[6] was set for December 9. Markham and Grey were to die on the

[4] *Ibid.*, 20.
[5] Quoted by Jardine, *Criminal Trials*, I, 520.
[6] Williams, *Court and Times of James the First*, I, 21.

same day. George Brooke perished on the 6th, his sentence commuted to beheading. A week before, Watson and Clarke, perhaps because they were priests, were hanged, drawn, and quartered according to the original sentence, being cut down alive and, as Carleton related, "very bloodily handled."[7] Contemplation of all that had happened and that was yet to happen caused Raleigh to lose his nerve. Between November 17 and December 13, the day set for his execution, he and his loyal Bess pled for his life with a complete lack of dignity and pride.[8] Bess's suppliance to Cecil was the pathetic, grief-stricken appeal of a brokenhearted woman; Raleigh's petitions for mercy to Cecil, the Commissioners, and the King were those of a fearful man. To be sure, Raleigh's appeal to the King was made in a day when kingship had a higher value than it now possesses— and Raleigh believed in kingship—but the following paragraphs reveal a groveling that is hard to reconcile with the man of courage:

"I know that, among many other presumptions gathered against me, Your Majesty hath been persuaded that I was one of them who were greatly discontented, and therefore the more likely to be disloyal. But the great God so relieve me and mine in both worlds, as I was the contrary; and as I took no greater comfort than to behold Your Majesty, and always learning some good and bettering my knowledge by Your Majesty's discourse.

"I do therefore, on the knees of my heart, beseech Your Majesty to take counsel from your own sweet and merciful disposition, and to remember that I have loved Your Majesty now twenty years, for which Your Majesty hath yet given me no reward. And it is fitter that I should be indebted to my sovereign Lord, than the King to his poor vassal.

"Save me, therefore, most merciful Prince, that I may owe Your Majesty my life itself. . . ."[9]

Whether one considers Raleigh's abject letters with anger or compassion that a man of his stature should so stoop to live, there can be little doubt that Raleigh himself was soon repelled

---

[7] *Ibid.*, 27.

[8] For Raleigh's letters to Cecil and the Lords, see Edwards, *Ralegh* (*Letters*), II, 278-80, 282-83, 406-07; HMC, *Salisbury MSS*, xv, 284-86 (Bess's letter is on p. 285).

[9] *Ralegh* (*Letters*), II, 280-81.

by what he had done. With death become a certainty—and evidently he seems to have thought he might die on the 9th with Cobham—he gradually accepted his fate; and, with his acceptance, his high, bold spirit returned. To Bess he wrote: "Get those letters, if it be possible, which I writ to the Lords, wherein I sued for my life. But God knoweth that it was for you and yours that I desired it [He had to save his pride], but it it true that I disdain myself for begging it. And know it, dear wife, that your son is the child of a true man, and who, in his own respect, despiseth Death and all his misshapen and ugly forms."[10]

This farewell letter was as genuine as the earlier farewell missive was spurious. Raleigh sent Bess his love that she might keep it rather than sorrows—griefs, he said, should go to the grave with him and be buried in the dust. He entreated her to to bear his death with a brave heart; her mourning could avail him naught who had become dust. He instructed her to pay whatever he owed all poor men. He bade her bring up their son in the fear of God, and asked her to remember the boy "for his father's sake that comforted you and loved you in his happiest times." Though he warned her against suitors for her money, he said he would not attempt to dissuade her from marrying again, "for that will be best for you, both in respect of God and the world." Now time rushed at him on swift, relentless feet: "I cannot write much. God knows how hardly I stole this time, when all sleep; and it is time to separate my thoughts from the world. Beg my dead body, which living was denied you; and either lay it at Sherborne, if the land continue, or in Exeter Church by my father and mother. I can write no more. Time and Death call me away. . . . My true wife, farewell. Bless my poor boy; pray for me. May the true God hold you both in His arms."[11]

His letter written, he did indeed try to separate his thoughts from the world. It was the night of December 8-9, the morning to bring Cobham's execution and perhaps his own, and the atmosphere heavy with impending death. Bishop Bilson of Winchester had attended Raleigh in recent days, and, without

[10] *Ibid.*, 286-87.
[11] For letter, see *ibid.*, 284-87.

eliciting anything significant by way of confession, political or spiritual, he satisfied himself that Raleigh was at least nominally Christian.[12] In these hours, religious feeling, rarely evident in his letters or poems beyond conventional expression, came upon him. It visited him as no flood of emotional regret or ecstatic renunciation of a world whose ill-treatment had finally surpassed his power to conquer it or his capacity to ignore it. Rather, it manifested itself in the form of a poem in which Raleigh wrought out a kind of anatomy of hope. The bitterness of his recent experiences continuing to color his thinking, he yet attained a certain humility, albeit one not entirely devoid of pride. The result is *The Passionate Man's Pilgrimage*, a poem beautiful in composition and noble in spirit:

> Give me my scallop shell of quiet,
> My staff of faith to walk upon,
> My scrip of joy, immortal diet,
> My bottle of salvation,
> My gown of glory, hope's true gauge,
> And thus I'll take my pilgrimage.
>
> Blood must be my body's balmer,
> No other balm will there be given
> Whilst my soul like a white palmer
> Travels to the land of Heaven,
> Over the silver mountains
> Where spring the nectar fountains;
> And there I'll kiss
> The bowl of bliss,
> And drink my eternal fill
> On every milken hill.
> My soul will be a-dry before,
> But, after, it will ne'er thirst more.
>
> And by the happy blissful way
> More peaceful pilgrims I shall see,
> That have shook off their gowns of clay,
> And go appareled fresh like me.
> I'll bring them first

[12] HMC, *Salisbury MSS*, xv, 306-09; Williams, *Court and Times of James the First*, i, 28.

To slake their thirst,
And then to taste those nectar suckets
At the clear wells
Where sweetness dwells,
Drawn up by saints in crystal buckets.

And when our bottles and all we
Are filled with immortality,
Then the holy paths we'll travel
Strewed with rubies thick as gravel,
Ceilings of diamonds, sapphire floors,
High walls of coral and pearl bowers.

From thence to Heaven's bribeless hall
Where no corrupted voices brawl,
No conscience molten into gold,
Nor forged accusers bought and sold,
No cause deferred, nor vain spent journey
For there Christ is the King's Attorney,
Who pleads for all without degrees,
And He hath angels, but not fees.

When the grand twelve million jury
Of our sins and sinful fury
'Gainst our souls black verdicts give,
Christ pleads His death, and then we live;
Be Thou my speaker, taintless pleader,
Unblotted lawyer, true proceeder;
Thou movest salvation even for alms,
Not with a bribed lawyer's palms.

And this is my eternal plea,
To Him that made Heaven, earth, and sea,
Seeing my flesh must die so soon,
And want a head to dine next noon,
Just at the stroke when my veins start and spread
Set on my soul an everlasting head.
Then am I ready like a palmer fit
To tread those blessed paths which before I writ.

Now, if ever, he was ready. Possibly he retained some vestige of hope that James, at the very last, would spare him, but he could not be sure. James had disdained his pleas; Cecil, those of Bess. Moved by his situation, the sister of Sir Philip Sidney, the Elizabethan chevalier and Raleigh's friend, sent her son, Lord Pembroke, to intercede with James. It was to no avail. The Scot would let the law take its course without interruption. Or so it appeared.

But appearances were deceiving. The King had no thirst for blood and decided to show clemency. At the same time, he possessed a sense of refined cruelty that now manifested itself. Perhaps the sudden popularity of Raleigh disturbed him. Perhaps he decided that enough persons had already been purged to serve as a warning to future plotters. Whatever his reasons, he made up his mind to spare the lives of the other condemned men but to let them go to the scaffold expecting to be executed. Accordingly, on the day following Brooke's execution, he drafted a warrant to Sir Benjamin Tichborne, Sheriff of Hampshire, to stay the executions. Keeping the general mercy warrant secret except for a Scottish lad, John Gibb, a groom of the bed chamber, he signed the individual death warrants for Grey, Markham, and Cobham. At the last moment, Gibb was to arrive from the King with the stay of execution. This was melodrama of a variety that would be deleted from current fiction as too blatant, but throughout his reign James liked melodrama and used it often.

The execution day for the condemned three arrived, Friday, December 9, dark with a misty rain falling—"A fouler day could hardly have been picked out, or fitter for such a tragedy."[13] Raleigh was instructed to stand by his window overlooking the green of Wolversey Castle at ten o'clock in the morning to observe the execution; his own hour was to come. Presently Sir Griffin Markham was conducted to the scaffold, his face sunken in melancholy. When one of his friends in the dense crowd about the scaffold offered him a napkin to cover his eyes, he threw it away with the comment that he could look upon death without blushing. Suddenly as Markham prepared to lay his

---

[13] Williams, *Court and Times of James the First*, I, 29.

head on the block, the Sheriff's attention was caught by a voice calling his name—and just in time to prevent the headsman from raising his ax. John Gibb, whose youth had caused him to be thrust out among the boys, failed to get Tichborne's ear and only saved Markham by frantically shouting to Sir James Hayes that he had a message from the King. Hayes quickly called out to Tichborne, who checked the headsman and climbed from the scaffold to confer with Gibb and receive the King's stay of execution. Then the Sheriff told Markham he was granted a two-hour respite, and led him to the great hall of the castle and locked him in. Grey next came on the scene, more composed and cheerful than Markham. Raleigh could not have helped seeing Grey's serene face as he prayed for a half-hour in the rain. Afterward, Tichborne, who had a sense of drama himself and who may have been instructed by Gibb to play up to the situation, told Grey that the order of execution had been changed, with Cobham now to die before him. Then he locked Grey in the great hall too.

What Raleigh thought when Cobham, his erstwhile friend, was led to the scaffold is interesting to conjecture. Did he wonder if Cobham was also to be given a temporary respite? Did he speculate on the kind of confession that Cobham would make? Had he been close enough, he would have seen that Cobham had a firmer grip on himself than during his trial, though he still held Raleigh responsible for everything. Certainly Raleigh could easily observe Cobham praying. In fact, Cobham so outprayed the friends present who prayed with him that one onlooker later muttered disgustedly, "He had a good mouth in a cry, but was nothing single."[14]

Sheriff Tichborne took over as Cobham finished. After telling Cobham there remained something still to be done, he ordered Grey and Markham to be brought back to the scaffold. When the three men stood before him, Tichborne spoke sternly to them on the heinousness of their offenses, the justice of their trials and condemnation, and the merited execution awaiting them. As they humbly admitted their faults, Tichborne's voice and manner suddenly changed. "Then," he announced in a loud, cheerful tone, "see the mercy of your prince, who of himself

[14] *Ibid.*, 30.

hath sent hither a countermand, and given you your lives."
Cheers and applause swept over the green, and the condemned
men practically dissolved in gratitude. Markham, like his con-
federate Copley, was to be exiled, while Grey and Cobham were
to be imprisoned.[15]

Of these matters Raleigh knew nothing. There were two
dramas that day, one on the castle green, the other in Raleigh's
mind. The first was visible to all, though not entirely audible to
Raleigh. About the second there was considerable curiosity. As
Carleton wrote to Chamberlain, "Raleigh, you must think, (who
had a window opened that way) had hammers working in his
head to beat out the meaning of this stratagem."[16] His bewilderment undoubtedly grew as the prisoners were led away, the
crowd dispersed, and the cold rain continued to fall on a scaffold
unstained with blood from the scenes of that day.

From bewilderment Raleigh passed to hope, faint but persistent, that the same mercy might be vouchsafed him. He was
not to be disillusioned. Before long he was informed that he
too was to be spared. Had he known what lay ahead, execution
at this time might not have seemed so dreadful. In any event,
his jailers soon took him back to London, where, on December
16, 1603, he began a term of imprisonment that was to last for
thirteen long years.

[15] For the "execution" scenes, see Carleton's letter in *ibid.*, 29-32; Cecil to
Winwood, Dec. 12, 1603. Winwood, *Memorials*, II, 10-11; Tichborne to the
Commissioners, Dec. 10, 1603. HMC, *Salisbury MSS*, XV, 319-20.
[16] Williams, *Court and Times of James the First*, I, 31.

# CHAPTER 18

# The Early Tower Years

RALEIGH entered upon the long years of his imprisonment troubled over his debts, the security of his wife and son, and the abrupt ending to his own career. He was almost fifty-two, a man, until a few months previously, of power, position, and wealth; he was now a relatively impoverished person of no consequence in the world of affairs. A man of smaller stature might have considered himself beaten and set himself simply to enduring the years until death overtook him. Cobham remained a prisoner until 1617, when, on account of his health, he was granted permission to go to Bath for treatments; he died two years later, a pauper. Grey, more fortunate, passed away in the Tower in 1614. Raleigh's fate might have been similar had he not continued to hope and work for his release, keeping up a barrage of appeals to the King, Cecil, and the Council in his behalf, and had he not occupied himself with a variety of intellectual enterprises, of which one, his *History of the World*, was a prodigious work for anyone, let alone a prisoner. He insisted on being treated with distinction, which included, eventually, living in a sumptuous apartment in the Tower with servants. The fact that his popularity and intellectual reputation were constantly growing undoubtedly impelled the government to refrain from being overly harsh with him now that he was helpless.

Nor can it be denied that Cecil was frequently kind. Though he made no real move to procure Raleigh's release, he managed for a time to keep Raleigh's estate from being utterly despoiled. Raleigh, of course, was no longer a menace to his own position or to the Stuart line; thus Cecil could afford to be generous so long as there was no question of freeing the prisoner. Cecil was not being deliberately cruel. He was simply a man who was unable to believe that he did not act consistently from motives that were wise and good and who probably lacked the moral courage to challenge authority that he himself had helped establish.

Raleigh's concern for his financial situation was very acute and became the subject of much correspondence. He had already lost the five main sources of his income: the Governorship of Jersey, the wine patent, the Wardenship of the Stannaries, the Rangership of Gillingham Forest, and the Lieutenantcy of Portland Castle. He was also obliged to give up the Duchy of Cornwall. The wine patent was an especially severe loss since the new monopolist, Nottingham—the Lord Admiral—claimed the arrears as well as the current returns. Bess Raleigh begged Cecil to speak to the Lord Admiral to relinquish at least part of what belonged to her and Sir Walter. "God knows that our debts are above three thousand pounds," she cried, "and the bread and food taken from me and my children will never augment my Lord's table, though it famish us."[1] To add to the misery of the fallen, the Commissioners closed in on Sherborne; they sold the livestock, cut down the woods, and started to dismantle the house itself. The result was utter demoralization, with tenants refusing to pay their rents and debtors defaulting. Truly, as Raleigh told Cecil, "I perish every way."[2]

Fortunately Cecil came to the rescue. The Lord Admiral was persuaded to be less avaricious, and the despoilment of Sherborne was halted. On July 30, 1604 Sir Alexander Brett and George Hall received from the Crown in trust a six-year lease of Sherborne and ten other manors in Somerset and Dorset, the funds collected by the trustees to be used for the maintenance of Bess and young Walter.[3] Bess considered herself mistress of Sherborne for a while, and was still there in 1605, having the rusty armor scoured when the famous Gunpowder Plot to blow up the Houses of Parliament was discovered. There were not wanting people who contended that her house-cleaning activity must somehow be connected with the more drastic intentions of Guy Fawkes and his Catholic conspirators.

When she was not at Sherborne, Bess took her son Walter and lived with Raleigh in the Tower, where residence had its hazards. During the Easter festivities of 1604, James wanted to see some bull-baiting in the Tower yard. Since prisoners

---

[1] HMC, *Salisbury MSS*, XVI, 456-57; Edwards, *Ralegh (Letters)*, II, 408-09.
[2] *Ralegh (Letters)*, II, 293. See also letter to Commissioners in *ibid.*, 298-300; HMC, *Salisbury MSS*, XVI, 454-55.
[3] *Cal. S.P. Dom., 1603-1610*, 138.

were often freed as a mark of clemency on the occasion of such visits, Raleigh, Cobham, and Grey were removed to the Fleet Prison until the King and his guests had thoroughly enjoyed themselves; then, as an indication of his generosity, James ordered the prisoners remaining in the Tower liberated. When the royal party had departed, the important prisoners were returned. They soon discovered that the royal guests had left the plague in the Tower, and Raleigh bitterly lamented of "My poor child having lain this 14 days next to a woman with a running plague sore, and but a paper wall between—and whose child is also this Thursday dead of the plague."[4] The menace was so great that Bess whisked Walter out of the Tower altogether. Raleigh hoped Cecil might secure his removal, too, since the Tower dampness and the river mists had affected his own health. He suffered "daily, in danger of death by the palsy; nightly, of suffocation, by wasted and obstructed lungs."[5] But pleas brought no favorable response from Cecil or the King. Presently Bess rented a house on Tower Hill to be near her husband but away from the plague; there, in the winter of 1604-1605, she gave birth to Carew Raleigh.

Later in 1605 Raleigh and Bess had an altercation over Sherborne that revealed the degree of tension under which both had been living. During the drawing up of the deed of transfer of Sherborne and other properties to young Walter Raleigh in 1602, the engrossing clerk had omitted the important clause, "shall and will from henceforth stand and be thereof seized." Though Raleigh had no regard for Popham and Coke as individuals, he respected their knowledge of the law of property, and at his own request they investigated the conveyance. They informed Cecil in June 1605 that the omission of the clause, though clearly accidental, made the conveyance invalid; hence the provision by which Sherborne was to be administered by Brett and Hall was likewise invalid.[6] Her nerves already frazzled from the blows of the last two years, Bess lost control of herself and in loud accents accused Raleigh of negligence. Earnestly Raleigh begged Cecil to salvage his estate, otherwise

[4] Edwards, *Ralegh* (*Letters*), II, 315.
[5] *Ibid.*, 314-15.
[6] *Ibid.* (*Life*), I, 468-69; HMC, *Salisbury MSS*, XVIII, 242-43.

"I shall be made more than weary of my life by her crying and bewailing who will return in post, and nothing done. She hath already brought her eldest son in one hand and her suckling child in another, crying out of her and their destruction; charging me with unnatural negligence, and that having provided for my own life I am without sense and compassion for theirs. These torments, added to my desolate life, . . . are sufficient either utterly to distract me or to make me curse the time that ever I was born into the world. . . ."[7]

Cecil, who had recently become Earl of Salisbury, ignored the appeal. Bess then made her own appeal to the King, who agreed that the clerk's error should not jeopardize the Sherborne property, and directed Cecil to have a new grant properly drafted. This request Cecil also ignored, ultimately to the Raleighs' great misfortune.

However, life was not entirely a burden for Raleigh. Sir George Harvey, at first unfriendly, became intrigued with, then kindly disposed toward his famous prisoner. When Raleigh evinced an interest in botany, Harvey, as Lieutenant of the Tower, gave him a garden plot. Later, when Raleigh's interest in chemistry grew keen, Harvey let him construct a furnace for assaying metallic ores and a tiny laboratory for making his distillations and analyses. Raleigh learned to make fresh water out of salt water, though the secret accompanied him to his grave. He also made a cordial of strawberry water that was very popular with the ladies, while his "great cordial," a fantastic compound of animal, vegetable, and mineral matter, remained a common remedy for nearly a century.[8] Many visitors came to chat with him, while numerous people who came to look at the animals in the Tower zoo hoped for a sight of the distinguished prisoner. One day in 1605 the Countess of Beaumont, the French ambassador's wife, arrived with Lady Effingham, the Lord Admiral's daughter, to view the Tower lions. On their way to the cages they passed Raleigh working in his garden.

[7] HMC, *Salisbury MSS*, XVII, 624; Edwards, *Ralegh (Letters)*, II, 318.

[8] The famous nostrum is described by J. Knott, "Sir Walter Ralegh's 'Royal Cordial,' " in *American Medicine*, New Ser., VI (1911), 157-67. Sir Francis Bacon was so impressed with Raleigh's interest in chemistry that he considered employing him in his *Great Instauration*. See A. W. Green, *Sir Francis Bacon, His Life and Works*, 214.

Stopping to chat with him, the Countess asked if he would send her a little of the balsam he had brought back from Guiana. This he courteously promised to do, and made Captain White-locke, a mutual friend who accompanied her, his messenger. Little incidents like this one helped to relieve the tedium.

Imprisonment, however, was still imprisonment, and Raleigh was exposed to a number of disturbing factors, not the least of which was the appointment of Sir William Waad in August 1605 to succeed Harvey as Lieutenant of the Tower. Waad wanted Raleigh's garden for himself and thought a wall should be constructed to lessen Raleigh's chances of escape. He complained to Cecil that in the garden Raleigh had "converted a little hen-house to a still-house, where he spends his time all the day in distillations."[9] Waad was perhaps a little fearful of these experiments. He became even more suspicious of his prisoner when the Gunpowder Plot was discovered. Despite his incarceration, Raleigh was called before the Lords for questioning as a possible conspirator in the Plot. When he returned from his examination, he found that Waad had begun to build a brick wall to hem him in. He was more amused than annoyed, and used to walk out on top of the wall in plain view of people who came to look at him as much as to gaze at the whelping lioness, a seven-day wonder in the Tower zoo. These promenades on the wall greatly angered Waad, who spoke bitingly of Raleigh's "cunning humour."[10]

The following year, 1606, Raleigh's health seriously deteriorated. Though—except in literature—modesty was hardly one of his virtues, even to the extent of his bodily ailments, there is little doubt about his decline in the winter. In March his physician, Dr. Peter Turner, reported to Cecil that Raleigh's left side was cold and numb, the fingers of the left hand were contracted, and his tongue was affected. Turner recommended that the patient be moved to warmer lodgings, preferably to "a little room which he hath built, in the garden adjoining to his still-house."[11] While Raleigh seems eventually to have been moved, there is little evidence that at this time Turner's recom-

[9] HMC, *Salisbury MSS*, XVII, 378.
[10] *Ibid.*, 548.
[11] The physician's report is in PRO, *S.P. Dom.* (James I), 19/112.

mendation was acted upon. Perhaps the delay occurred as a result of the arrival of spring weather and a diminution of the paralytic symptoms, perhaps as a result of the continued enmity of Waad.

That same year, several attempts were made to intercede for Raleigh. Queen Anne, who considered herself helped during an illness by the prisoner's "great cordial," became his firm friend, but her husband ignored her words in Raleigh's behalf. In the course of the year, her brother, the King of Denmark, made a formal visit to London. The visit turned into an elaborate round of feasting and drinking bouts, and Christian IV, with an appetite and a thirst like a Viking of old, acquired a redoubtable reputation for conspicuous consumption. Before he arrived, James surmised that Anne had prompted her brother to speak in Raleigh's behalf, for, soon after he appeared, James drew him aside and said, "Promise me that you will be no man's solicitor." Despite James's wishes, Christian, who had his eye on Raleigh for admiral of his fleet, asked for a pardon. James paid as little heed to him as to his sister. Though the failure was a bitter blow, Bess Raleigh did not give up hope that the King would be merciful. She hastened to Hampton Court Palace in September, fell on her knees before James, and begged his intercession. He brushed past her without word or look; for all he cared, Raleigh could rot.

The Raleighs rarely regarded rebuffs as final. Raleigh continued his experiments, Bess persisted in driving into the Tower in her coach much to Waad's indignation. Neither relinquished hope that, one day, the Queen or Cecil might persuade the King to show clemency. Meanwhile, pending a softening of James's heart, they were exposed to Waad's petty tyranny. One manifestation of this was the new system of regulations introduced in July 1607. Henceforth, when the late afternoon bell rang in the Tower, prisoners and their servants were to retire to their chambers and remain there for the night. Wives of prisoners might see their husbands at convenient times but not after the afternoon bell, nor were they, from now on, to enter the Tower with their coaches. Wrathfully the Raleighs complied with Waad's regulations; to defy them would have given him indescribable satisfaction and a magnificent opportunity to be something worse than spiteful. They consoled themselves by falling back on their invincible hope of Raleigh's release.

In this year, 1607, Raleigh witnessed from afar two events that must have afforded him considerable pride. One was the matriculation of Walter on October 30 at Corpus, Oxford, where his chief tutor was a young cleric of great talent, Dr. Daniel Featley. Months earlier, Raleigh had probably observed from his famous walk the departure of the three little ships that, on May 24, landed the emigrants who were to found Jamestown, Virginia.[12] Though his conviction in 1603 had caused the rights included in his patent to revert to the Crown, Raleigh followed with mounting interest and anguished frustration the development of a permanent colony. True, the work which he had started was being carried on by others, but at least they were building on his experience and the information he and those associated with him had acquired. In fact, from 1603 on, several groups had been at work: London merchants, headed by Sir Thomas Smythe, who had been among Raleigh's grantees in 1589; a group from Plymouth, chiefly Sir John Popham, Sir Ferdinando Gorges, and Humphrey Gilbert's sons; a body of Bristol merchants under Richard Hakluyt; and several individuals, including the Earl of Southampton, who planned to establish a Catholic colony but who gave up the idea after the Gunpowder Plot. The first three groups formed the Plymouth Company, to exploit the New England area, and the London Company, to develop the southern area. It was the latter company, guided in part by Hakluyt's suggestions and issuing instructions resembling those which Raleigh had given Lane, that dispatched the *Sarah Constant*, the *Goodspeed*, and the *Discovery* with the Jamestown settlers.

Though unable to participate, Raleigh realized that his efforts of years past were now bearing fruit, that, thanks to his work and the interest he had inspired, the business of colonization had at last an admirable chance of prospering. In the enlargement and reorganization of the London Company in the next few years, both he and Thomas Hariot were called on for advice and information. Disturbed, the Spanish ambassador in 1609

[12] A. Brown, *The First Republic in America*, 24-27; W. E. Dodd, *The Old South*, 22.

told Philip III of Spain that Raleigh had written a paper which the Council of Virginia followed. The old magician, though still in the Tower, had thus not lost his ability to inspire respect among Englishmen and fear in the hearts of Spanish official-dom.[13]

While Raleigh languished in prison, the King and his Parliament had tangled over many issues in a struggle that was to continue for decades until parliamentary privilege won out over royal prerogative, monarchial absolutism, and divine right. Of the four problems that proved so controversial during James's reign—money, religion, foreign policy, and control of the courts—the money problem proved especially vexing to both King and Parliament. James's need of money was real, more real than Parliament would concede, but part of his need occurred as a result of his own extravagance; and few eccentricities of James gave greater offense than his addiction to attractive young men, to whom he gave titles, estates, and extraordinary privileges. His first great favorite in England was a Scot named Robert Carr, who broke his leg in the tilting yard and lay helpless and handsome under the amorously admiring eyes of the King. So captivated was James that he soon knighted Carr and eventually made him Earl of Somerset.

But rank without land lacked substance, and James looked about for an estate for his beloved. Sherborne, to which Raleigh possessed an invalid title, occurred to him as a likely possibility. As a matter of fact, it was Cecil, proving unfriendly again to Raleigh, who suggested Sherborne for Carr. The King, of course, was enormously pleased: "The more I think of your remembrance of Robert Kerr for yon manor of Sherborne, the more cause I have to conclude that your mind ever watcheth to seek out all advantages for my honour and contentment...."[14]

James began action in late 1607 through the Court of Exchequer, which in January 1608 asked Raleigh to show proper title by which Sherborne should revert to his heirs. All Raleigh

[13] For the colonial matters, see *ibid.*, 19-23; Quinn, *Raleigh and the British Empire*, 226-36; Andrews, *Colonial Period of American History*, I, 83-101; Craven, *Southern Colonies in the Seventeenth Century*, 57 ff.

[14] *Hatfield MSS*, 134, fol. 149. Quoted by Thompson, *Ralegh*, 248. Carr's fascination for James was probably physical and is well described by Willson, *James VI and I*, 336-37.

could produce was the dubious conveyance. Though counsel was assigned him, it could find no basis of defense acceptable to the court, so fatal had been the engrossing clerk's error. The Exchequer, however, waited until October 27 before giving judgment in the King's favor. Raleigh had no choice but to let Bess accept £5,000 which the King offered in exchange for her interest and young Walter's in the estate during Raleigh's lifetime. Eventually James softened the blow. He authorized Lawrence Keymis to survey the land, and appointed Sir Arthur Throgmorton, Bess Raleigh's brother, as a trustee. He then obtained a renunciation of the £5,000 agreed upon and promised to pay an annual pension of £400 for the duration of the lives of Bess and her son. In addition, he granted the Raleighs a capital sum of £8,000. The provisions could thus have been much harsher, even allowing for the lack of regularity in paying Bess Raleigh's pension. On the other hand, the financial loss to the Raleighs was severe.

Neither Raleigh nor Bess wished to acknowledge defeat. Raleigh actually abased himself to address an appeal to Carr, begging him not "to give me and mine our last fatal blow, by obtaining from His Majesty the inheritance of my children and nephews, lost in law for want of words."[15] Carr ignored the letter. Taking her courage in hand, Bess again confronted James at Hampton Court and entreated him to have compassion upon her and hers. As her son Carew scornfully remarked to the Long Parliament, forty years later, the only answer the King gave was, "I mun have the land, I mun have it for Carr." According to Carew, Bess then fell on her knees and in bitterness of spirit besought God to look upon the justice of her cause and punish those who wrongfully exposed her and her children to beggary and ruin.[16] Possibly James was out of earshot, else, because of her words, she might have joined her husband in the Tower as a prisoner.[17]

On January 9, 1609 Sherborne passed out of the Raleighs' hands into those of the worthless favorite. Thanks to the over-

[15] Edwards, *Ralegh* (*Letters*), II, 326-27.
[16] *Works*, II, 788.
[17] For a full discussion of the financial arrangements of the estate, see Gardiner, *History of England*, VIII, 43-49; Stebbing, *Ralegh*, 260-64.

sight of the clerk and of Raleigh's own attorney who handled
the conveyance, the case had been hopeless from the start. If
Raleigh was negligent in checking the conveyance at the time,
neither James, who seized the estate for Carr, nor Cecil, who
suggested it for the young Scot, was without guilt in the wrong
done to Bess and her children. It is unlikely that either was
disturbed in his conscience; the King's eagerness to delight his
favorite was hardly less than Cecil's desire to please the King
by a show of loyalty. Besides, both shared the view that perhaps
the intervention of the Almighty was evident in the affair. As
John Chamberlain wrote Carleton the day after Carr received
Sherborne:

"Sir Walter Raleigh's estate is fallen into the King's hands by
reason of a flaw in the conveyance, who hath bestowed it on
Sir Robert Carr . . . and though the Lady Raleigh have
been an importunate suitor all these holidays in her husband's
behalf, yet it is past recall, so that he may say with Job, 'Naked
came I into the world, and naked will I go out.' But above all,
one thing is to be noticed, that the error or oversight is said to be
gross, that men do merely ascribe it to God's own hand that
blinded him and his counsel."[18]

The confiscation of Sherborne had a striking effect not only
on Chamberlain but also on the playwright, John Webster. In
*The White Devil*, written about 1609, there is almost certainly
a reference to the way in which many contemporaries viewed
the Crown's action. Speaking against whores, the Cardinal
Monticelso declares:

> They are those brittle evidences of law
> Which forfeit all a wretched man's estate
> For leaving out one syllable.[19]

Henceforth dependent largely on his wife, Raleigh was now
closer than ever to the impoverishment he dreaded. Cecil had
played him false, and the King clearly had no intention of
releasing him. Fortunately Bess stood by him, and fortunately

[18] Williams, *Court and Times of James the First*, I, 86; *Chamberlain Letters*,
I, 280.
[19] J. Webster, *The White Devil*, act III, scene ii, lines 93-95; *Notes and
Queries*, CXCIII, 427-28.

too he possessed magnificent mental resources on which he was already starting to draw. He was soon deep in the greatest sustained achievement of his life. It would require more than a mere imprisonment to extinguish the vitality of his intellect or the vigor of his spirit.

# CHAPTER 19

# The Later Tower Years

WHILE Raleigh was in the Tower, few things afforded him greater pleasure or lent more direction to his thinking than the friendship of James's heir to the throne, Prince Henry. About ten years old when James came to England, Henry was described by the Venetian ambassador as "little of body, and quick of spirit . . . ceremonious beyond his years, and with great gravity. . . ."[1] He grew up still serious but a lover of sports of all kinds, courageous and high-spirited. He was frank, open, and manly, neither like nor liking his father. About 1607 or 1608, Queen Anne began to bring him to visit Raleigh. Anne evidently saw in the prisoner in the Tower a man who could serve as a greater inspiration and counsellor to her son than could her husband with his unkingly bearing, his small nature, and his notorious affection for Robert Carr. For all her capriciousness, her love of revelry, and her extravagance, Anne has to be forgiven much. Life with James Stuart was attended by more than the usual trials of a royal marriage. Perhaps seeing young Henry become the warm admirer of her husband's prisoner was as solidly satisfying to her as to Henry, though for different reasons. Certainly there was no doubt that Henry was impressed with Raleigh. Nor, according to contemporary rumor, did he conceal his opinion that "No one but my father would keep such a bird in a cage." Raleigh was delighted with the Prince. In him lay not only a hope of eventual release but the opportunity of shaping a vigorous mind and will that would restore to England the prestige lost since James's accession and his inglorious peace with Spain. With Henry's encouragement, and now that Bess was forbidden the Tower after five o'clock, he spent the long evenings and much of the days in composition. While he did not entirely neglect his chemical experiments, he wrote furiously on a host of topics. After all, the education of a prince had fallen

[1] *Cal. S.P. Venetian*, *1603-1607*, 74.

in good part on his shoulders, and none could call him delinquent in the variety or volume of his labors.[2]

His compositions fall roughly into five categories: political and economic problems of current importance, problems of political philosophy, ethical and metaphysical problems, military and naval matters, and historical subjects. Merely listing according to category some (not all, by any means) of the essays he wrote reveals in their diversity the widespread interests of the man's mind:

### I. CURRENT POLITICAL AND ECONOMIC PROBLEMS

*On a Match between Lady Elizabeth and the Prince of Piedmont*
*On a Match between Prince Henry and a Daughter of Savoy*
*Observations Touching Trade and Commerce*
*Causes of the Magnificency and Opulency of Cities*

### II. PROBLEMS OF POLITICAL PHILOSOPHY

*Maxims of State*
*The Cabinet-Council*
*The Prerogative of Parliaments*
*On the Seat of Government*

### III. ETHICAL AND METAPHYSICAL PROBLEMS

*The Sceptic*
*A Treatise of the Soul*
*Instructions to His Son and to Posterity*

### IV. MILITARY AND NAVAL MATTERS

*A Discourse of War in General*
*A Discourse of the Invention of Ships, Anchor, Compass, etc.*
*Observations on the Navy and Sea Service*

### V. HISTORICAL SUBJECTS

*The Reign of William the First*
*A Discourse of Tenures Which Were Before the Conquest*

[2] See the brilliant, perceptive account in Waldman, *Raleigh,* 184-94.

Raleigh wrote most of this material with Prince Henry in mind. The Spanish faction among English statesmen had grown with James's well-known pacifism, the dying-down of the robust Elizabethan temper, and the extension of Philip III's pension system, which, one should remember, included Cecil on its ledgers. James embraced the idea of strengthening his policy by marrying his daughter Elizabeth to the son of a Spanish satellite prince, the Duke of Savoy, and Prince Henry to the Duke's daughter. Asked for his opinion by Prince Henry, Raleigh gave it in two detailed essays which bear the imprint of his lifelong antagonism to Spain. The proposed match, he pointed out, would place a heavy burden on England. Defense of Savoy against Spain would be impossible, if indeed the Duke could ever be persuaded to fight Philip III, while Savoy could give England no aid worth mentioning. On the other hand, the Savoyard link might force England to remain neutral while Spain disposed of the Netherlands in her own time and leisure. "Hispaniolized" Englishmen, as Raleigh described the Spanish faction, would do a disservice to England to treat with lenience and regard with fear a nation like Spain. The marriages, moreover, would be of a mixed religious nature, and England would lose her position as champion of Protestantism. Princess Elizabeth would do far better to take as her husband the ruler of the Palatine, a Protestant.

As for Henry, while Raleigh did not presume to suggest a wife for him, the Prince later declared that rather than have two religions in his bed, he too would find a mate among the Protestant Germans. Perhaps Raleigh's scornful words lingered as, after disposing of the arguments for the marriage, the prisoner of the Tower declared: "What then remains of profit to our prince. . . ? A sum of money and a beautiful lady: for beauty was never so cheap in any age, and it is ever better loved in the hope, than when it is had. For the millions of crowns offered . . . when all those dukes, lords, and great ladies, which will attend the princess in her passage hither . . . when the preparations, triumphs, and feastings are paid for, there will remain nothing but a great increase of charge, and perchance a great deal of melancholy."[3] It is scarcely cause for

[3] *Works*, VIII, 246.

wonder that James and Cecil fumed at Raleigh, particularly as the marriage negotiations broke down.

Raleigh's political philosophy as embodied in his essays was essentially a faith in what was later known as enlightened despotism. He believed in the prerogatives of kingship to the extent that he even defended King John for taking so strong a stand at first against signing the Magna Carta, which tended "to the alteration of the whole commonwealth."[4] In his opinion, Archbishop of Canterbury Stephen Langton, who produced the charter, was a traitor, while the nobles who supported the Archbishop behaved "in rebellious and outrageous fashion." The likely fact that he hoped James would show him more favor by his intellectual support of kingship does not necessarily signify that he was truckling to James. Raleigh had never been a real democrat—quite the contrary. On the other hand, he did not hesitate to point out in *The Prerogatives of Parliament* that a king's love for his people should be unfailing and that no more unfortunate fate could happen to him than to have a falling-out with the House of Commons.[5] In *The Cabinet Council*, which unmistakably shows a careful reading of Machiavelli's *The Prince*, Raleigh set forth the requirements of a good king: he must be wise, brave, strong, virtuous, and just. If he lacks but one of these attributes, his rule will suffer and the result may be his ruin: "virtuous and vicious examples of princes incite subjects to imitate the same qualities."[6] Slyly Raleigh also slipped in the observation that "The way whereby a prince eschews the hate of subjects is not to take from them their lands or goods"; confiscation can make him "odious."[7] John Milton thought so highly of *The Cabinet Council* that he had it printed for the first time in 1658.

In his discourses on ethical and metaphysical problems, Raleigh revealed the worldliness of his life and his dependence upon expediency. *The Sceptic* is a superficial, disappointing essay saved from insignificance only by its definition: "The sceptic doth neither affirm, neither deny any position, but doubteth of it, and opposeth his reasons against that which is

[4] *Ibid.*, 161.
[5] *Ibid.*, 155.
[6] *Ibid.*, 150.
[7] *Ibid.*, 121.

affirmed or denied, to justify his not consenting."[8] This definition was roughly Raleigh's initial position on any question. His
was the independent, inquiring mind that had first to consider
a point of view in all its aspects and colorings before committing
himself. It was this persistence in weighing, in evaluating, in
testing for validity, that helped set men against him in an age
when conformity was not simply desirable but, in so many
respects, mandatory.

In his *Treatise on the Soul*, much of which has previously
been considered in connection with the charge of atheism,[9] he
somewhat raised the standard of performance. The essay reveals
great erudition, some insight, but little originality. The soul,
he concluded, is the image of God and, in will and reason, is
immortal. But even here Raleigh's materialism finds expression.
We worship God, he said, "because our souls are made to his
image, and we know he is *a rewarder of them that serve him. . . .*
Now to what end were religion, if there were no reward? and
what reward is there, if the souls do not live for ever? for in
this life the reward of the godly is but small."[10] The notion
that a man might live his own life in love of God without hope
or desire of recompense was simply beyond Raleigh's experience, perhaps even his comprehension. Still, in a fine froth
of feeling and words, he challenged the denials of certain
learned men in history that women have souls. On the contrary,
"women have souls eternal, endowed with reason, wise, sober,
temperate, and holy, redeemed by Christ, sanctified by His
Spirit, and chosen by the Father to the everlasting kingdom of
heaven."[11] It is a magnificent concession, given in all soberness,
so perhaps one can forgive him much of his materialism.

Or can one? His essay *Instructions to His Son and to Posterity*
raises at least a doubt. In ten brief chapters Raleigh spoke as a
worldly man giving advice to his son. He urged Walter to
choose virtuous persons as friends; to beware of flatterers since
they are the worst kind of traitors; to avoid quarrels and
loquacity and lying; to put up with no waste by servants; to
avoid spending money before in possession of it; to suffer for

[8] *Ibid.,* 548.
[9] See Chapter 7.
[10] *Works,* VIII, 591.
[11] *Ibid.,* 573-74.

no man's faults; to beware of extravagance in dress; to seek not riches by evil means; to refrain from drunkenness; to serve God and let Him be the Author of one's actions. This is all very admirable, and few knew better than Raleigh the consequences of not following some of this advice.

But Raleigh also had words of wisdom concerning his son's choice of a wife, and here one encounters some opinions of women that are, to say the least, not overly charitable. The danger in selecting a wife is that she may be beautiful, for, in all eras, men, wise and foolish, have been betrayed by beauty. Marry not beauty, therefore. Especially beware of marrying a combination of beauty and poverty since "love abideth not with want." Marry, rather, for convenience, for estate rather than love. Furthermore, it is better that, once married, "thou be beloved of thy wife, rather than thyself besotted on her."[12] Yet one should not be sour or stern to her, or deny her half the estate while one lives. On the other hand, a man should be sure to leave his estate to his children and only what necessity dictates to his wife, who, if young, will probably remarry if widowed.

Again, this was the practical worldling, the materialist, emerging in Raleigh. But did he really believe all he advised? He who said, "no man is esteemed for gay garments but by fools and women,"[13] had been the most resplendent courtier of his day and reveled in his magnificence. He who bade his son marry so circumspectly had jeopardized his own career and spent long weeks in the Tower for marrying so uncircumspectly. He who stressed a preference that a wife love her husband was devoted to his own wife, remained faithful to her in an unfaithful age, and, while awaiting what he presumed was his execution, wrote her a letter so beautiful in sentiment and expression that it became a classic almost at once. Truly, as one of his most perceptive biographers has so aptly observed, "though he preached like Polonius, he could act like Laertes."[14] It is his deeds set against his admonishments that causes one to marvel at the humorless cynicism and to prefer the erring man to the juiceless counsellor.

[12] *Ibid.*, 559.
[13] *Ibid.*, 567.
[14] Waldman, *Raleigh*, 187.

He was on surer ground when he turned to war and ships and the navy. Prince Henry shared with him a love of the latter two, and, inspired by the boy's interest, Raleigh wrote on these subjects in terse, graphic English that is a model of lucidity and precision. He even assisted Phineas Pett, the outstanding naval architect of the day, in building a ship, *The Prince Royal*, for Henry, giving detailed suggestions for her construction.[15] The design and construction of the vessel were so skillful and sound that, with Henry's brother Charles aboard, she later weathered a Channel gale in which many other craft went to the bottom. It seems highly likely that Raleigh intended his naval essays as part of a larger work, *The Art of War by Sea*.[16] In the essays, and scattered here and there in his *History of the World*, he made valuable suggestions on naval tactics and ship construction. To be sure, he has been criticized, for his knowledge of nautical history was by no means infallible. Furthermore, as Sir Julian Corbett has said, though in what seems a rather extreme statement of the case, "He could not believe that seamen could work a gun nor could he see the ship as a gun carriage. It was still for him a fortress carrying men in which the guns were mainly of use to effect an entrance into a rival fortress."[17] This is perhaps doing Raleigh less than justice for, regardless of his shortcomings, he was, as a distinguished naval scholar remarked, "as a theorist . . . the first strategist of his day."[18] He was also an acute observer, one of the first sea fighters of his nation to draw up a systematic treatise on tactics and ship construction for the Royal Navy based on his experiences and observations, and one of the few men in either the sixteenth or seventeenth century who could write in intelligible English on a subject so technical as naval science.

Far and away his outstanding work while in the Tower was his *History of the World*. This monumental work, filling six substantial volumes in the Oxford edition of 1829, was first printed in 1614 after seven years of research and writing. In his preface Raleigh said that he undertook the work expressly "for the service of that inestimable prince Henry, the successive

[15] Edwards, *Ralegh* (*Letters*), II, 330-32.
[16] *Ibid.*, I, 504; II, 498.
[17] Corbett, *The Successors of Drake*, 434, 424-35, *passim*.
[18] Oppenheim, *Monson's Naval Tracts*, II, 67.

hope, and one of the greatest of the Christian world. . . . It pleased him to peruse some part thereof, and to pardon what was amiss."[19] Raleigh thought of writing a universal history to the time of the Roman invasion of Britain; afterward, he proposed to confine himself largely to English history with an occasional excursion into Continental. His was a magnificent conception, a staggering task even for a professional scholar, a healthy person, and a free man. Raleigh was none of these, yet he pursued his objective without flagging until, his princely patron suddenly dying, his zeal for the work burned out. By that time, he had brought his account from the Creation to the Roman conquest of Macedon, but 133 B.C. was quite far removed from the modern world. Still, he had no intention of bringing his history into the seventeenth century despite the fact that he would have pleased readers since he had been "permitted to draw water as near the well-head as another." His answer to such criticism was that "whosoever, in writing a modern history, shall follow truth too near the heels, it may happily strike out his teeth."[20] He preferred to write of an older era, though this did not prevent him from alluding to contemporary experiences, particularly his own, by way of comparison and illumination. But to bring his work up to date? He had had enough teeth struck out during his lifetime!

For the general reader of the twentieth century, the *History of the World* is a strange and forbidding work, holding terrors even for the scholar. It contains, particularly in the first part, a wealth of scholarship of the most minute detail and nowhere more evident than in the first chapter dealing with the Creation and in the geographical and historical account of the Ten Tribes of Israel. On and on Raleigh takes one in a leisurely but tortuous way through the rise of one empire to its conquest by another. One reads of the imprisonment of the Israelites by the Babylonians, the displacement of the latter by the Persians, the struggles of the Persians with the Greeks, the interminable Greek city-state rivalries, and the rise of Macedon and the Asiatic conquests of Alexander, the conquest of Carthage and Macedon by the Romans. When Raleigh arrives at Greece, and

[19] Preface, in *Works*, II, lxiv.
[20] Preface, in *ibid.*, lxiii.

particularly at the period of Roman supremacy, his interest in his material seems to increase, and his style moves in a less stately manner. As David Hume remarked in the eighteenth century, "If the reader of Raleigh's History can have the patience to wade through the Jewish and Rabbinical learning . . . , he will find, when he comes to the Greek and Roman story, that his pains are not unrewarded."[21]

The *History* is no mere chronicle, nor was it written as a research project with a microscopic eye for documentation. To be sure, much of it makes tedious and profitless reading for us. History is written nowadays with a different conception, structure, use and evaluation of evidence, and interpretation. But, as Sir Charles Firth has pointed out, the differences should not obscure one's vision to the value of Raleigh's work as a history.[22]

The *History* and its method were strongly influenced by Raleigh's conception of history. With Cicero, he considered that the "end and scope of all history" is "to teach by example of times past such wisdom as may guide our desires and actions."[23] History thus helps us to learn from other men's misfortunes, permitting us to profit by their example. At the same time, Raleigh shared with others of his age, particularly the Puritans, the view that God ordained what happened—"God, who is the author of all our tragedies, hath written out for us and appointed us all the parts we are to play."[24] God moves through history, manifesting His goodness in all life and loving the goodness He does. If men would but put aside their vanity and frantic self-seeking, they would hear His voice and, if wise, heed His will. It was Raleigh's belief in the task of the historian to point out the manifestations of Providence that impelled him to begin where he did. As he said, "The examples of divine providence, everywhere found . . . have persuaded me to fetch my beginning from the beginning of all things; to wit, creation."[25] From the Creation on, Raleigh illustrates in each of the ancient governments and civilizations the workings of a Divine Providence. The *History* thus possesses a thread of unity that becomes more

---

[21] D. Hume, *History of England*, IV, 377.
[22] Sir C. Firth, *Essays Historical and Literary*, 34.
[23] *History of the World*, bk. II, ch. xxi, sec. 6 (*Works*, IV, 616).
[24] Preface, in *ibid.*, II, xlii.
[25] *Ibid.*, xliii.

evident as Raleigh moves out of the East into the classical civilizations of Greece and Rome.

Admitting that he could "never be persuaded that God hath shut up all light of learning within the lantern of Aristotle's brains,"[26] Raleigh indulges in considerable moralizing and personal reflection. The conquerors of the earth, the greatest oppressors, were, like "the most undertrodden wretches," subject to God, who governed "all alike with absolute command."[27] If monarchs but realized how variable and how unstable was Fortune, they might show more sympathy and compassion for those they ruled. Unfortunately men seek the power, without the moderation, of God; the result is misery. Kings put off God and only fear death.

For Raleigh, death had a persistent and extraordinary attraction. It was not simply that death had stood at his elbow during much of a tumultuous life. Rather, he had some strange affinity for a force that in the end was triumphant. Life was essentially tragic but veiled in a mystery, now unimaginably repugnant, now infinitely intriguing and perhaps comforting in prospect. Not that Raleigh wooed death as one for whom life held no more relish; but as one who had soared and plumbed in life, he recognized in death a judgment of life in all its strivings and tinsel that was somehow fitting. In another vein, he spoke of life, as did so many Elizabethans, as a play, whereas death was the reality, the ultimate which made life look a little silly. It is death "that puts into man all the wisdom of the world, which God, with all the words of His Law, promises, or threats, does not infuse."[28] All indeed is vanity, but who believes it until death reminds us? Only death can make a man truly know himself. Death humbles the proud and insolent, and proves the rich man a beggar. One of the most striking prose passages in English literature is his famous apostrophe to death:

"O eloquent, just and mighty Death! whom none could advise, thou hast persuaded; what none hath dared, thou hast done; and whom all the world hath flattered, thou only hast cast out of the world and despised; thou hast drawn together

---

[26] *Ibid.*, xlv.
[27] *History of the World*, bk. v, ch. vi, sec. 12 (*Works*, VII, 896).
[28] *Ibid.* (*Works*, 900).

all the far-stretched greatness, all the pride, cruelty, and ambition of man, and covered it all over with these two narrow words, *Hic Jacet!*"[29]

It is the occasional passages of gorgeous prose, the interesting speculations, and the reminiscences used as illustrations that help sustain one's interest in the *History*. The reminiscences in particular bring one up short. In the midst of relating one of Alexander's feats in securing a position by means of a fire that forced back his foe, Raleigh suddenly says, "I saw in the third civil war of France certain caves in Languedoc. . . ."[30] Then he tells how the Huguenots were able to smoke their enemies out of the caves. In speaking of the difficulties the Romans had in transporting troops to Africa with an inferior fleet, Raleigh launches into a discussion of seapower in the war with Spain and declares that without her fleet England could not have prevented the Spaniards from invading the country.[31] Land fortifications were not a sufficient defense, as Raleigh related from his personal experience during the Islands Voyage—"I landed those English in Fayal myself."[32] Similarly, at the taking of Cadiz, "The fort St. Philip terrified not us in the year 1596."[33] Forthright, frank statements of personal experience and the ancient wars suddenly come alive in the illumination of modern parallels drawn from the history of England, Spain, Holland, France, and Italy.

The *History* had an enormous success. It went through ten editions in the seventeenth century, one in the eighteenth, and two in the nineteenth. There have also been three abridgments and two attempts at continuation.[34] Princess Elizabeth, married to Frederick the Palatine prince who was chosen by the Protestant nobles of Bohemia to be their king, carried a copy with her to Prague; it was captured by the Spaniards in 1620 when she was forced to flee the city, was recovered by the Swedes in 1648, and is now safely domiciled in the British Museum. John Hampden was a close student of the *History*. Milton also became a

---

[29] *Ibid.* (*Works*, 900).
[30] *Ibid.*, bk. IV, ch. ii. sec. 16 (*Works*, V, 355).
[31] *Ibid.*, bk. V, ch. i, sec. 9 (*Works*, VI, 97).
[32] *Ibid.* (*Works*, 103).
[33] *Ibid.*, sec. 10 (*Works*, 109).
[34] See T. N. Brushfield, *The Bibliography of Sir Walter Ralegh*.

great admirer of it, made extracts for his copybook, and showed what was evidently a pretty thoroughgoing interest in a number of Raleigh's writings. Cromwell suggested that his son Richard read the *History* as "a body of History" that would add more to his understanding than "fragments of story";[35] the great Oliver deplored purely factual narratives that did not point out the "strange windings and turnings of Providence" and the "very great appearances of God."[36] Even the rationalist philosopher John Locke commended the *History*. The fact that Raleigh was identified with the opposition to the Stuarts made his memory and his writings popular with the Parliamentary opponents of James I and Charles I. Puritans, forgetting their hatred of him as the man they considered responsible for the death of the Earl of Essex, also claimed him by virtue of his view that history teaches the moral lesson that God punishes the sinful. That Raleigh was no republican and certainly no Puritan troubled his admirers not at all. Thus, long after his death, men thought of him as they wanted to think of him, even as they had during his lifetime, though with this difference: the posthumous opinion was, in the main, laudatory.

But, of course, he did not escape criticism for his *History*. To those who wondered how he had accumulated such erudition, Raleigh, in a grim jest, pointed to his years of enforced leisure in which he had become a voracious reader. On the other hand, it is not surprising that he received help on some of the more than six hundred sources he refers to in the *History*. He acknowledged his ignorance of Hebrew and preferred Greek authors in Latin versions. Sir Robert Cotton and friends loaned him many books, and experts gave him the benefit of their specialties. Ben Jonson said that "The best wits of England were employed for making his Historie."[37] Because of these manifold contributions, some critics have sought to belittle his efforts, the most preposterous comment being that of Algernon Sidney: "An ordinary man with the same help might have performed the same thing."[38] The widow of the divine, Dr. Robert

---

[35] T. Carlyle, *Oliver Cromwell's Letters and Speeches*, Letter CXXXII, Vol. I, pt. v, 53.

[36] *Ibid.*, Speech I, Vol. I, pt. vii, 301.

[37] B. Jonson, *Works*, IX, 384.

[38] A. Sidney, *Works*, 398.

Burhill, a friend of Raleigh, told Aubrey that "all or the greatest part of the drudgery of his book, for criticisms, chronology, and reading of Greek and Hebrew authors, was performed" by her husband.[39] Isaac D'Israeli, father of the great Dizzy, gave an uncritical approval to this report, a report which has since been convincingly refuted.[40] No doubt Raleigh made good use of Burhill, as he did of Jonson, who wrote a portion on the war between Rome and Carthage which Raleigh altered.

With the eighteenth century, the *History* began to lose its appeal. Yet Dr. Samuel Johnson, though critical of the work as history, praised "the elegance of his style,"[41] while Hume, even more critical of Raleigh's treatment, considered him "the best model of that ancient style. . . ."[42] Though Raleigh continued to be criticized in the nineteenth century—notably by Matthew Arnold and the Catholic historian, the Reverend John Lingard —Lord Acton, the great Catholic editor of the *Cambridge Modern History*, still found him valuable. "I venerate that villainous adventurer, for his views on universal history," he wrote a friend.[43] These views, primarily that history teaches by example, that the workings of Providence are manifest in men's lives, and that punishment falls upon the evildoers, impressed even Edward Gibbon, the greatest historian in the English language and a man scarcely noted for his religious enthusiasm. "I shall not, I trust, be accused of superstition," he said apropos of these views, "but I must remark that, even in this world, the natural order of events will sometimes afford the strong appearances of moral retribution."[44] As one contemplates certain developments within the past twenty years in the history of the world, it is not difficult to agree with Gibbon, and thereby at least in part with Raleigh.

The sharpest contemporary criticism came from the very individual whom, next to Prince Henry, Raleigh wished most to impress favorably, the King. Through the Archbishop of Canterbury, he ordered the *History* suppressed in December

---

[39] Aubrey, *Brief Lives*, II, 194.
[40] I. D'Israeli, *Curiosities of Literature*, IV, 9; B. Corney, *Curiosities of Literature Illustrated*, 59.
[41] Quoted by Strathmann, *Ralegh, A Study in Elizabethan Skepticism*, 257.
[42] Hume, *History of England*, IV, 377.
[43] Quoted by Firth, *Essays*, 60.
[44] Quoted by *ibid.*, 50.

1614. John Chamberlain told Dudley Carleton that the *History* was called in because Raleigh was "too saucy in censuring princes,"[45] an explanation borne out in another account that James was indignant at his having spoken "irreverently" of Henry VIII.[46] Kings identified themselves with rulers in other countries and other ages when writers aired views antagonistic to those rulers. Thus Elizabeth took offense at the Essex-inspired performance of *Richard II* by Shakespeare's company. James might well have identified himself with any number of ancient princes whom Raleigh criticized, let alone Henry VIII. Actually all James needed was to let his royal sensibilities be offended at Raleigh's general observations on princes in the preface to the *History*. However, the suppression did not last long. The government tore out the title page with the author's name and portrait, a man "civilly dead," and soon let the book reappear with everything else untouched. Actually, the marvel, as Sir Charles Firth remarked, was that the government ever rescinded the suppression order.[47]

The temporary suppression of the *History* was not the first instance of the government's displeasure while Raleigh was in the Tower. Not only was he called up for examination in connection with the Gunpowder Plot, but the government seems to have become suspicious and resentful of the influence he exercised over Prince Henry. Consequently, when Lord Grey complained in 1611 that his fellow prisoners enjoyed more privileges than himself, Raleigh being permitted a garden and a gallery, the Councillors again questioned Raleigh.

Precisely what was discussed at the session is not known for a certainty, but that it was an emotional occasion is clear enough. Raleigh admitted that Cecil used "sharp words" toward him, "terms . . . which might utterly despair anybody else,"[48] while Henry Howard wrote Robert Carr: "We had a bout with Sir Walter Raleigh, in whom we find no change, but the same boldness, pride and passion, that heretofore hath wrought more violently, but never expended itself in a stronger passion.

---

[45] *Chamberlain Letters*, I, 568.
[46] Osborne, *Traditional Memorials on the Reign of King James*, 431.
[47] Firth, *Essays*, 55.
[48] See his letter to Sir Walter Cope, incorrectly dated 1610 instead of 1611, in Edwards, *Ralegh (Letters)*, II, 328-29.

Hereof his Majesty shall hear when the Lords come to him. The lawless liberty of the Tower, so long cockered and fostered with hopes exorbitant, hath bred suitable desires and affections."[49] It must indeed have exasperated so rancorous a soul as Howard to find the object of his inveterate enmity still unchastened. But Raleigh possessed a strength of spirit beyond the ability of either Howard or Cecil to appreciate.

Cecil, however, had little desire henceforth to appreciate anyone's misfortunes other than his own. The King was angry with him for his failure to reach a financial agreement with Parliament favorable to the Crown. Carr intrigued vigorously for his downfall, and in this he had the support of Henry Howard, who was eager to see his niece, Frances Howard, divorce the new Earl of Essex for alleged impotence in order to marry Carr. Francis Bacon was stirring restlessly as Cecil continued to dominate policy. More dangerous than even these opponents was the accumulation of physical afflictions that beset him in the winter of 1612: an abdominal tumor, rheumatism, ague, scurvy, dropsy, and melancholia.[50] Finally he died on May 24, at the age of forty-eight, almost friendless and unlamented.

In the general belief that, because of his amours, he perished of syphilis, a rash of ribald and scurrilously critical verses broke out, expressing the satisfaction felt by so many at his demise. To Raleigh has been ascribed a coarse "Epitaph" on Cecil that, despite its awkwardness, still wants proof not to have been his. Certainly it expresses feelings that Raleigh might well have come to indulge toward the man who had so grievously wronged him:

Here lies Hobinall our pastor whilere,
That once in a quarter our fleeces did sheer;
To please us, his cur he kept under clog,
And was ever after both shepherd and dog;
For oblation to Pan, his custom was thus,
He first gave a trifle, then offered up us;
And through his false worship such power he did gain,
As kept him on the mountain, and us on the plain.

[49] PRO, *S.P. Dom.* (James I), 65/26.
[50] Cecil, *Cecil*, 333.

Where many a hornpipe he tuned to his Phyllis,
And sweetly sung Walsingham to his Amaryllis.
Till Atropos clapt him, a pox on the drab,
For (spite of his tarbox), he died of the scab.

Though James had wearied of Cecil, he was so angered when he saw the composition that he said he hoped the man who wrote those lines would die before he did. If the author was truly Raleigh, his wish was gratified.

With Cecil's departure, Raleigh saw an insurmountable obstacle to his release removed. Now more than ever, he pinned his hopes on Prince Henry, whom Howard disliked and feared. Similarly, both Henry and Queen Anne esteemed more than ever the old lion in the Tower. Henry, moreover, objected strongly to his father's having given Sherborne to Carr, and expressed the wish that James would bestow an estate of such beauty upon himself instead. Accordingly, the King, who stood somewhat in awe of his strong-willed son, complied, buying back Sherborne for £20,000. It was said that Henry fully intended to give it back to Raleigh on the latter's release,[51] and that he had also wrung from his father a reluctant promise that Raleigh should be freed by Christmas. Unfortunately, Henry, who loved to swim in the filthy Thames, caught what is now known to be typhoid fever in October. Apparently recovered, he played tennis, caught a chill, and suffered a relapse. On November 6, 1612, he was dying. Utterly distraught, the Queen sent to Raleigh for his "great cordial." She had wanted it days before, but the government refused to let her ask the prisoner's aid until it was clear that the ministrations of physicians were hopeless. Although the cordial revived Henry long enough for him to speak, he died before the day was out.

His death was a staggering blow to Raleigh. He lost interest in his *History* except to see it through the press. Although he had intended to continue it, he could not. As he said of the volumes that would remain unwritten, "besides many other discouragements persuading my silence, it hath pleased God to take that glorious prince out of the world to whom they were directed."[52] Henry's demise meant, too, that Sherborne was

---

[51] Carew Raleigh's statement is in *Works*, VIII, 788.
[52] *History of the World*, bk. V, ch. vi, sec. 12 (*Works*, VII, 901).

forever lost to him; James sold it back to Carr for £25,000, far in excess of what he had paid the Raleighs for it.[53] Furthermore, the King chose not to free him by Christmas. Worse still for Raleigh was the irreparable loss of a promising young ruler to whom he had been a mentor and almost a father. The heart went out of him as, in the closing sentence of his *History*, he lamented with Job, "My harp has been turned into mourning and my organ into the voice of those who weep."[54]

Death and misfortune began to strike others. Raleigh's fellow prisoner, Lord Grey, died in the Tower in 1614. In the same year Henry Howard also died. A learned but cynical, detestable person, he died soon enough to avoid the disgrace that should have been his to share with his niece. Together with Robert Carr, he had been an accessory to Frances Howard's efforts to drug Essex's son into impotency and thereby win a divorce. Thanks to a special commission appointed by James, she won the divorce in which she produced a wealth of manufactured detail of an obscene nature that disgusted decent-minded people, and then married Carr, who was, at the time, Viscount Rochester and, later, Earl of Somerset. Sir Thomas Overbury, a friend of Somerset, detested Frances and spoke of her and her family in terms so frank that she never forgave him. Adroitly spreading slander that if Somerset dominated the King, Overbury was Somerset's master, she so roused James's anger that he insisted Overbury serve abroad. When Overbury refused, he was sent to the Tower. Once he was there, both Howard and Carr endeavored to keep him in prison for reasons of their own, while, unbeknownst to them, Frances Howard decided to poison him. To make their control over him more complete, the two noblemen secured the dismissal of the Lieutenant of the Tower, Sir William Waad, who, though impossible in his treatment of Raleigh, was honest according to his lights; in Waad's stead, the conspirators obtained the appointment of a compliant tool, Sir Gervase Helwys. Then, through intermediaries, Frances had poison slipped into Overbury's food; he died in September 1613. Soon realizing what had happened, Howard skillfully sought to cover up the crime, but a year later, with Sir Ralph

[53] Gardiner, *History of England*, II, 48-49.
[54] *History of the World*, bk. v, ch. vi, sec. 12 (*Works*, VII, 901).

Winwood becoming Secretary, Helwys confessed, and the whole plot came to light. As a result of the trials, numerous people were executed, including Helwys. The Somersets, tried early in 1616, were also sentenced to death. Rank and influence, however, still counted heavily. Frances, far more guilty than her husband, was pardoned, while the Earl's sentence was commuted to imprisonment in the Tower, where the Countess joined him.

With his enemies falling upon hard days or dying off, Raleigh began to pick up hope again. The Overbury murder alienated large sections of the population, particularly the Puritans of the middle class that was becoming powerful in Parliament. Sensing that alienation, and believing that Sir Ralph Winwood, who was friendly to him, would look with favor upon his efforts, Raleigh revived his Guiana project. In his original voyage, Raleigh had learned through Lawrence Keymis of a gold mine that had been pointed out to him by an Indian, Putijma. When Keymis sailed again in 1596, the Spaniards had occupied the Indian settlement at the Caroni, thereby blocking the approach to the mine. A search for Putijma failed to disclose him, but Keymis returned to England still convinced the mine was real and valuable. As Raleigh languished in the Tower, this mine grew in importance, the more he thought of it. Although he was still certain of the strategic and economic value of Guiana as a colony, he spoke now of the gold that could be found there, for he suspected that, with James in financial straits, the lure of gold might prove so attractive to the King that he would release him from prison to go after it. From 1609 on, the scheme started to possess his imagination.

Letters to Cecil and others may have won Raleigh no consideration of release, but Guiana so interested both the King and Cecil that they authorized a voyage in 1609 by Robert Harcourt and one in 1610 by Sir Thomas Roe. Actually these were by no means the only Englishmen to visit Guiana since Lawrence Keymis arrived in 1596, for many English traders, as well as Dutchmen, frequented both Port of Spain in Trinidad and San Thomé, the settlement built near the Caroni after Raleigh's departure.[55] Thanks to Raleigh's Guiana interest,

[55] See J. A. Williamson, *The English in Guiana.*

which had aroused his own enthusiasm, Prince Henry was eager to see his father send out Harcourt. Accordingly, Harcourt went with James's blessing, and, although he had no commissioned right of annexation, he took possession, in James's name, of all the land between the Amazon and Orinoco "not being actually possessed and inhabited by any Christian Prince or State."[56] The next year, James and Cecil dispatched under Roe, a friend of Raleigh's, an expedition to which Raleigh and the Earl of Southampton, Essex's old friend and now Raleigh's as well, contributed substantially. Roe, who despised the Spaniards for their insolence and their weakness, reported the area between the two great rivers to be seething with discontent between Spaniards and natives and between rival Spanish factions. Roe also stated his conviction that Manoa and El Dorado did not exist.[57]

Although Cecil's interest henceforth diminished, Raleigh still clung to the Guiana dream. He protested to Queen Anne that nothing was being done about Guiana.[58] After Cecil's death, he wrote the Council entreating them to send out an expedition of two ships under the general charge of Keymis. If Keymis failed to return with a half-ton of gold, he, Raleigh, would assume the total expenses incurred by the expedition; but if Keymis brought back the half-ton, Raleigh was to have his liberty.[59] The government turned down the proposal, probably because the war risk was great and Somerset was still strongly in favor of a pro-Spanish policy. But now with Somerset in trouble because of the Overbury murder and the King discovering, in late 1614, a new favorite in handsome young George Villiers, Raleigh began to press his case. Around Villiers and the old Spanish hater, Winwood, an anti-Spanish faction gathered that denounced Somerset and his pro-Spanish tendencies. Taking advantage of the change in the situation, Raleigh wrote a vigorous letter to Winwood, speaking again of the riches of Guiana and hoping for an opportunity to "die for the King, and not by the King. . . ."[60]

---

[56] Harcourt's account is in *Purchas*, XVI, 358-402.
[57] Roe's letter to Cecil, in PRO, *S.P. Colonial* (James I), 1/25.
[58] Edwards, *Ralegh (Letters)*, II, 334-35.
[59] *Ibid.*, 337-39.
[60] *Ibid.*, 339-41.

Raleigh saw that Winwood would need support. Why not appeal, therefore, to the new favorite? James could deny Villiers, his beloved "Steenie," nothing, and Villiers could deal no more effective blow to Somerset and the pro-Spanish faction than to secure the release of the one man whom, next to Drake, the Spaniards had dreaded above all; but whereas Drake was long dead, Raleigh was still very much alive in the Tower. There is a story, unsubstantiated but by no means unlikely, that Raleigh bribed Sir William St. John and Sir Edward Villiers, a half-brother of George, with £750 apiece to intercede with the favorite.[61] Certainly this was an infallible way of securing attention at Court. Both Winwood and George Villiers spoke with the King and on March 19, 1616 the Lieutenant of the Tower received from the Crown a warrant releasing Raleigh from his imprisonment in order to prepare for a voyage to Guiana.[62] He was still not technically free—that had to wait until January 30, 1617—nor could he go anywhere without a keeper or attend Court or any public assembly without special license. But at least he could now walk out of the Tower, nearly a free man.

Ironically enough, on March 27, barely more than a week after he left, his former lodgings received new occupants. As Sir George Carew, now Lord Carew, wrote Sir Thomas Roe, who had been appointed the first English ambassador to the Grand Mogul in India, "The Countess of Somerset hath a pardon, but she remaineth in the Tower in Sir Walter Raleigh's lodging." Originally assigned to the chamber where her victim, Overbury, had died, she pled so passionately for another lodging that the Lieutenant gave her Raleigh's. Presently Carew sent Roe another tidbit, namely, that the Somersets "lodge together, he lies in the Bloody Tower, Sir Walter Raleigh's ancient lodging, and she in Sir Walter's new building."[63] Thus the niece of Henry Howard, Earl of Northampton, Raleigh's

[61] For discussion of its validity, see Gardiner, *History of England*, II, 381 n. 1. Though the political situation was likely to find Villiers receptive to Raleigh's release, he needed strong persuasion to attempt to overcome James's conviction of thirteen years' standing. St. John was hardly so friendly to Raleigh as Gardiner implies.

[62] For warrant, see Edwards, *Ralegh* (*Life*), I, 563.

[63] For letters, see *Letters of George Lord Carew to Sir Thomas Roe, 1615-1617*, 39, 44.

deadly enemy, and her husband, to whom the King had given Sherborne and whose pro-Spanish policies had probably helped prolong Raleigh's imprisonment, had now taken his place in prison.

Had Howard lived two years longer than he did, he might have found the Tower gates opening for himself. This would have been not only for his part in the Overbury scandal[64] but also for another offense. The final damning allegation in Raleigh's trial had been Cobham's statement that Raleigh had been offered a Spanish pension. The King learned for the first time, as a result of the Overbury case, that Howard had been the recipient of such a pension for years. He discovered too, to his shock, that his greatest minister, Robert Cecil, Earl of Salisbury, had also been long in the pay of Spain, receiving an annual pension equal to the amount Raleigh was alleged to have been offered and had insisted that he refused. Perhaps, had death spared Cecil as well as Howard, the two noblemen would have shared each other's company in the Tower on the charge of treason. That indeed would have been a handsome vindication for the sick, feeble man of sixty-four—aged beyond his years—who emerged from the Tower on March 19, 1616, after little less than thirteen years of imprisonment.

[64] One of the finest accounts (unfortunately not documented) of the Overbury murder is by W. McElwee, *The Murder of Sir Thomas Overbury*.

# CHAPTER 20

# The Tragic Expedition

RALEIGH spent the first days after his release going about London like any tourist, looking at the changes that had occurred during his enforced absence.[1] Probably few recognized the tall, grey-haired man who limped along with a cane. He had recently suffered a stroke and paused frequently to rest himself. No doubt he stared with mixed feelings at Cecil's "New Exchange" near his old home at Durham House. Though forbidden the Court's precincts, he took advantage of the Court's absence at the time to ignore the prohibition and stroll around. The new Banqueting House at Whitehall probably drew his eye; how many times he had dined with the Queen in the old building torn down in 1606. Inside the Abbey, no doubt he noted the carved canopy and inscription to the two sisters who had been queens, Mary and his Elizabeth. Perhaps he also observed the tombs to two fellow-warriors, Henry Norris and Francis Vere.[2] So many of the friends and enemies of the old days were gone. Did he feel alone in this new world, this sober Jacobean merchandising world with its boorish King and his corrupt Court, of whom so many truckled to the Spaniards? As one commentator wrote regretfully, Raleigh was "the only man left alive that had helped to beat them in the year 1588."[3] Had it all been for naught, the long struggle against the ancient foe and the great days against the Armada and at Lisbon, Cadiz, and Fayal? Perhaps the old man (quite old indeed for the seventeenth century) thought with grim humor that one still "civilly dead" could rise from his grave and strike yet a final blow for England's honor, even if it was only to sneak a few hundredweight of gold from under the eyes of the insolent Dons.

The Spaniards had been represented in London for the last three years by a most unusual person, Don Diego Sarmiento

---

[1] *Chamberlain Letters*, I, 617.
[2] For detailed speculation on places seen, see Edwards, *Ralegh* (*Life*), I, 564-65.
[3] Osborne, *Traditional Memorials on the Reign of King James*, 428.

de Acuna, better known to history by the title he was to receive, Count Gondomar. There is a story that he held a grudge against Raleigh for the capture of his kinsman, Pedro Sarmiento de Gamboa, back in 1586. Though Gondomar's pedigree fails to reveal any relationship to Raleigh's prisoner,[4] one, of course, may still have existed. But an uncertain kinship aside as a cause for grievance against Raleigh, Gondomar hated Raleigh as he had hated Drake, as indeed he had hated all the great Elizabethans who had reduced the substance of his country's strength to a shadow. He had held important civil and military posts in Spain during the English offensives beginning in 1589. He knew from his own experience the dangerous possibilities in letting the dreaded "Guateral" loose on the high seas. Hence, while not ruling out the possibility of a personal resentment, one can only say that none was needed to incite the Spaniard's fear and anger; he considered territory claimed by Spain to be in grave danger.

Gondomar set himself the task of ruining Raleigh's chances of success, and he brought a formidable array of weapons to its accomplishment. Tall and lean, long-faced and black-haired, he possessed an austere, almost savage aspect that intimidated James. But this was only one side of Gondomar. He could unbend to joviality, even to clownishness and horse-play. This facet delighted James, who liked nothing better than to be amused, unless it was to be flattered—and Gondomar, a facile conversationalist, could flatter with consummate skill, playing particularly to the King's vanity about his scholarly and diplomatic ability. Gondomar professed a love of English literature, and collected English books, tapestries, and gold and silver plate. Once, when the King was short of cash, Gondomar slyly presented him with 2,000 ounces of plate; James would not have been a King or a Scot had he not appreciated both such a gift and the giver. Astute, bold, and intensely proud, the Count served his master, Philip III, with extraordinary ability and devotion.

From the very first, Gondomar established a moral superiority over James. Determined to convince the King that he repre-

---

[4] Edwards, *Ralegh* (*Life*), I, 569 n.

sented a nation once again powerful, he preferred a complaint immediately upon his arrival in London. The naval authorities had treated him somewhat less than diplomatically when his ship deliberately failed to acknowledge English supremacy by dipping its flag. So effective was his protest that James reprimanded the Governor at Plymouth and the Admiral for insisting upon an obsolete observance and for conducting themselves in an unseemly manner. This was only a sample of Gondomar's ability to impress James. The Spaniard played the game shrewdly, knowing when to speak and when to persuade by silence. He was firmly resolved to see that England broke its alliance with France, the Netherlands, and the Protestant German princes. To that end he wooed James's interest in Spain and used English ministers and the King's favorites with masterly adroitness. He was so successful that, aided by a temporary confusion in the French government, he saw James end the French alliance but two months after Raleigh's release from the Tower. Gondomar again began to talk in beguiling accents of a subject he had proposed before, a marriage between Prince Charles and the Spanish Infanta. It was an idea that, ere many months had passed, was to captivate both Charles himself and his father's favorite, Villiers. That the project eventually failed was hardly the fault of Gondomar, who wrote to James from Madrid a letter, which, allowing for some slight exaggeration, reveals his importance in the years 1613 to 1619: "That a Spaniard should have been and should still be a Councillor, not merely in your Majesty's Privy Council, but in your private Closet itself, doth not only exceed all possible merit of mine, but also exceeds all the services that I can possibly have been able to render Your Majesty."[5]

Raleigh's release alarmed Gondomar. He informed Madrid of Raleigh's hopes of finding gold, and protested to James, insisting that Guiana belonged to Spain and that Raleigh, planning to go in force, must intend to turn pirate rather than dig gold in Guiana. If only the latter, the Spaniards, said Gondomar, would willingly give him protection, let him dig in

[5] *Tanner MSS*, LXXIII, 160 (Bodleian Library, Oxford). Quoted by Edwards, *Ralegh (Life)*, I, 573. An excellent detailed analysis of Gondomar and his ascendency over James appears in Willson, *James VI and I*, 362-64.

peace, and permit him to return with what he discovered. Learning of this offer, Raleigh wisely declined it. He remembered all too well how, in the early days of Elizabeth's reign, Sir John Hawkins had accepted an invitation to trade with the Spanish West Indies and had nearly lost his squadron to Spanish treachery; more recently a British merchant named Hall had lost thirty-six of his men, whose throats were cut by the Spaniards.[6]

Gondomar continued to press James, but his success at this time was by no means complete. While the King wanted any gold Raleigh might acquire, acceptance of a Spanish escort was a tacit acknowledgment of Spain's claim to Guiana; and even the peaceful James was not disposed to go that far. It has been argued with considerable persuasiveness[7] that James may have believed Raleigh's contention that the Orinoco area was now British territory in which the Spaniards were squatters and that the King might have supported Raleigh if Raleigh was attacked by Spaniards in the course of working the mine. In short, James would have approved defensive action had the gold extracted been of sufficient quantity and value. This may well be true, for James certainly needed money. On the other hand, he listened to Gondomar and insisted that Raleigh keep the peace. In the commission that he gave Raleigh, one sealed not by the Great Seal but by the Privy Seal only, he erased the usual words to the recipient, "trusty and well-beloved" and placed him "under peril of the law."[8] Spanish lives and property lost on the expedition meant Raleigh's life.

It was a strange arrangement. James knew there were Spaniards in the territory in which the mine was located and that they were not likely to let Raleigh work without interference. Raleigh knew this too, though he may well have believed on the basis of Keymis' information that there was no permanent settlement in the immediate vicinity of the mine. It was reported that while he was conversing with several lords one day, one of them expressed doubt that Raleigh would be "prizing" if he could do it "handsomely." "Yea," Raleigh replied, "if I can light right on the Plate Fleet you will think I were mad if I

---

[6] For Raleigh's point of view, see *Works*, VIII, 499-500, 501.
[7] V. T. Harlow, *Raleigh's Last Voyage*, 25-26, 35-44.
[8] For commission, see T. Rymer, *Foedera*, XVI, 789.

should refuse it." To this, Francis Bacon rejoined, "Why, then you will be a pirate." "Tush, my Lord," said Raleigh, "did you ever hear of any that was counted a pirate for taking millions?"[9] This was the old Elizabethan buccaneer jesting in terms of an age long past. It was incautious jesting too since Bacon was an opponent of the anti-Spanish Winwood. Still, money seems to have a way of talking if there is enough of it, and the Plate Fleet in 1618 brought to Spain a golden harvest valued at £2,545,454. Had Raleigh brought back to England a reasonable fraction of that amount, it is doubtful that James would have tried him for piracy. Besides, he would have had the support of the anti-Spanish faction of the Privy Council, men like Winwood, George Carew, and the Archbishop of Canterbury, who preferred war to the prospect of a Spanish marriage alliance.

Though Raleigh gambled with fate all his life, it is doubtful if ever a gamble for such stakes had less chance of success. Not only was he expressly forbidden to become involved in hostilities with the Spaniards; the King also promised Gondomar that if Raleigh attacked or plundered Spanish subjects, he would be turned over to the Spanish authorities to be hanged in Madrid. Furthermore, the King required of Raleigh a complete record of his ships and the number and caliber of their guns, the ports at which he proposed to stop, and the estimated dates of his arrival. This information the King passed on to Gondomar, who forwarded it to Spain. Though Raleigh knew of James's action, he kept up his courage. As Carew wrote Roe in India, "The alarm of his journey is flown into Spain, and, as he tells me, sea forces are prepared to lie for him, but he is nothing appalled with the report, for he will be a good fleet and well manned."[10] To add to his troubles, James refused to issue him a pardon, so that, although in charge of his fleet with power of life and death over men of his command, he still sailed with the sentence of death hanging over him. The old story that Bacon assured him that his commission was in itself a sufficient pardon sounds unlikely, coming from a great legal mind like the Lord Chancellor's unless Bacon meant to deceive him, which was at least a possibility, though an unlikely

[9] J. Spedding, *The Life and Times of Francis Bacon*, II, 291.
[10] *Letters of George Lord Carew*, 71.

one.[11] His friends, moreover, the Earls of Arundel and Pembroke, had to stand as sureties for his return, and Raleigh promised that, whatever happened, he would come back to England. What seems increasingly evident is that, aided by Gondomar, James deliberately helped Raleigh involve himself in a situation in which the odds were overwhelmingly against his escaping without hostilities; and if hostilities occurred and he survived them, he would be executed for breach of his commission. The only way out of the trap was for him to bring back enough gold, a most unlikely circumstance.

For a time Raleigh's destination puzzled Continental contemporaries, and both Savoy and Venice made overtures to him for his services. Savoy, Spain's satellite now turned friendly, was particularly eager to get him to sail with his squadron, accompanied by ships of the Royal Navy and Huguenot and Dutch ships, to Genoa, a pro-Spanish city, and compel its submission. The Savoyard ambassador, Scarnafissi, was the first to broach the subject—not Raleigh—in conversations with Winwood as an anti-Spanish alliance that might be joined by Venice; and indeed the "Queen of the Adriatic" was deeply interested in the redoubtable "Sir Vate Ralo."[12] James knew of the project and let Scarnafissi talk to Raleigh. He was weary of the Spaniards' delay in the marriage alliance, and if they realized that powers hostile to Spain were dickering for the use of Raleigh, they might hasten to give a definite answer. If the answer was favorable, he could always stop Raleigh from going to the Mediterranean and let him sail for Guiana, where, thanks to Gondomar's information, the Spaniards would be already prepared for him.[13] That Raleigh himself would have been willing to strike at Genoa is probable; it would be another solid blow at the Spain he hated.

Not only Savoy and Venice but France as well was interested in what Raleigh was planning. Dreading a possible attack upon his country's coast in alliance with the Huguenots, the French ambassador, des Marets, went on March 15, 1617 to Raleigh's

[11] Jardine, *Criminal Trials*, II, 518-19.
[12] *Cal. S.P. Venetian, 1615-1617*, 210, 413-17; Edwards, *Ralegh (Life)*, I, 575-79.
[13] For James's policy, see Harlow, *Raleigh's Last Voyage*, 27-29; Gardiner, *History of England*, III, 48-53.

flagship, the *Destiny*, which was fitting out in the Thames. This visit was made, moreover, with the knowledge of the English government. Des Marets had heard that Raleigh was indignant about Sherborne, which had recently been given to the former ambassador to Spain, Sir John Digby. Though des Marets expressed sympathy for him because of his imprisonment and loss of property, Raleigh was polite but cautious. The Frenchman, however, discovered no such design on the French coast as he and the great French minister, Richelieu, had feared. The latter was greatly relieved, of course, but although his opinion of Raleigh was divided ("a great sailor and a bad captain"), he wondered if some use could not be made of him. In a subsequent conversation with Raleigh, des Marets thought he discerned such a dissatisfaction with the Stuart government that Raleigh could be persuaded to enter French service.[14] How true this last was at the time is a matter of some doubt. Certainly for the present, Raleigh did not accept the French commission offered by Admiral de Montmorency permitting him to send prizes into French ports. But he was very willing—again with the knowledge of his government—to associate the French with the Guiana project since this was a way out of a difficult situation. Had he been able to obtain the assistance of the French, he might have succeeded in having them displace the Spaniards at San Thomé and thus would have reached the mine without a clash between the English forces and the Spaniards. As one scholar of the expedition has pointed out: if, under those circumstances, Raleigh had brought home his gold, all would have been well. If he had returned with gold over the bodies of dead Spaniards, he could have run into a French port and safely awaited a development of James's intentions. But to have arrived in France without gold and at the cost of hostilities would have meant permanent exile from England, while to have returned to England was to have hazarded his life.[15]

Meanwhile, the Genoa project having been abandoned, sailing time approached for the voyage to Guiana. The Venetian

[14] Des Marets's report is quoted in part by Edwards, *Ralegh* (*Life*), I, 595-96; see also *ibid.*, I, 591-97.

[15] Harlow, *Raleigh's Last Voyage*, 29-30; PRO, *S.P. Dom.* (James I), 103/16.

ambassador wrote home that the Council had informed the Savoyard ambassador of the King's intention not to entrust Raleigh with the Genoa command since he was determined to send the Admiral to the Indies. But the Venetian added that the chief reason James was unwilling to use Raleigh at Genoa "may possibly be his disinclination to meddle with an affair which may so greatly offend the Spaniards, as even if the attempt succeeded he would never trust him to give him his rightful share of the gain."[16] This is a fairly accurate estimate of James: fearful and greedy. Still, the King had reason for not wishing to alarm the Spaniards. The Spanish government had informed Gondomar of Philip III's intention of going ahead with the treaty; and now James talked of sending Digby to Madrid to discuss the treaty terms.[17]

Sick at heart that his country was falling into the Spanish embrace and eager to be off, Raleigh hastened his preparations. His expedition cost an enormous sum of money, and to the last moment he was busy trying to pay for it. The entire joint stock amounted to nearly £30,000. Many of the gentlemen volunteers put up £50 apiece. A number of people invested more substantial amounts, including the Earl of Huntingdon, Bess Raleigh's relative, and the Earl of Arundel, Raleigh's friend. From the Sherborne money Raleigh called in £3,000 of the £5,000 loaned to the Countess of Bedford. He sold almost all the personal property he possessed to raise the necessary funds. Bess sold the handsome estate of Mitcham in Surrey to Thomas Plumer, member of Parliament for Hertfordshire, for £2,500. The Crown also contributed £175 in tonnage money for the usual encouragement of shipbuilding.[18]

For his great expense Raleigh had an expedition more impressive in number of ships than in their quality or that of their crews. He had in the Thames seven ships, of which the brand-new *Destiny*, his flagship, was largest at 440 tons with 36 guns and the *Page* was smallest at 25 tons with 3 guns. When he reached Plymouth, several other small craft were to join him. He had 431 men in the Thames squadron, most of them of

[16] *Cal. S.P. Venetian*, *1615-1617*, 434.
[17] Gardiner, *History of England*, III, 53, 58-61.
[18] For financial arrangements, see *Works*, VIII, 481; Edwards, *Ralegh (Life)*, I, 566-67; II, 372; *Notes and Queries*, 2nd ser., IX, 331-32, 1st ser., XI, 262.

wretched quality. Many of the gentlemen volunteers were hardly better, drunkards and wastrels lured by adventure and the chance of gain. Fortunately there were a few who were more reliable, men like Sir Warham St. Leger, whose father Raleigh had known in Ireland; George Raleigh, his nephew; William Herbert, one of his innumerable cousins and a relative as well of Lord Pembroke; Captain North, brother of Lord North; and Edward Hastings, the Earl of Huntingdon's brother.

Captain of Raleigh's own flagship was young Walter Raleigh, about twenty-two years old. Walter, called "Wat" by his father, had been a reckless, impulsive youngster whose conduct had often worried Raleigh. Once during a dinner in the Tower at which the Raleighs were the guests of another distinguished prisoner, the Earl of Northumberland, Wat, greatly daring and acting contrary to his father's explicit instructions, interrupted the conversation to mention a quarrel he had had that morning with Raleigh. At this, Raleigh slapped his son across the mouth. Though Wat dared not hit back at his father, he slapped the face of the man next to himself and exclaimed, "Box about: 'twill come to my father anon."[19] His Oxford career was given more to having a good time than to studying, though he attained considerable fluency in Latin, some knowledge of philosophy, and skill with the lute. In 1613 Raleigh sent him to France and engaged as tutor Ben Jonson, like himself a man of the Renaissance and one who had helped him with the *History of the World*.

If Jonson was expected to use a firm hand with Wat, he was a poor choice. A lover of wine and good fellowship, Jonson succumbed one day in Paris, as Wat slyly kept his glass brimming with Canary. When Ben finally drooped into unconsciousness, Wat stretched the burly playwright on a cart and hired men to haul the vehicle, while he followed "through the streets, at every corner showing his governor stretched out, and telling them that was a more lively crucifix than any they had." This performance had its hazards in the midst of a Catholic population, but evidently it amused the French.

[19] Aubrey, *Brief Lives*, II, 185.

Though Bess Raleigh smiled when she heard what happened, remarking that Wat's behavior was so like that of his father when he was young, Raleigh deplored the incident. The only consolation was that Wat did not relish drunkenness himself; though no teetotaler, Raleigh hated drunkenness.[20]

Two years later, Wat again visited the Continent. This time, he left England in a hurry since he had wounded a friend of the Lord Treasurer, the Earl of Suffolk, in a duel.[21] From his service on this occasion with Prince Maurice in the Netherlands, he returned eager to assist his father to prepare the expedition to Guiana. Though more mature, he still manifested the same qualities of courage and rashness that had impelled Raleigh to indite to him, when a child, one of the strangest poems ever written by a father for a son.[22] Raleigh, however, dearly loved his impulsive son despite his awareness of Wat's deficiencies.

The *Destiny* left the Thames on March 26, 1617 and on the 29th Raleigh rode to Dover to join her. Gondomar had opposed his leaving up to the very day before, but the Privy Council overruled the ambassador and let the old warrior sail. Interestingly enough, but a few days before Raleigh left London on this tragic expedition, the lovely "Virginian woman," reigning sensation of London for weeks, died. Brought to England as wife of John Rolfe and introduced at Court by Captain John Smith, Pocahontas succumbed to overstrain, illness, and unhappiness after James ordered her back to Virginia against her will. It is doubtful if she and the man who had done so much

[20] M. Chute, *Ben Jonson of Westminster*, 198-204, for Continental tour.

[21] *Letters of George Lord Carew*, 10; L. P. Smith, *Life and Letters of Sir Henry Wotton*, II, 79.

[22] "Sir Walter Raleigh to His Son":

Three things there be that prosper up apace
And flourish, whilst they grow asunder far,
But on a day, they meet all in one place,
And when they meet, they one another mar;
And they be these, the wood, the weed, the wag.
The wood is that, which makes the Gallow tree,
The weed is that, which strings the Hangman's bag,
The wag, my pretty knave, betokeneth thee.
Mark well, dear boy, whilst these assemble not,
Green springs the tree, hemp grows, the wag is wild,
But when they meet, it makes the timber rot,
It frets the halter, and it chokes the child.
    Then bless thee, and beware, and let us pray,
    We part not with thee at this meeting day.

to interest England in the wonderful country in which she was born ever met since Raleigh was denied access to the Court and to public places where she created such a stir.

From the very start, trouble hounded the expedition. One ship, the *Star*, was detained at the Isle of Wight while its Captain, John Pennington, hurried back to London to raise money from Bess Raleigh for bread. Another, the *Husband*, under Captain John Bailey, incurred a similar experience. Waiting at Plymouth for these two laggards, Raleigh was joined by seven more craft, four of them commanded by Sir John Ferne, Captains Richard Wollaston and John Chudleigh, and his faithful friend, Lawrence Keymis, the former Balliol scholar-explorer. For another of his captains, Thomas Whitney, Raleigh had to sell a great deal of his plate to raise funds, while he finally succeeded in coming up with £300 for the needy Ferne.

While all this was going on, Raleigh published on May 3 his famous orders to his fleet. To a certain extent they resembled those Medina-Sidonia issued to the Armada captains before the galleons sailed on their ill-fated voyage. Like the grandee's, Raleigh's orders were highly moral and severe. Divine service was to be held twice a day, before dinner and before supper. Swearing, stealing, and gambling were prohibited. Proper battle discipline was defined, and prompt obedience to orders demanded. With his own experience in the tropics in mind, Raleigh forbade the men to eat fruit avoided by birds or beasts or to touch new flesh that had not been salted for several hours. He enjoined them, for fear of alligators and crocodiles, to swim only where the Indians swam. He insisted that they show every courtesy to the Indians, and tersely declared that "no man shall force any woman, be she Christian or heathen, upon pain of death." Even the critical King could not have objected too strenuously to these orders, though he would probably have raised an impatient question or two on Raleigh's allusions to "the enemy" and to the section dealing with battle discipline when this was presumed to be a peaceful expedition.[23]

After long delays Raleigh sailed on June 12. Almost at once contrary winds threw him back into Plymouth. Again he tried, and back the winds blew him to Falmouth. A third time he

[23] See *Works*, VIII, 682-88, for orders to the commanders.

ventured forth, and a gale caught him off the Scilly Islands, sinking a pinnace. Raleigh now took refuge in the harbor of Cork to rest and refit. Old friends and old enemies, including Lord Barry and Lord Roche, received him hospitably, as did Richard Boyle, now Lord Boyle, who had bought Lismore and was making the estate marvelously productive. Though Raleigh enjoyed himself, he became increasingly impatient as the winds kept him land-bound from June 25 on. He was practically out of money, his crews were growing restless, and the best part of the season was fast passing. Well aware of the mounting hazards of his voyage, Raleigh told Boyle he had no choice but "perish or prosper";[24] and the chances of his prospering diminished with the passing of every summer day in inaction.

Finally, however, the weather turned favorable, and Raleigh sailed into blue water on August 19. Off Cape St. Vincent, on the 30th, he caught up with four French ships carrying fish oil. Actually Captain Bailey captured them and seized a net, a pinnace, and several pipes of oil. Bailey wanted to keep the ships as prizes since they had seized property from the Spaniards in the West Indies. Raleigh refused, insisting that he had no authority to take French subjects and that Frenchmen had as much right as Englishmen to plunder the Dons beyond the line running south of the Canaries and west of the Azores. Bailey was angered by the decision and liked no better Raleigh's action in paying the French for what he needed.

On September 7 Raleigh anchored off Lancerota in the Canary Islands. What he wanted was water and provisions, but the islanders, who had been ravaged by Barbary pirates, considered him just another Turk. Though the Governor promised to make supplies and water available, none were forthcoming. When Raleigh landed men, the Spaniards killed three of them. Though their comrades roared for a chance to retaliate, Raleigh held them tightly in hand. Not only was he reluctant to violate his instructions but he knew that, if he revenged the attack, the master of an English merchant ship in the harbor, having unloaded his cargo, would be ruined.[25]

With Raleigh leaving to hunt a more hospitable haven,

---

[24] Stebbing, *Ralegh*, 312.
[25] *Works*, VIII, 484.

Captain Bailey deserted for England, where, on arriving, he declared Raleigh to be a pirate. In reality, he was aggrieved at Raleigh's refusal to let him become a pirate himself and confiscate the French ships. There was such a celerity in both London and Madrid to enlarge on his report that some have thought he was one of Gondomar's paid agents, but there is no evidence of this.[26] Sir Thomas Lake, a Privy Councillor, called on the Spanish ambassador to convey the King's regrets and those of "all good people" at the incident. Gondomar himself entreated Philip III to send the fleet to punish Raleigh and bring him to Seville, where he should be executed in the Plaza as a necessary step for the preservation of the peace with England, France, and Holland.[27]

Despite the attitude of Councillors Lake and Digby, the Council as a whole was less easily taken in by Bailey,[28] but many in places high and low had a field day of the "I told you so" variety. Carew wrote Roe in India that he thought Bailey would eventually be "sorry and ashamed both of his return and for the scandal which his report hath cast upon his general; in the meantime there is a doubtful opinion held of Sir Walter, and those that malice him boldly affirm him to be a pirate, which, for my part, I will never believe."[29] Notwithstanding the loyalty of Councillors Carew and Winwood, a more powerful opinion than either of theirs was working against Raleigh. Lake wrote Gondomar on October 21 that Sir Thomas Erskine, now Viscount Fenton and Raleigh's successor as Captain of the Guard, had sent him a letter stating that "His Majesty is very disposed and determined against Raleigh, and will join the King of Spain in ruining him, but he wishes this resolution to be kept secret for some little while, in order that, in the interim, he may keep an eye on the disposition of some of the people here."[30]

While clouds of hatred and vengeance were gathering in England—clouds dissipated slightly when the captain of the

---

[26] Harlow, *Raleigh's Last Voyage*, 54.

[27] Correspondence in Hume, *Ralegh*, 228-32.

[28] Bailey's hearing before the Council is printed in *Acts of the Privy Council*, *1618-1619*, 7-8; S. R. Gardiner, "Documents Relating to Sir Walter Raleigh's Last Voyage," in *Camden Miscellany*, v, 7-13; Harlow, *Raleigh's Last Voyage*, 155-57.

[29] *Letters of George Lord Carew*, 129.

[30] Printed by Harlow, *Raleigh's Last Voyage*, 155; Hume, *Ralegh*, 232.

English merchantman in Lancerota returned to embarrass King, Councillors, and particularly Bailey with a true account of Raleigh's behavior[31]—Raleigh put into Gomera in the Canaries. Although an interchange of shots at first occurred, no one was hurt, and Raleigh's plea for water was eventually granted. It helped, of course, that the Governor's lady was half-English (her mother a born Stafford), that Raleigh sent her a gift of a half-dozen pairs of gloves, and that he held his men in rigid discipline. In return, she sent him baskets of oranges, lemons, pomegranates, and figs for himself and the ill men aboard his ships. This was a bounty, said Raleigh, "better welcome to me than 1,000 crowns would have been."[32] Gallantly he countered with gifts that included amber, ambergris, rosewater, and a picture of Mary Magdalene. Utterly captivated, the Governor's lady again responded with fruit, hens, and white bread, while, before the fleet sailed, the Governor gave Raleigh a letter to Gondomar testifying to his "noble" behavior. This was by all odds the pleasantest incident in a voyage that rapidly became a nightmare of misfortune.

The sickness that had laid hold of Raleigh's fleet let up during the stay in the Canaries but on September 24, with the ships bound west for Guiana, it descended with violence. By nightfall the *Destiny* alone counted fifty men on its sick list. While men suffered and died of the raging fever, a hurricane off the Cape Verde Islands battered the wallowing, half-manned ships, one going to the bottom. Following the winds and torrents of rain came one of those stifling, blistering calms that made life aboard sailing ships in those latitudes a torrid torment. As the hot weather seemed to favor the strange affliction, corpses were thrown overboard daily now from all vessels. The month of October was one long agony. Raleigh himself came down with fever, spending twenty-eight days in his cabin and living on the Canary Islands fruit, without which he would have died. By the time the fleet dropped anchor off the mouth of the Caliana (now the Cayenne) River in Guiana, he had lost forty-

[31] *Acts of the Privy Council, Colonial Ser.*, *1613-1680*, 16, 26.
[32] Raleigh's Journal, in *Cotton MSS*, Titus B, VIII. It is printed in Schomburgk's edition of Raleigh's *Discoverie of Guiana*.

two men on the *Destiny* alone and scores on the other vessels.[33]

That same day on which the anchors splashed into the river mud, November 14, Raleigh picked up a quill in his feeble fingers and wrote Bess of his losses. These included his general, the latter's second-in-command, his surgeon, his master refiner, his provost marshal, the Governor of the Bermudas, and a beloved servant, John Talbot, who had served him faithfully through the long Tower years: "Sweet Heart, I can yet write unto you but with a weak hand, for I have suffered the most violent calenture, for fifteen days, that ever man did, and lived: but God that gave me a strong heart in all my adversities, hath also now strengthened it in the hell-fire of heat." Weakened as his force now was, Raleigh still felt it was strong enough for the task he had undertaken "if the diligent care at London to make our strength known to the Spanish king by his ambassador have not taught the Spanish king to fortify all the entrances against us. Howsoever, we must make the adventure. . . ." There were but two saving graces in the present situation. One was that their beloved Wat never enjoyed better health. The other was that the Indians who had come out to him remembered him from 1595 and were eager to obey him: "my name hath still lived among them," he said gratefully.[34]

Raleigh sent news of his arrival to England by one of his ailing captains, Peter Alley. With Alley went an anonymous account entitled, "Newes of Sir Walter Rauleigh from the River of Caliana." Composed by one of the gentlemen adventurers, it sang the praises of Guiana. Unfortunately it was not published until long after Alley reached Portsmouth in February 1618, and thus could not counteract the effect produced by that worthy. For, like a Jeremiah, Alley bemoaned the misfortunes and discontent of the expedition. Naturally Gondomar was greatly encouraged by what Alley had to report, while Raleigh's friends were correspondingly cast down.

Meanwhile Raleigh prepared for the expedition up the Orinoco. First, the ships had to be reconditioned after the long, rough voyage, and the men restored to health. Gravely weak-

[33] Account of the voyage is in his Journal, and in a letter to his wife, in Edwards, *Ralegh (Letters)*, II, 347-49.
[34] *Ibid.*

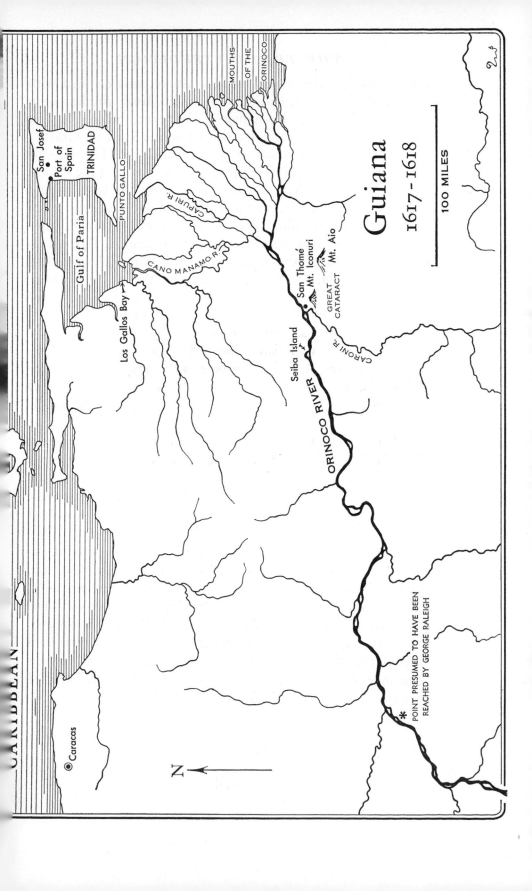

CARIBBEAN

San Josef
Port of Spain
TRINIDAD

PUNTO GALLO

Gulf of Paria

CANO MANAMO R.

CAPURI R.

MOUTHS
OF THE
ORINOCO

Los Gallos Bay

Caracas

N

Seiba Island

San Thomé
Mt. Iconuri
GREAT
CATARACT
Mt. Aio

CARONI R.

ORINOCO RIVER

Guiana
1617–1618

100 MILES

*
POINT PRESUMED TO HAVE BEEN
REACHED BY GEORGE RALEIGH

ened himself, Raleigh was brought ashore, where, plied with game and pineapples, and sleeping in the fresh air, he began to recover.[35] It was December 4, however, before he left Cayenne for the Triangle Islands (now the Isles of Health) and got down to the actual work of organization. He was still too ill to lead the expedition up-river in person, and the sickening frustration may have been responsible for the fever's again closing down upon him. St. Leger, who should have then taken the leadership, was also very ill. The overall command thus devolved upon Lawrence Keymis, with George Raleigh in direct command of the land forces and Wat Raleigh going along as a captain. The five vessels drawing the least water were then chosen and an expeditionary force of 250 soldiers and 150 sailors was formed for the dash to the mine.

As if for the first time, the men awoke to the urgency of action. There were Indian rumors of a hostile fleet gathering to trap them in the Orinoco mouth while they were up-river looking for gold. Everyone knew, moreover, that Spain had been given complete data on the expedition. Ironically, as has been established by recent research,[36] the Spanish settlement of San Thomé near the mine was not reinforced until six weeks after Raleigh had left Guiana, and then from colonial sources, not from Spain itself. But fear of Spanish vengeance haunted the expedition. The great obstacle to its despatch was the possibility of entrapment. Even had Raleigh not been too ill to lead the expedition, he might have had to remain at the river's mouth. Grumble at him and his discipline though they did, his men trusted him to protect them. Nor would he let them down. As he told Keymis, ". . . you shall find me at Puncto Gallo, dead or alive; and if you find not my ships there, yet you shall find their ashes; for I will fire with the galleons if it come to extremity, but run away I will never."[37] None knew better than Keymis that the lame, fever-worn veteran, active now when most men of his age were sitting by their hearths dreaming of yesteryear, would stand by his men to the last.

[35] Journal, Nov. 17, 1617.
[36] A. Latham, "Sir Walter Raleigh's Gold Mine," in *Essays and Studies*, New Ser., IV (1951), 98-99; Harlow, *Raleigh's Last Voyage*, 325.
[37] *Works*, VIII, 490.

Assured of Raleigh's protection to his rear, Keymis departed on December 10 with a month's store of food and detailed instructions. He was "to suffer the captains and companies of the English to pass up to the westwards of the mountain Aio, from whence you have no less than three miles to the mine; and to lodge and encamp between the Spanish town and you, if there be any town near it; that being so secured, you may make trial what depth and breadth the mine holds, and whether or not it answers our hopes." If the mine proved not so rich as to be worth holding, Keymis was to bring back but a basket or two of ore to satisfy the King that Raleigh's design was not imaginary, "though not answerable to His Majesty's expectation." Raleigh also warned Keymis to be well advised how he landed, particularly if the enemy appeared to be reinforced, "for I know (a few gentlemen excepted) what a scum of men you have; and I would not for all the world receive a blow from the Spaniards to the dishonour of our nation."[38] Raleigh's "scum of men" sounds a little like Wellington's appraisal of the British enlisted men, but of the two disparaging remarks, Raleigh's was the truer.

While Keymis took the expedition on its search for gold, Raleigh sailed for Puncto Gallo (now Point Hicacos), southwest of Trinidad. Back and forth he cruised off the coast of Trinidad, keeping watch by sea for the expected Spanish fleet. His attempts to trade with the Spaniards were met by a hail of shots from which he suffered two casualties. Thereafter he ignored the Spaniards and the sniping they indulged in as he went about boiling pitch from the great pitch lake and collecting balsams and other plants with medicinal properties. His mind was less on these activities and his cruising than on the expedition. His Journal reveals the anxiety he felt; his son's life was in danger and his own reputation and life were at stake. The first news he had was a jungle rumor from an Indian that the English had occupied San Thomé. This did not sound promising, and Raleigh lived in the throbbing heart of suspense until February 13, 1618, when a letter from Keymis, dated January 7, arrived. As Raleigh read, his fine hopes and buoyancy collapsed, heartbreak and near-despair possessed him, and the

[38] *Ibid.*, 489-90.

Journal came to an abrupt end on that day. For Keymis reported that a clash with the Spaniards had occurred, San Thomé was occupied, and Wat Raleigh had been killed in action.

The story of the expedition has been told many times over in biographies and special studies, but new information is constantly being revealed. The most complete recent study is *Raleigh's Last Voyage* by Vincent T. Harlow, who, in 1932, brought together the more important relevant documents. In addition to this study, Miss Agnes Latham has contributed an excellent article as recently as 1951 based on some newly discovered correspondence. Very likely further materials will turn up, but it is doubtful if they will appreciably alter the account of the expedition as given by Mr. Harlow and Miss Latham. There is no intention of relating here in detail the unhappy adventures of that fateful expedition, but a general account is desirable that one may perceive the dreadful irony in the Raleighan drama that was about to rise to its extraordinary climax.

What has invariably complicated any clear understanding of the expedition is that Raleigh and Keymis were thinking of two mines. When Raleigh was in Guiana in 1595, he discovered on the ground certain auriferous stones in the vicinity of Mount Iconuri, one form in which gold has since been found in Guiana. After San Thomé was settled by the Spaniards only a few miles from the Iconuri "mine," Raleigh and Keymis began to build their hopes on a mine twenty miles down-stream and inland near Mount Aio. Neither had seen this second mine, but Raleigh knew of the mountain and the Indian guide Putijma had told Keymis in 1595 that a rich mine existed there; another guide repeated the same in 1596. Still, for Raleigh to speak of two mines would have made his claim seem hopelessly absurd to a skeptical monarch. He therefore alluded to only one mine, and there seems little doubt that he had in mind the Mount Aio mine. A Raleigh-James partnership in relation to this mine was possible since, theoretically, it was far enough away from San Thomé for Raleigh's force not to become embroiled with the Spaniards.

The tragedy of Raleigh's absence became manifest as the expedition moved up-river. The English had ample evidence of unrest among the Indians at Spanish rule. Furthermore, as

Roe had pointed out, seven years earlier, the Spaniards were by no means united, and Raleigh and Keymis could not have helped knowing that there was a strong trading faction in San Thomé friendly to the English and opposed to the rule of the authorities.[39] Though Raleigh's old antagonist, Berrio, was dead, his son, as Governor-General of New Grenada, had authority over Guiana and Trinidad, while, only recently, Diego Palomeque de Acuna, for whom the claim has been made that he was one of Gondomar's many cousins, had been appointed administrator of these provinces. Palomeque had received from Madrid a copy of the list of ships with their destination that James had requested of Raleigh and had given to Gondomar. Palomeque was determined to prevent any trading with the English and to make it impossible for Raleigh to achieve his purpose. Evidently Keymis became aware very early from Indian reports that a number of the Spaniards were willing to betray the unpopular Palomeque and open San Thomé. He seems to have balanced this likelihood of defection against the hazards of marching miles inland to the hypothetical Mount Aio mine with an enemy already alerted to his presence and numbers, and possibly harassing him with occasional sniping. Raleigh might have tried the Mount Aio mine in any event and, if his search proved fruitless, have then gone on to San Thomé. Keymis decided differently. He knew personally of the auriferous stones near Iconuri, while part of San Thomé was obviously ready to welcome him. He therefore ignored Raleigh's order, put his men ashore on January 2, 1618, but a few miles below San Thomé, and sent three of his ships through the channels to anchor opposite the town, where the Spaniards fired on them about nine o'clock in the evening.[40]

Though the ships did not reply, the English ashore probably wondered whether they should take San Thomé or slip by it if they could do so without fighting. Greatly superior to the Spaniards in the town, they could have kept them at bay with part of their forces and sent the rest to the mine. It is also possible that, owing to their divisions of opinion, the Spaniards might

[39] Harlow, *Raleigh's Last Voyage*, 70-76.
[40] Thompson, *Ralegh*, 318-22, contains an excellent analysis of the situation, particularly of Keymis' actions.

have surrendered the town without a direct assault had the English kept a proper distance and allowed the faction friendly to them sufficient time to take over. As it was, they were close enough to be considered menacing, and the Governor directed one of his captains, Geronimo de Grados, to lay an ambush. In his *Apology*, written after his return to England, Raleigh said that the English did not realize how close they were to the town and intended to rest for the night, presumably before hunting for the mine on the morrow.[41] The Spanish friar, Pedro Simon, who wrote about the Spanish side of the encounter a few years later, insisted that the English were planning to attack the town.[42] In reality, it was difficult, though not impossible, to proceed to where the mine supposedly lay except through the town; aware of this, a dozen Spanish regulars made a surprise attack upon the English about one o'clock in the morning.

At the wild yells of *"Perros Ingleses!"* (English dogs), the English became terrified. Momentarily, because of the panic, there was danger of their being routed by the handful of Spaniards. Then the officers succeeded in rallying the men, Wat Raleigh being particularly effective. Wat led a counterattack at the head of a company of pikemen, while the Spaniards fell back upon their main force under Palomeque. The English pursued until they were at the edge of the town before realizing it. Sight of Palomeque and his regulars brought them to a halt, but only for a moment. Springing forward with "unadvised daringness," as an unfriendly English critic, Captain Parker, remarked,[43] Wat cried out, according to the *Declaration* that King James caused Francis Bacon to issue in their review of Raleigh's case, "Come on, my hearts! This is the mine you must expect! they that look for any other are fools!"[44] There seems little reason to doubt that Wat uttered such words; he was rash and impetuous, and evidently could see no point in trying to avoid further hostilities now that the fighting had actually broken out. Dashing ahead of his company, sword in hand, he threw himself at the Spaniards. Almost at once a ball pierced his body, and, as he fell, a musket butt crashed

[41] *Works*, VIII, 490-91.
[42] Harlow, *Raleigh's Last Voyage*, 164-66.
[43] *Ibid.*, 231.   [44] *Ibid.*, 344.

against his skull. Though fatally wounded, he called out to his countrymen, "Go on! The Lord have mercy upon me, and prosper your enterprise."

Keymis plunged on and took the town. Though the Spaniards managed to evacuate the inhabitants to the strong island of Seiba, where the Caroni joins the Orinoco, they had lost five officers, including Palomeque, who may have been killed by a Spaniard. The English had also lost four officer casualties, in addition to Wat, whom they buried before the high altar of the church in a lavish ceremony of mourning. Not until January 7, however, did Keymis summon up enough nerve to write to Raleigh the dreadful news of Wat's death in the disastrous attack on San Thomé.[45]

Keymis had much to account for: the forbidden attack on San Thomé and Wat's death. He could not have helped knowing the grief and ruin that awaited Raleigh. In his desperation, he sought for a plausible explanation and came up with a tale that San Thomé had been moved twenty miles down-stream so that, in attempting to locate the Iconuri mine, he had stumbled upon the town and had become involved with the Spaniards through sheer accident. Raleigh believed the tale in defending himself, and in the *Declaration* the Crown later jested how conveniently San Thomé seemed to move twenty miles back and forth; Raleigh was obviously a liar.[46] In reality, the liar was the well-meaning but incompetent leader, Keymis, who, in letters of January 24 and February 9,[47] mentioned the change of site, and may have done so in his original of January 7,[48] of which only a fragment survives in Raleigh's *Apology*. Recent research, first by Mr. Harlow and latterly by Miss Latham, has pretty well confirmed the Spanish friar, Simon, in his contention that the town had not been reestablished twenty miles down-stream.

The town now in his hands, Keymis hardly made what could be called an attempt to find a mine. He left a garrison in San

---

[45] For a Spanish account of the battle, see Simon's version in *ibid.*, 166-70; for Raleigh's account, see *Works*, VIII, 490-92, 505.

[46] *Works*, VIII, 490-91; Raleigh to the King, Sept. 24, 1618. Harlow, *Raleigh's Last Voyage*, 277; *Declaration*, in *ibid.*, 344. San Thomé had four sites in the course of its history but did not move from its original site until 1647. *Ibid.*, 357-67.

[47] Latham, in *Essays and Studies* (1951), 106-11.

[48] Keymis mentions the 7th, Raleigh the 8th.

Thomé and sailed up-river. As he passed the island of Seiba, the small guard protecting the refugees of San Thomé fired on him. Keymis gave Raleigh to understand that the fire came from the mainland and that the Spaniards were guarding the mine in too great strength for him to force it. Raging, Raleigh wrote Winwood, when he learned of Keymis' troubles, "I told him that, seeing my son was lost, I cared not if he had lost an hundred more in opening the mine. . . ."[49] But Keymis had no intention of looking seriously for a mine that in reality he had never seen. Instead, he and George Raleigh went on what amounted to an exploring expedition up-stream, perhaps 200 miles from San Thomé, though the Spaniards said 300, Chaplain Jones 180, and Keymis 120.[50] When the force returned, considerably reduced by sniping from both Spaniards and Indians, they found San Thomé burned to the ground by the terrified English garrison. Shortly after leaving the town for good, Keymis mentioned to his lieutenants another way to the Mount Iconuri mine, but they treated him with scorn. They were persuaded that the mine was a fiction; "it could not be," as Miss Latham observes, "at once three hundred miles above San Thomé and twenty miles below it."[51] Almost in panic the weary, disgusted survivors of the expeditionary force—150 out of 400 men—fled to the sea, reaching the fleet on March 2.

The interview between Raleigh and Keymis was painful for both. Naturally Raleigh wanted to hear everything possible about his son's death. Naturally, too, he demanded a complete report on the search for the mine. The explanation that Keymis gave for not finding the mine was incredible to him. Not only did Keymis speak of the thick woods, the hills, and the Spaniards as obstacles; he said also that his fear of Raleigh's death from illness or grief convinced him that it would be a greater error to find the mine and thereby reveal its location to the Spaniards than to excuse himself to his own men for not finding it![52] Coldly furious, Raleigh reproached Keymis for disobedience, and expressed the hope that he might satisfy the King with his excuses

[49] Edwards, *Ralegh* (*Letters*), II, 356.
[50] Harlow, *Raleigh's Last Voyage*, 207, 235.
[51] Latham, in *Essays and Studies* (1951), 104.
[52] *Works*, VIII, 493-94.

better than he could his own Admiral. Keymis went to his cabin, depressed and conscience-stricken.

Several days later Keymis came back to Raleigh with a letter to the Earl of Arundel, in which he again used the same arguments and excuses. He also asked Raleigh at this time to accept his apology. But Raleigh's grief made him harsh; it is understandable but regrettable, since Keymis, for all his faults, was a worthy man. "You have undone me by your obstinacy," Raleigh said, "and I will not favour or colour in any sort your former folly." When Keymis asked if that was indeed his resolution and Raleigh told him it was, Keymis replied, "I know then, sir, what course to take."

Shortly afterward Raleigh heard a pistol shot. Instantly he sent men to inquire who was responsible for it. Keymis replied from his cabin that he was cleaning his weapons and had fired a pistol that had been long charged. Satisfied, Raleigh returned to his cabin desk. But, a half-hour later, Keymis' cabin boy entered to find his master stretched on his bed with a long knife through his heart. Beside him lay the pistol, whose bullet had merely glanced off a rib. He had been a faithful follower to Raleigh but a kind of nemesis too, whose testimony in 1603 had been damaging, whose gold mine had been more shadow than substance, and whose disobedience ruined Raleigh. Usually the soul of kindness to men who were loyal to him through the years, Raleigh in his despair found little that was considerate to say of the former Balliol scholar.[53]

From this point on, Raleigh seems to have become so distraught as to have lost control of his captains. Captured Spanish documents revealing evidence of gold-workings nearby prompted him to try to organize another expedition, but his captains refused. They were weary and disillusioned, and fearful too of Spanish reinforcements due soon to arrive. Bewildered, Raleigh sailed for the Leeward Islands, where his fleet started to break up. Captain Whitney, for whom he had sold his plate to get his ship to sea, deserted to prey upon Spanish shipping; he was joined by Captain Wollaston. Raleigh sent one ship home with the unfit. To hold the others, he talked wildly of cleaning and revictualing in Newfoundland and returning to

---

[53] Keymis' suicide is related in *ibid.*, VIII, 494-95.

Guiana, of having a try at the Plate Fleet, of seizing other Spanish ships and bringing them into French ports. These, however, were but the desperate, feverish fantasies of a man who knew he was doomed—even Whitney and Wollaston had reminded him that death awaited him at home. By the end of March, a few of the captains followed the example of the two deserters, others sailed directly for England, and the *Destiny* remained alone, her crew on the verge of mutiny.

Off St. Christopher, Raleigh wrote Winwood on March 21 about the disasters. He was bitter over the King's valuing him so little as to command him to hand over the data concerning his ships and their destination. His bitterness was understandable, for Keymis had brought back from San Thomé an identical copy of the list he had submitted to James. What was to become of him, he said he knew not: "I am unpardoned in England, and my poor estate consumed." He begged Winwood "to take some pity on my poor wife, to whom I dare not write. . . ."[54] Unknown to him, Winwood, whom he wished to comfort his wife and on whose support in the Council he could depend, had died of a fever the previous October.

The next day he summoned the courage to write Bess a letter at once eloquent in composition and touching in sentiment: "I was loathe to write, because I knew not how to comfort you; and, God knows, I never knew what sorrow meant till now. All that I can say to you is, that you must obey the will and providence of God; and remember, that the Queen's Majesty bore the loss of Prince Henry with a magnanimous heart, and the Lady Harrington of her only son. Comfort your heart (dearest Bess), I shall sorrow for us both. I shall sorrow the less, because I have not long to sorrow, because not long to live. I refer you to Mr. Secretary Winwood's letter, who will give you a copy of it, if you send for it. Therein you shall know what hath passed. I have written but that letter, for my brains are broken, and it is a torment for me to write, and especially of misery. I have desired Mr. Secretary to give my Lord Carew a copy of his letter. I have cleansed my ship of sick men and sent them home. I hope God will send us somewhat ere we return. Commend me to all at Lothbury. You shall hear from me, if I live, from the New-

[54] Edwards, *Ralegh* (*Letters*), II, 350-58.

foundland, where I mean to make clean my ships and revictual; for I have tobacco enough to pay for it. The Lord bless and comfort you, that you may bear patiently the death of your valiant son."

Although Raleigh intended to write no more, his grief and anger suddenly impelled him to add a postscript several times as long as the body of the letter. In this postscript he repeated in less restrained language much of what he had already written to Winwood: the disobedience of Keymis, the King's strange conduct, and his captains' desertion. "I protest before the majesty of God," he said passionately, "that as Sir Francis Drake and Sir John Hawkins died heartbroken when they failed of their enterprise, I could willingly do the like, did I not contend against sorrow for your sake, in hope to provide somewhat for you; and to comfort and relieve you."[55]

Soon after writing these letters, Raleigh sailed for Newfoundland. Part of his crew actually mutinied, some wanting to seize Spanish prizes, others determined not to return to Guiana come what may, and none daring to go back to England. Raleigh was forced to compromise with them: he would sail for Kinsale in Ireland, land the mutineers there without taking action against them, and return with the loyal crewmen to Plymouth. This plan proving acceptable, he set his course for Kinsale, where he arrived on May 26.

Three days before, Captain Roger North of Raleigh's fleet had told James the dismal story of the expedition. Gondomar at once reminded the King of his promise to deliver Raleigh to Madrid to be hanged, the King swore he would be true to his word, and the Lord Admiral issued instructions for Raleigh and the *Destiny* to be seized as soon as the ship entered English waters. On June 21 their victim steered bravely into the lovely, landlocked harbor of Plymouth. Raleigh had kept his promise to the Earls of Arundel and Pembroke, who had pledged surety for him: he had returned.

By a stroke of irony, this was the twenty-second anniversary of the day when, magnificent and redoubtable, he had led the English fleet to the glorious victory at Cadiz.

[55] *Ibid.*, 359-63.

# CHAPTER 21

# The King's Welcome

THOUGH Raleigh knew that returning to England was hazardous, he was ignorant of the lengths to which the King had already gone, or was yet willing to go, to assure his doom. There is a story that when London learned of the burning of San Thomé, about ten days after Madrid had the news, Gondomar burst in upon the King and almost startled him to death by shouting, "Piratas! Piratas! Piratas!"[1] Though the story may be apocryphal, no doubt exists of James's anger at Raleigh, and it was at Gondomar's suggestion that he issued the proclamation of June 9.[2] Promulgated on the 11th, this proclamation, which in the same breath invited persons having evidence against Raleigh to give it, denounced the "hostile invasion of the town of S. Thomé" and said that Raleigh had "maliciously broken and infringed the Peace and Amity, which hath been so happily established, and so long inviolably continued."[3] Raleigh was thus neatly prejudged.

Gondomar, who was about to leave for home, was ordered to remain for a time until he had witnessed the "thorough completion" of Raleigh's punishment.[4] In an express to his ambassador, Philip III bade Gondomar "to exaggerate as much as you can Raleigh's guilt and try to get the King to make a great demonstration." But Philip was shrewd. He urged Gondomar not to threaten James "but make him understand that I am offended, and that if a proper remedy be not forthcoming at once, we shall make reprisals and seize English property in Spain."[5] Gondomar needed no urging; now he cajoled, and now he warned James. Though the latter occasionally became testy at Gondomar's relentless attentions, he dared not antagonize the Spaniard since he sorely wanted the ambassador's help

[1] Howell, *Epistolae Ho-Elianae*, 23.
[2] *Cal. S.P. Venetian, 1617-1619*, 244.
[3] The proclamation is printed in Harlow, *Raleigh's Last Voyage*, 245-46.
[4] *Cal. S.P. Venetian, 1617-1619*, 253.
[5] Quoted by Hume, *Ralegh*, 249-50.

in sealing the marriage alliance. With Villiers's encouragement and the King's acquiescence, Gondomar bade the English Privy Council wait on him, reminding the Councillors of James's promise to send Raleigh to Madrid and threatening reprisals if this was not done.[6]

At subsequent meetings of the Council, however, opposition grew at committing Raleigh to the Spaniards; it was considered derogatory to England's pride. Carew especially, but even Bacon, fought to keep him in England. But Villiers was insistent and, at James's direction, the favorite wrote Gondomar on June 26 that justice would be done. Carew refused to give up; again and again he spoke in Raleigh's behalf. "I may as well hang him," James admitted to Carew, "as deliver him to the King of Spain; and one of these two I must do, if the case be as Gondomar has represented it." When Carew still pressed him, James stammered angrily, "Why, the most thou canst expect is that I should give him a hearing."[7] The faction on the Council friendly to Raleigh provoked James so deeply by its defense of him that on one occasion the King burst out that he would do as he pleased, "without following the advice of fools and badly disposed persons."[8]

Gondomar's work was now about done. He had an audience with the King on July 3, as a consequence of which the proclamation of June 9 was repeated.[9] He left London on July 15 like a conqueror, a magnanimous and condescending conqueror too. A day or two before he departed, a roaring mob of several thousand swarmed over to the Spanish embassy in the Barbican after one of the embassy staff had carelessly ridden down a child in Chancery Lane. Only the appearance of the Chief Justice and the Lord Mayor with his aldermen prevented the mob from tearing the place to pieces. Gondomar was away at the time, dining with the Earl of Worcester, but James personally apologized to him and compelled the Lord Mayor to bring the ring-

---

[6] See Gondomar's report to Philip III, in *ibid.*, 257-58. For Gondomar's pressure on James, see also Willson, *James VI and I*, 374-75.

[7] Lorkin to Puckering, June 30, 1618. Quoted by Gardiner, *History of England*, III, 135.

[8] Quoted by D. H. Willson, *The Privy Councillors in the House of Commons*, *1604-1629*, 20.

[9] *Cal. S.P. Venetian*, *1617-1619*, 253.

leaders to justice. Before leaving, however, Gondomar graciously asked the King not to punish the rioters. The King chose to ignore the request until it was seconded several weeks later by Sanchez, the Spanish secretary who remained in London after Gondomar had gone.

Gondomar never saw Raleigh after the latter's return to England; he was off for Spain before Raleigh reached London. Nor, in view of his success in persuading James, did Gondomar need to remain longer. Though he had won out over Raleigh, there is no evidence that Raleigh bore him personal animosity. Since in Raleigh's eyes Gondomar represented the national enemy and was a redoubtable opponent to boot, Raleigh seems to have expected him to resort to almost any measures to accomplish his ruin; Raleigh would have done the same himself in Gondomar's place. Raleigh reserved his hatred and contempt, rather, for those of his own countrymen who played him false. And there were so many.

Meanwhile he faced an odd situation down in the West Country. His meeting with Bess, who came to Plymouth when news of his arrival reached London, was an experience not unmixed with sadness, but, whatever the private grief they shared, they faced the curious world with coolness. She brought him information of the hostility in London, to which he resolved to repair in her company and in that of one of his loyal captains, Samuel King, as soon as he completed some local business. He went about the city without interference by any Crown officer. He took advantage of the liberty he enjoyed to write two letters to Carew, explaining the circumstances of the expedition and stressing what he firmly believed, namely, "that Guiana be Spanish territory can never be acknowledged, for I myself took possession of it for the Queen of England, by virtue of a cession of all the native chiefs of the country. His Majesty knows this to be true, as is proved by the concessions granted by him under the great seal of England to Harcourt." Raleigh was quite right in his implication. If Guiana had been territory unquestionably Spanish, the King had no right to permit the expedition to sail in the first place. Whatever Raleigh's guilt in not adhering strictly to his commission, James was even more culpable, not so much, as Gardiner contends, for refusing to investigate conditions under which the voyage was to be made as for imposing conditions which made success virtually impossible to achieve.[10] His letters mailed, Raleigh set out for London in the second week of July.

Raleigh and his little company had traveled only as far as Ashburton, twenty miles beyond Plymouth, when they were met by Sir Lewis Stukely, a cousin, Vice Admiral of Devon, and the officer ordered to arrest him. According to Samuel King, when Stukely told Raleigh he had come to apprehend him and his ship, Raleigh replied facetiously that he had saved Stukely the labor and had arrested himself.[11] Stukely, who carried only verbal orders, directed the party back to Plymouth, while he waited for his written commission and supervised the sale of the *Destiny's* supplies. He paid so little attention to his distinguished prisoner, sometimes not seeing him for days, that it seemed as if the government were almost encouraging him to escape in order to save itself from the embarrassment of another trial, a trial—unlike that of 1603—of a popular hero.[12] Actually Stukely may have shared the belief of people in London that Raleigh was still ill and so left him alone.[13]

Whatever the reason for his neglect, Bess Raleigh took advantage of it to beg her husband to flee the country; unlike Raleigh, she was under no illusions of what the King's enmity portended. Raleigh was more naïve, for he had recovered enough of his spirits to convince himself that all was not lost. He believed that James had been a partner in the enterprise by authorizing it and that this was a mitigating circumstance. What had happened was regrettable but, at worst, the affair at San Thomé was provoked by Spaniards trespassing on territory rightfully England's. Finally, however, he listened to Bess, and Samuel King hurriedly dickered with the captain of a French bark to take Raleigh to France. Then, one night, Samuel King rowed Raleigh out to the ship. When they drew close to the craft, the idea of flight suddenly became so intolerable to Ra-

[10] Harlow, *Raleigh's Last Voyage*, 249. Letters in *ibid.*, 247-53; Edwards, *Ralegh* (*Letters*), II, 375-80. For Gardiner's view, see his *Prince Charles and the Spanish Marriage*, I, 53.
[11] W. Oldys, *Life of Sir Walter Ralegh*, in *Works*, I, 519.
[12] Thompson, *Ralegh*, 345.
[13] *Cal. S.P. Venetian, 1617-1619*, 253.

leigh that he ordered King to return.[14] Another night, he almost succumbed again to the entreaties of Bess and King, but, in the end, he conquered his disgust and fear and refused to take refuge in France. When Stukely received a peremptory order from the Council on July 25 to bring the prisoner on to London, Raleigh went without protest.[15]

Accompanying the party was a French physician, one Dr. Manourie. He has been considered by a number of scholars to have been a quack, but, in seventeenth-century medicine, the dividing line between a genuine physician and a charlatan was somewhat obscure. What is more certain is that he was hired by Stukely as both attendant and spy. Raleigh, as usual overly trustful, regarded Manourie as a possible friend. He seems to have become increasingly impressed with him as the two men chatted about chemistry. Manourie forgot little and embroidered what he remembered. When, by a curious irony, they passed near Sherborne, Raleigh remarked, "All this was mine, and it was taken from me unjustly."[16] However true the comment, it was rashly made, for Manourie included it in his report which the government used against the prisoner.

Freedom was fast running out for Raleigh, and belatedly he realized it. Having chosen not to escape, he now sought time to prepare his defense. To do so, he resorted to a device generally considered unworthy of him. Perhaps it was beneath him, but the time had come for desperate measures, and Raleigh possessed a flair for theater that made the device appealing to him.

The King was in or near Salisbury on his annual progress, as the summer tour was called, and Raleigh wanted him to read the document he intended to write. He must therefore find time at Salisbury for composition. "Give me a vomit," he requested Manourie; "it is good for me to evacuate many bad humours,

---

[14] King's narrative in Oldys' *Ralegh. Works*, I, 520-21; *Declaration*, in Harlow, *Raleigh's Last Voyage*, 347.

[15] See order and related matters in *Acts of the Privy Council, Colonial Ser., 1613-1680*, 19-30; quoted in part by Gardiner, *History of England*, III, 138 n; printed by Harlow, *Raleigh's Last Voyage*, 254. See also Stukely's *Apology* in *Works*, VIII, 784.

[16] *Declaration*, in Harlow, *Raleigh's Last Voyage*, 348. Original in the third person.

and by this means I shall gain time to work my friends, give order for my affairs and, it may be, pacify His Majesty." Otherwise, he said, as soon as he reached London, the Crown would place him in the Tower, and cut off his head. He could not escape this fate without counterfeiting sickness, "which your vomits will effect without suspicion."[17] At Salisbury he staggered and, apparently very dizzy, hit his head against a pillar. The next morning, Bess Raleigh and her retinue of servants went on to London, accompanied by King. Raleigh remained behind, frightening everyone except Manourie by thrashing about naked on all fours, gnawing at the rushes on the floor, and, with perfect timing when Stukely dashed into the room, going into such convulsions from the emetic that Stukely actually helped rub him. Raleigh later said he had made a perfect physician of his cousin. Subsequently, at Raleigh's request, Manourie supplied him with an ointment that caused him to break out on the face, arms, and chest into purple spots with yellow heads. The rest of his skin became greatly inflamed. He had hoped to resemble a leper; at the very least, he appeared smitten with some dreadful plague. Stukely rushed over to the Bishop of Winchester, Lancelot Andrews, who sent physicians to examine Raleigh. Though his affliction baffled them, they wrote a statement that to move him would be dangerous. Manourie signed the statement.

By this stratagem Raleigh gained several days of grace, days in which he was ostensibly fasting but was actually dining off mutton and bread which he had Manourie smuggle in to him. His enemies later reproached him for contriving such a trick and for being "very jocund and merry with Manourie."[18] Raleigh had no regrets. He explained that "David, a man after God's own heart, yet, for safety of his life, feigned himself mad, and let the spittle fall down upon his beard, and I find not that recorded as a fault in David, and I hope God will never lay it to my charge, as a sin."[19] It was undignified, messy, and uncomfortable to himself, as well as exceedingly embarrassing to others at the time; even so, it was not without comedy and was

[17] *Declaration, ibid.*, 348.    [18] *Ibid.*, 350-51.
[19] See speech on scaffold, in *Works*, VIII, 777. The Scriptural allusion is to I Samuel, 21:13.

certainly no gross offense, though the government took a decidedly critical view of his behavior when it learned the truth.

Raleigh made use of his hard-earned respite at Salisbury by producing his famous *Apology*.[20] Written at white heat, the document contains most though by no means all of what we know about his fateful voyage to Guiana. It is a vigorous defense, not entirely immune to criticism but generally sincere and powerfully expressed. Raleigh held that if the ventures of many of the greatest rulers of Europe had often miscarried—and he cited numerous instances—it was not strange that a private individual like himself, imprisoned for thirteen years and unpardoned, should have failed in his enterprise because of other men's errors. He strongly emphasized England's right to Guiana by cession of the native chiefs, by his conquest of it in 1595, and by the King's own action in sending Harcourt and himself there. He could explain the assault on San Thomé only on the grounds that it had been moved and that the Spaniards had attacked Keymis first. Bacon in the *Declaration* later ridiculed this explanation, particularly that San Thomé had been moved, but Raleigh believed Keymis' story. As to the accusations being hurled against him, he pointed out in Salisbury that he was certainly not guilty of using French ships, nor had he molested the Plate Fleet. As for his men having attacked San Thomé and failing to find a gold mine, Raleigh vigorously answered both charges. The Spaniards had attacked the English first, and the English leaders had most definitely tried to find gold. On the other hand, he was not directly responsible for either the attack or the failure to discover gold, since he was at the time many miles from the area in question. His enemies, of course, asserted that there had never been a gold mine in the first place. Raleigh therefore had to convince people not so much that a gold mine existed as that he truly believed it did and that he had not invented the myth of a mine in order to secure release. If Keymis had brought back a basket or two of ore, as Raleigh had hoped he might, he would have felt more confident in facing his critics. That gold does exist in the area Keymis had traversed and near the surface in flat slate has been

[20] *Works*, VIII, 479-507.

proved,[21] but that either Keymis or Raleigh knew of any mine beyond hearsay or acquaintance with the auriferous rocks in 1595 is dubious despite Raleigh's statement of having seen a mine himself. "The mine," writes Miss Latham, "was a bait."[22] This seems quite likely indeed—a bait to commit England to a deeper interest in Guiana than merely that of gold—but this does not necessarily signify that Raleigh did not firmly believe he would find gold.

As for San Thomé, with its penchant for moving, it was located in territory that was open to dispute, notwithstanding the claims of Gondomar. Trading in the Orinoco was largely carried on by Dutchmen and Englishmen, and Spanish political control was so lacking that, ten years after Raleigh's death, an Anglo-Dutch expedition tore down San Thomé and rebuilt it. Mr. Milton Waldman called attention, more than twenty years ago, to the way in which Raleigh was vindicated in the Blue Books published between 1896 and 1899 by the British Foreign Office when the government submitted its dispute over the boundary between British Guiana and Venezuela to arbitration at the behest of the United States.[23] In its review of Guiana, the government found that, between 1596 and 1720, the Spaniards had not expanded beyond the immediate confines of the various sites of San Thomé. This was confirmed for part of the time by the report of the American commission, which declared that "There is no perfect evidence of the existence before 1648 of any other Spanish settlement than San Thomé in the region between the Orinoco and the Essequibo, or any other than a temporary occupation of any position in that region."[24] Raleigh was thus confirmed, albeit belatedly, in his contention that Spain did not control the Orinoco country. To him San Thomé, lying on the right or south bank of the Orinoco and therefore on territory that he had claimed for England a year before its founding, was evidence of usurped possession. That Raleigh was

[21] Observed by the Marquis of Salisbury on November 26, 1895. See also U.S. Commission on Boundary between Venezuela and British Guiana *Report*, VII, 434; Harlow, *Raleigh's Last Voyage*, 81 n; C. L. Foster, in *Quarterly Journal of the Geological Society* (1869); Latham, in *Essays and Studies* (1951), 97.

[22] Latham, *Essays and Studies*, 106.

[23] Waldman, *Raleigh*, 224-25; Foreign Office *Blue Books* on Venezuela-British Guiana Boundary Dispute.

[24] U.S. Commission *Report*, I, 45.

a trespasser, as asserted by James, was absurd. But, to ruin Raleigh, James chose to repudiate the Orinoco region with all its vast resources.

While Raleigh was in Salisbury, the King appeared and, angry at the prisoner's slow progress to London, ordered Stukely to get on with his task. The little cavalcade then moved on to Brentford, Manourie later averring that on the way Raleigh spoke in an ungracious manner of the King, an interpretation which depends, of course, on the meaning of "ungracious" in a convinced monarchist whose release was conditional on the King's good will. It was contended in the *Declaration* that Raleigh attempted through bribery at this time to persuade both Stukely and Manourie to assist him in escaping.[25] This is possible since he could now have entertained few illusions that the government would free him once he reached London. While he was at Brentford, David de Novion, the Sieur de la Chesnée, who served as interpreter to Le Clerc, the French ambassador, visited him and told him that Le Clerc was eager to see him. Getting wind of the visit, the government evidently decided that the French "plot" should be permitted to develop in order to ascertain what the French interest in Raleigh involved in the political sphere and perhaps thereby to establish a real case of treason against him. Hence Raleigh was not imprisoned at once in the Tower but was allowed to go to a residence maintained by his wife on Broad Street, where he arrived on Friday night, August 7.

There is no doubt that Raleigh was seriously considering escape. He was aware at last that a return to London meant death or indefinite confinement, and in neither fate could he see himself useful in achieving what seems to have been his objective, the ending of the Spanish colonial monopoly and its replacement by an English tropical empire. From Salisbury he had sent Samuel King ahead with Bess to make arrangements. King knew that a former boatswain of his, a man named Hart, owned a ketch. On his arrival in London, King sent Cottrell, who had served Raleigh in the Tower, to get in touch with Hart and to instruct him to have his ketch stand by at Tilbury. As it happened, King placed too much faith in Cottrell's apparent devo-

---

[25] *Declaration*, in Harlow, *Raleigh's Last Voyage*, 352-54.

tion to Raleigh and in Hart's presumed loyalty to himself. Both betrayed what they knew—and they knew too much—to one of Stukely's relatives, William Herbert, who revealed his information to Sir William St. John, half-brother to the royal favorite, George Villiers, Duke of Buckingham. St. John had been one of the two men who, for a price, had helped secure Raleigh's liberation from the Tower; now he was as willing to assist in putting him back in again. He and Herbert galloped to meet Stukely and Raleigh at Bagshot, where they informed Stukely of King's arrangements. To St. John's surprise, until he was later informed of the reason in London, Stukely showed only concern for Raleigh's safety, not fear of his departure. Stukely had received from Sir Ralph Naunton, Winwood's successor as Secretary and a man unfriendly to Raleigh, instructions to remain in Raleigh's confidence, come what may. Perhaps Stukely had already wormed out of Raleigh his intention of escaping.

Ignorant of the trap being set for him, Raleigh expressed a preference to leave in Hart's English ketch rather than accept aid by Le Clerc, who, with La Chesnée, visited him at Broad Street on the night of August 9. In the presence of nearly a dozen of Raleigh's friends, Le Clerc offered him assistance in reaching France and a hospitable welcome on his arrival. The French manifestly believed that Raleigh, alive and at liberty in France, could be a useful instrument in opposing the proposed Anglo-Spanish alliance. Though he graciously thanked Le Clerc for his invitation, Raleigh declined it; he had already made plans to leave in Hart's ketch that very night, and, by now, he had revealed them in detail to Stukely in the fatuous belief that his kinsman's professions of affection and eagerness to flee with him were sincere.

Later that night Raleigh made his attempt at a getaway, for which, unbeknownst to him, there was not the slightest chance of success. One of the greatest of Englishmen was being toyed with by men whose names have survived almost solely because of their treatment of him. Samuel King had two wherries ready at the Tower dock when Raleigh appeared, wearing a false beard and a hat with a green band, and accompanied by a page, Stukely, and Stukely's son. When Raleigh's cloak-bag and pistols were stowed away, Stukely turned to King and asked "whether thus far he had not distinguished himself an honest man." To this, King, who evidently was not so sure of Stukely as was Raleigh, replied "that he hoped he would continue so."[26] The party then climbed aboard, Raleigh and Stukely in one wherry, King and Hart in the other.

Before they had gone more than twenty strokes, they sighted another boat, larger and powerfully manned, following them. Startled, Raleigh turned to Stukely, who made light of it and encouraged the oarsmen to keep rowing. Later, his suspicions still not satisfied, Raleigh asked the men whether they would continue if ordered to stop in the King's name. It was not a wise question; the men became so frightened that they lay to on their oars. Raleigh then hastily told a tale of disagreement with the Spanish ambassador that made it necessary for him to board a ketch at Tilbury for the Low Countries. At this, Stukely fell to cursing that he had ever ventured his life and fortune with a man so filled with doubts and fears. He threatened to kill the boatmen if they did not go on. Near Greenwich, the movements of the pursuing craft again so excited Raleigh's suspicions that, when he voiced them to King in the other wherry, King told him that if they could but reach Gravesend, he was certain they could get to Tilbury. The boatmen, however, said that the delays had cost them the tide and that it would be impossible to arrive at Gravesend before morning. Finally, when they had rowed as far as Gallions Reach, about a mile beyond Woolwich, and Hart began to express doubts of being able to identify his own ketch, Raleigh concluded that he was betrayed, and ordered a return to Greenwich.

Their pursuers now hailing them in the name of the King, Raleigh and Stukely whispered together, Raleigh handing over several valuables to his kinsman and Stukely tenderly embracing him. But when they landed at Greenwich and the guards in the pursuing boat—men in the service of Herbert and St. John—quickly surrounded them, Stukely arrested both Raleigh and King. "Sir Lewis," said Raleigh sadly, at last and too late alert to the plot against him, "these actions will not turn out to your credit." When the prisoners were brought to the Tower

[26] King's narrative, in Oldys' *Ralegh. Works*, I, 534.

in the morning, Raleigh turned to Captain King, remarking that, although Stukely and Cottrell had betrayed him, King was in no real danger himself, since "it is I am the mark that is shot at." Then the faithful King, taken elsewhere, left Raleigh, as he said in concluding his narrative of the attempted escape, "to His tuition with whom I do not doubt but his soul resteth."[27]

It had been an unfortunate venture. Raleigh's enemies naturally rejoiced. A man who sought to escape the law must surely be guilty and now, by reason of his flight, he had compounded his offense. He wanted, as he admitted later, to remain in France until "the Queen should have been made means for his pardon and recalling."[28] London society knew that Anne hated the Spanish match for Charles and much preferred a French marriage alliance. What neither Raleigh nor many people knew was that Anne's influence over James had become so negligible as to be virtually nonexistent; certainly her wishes would have been unavailing in behalf of a man like Raleigh for whom the King bore a profound and unremitting hatred. On the other hand, Raleigh's capture always excited James's contempt. Aubrey remarked that James was "wont to say that he [Raleigh] was a coward to be so taken and conveyed, for else he might easily have made his escape from so slight a guard."[29] It is possible that he would have welcomed Raleigh's escape as a release from an embarrassing and delicate situation. But it is more likely that, in so speaking, he was indulging in a sentiment that was distinctly an afterthought; at the time he was probably delighted to have caught the old fox, as Essex had called him, in a nicely laid trap.

James was quite unaffected by the fact that Stukely's betrayal so vividly reminded men of the greatest betrayal in history that ever afterward they alluded to him as "Sir Judas" Stukely. Though rewarded with nearly £1,000 for his efforts and expenses, Stukely complained to the King of the critics who damned him. "On my soul," retorted the exasperated monarch, "if I should hang all that speak ill of thee, all the trees in my kingdom would not suffice."[30] It is a fitting commentary on the

[27] See *Works*, I, 533-37, for Oldys' account based on King's narrative.
[28] *Ibid.*, 531.
[29] Aubrey, *Brief Lives*, II, 188.
[30] Goodman, *Court of King James*, II, 173.

character of the men used to implicate Raleigh that, within a few weeks, both Stukely and Manourie were caught clipping gold coins and were condemned to death. Though James added nothing to his popularity by pardoning his tool, his act was unable to save Stukely from the fate pursuing him. Finding the West Country untenable because of the hatred for him, he scurried to cover in Lundy Isle. Rich and poor alike shunned him there, and he died a madman in August 1620.

Raleigh knew his case was becoming desperate, and he addressed a poem to the Queen, entreating her to intervene in his behalf:

> O had Truth power, the guiltless could not fall,
>     Malice win glory, or Revenge triumph,
> But Truth, alone, cannot encounter all!
>
> Mercy is fled to God, which Mercy made;
>     Compassion dead; Faith turned to policy,
> Friends know not those who sit in Sorrow's shade.
>
> For what we sometimes were, we are no more;
>     Fortune hath changed our shape, and Destiny
> Defaced the very form we had before.
>
> All love and all desert of former times
>     Malice hath covered from my Sovereign's eyes,
> And largely laid abroad supposed crimes.
>
> . . . . . . . . . . . . . . . . . .
>
> If I have sold my duty, sold my faith
>     To strangers, which was only due to one,
> Nothing I should esteem so dear as Death.
>
> But if both God and time shall make you know
>     That I your humblest vassal am opprest,
> Then cast your eyes on undeserved woe.

Sorely ill, half-deranged, Anne sat down and wrote to the only one she knew who had sufficient influence to avert the King's revenge, Buckingham. It was a pathetic little note, beseeching the favorite to give her an opportunity to entreat the King "that Sir Walter Raleigh's life may not be called in question. . . ."[31] But Buckingham was now, like his master, an advocate of the Spanish alliance, and Raleigh's life had practically become part of the price, though never mentioned as such.

But if Raleigh's life must now be taken, how to accomplish the task without making it look like murder was a real problem for the government. James was responsible for sending Raleigh off on an expedition which, thanks to the intelligence he had given the Spaniards, had had practically no chance of succeeding. If he executed Raleigh offhand, he would be condemning himself for his own participation. Puzzled, James turned to a board of six commissioners which included Bacon, Coke, and Naunton. Their hearings opened on August 17 and continued for weeks.

There were three approaches developed in the hearings: treason in complicity with the French, piracy, and trespass. Of the justice of the last two points, a number of scholars, particularly Bacon's biographer, James Spedding, were convinced. On the other hand, James and his colleagues were by no means so certain. Allegations that he took no mining equipment along with him, Raleigh countered by contending that he had invested £2,000 in such material. He may have talked recklessly of taking the Spanish Plate Fleet, but his conduct at Lancerota and Gomera was the reverse of piratical. In fact, he tried in the West Indies to prevent his ship captains from going off on maurauding expeditions of their own. Certainly, as Mr. Waldman has pointed out, he had precisely the right kind of crews to have joined him if he had wanted to turn pirate.[32] The basis of the claim lay, of course, in the accusation that the mine was a myth. A myth it may have been but not in Raleigh's mind; there it had become a reality that no circumstance or testimony could shake. Furthermore, it would be difficult for the government to hang the ill and absent Raleigh for the attack on San Thomé and not to try the members of the expedition who had actually participated in the attack—captains whom the government used to testify against the prisoner.

As for the trespass charge, it involved the location of the mine, the site of San Thomé, and the fate of that town. As in-

[31] Edwards, *Ralegh* (*Letters*), II, 487.
[32] Waldman, *Raleigh*, 220.

dicated previously, the government developed the imaginary existence of the mine, its surprising movability, and the attack on an innocent people. But the Crown could prove nothing that Raleigh did not counter with considerable effectiveness. The commissioners made what was probably a mistake in procedure in insisting that he had never intended to go to the mine at all but merely sought his liberty. In a somewhat confused but strong-toned letter to the King, Raleigh let his enemies know what he thought of this contention:

"If I had spent my poor estate, lost my son, suffered, by sickness and otherwise, a world of miseries; if I had resisted with the manifest hazard of my life the rebels [robberies?] and spoils which my companies would have made; if when I was poor I could have made myself rich; if when I had gotten my liberty, which all men and Nature itself doth so much prize, I voluntarily lost it; if when I was master of my life I rendered it again; if, though I might elsewhere have sold my ships and goods, and put five or six thousand pounds in my purse, I have brought her into England—I beseech Your Majesty to believe that all this I have done because it should not be said to Your Majesty that Your Majesty had given liberty and trust to a man whose end was but the recovery of his liberty, and who had betrayed Your Majesty's trust."[33]

What the commissioners simply could not believe was that Raleigh sincerely wanted England to establish an empire in tropical America. They saw in the inspiration and conduct of the expedition personal motives alone, and corrupt ones at that— they had to look at the situation in this light, for basically they were not a board of impartial judges but a body of accusers. But if Raleigh had erred, the King was not above reproach in having agreed to let him sail—this point even the commissioners may have realized, for they seemed more desirous of pushing the alleged plot with the French.

This plot they pursued with an avidity that suggests they thought they might turn up something genuinely treasonable. Raleigh, it was known, had conversed with des Marets, the French ambassador in 1617, who had visited him on the *Destiny* before he left for Guiana. The French commission, of which

[33] Edwards, *Ralegh* (*Letters*), II, 369.

much was made, was, however, offered him by Admiral de Montmorency, not by the French government—certainly no copy of an official French commission survives in the French archives. It is doubtful that Raleigh seriously entertained the idea of capitalizing on the Montmorency commission apart from the advantage that might ensue from French assistance in the expedition which he vainly hoped would materialize through the agency of a French friend, Captain Faige, and the anti-Spanish party in France. Furthermore, with the possibility of the French participating, he was naturally interested in having access to a French port. His critics, contemporary and subsequent, argued that Raleigh intended to use the French connection to desert to France should the expedition fail.[34] Whatever his original intentions, the fact remains that he did not do so. As he informed the King, "My mutineers told me, that if I returned for England I should be undone; but I believed more in Your Majesty's goodness than in their arguments."[35] Raleigh would have done well, from the point of saving his own life, to have listened to his mutineers, but he did not really believe that James had a case for hanging against him, nor did he desire to break his pledged word to Arundel and Pembroke to return.

The English examiners became so interested in the "plot" that they questioned La Chesnée, who naturally denied that he had ever spoken to Raleigh on the subject of escape. Enraged at his denial, the government locked him up and examined the ambassador himself, Le Clerc, at Hampton Court. When Le Clerc likewise denied any dealings with Raleigh, the Council suspended him from his duties.[36] This action angered the French government. Indeed, as the Venetian ambassador reported, "The disagreements between these two crowns augment daily."[37] As evidence of their resentment, the French retaliated by treating the English ambassador, Sir William

[34] See, in particular, S. R. Gardiner's unfriendly summation of the case, "The Case against Sir Walter Raleigh," in *Fortnightly Review*, VII (May, 1867), and New Ser., I. Edward Thompson calls Gardiner's essay "notorious"; certainly it is not among the great historian's more judicious writings. Thompson, *Ralegh*, 361; Waldman, *Raleigh*, 219-20; Edwards, *Ralegh* (Letters), II, 344-47.

[35] Edwards, *Ralegh* (Letters), II, 369.

[36] See Harlow, *Raleigh's Last Voyage*, 285-94.

[37] *Cal. S.P. Venetian, 1617-1619*, 334, 339-40.

Beecher, in such a manner that he did not know whether he was regarded as a prisoner or was still a free man. Whatever his status, he left London in no doubt that the French considered Raleigh a prisoner more "to content the Spaniards, than for any interest of His Majesty."[38]

The commissioners found themselves so baffled in building up a case against Raleigh that they resorted to a device, disgusting but not unusual, to strengthen their hand. The Lieutenant of the Tower was Sir Allen Apsley, a man not unfriendly to Raleigh and one who had assumed personal responsibility for him. Apsley was now displaced as special custodian, though not as Lieutenant, by the Keeper of the State Papers, Sir Thomas Wilson, whose duty was to ingratiate himself into Raleigh's confidence and keep a complete record of all his conversation. Cecil had used him as a tool often and successfully, so this sort of assignment was an old story to the spy. Wilson was a slippery, arrogant, rather pious-mannered individual who seems to have felt an honest pride in doing his work with competence and for whom no task was too base. He was to attend Raleigh constantly from morning till night, sharing his meals and even his devotions.

Wilson entered into his association with the prisoner, confident of his ability to induce Raleigh to speak without inhibition. For once in his life, however, Raleigh was reasonably discreet and not too trusting. Perhaps he suspected that Wilson was disposed to be a little too friendly. Perhaps Wilson overestimated his capacity for deception. At any rate, Wilson kept copious notes which he sent to Naunton. "I told him," wrote Wilson of Raleigh, "that if he would but discover what he knew, the King would forgive him, and do him all favours." But the notes revealed little that the government did not already know or suspect. At times it seemed as if Raleigh was alert to Wilson's function and gulled him along, coming to the point of admitting something exciting, then explaining it away so skillfully that he confused and exasperated Wilson. The spy's notes frequently alluded to the prisoner as "arch hypocrite," "arch imposter," and similar appellations. Having moved Raleigh into an upper and more secure apartment, he told Naunton that although the

[38] Quoted by Edwards, *Ralegh* (*Life*), I, 673.

"safer and higher lodging . . . seemeth nearer heaven, yet is there no escape but into hell." Once he suggested that if his methods were unsuccessful, "a rack or a halter" should be used. Raleigh's interest in science vexed the sanctimonious Wilson, who objected that "the things he seems to make most reckoning of are his chemical stuffs, amongst which there is so many spirits of things, that I think there is none wanting that ever I heard of, unless it be the Spirit of God."[39]

Ever since his return, Raleigh had not been well, never having completely recovered from his illness during the expedition. In the Tower, fever and ague attacked him, and his left side swelled. Wilson, in his reports, ridiculed Raleigh's "puling, pining, and groaning." To be sure, Raleigh had often faked illness and was never one to suffer in silence, but there is no doubt that he was utterly miserable. He told Bess, "My swollen side keeps me in perpetual pain and unrest." Anxiously she sought to comfort him by assuring him that " 'Tis merely sorrow and grief that with wind hath gathered into your side."[40] But she was worried about him, all the same, and not simply about his health of the moment. It was becoming all too clear that the government was determined to get rid of him. Nor was she herself altogether free, for she too was confined briefly that fall, and her letters and Raleigh's to each other were opened and copied.

Eventually the government realized that this surveillance was accomplishing little. Raleigh refused to concede that Guiana was Spanish, that the King had recognized Spain's right to Guiana, that he held a commission from the French Crown, or that he talked with La Chesnée at Brentford on any subject other than escaping. Wilson complained that Raleigh was becoming "reserved" with him, and he begged the King to employ him more usefully among the state papers again than in continuing with "this arch imposter."[41] Hence, on October 15, James released Wilson from his charge, and also liberated

[39] Wilson's notes are in PRO, *S.P. Dom.* (James I), 99/9. 10, 10 i, 12, 12 i, 25, 48, 58, 58 i, 59, 59 i, 62, 62 i, 69, 73, 77, 96, 96 i and ii, 103/16. They are partially or wholly printed by Harlow, *Raleigh's Last Voyage*, 261-84.

[40] Edwards, *Ralegh (Letters)*, II, 370.

[41] PRO, *S.P. Dom.* (James I), 103/16.

Raleigh's wife.[42] There is no record of Raleigh's having any regrets at the spy's departure.

The King's action was probably motivated by the Spanish embassy's having received, that same day, notification from Madrid of the Spanish government's decision. Philip III instructed the embassy to notify James that Raleigh should be put to death in England, not in Spain.[43] The decision was a shrewd one since it removed much of the opprobrium from Spain and placed it squarely on James's shoulders. That James accepted the decision without fudging goes without saying. The alliance negotiations had entered a difficult stage, and he was eager to give the Spaniards an earnest of his sincerity; Raleigh's life could well serve this purpose.

But the problem of how, legally, to execute Raleigh still remained. James believed that a trial of some sort was necessary, though he had doubts that, under the law, any court could try a man already under the sentence of death. In response to his request, his commissioners—Coke drafting the report—on October 18 offered alternative suggestions. Raleigh, they concluded, could not be tried for an offense committed while already attainted; he should therefore be executed under the sentence of 1603. Though there was no question that he could be executed solely upon a warrant to the Lieutenant of the Tower, the Crown would be well advised to publish the offenses for which he was to be put to death inasmuch as fifteen years had elapsed since the sentence, he had in the meantime held the King's commission, and his latest offenses were not common knowledge. The second suggestion was quite different. Raleigh could be called before a mixed group of the Council and the Judges, with certain noblemen and gentlemen present to observe. Coke and others would speak for the Crown, Raleigh would be given a chance to defend himself, and the witnesses against him should be produced. Afterward he would be returned to prison, with execution following at the King's convenience.[44]

---

[42] *Ibid.*, 103/36.   [43] *Ibid.*, 99/74.

[44] J. Spedding, *The Letters and Life of Francis Bacon*, VI, 361-62; Harlow, *Raleigh's Last Voyage*, 295-96. Mrs. Bowen (*The Lion and the Throne*, 415) suggests that Coke's appointment to the commission was "a tormenting assign-

If the commissioners, in weighing the second suggestion, felt that the case against Raleigh was strong enough to bring out into the open,[45] the King was of another mind. Though he considered the first suggestion too abrupt in procedure, the second alarmed him. Such an arraignment would make Raleigh "too popular," and James pointed fearfully at the trial of 1603, where, he reminded the commissioners, Raleigh "by his wit ... turned the hatred of men into compassion of him."[46] James then projected a compromise course. Raleigh should be brought before the commissioners who had examined him in the late summer and early fall, confronted with his principal accusers, permitted to speak in his own defense, and then instructed to prepare himself for death. What James failed to perceive was that the people who resented a Spanish alliance would see in Raleigh one who had been condemned secretly from fear of what he might say against the alliance in a public hearing. The King, however, agreed that a *Declaration*, setting forth Raleigh's crimes and offenses, should be published. But publication was to be posthumous, for no time should be wasted in getting rid of the miscreant. James demanded that a warrant of execution be sent down for him to sign.[47]

Accordingly, on October 22, Raleigh was summoned before the commissioners. Though one is dependent on the few rough notes kept by Sir Julius Caesar, Master of the Rolls and one of the commissioners, the proceedings are reasonably clear. The Attorney General, who was now Sir Henry Yelverton, and the Solicitor General, Sir Thomas Coventry, developed his offenses. Yelverton pointed out his "faults" committed before, during, and after the expedition. He emphasized in particular that Raleigh had never intended to find a mine, that he purposed to create a state of war between England and Spain, that he abandoned and endangered his men, and that he was unfaithful to both the King and his men. For his part, Coventry denounced

ment" owing to his having come to share Raleigh's hatred of Spain and to his loathing the possibility of a royal match.

[45] Gardiner, *History of England*, III, 146; Spedding, *Letters and Life of Bacon*, VI, 362.

[46] Spedding, *Letters and Life of Bacon*, VI, 363; Harlow, *Raleigh's Last Voyage*, 296-97.

[47] *Ibid.*

Raleigh for his efforts to escape both before and after the order of arrest, his deception as at Salisbury, his speeches "full of contumely" about the King, and his attempts "to corrupt" Stukely and Manourie.

Raleigh's replies were of the nature of a general denial. He declared that "he verily thinketh that His Majesty doth in his conscience clear him of all guiltiness" of his original conviction, and he cited in support a hearsay remark that James was critical of Middlesex juries and Justice Gawdy's deathbed observation that "the justice of England was never so depraved and injured" as in his "condemnation." For that matter, there is some doubt that James really did believe Raleigh guilty of the 1603 treason; if truly he did, then, as a Raleigh scholar has pointed out, it was "an astounding action" to let him go to Guiana so powerfully armed when he might not return to England.[48]

With his general statement as a preface, Raleigh developed his defense. He denied all four charges listed by Yelverton, the last two without explanation. As for Coventry's charges, Raleigh denied that he attempted to escape until after his arrest and, though he admitted to faking illness, he excused himself by citing David's example. Furthermore, while he acknowledged that once he had said he had been deceived in his confidence in the King, he also asserted that he had never spoken critically of James on any other occasion. Monarchist though Raleigh was, James's treatment had evidently forced him to tell Manourie at least this one blunt opinion of the royal Scot. The alleged attempt at "corruption" he ignored. True, when confronted with Captains St. Leger and Pennington, he admitted that he proposed "the taking of the Mexico fleet if the mine failed." On the other hand, this intention had clearly been expressed as a means of keeping his crews together and, if the old adage that "actions speak louder than words" means anything, the fact remains that he did not molest the Plate Fleet.[49]

Raleigh's assertions, delivered with dignity and eloquence, fell upon barren ground. Speaking for the commissioners, Bacon expatiated upon the injury Raleigh had inflicted upon Spanish

[48] Thompson, *Ralegh*, 365.
[49] For hearing, see *Camden Miscellany*, v (1864), 9-13. The proceedings are misdated as of Aug. 17; see Gardiner, *History of England*, III, 147 n. 2.

lives and property and the manner in which he had abused the King's confidence. The new Lord Chancellor, who was eventually to lose that great office for accepting bribes, concluded by solemnly informing Raleigh that he must die.[50] The Council, however, made one concession to him two days later: he should be beheaded instead of hanged, drawn, and quartered according to the original sentence in 1603.

After the hearing on the 22nd, the King's Bench was instructed to authorize an execution of the 1603 sentence of treason. The Justices insisted that, according to proper legal form, the prisoner must be produced to show cause, if any existed, why the sentence should not be carried out. On October 28, therefore, Raleigh was roused early in the morning and brought before the Justices.

Heretofore always fastidious, Raleigh had become careless of his appearance, no doubt the effect of his hopeless situation and of his illness. Feverish and shaking with ague, he walked uncombed in the procession that moved from the Tower to Westminster. As he passed through a corridor, an old servant stared in dismay at his master's rumpled white hair, and asked to comb it. "Let them kem it that are to have it," Raleigh replied with a smile. Then, as his servant looked sad, he asked, still smiling, "Dost thou know, Peter, of any plaster that will set a man's head on again when it is off?"[51]

Before the King's Bench, Raleigh, looking older than his years, disheveled, stooped, lame, and shivering with a chill, appeared quite unlike the splendid, almost legendary hero of the great days of Elizabeth. To those who stared at him, greatness had become incredibly tragic in its eclipse. Attorney General Yelverton, no Coke in ability but no Coke in brutality either, fell under the spell of the metamorphosis that had occurred in the person before him. Though he called for execution of the judgment of 1603, as was his duty, he delivered himself of rather an extraordinary observation: "Sir Walter Raleigh hath been a statesman and a man who, in respect of his parts and quality, is to be pitied; he hath been as a star at which the world

[50] Spedding, *Letters and Life of Bacon*, VI, 365. For a Spanish account of how Raleigh received the pronouncement, see Hume, *Ralegh*, 282-83.
[51] John Pory to Carleton, Oct. 31, 1618. PRO, *S.P. Dom.* (James I), 103/61.

hath gazed; but stars may fall, nay, they must fall when they trouble the sphere wherein they abide."[52] For an Attorney General, this was far removed from the "thou viper" maledictions of Sir Edward Coke.

After the Clerk of the Crown read the record of the conviction and judgment, Raleigh was asked if there was any reason why execution should not be awarded. He mentioned, in drawing himself up to reply, that his voice was weak because of his illness and the ague, but the Chief Justice, Sir Henry Montague, assured him his voice was "audible enough." Raleigh then said he had hoped and presumed the previous judgment could not now be used against him in view of the fact that he had been granted a commission with the power of life and death over others. But as he began to explore this subject further in connection with his Guiana voyage, Montague stopped him, telling him that nothing touching the voyage was pertinent. He had been condemned for high treason, and for this offense, unlike a felony, he must "show a pardon by express words, and not by implication." Raleigh accepted the opinion with calmness, though he could not forbear remarking, in connection with the 1603 judgment, "I presume that most of you that hear me know how that was obtained; nay, I know His Majesty was of opinion that I had hard measure therein. . . ."

Though Raleigh was not greatly exaggerating, it was hardly surprising that Montague refused to let the statement pass. He told Raleigh he had received an honorable trial, and reminded him that, for fifteen years, he had been "a dead man in the law, and might at any minute have been cut off" but for the mercy of the King, whose "justice" had been "stirred up" by Raleigh's "new offences." Unlike Lord Chief Justice Popham in 1603, Montague was a very decent man. He tried to comfort Raleigh, urging him not to fear death and praising him as "valiant and wise." Moreover, he laid the ghost of the atheism charge of 1603 when he said, "Your faith hath heretofore been questioned, but I am satisfied you are a good Christian, for your book, which is an admirable work, doth testify as much." Still,

[52] Jardine, *Criminal Trials*, I, 499.

though a humane person, Montague had also a duty to perform: he ordered execution.[53]

The end was now very near, for James signed the death warrant and demanded that the execution take place the next morning. He was unmoved by all appeals, whether from the Queen, Lord Carew, the Bishop of Winchester, Raleigh's young son Carew, or even a Spanish Dominican lately arrived in London, who believed Raleigh's death would alienate the minds of Englishmen "if he were sacrificed to the malice of the Spaniards."[54] The King was tired of the whole business. That there was anything shameful in the affair seems not to have occurred to him, unless the shame was Raleigh's. He was far too interested in marrying Charles off to the Spanish princess to be troubled by a matter of justice involving one of the greatest of Englishmen who happened to be an obstacle to amicable relations with Spain.

Could James have looked ahead, he might have stayed the headsman's ax on the morrow. For afterward, according to one report, London was "full of the worthy end of Sir Walter Raleigh. His Christian and truthful manner made all believe that he was neither guilty of former treasons nor late practices, nor of unjustly injuring the King of Spain."[55] Another keen observer asserted that "his death will do more harm to the faction that procured it than ever he did in his life."[56] Two years later, a satire in manuscript, *Vox Spiritus or Sir Walter Raleigh's Ghost*, by Captain Thomas Gainsford, enjoyed such popularity in private circulation that Naunton and Buckingham bent every effort to suppress it.[57] Most ironical of all, but five years after Raleigh's execution, the proposed marriage alliance failed to materialize and Charles and Buckingham returned from a humiliating courting venture to Spain to lead the party clamoring for action against that country. In the bonfires of rejoicing and the prayers of thanksgiving and exultation throughout England was to be seen, for Raleigh's friends, the vindication of all

---

[53] For hearing, see *ibid.*, 499-502; Harlow, *Raleigh's Last Voyage*, 302-05.
[54] *Chamberlain Letters*, II, 178.
[55] *Cal. S.P. Dom., 1611-1618*, 588.
[56] *Ibid.*, 589.
[57] Thompson, *Ralegh*, 388.

Raleigh himself had said of Spanish policy and the Spanish alliance.

Though surprised at the suddenness of his execution hour, Raleigh retained his composure. In fact, the announcement seemed to tap a vein of ironical humor. When being removed from Westminster Hall to the Gatehouse nearby, where he was to spend his final night on earth, he saw an old acquaintance, Sir Hugh Beeston of Cheshire, standing in the throng. Almost gaily Raleigh asked him if he intended to be present in the morning. When Beeston replied that he would certainly be on hand, Raleigh retorted with mock concern, "I do not know what you may do for a place. For my part, I am sure of one. You must make what shift you can."[58] Similar, though on a note more grim, was his reply to a kinsman, Francis Thynne, who was one of the many who hastened to the Gatehouse to bid farewell. "Do not carry it with too much bravery," urged Thynne, a sober man. "Your enemies will take exception, if you do." "It is my last mirth in this world," Raleigh countered with a wry smile. "Do not grudge it to me. When I come to the sad parting, you will see me grave enough."[59]

[58] T. Birch, *Court and Times of James I*, II, 97.
[59] John Pory to Carleton, Oct. 31, 1618. PRO, *S.P. Dom.* (James I), 103/61.

# CHAPTER 22
# The Final Victory

RALEIGH's statement to Thynne was the soberest of truths, for grave enough he was, and sad indeed the parting, when Bess visited him that night for the last time in their lives. Those were moments of anguish, of which it is difficult to speak and into which it is almost an intrusion, even at this distance in time, to probe. Bess had learned that the Council, though forbidding her to intercede further with the King, would let her have her husband's body to bury; this was at least a precious, if futile, concession. But to talk of death was too dreadful, and, seeing her grief, Raleigh deliberately turned her thoughts to her future task of vindicating his good name before the world. As they were speaking, the clock in the Abbey tolled the hour of midnight, and Bess rose to go in order to allow him to rest for the ordeal of the morrow. Yet as she clung to him in a last embrace, she momentarily lost the rigid control of her feelings and sobbed brokenly. Then she got hold of herself and told him the Council would let her have the disposal of his body. "It is well, dear Bess," he replied with a tender smile, "that thou mayst dispose of that dead which thou hadst not always the disposing of when alive."[1] With that, she left, deeply shaken. Lord George Carew and his wife, who had accompanied her, brought her back with them to their home.

On arriving, Bess had one more task before trying to sleep. Quickly she dashed off a note to "my best brother," Sir Nicholas Carew, at Beddington: "I desire, good brother, that you will be pleased to let me bury the worthy body of my noble husband, Sir Walter Ralegh, in your church at Beddington, where I desire to be buried. The Lords have given me his dead body, though they denied me his life. This night [it was already early morning] he shall be brought you with two or three of my men. Let me hear presently. God hold me in my wits."[2]

[1] *Chamberlain Letters*, II, 180.
[2] Edwards, *Ralegh* (*Letters*), II, 413.

As it turned out, Raleigh's body was for some unknown reason not buried at Beddington but was conveyed directly from the scaffold to St. Margaret's Church and interred before the Communion table. His head was wrapped in a velvet bag, which was enveloped in a velvet robe, and brought to Bess Raleigh's house in a black mourning coach she had ordered for the occasion. She had the head embalmed, and kept it until her death, when it passed to her son, Carew; its fate thereafter is not known.

After his wife's departure from the Tower, Raleigh, like Bess, picked up his quill and wrote, penning two testamentary notes. One was a business note expressing his regret that, when entertained by Lord Boyle before leaving for Guiana, he said something prejudicial to his old colleague, Henry Pyne, about a lease controverted between Boyle and Pyne; he wished now to be neutral. In the same note, he expressed his hope that Bess would care, within her means, for the widows of two of his former servants who would otherwise perish. He also expressed his wish that Stukely be forced to give an account of the tobacco aboard the *Destiny* that he had sold at Plymouth. In the second note, Raleigh denied nine accusations made in connection with the Guiana voyage and his return; he intended to develop a number of these in the speech which he had received permission to make from the scaffold. Among these nine points was a vigorous disavowal that he had ever spoken disloyally or dishonorably of the King. At the same time, he could not help adding what was, in part, the bitter truth, that "if I had not loved and honored the King truly, and trusted in his goodness somewhat too much, I had not suffered death."[3]

These matters attended to, what now did Raleigh think of? Of Bess, surely, who was to live until 1647, long enough to see James die discredited and the country plunged into civil war partially because of his and Charles I's folly, and only two years before Charles himself lost his head. Of Carew, too, Raleigh undoubtedly thought, his surviving son who was to shelter Bess and who was to enjoy an unspectacular but honorable career. Thinking of his family probably became too painful; death was pressing close and its utter finality required courage

[3] The testamentary notes are in *ibid.*, 493-95.

to meet it. The death watch evoked a poetic mood and, according to tradition, Raleigh wrote:

> Cowards may die. But courage stout,
> Rather than live in snuff, will be put out.

This, however, was not enough—Roman perhaps, but scarcely fitting or distinguished. Then he recalled a love poem he had inscribed long years ago, the last stanza of which began with:

> Oh cruel Time, which takes in trust. . . .

This he changed slightly, and thoughtfully added two final lines that turned a love poem into an expression of religious faith:

> Even such is Time! who takes in trust
>     Our youth, our joys, and all we have,
> And pays us but with earth and dust:
>     Who in the dark and silent grave,
> When we have wandered all our ways
> Shuts up the story of our days.
>     But from that earth, that grave, that dust,
>     The Lord shall raise me up, I trust.

Raleigh wrote these lines in the flyleaf of his Bible and gave the Bible to the divine who attended him in the fading hours of the night, Dr. Robert Tounson, Dean of Westminster and later Bishop of Salisbury.

Raleigh baffled Tounson by being so untroubled. In fact, he made so light of death that Tounson reproached him for it. Raleigh replied that he did not fear death, and greatly preferred to die by the ax than by a wasting fever. Tounson, however, continued dubious of the reason for "this extraordinary boldness." After Raleigh received the Communion and, "very cheerful and merry," said he hoped to convince the world he died an innocent man, Tounson taxed him with obliquely impugning the King's justice. Raleigh conceded that justice and the law compelled his death, but he insisted that he was innocent in fact and that all who had heard his answers truly thought so too. Tounson, who was a brisk, businesslike cleric, an ambitious man not above being presumptuous, then reminded him that he had been regarded as "a great instrument" of Essex's death and that he should repent and ask God's forgiveness. Evidently making a mental note to say something about Essex on the scaffold, Raleigh told Tounson that the Earl "was fetched off by a trick." Though Tounson neglected to relate what the "trick" was, it may have pertained to a ring that Elizabeth had once given Essex with the assurance that if he returned it with any specific request, she would grant that request. According to tradition, Essex sent the ring to the Queen with a plea for his life, but Lady Nottingham deliberately refused to pass the ring on to Elizabeth, who later reputedly told the Frenchman, Biron, that she let Essex die because he was too proud to beg for his life.[4]

Presently dawn came, Friday, October 29, 1618. To Tounson's amazement, Raleigh ate a hearty breakfast, smoked a pipe of tobacco, and made no more of his impending death than if he had been about to take a journey. This was the final day of a rich, full life and, like an old actor on stage for the last time, Raleigh was determined to leave an imperishable memory of himself. Rejecting his recent slovenliness, he dressed carefully and decorously. He wore ash-colored silk stockings, black taffeta breeches, a hair-colored satin doublet over a black wrought waistcoat, a ruff band, and a black velvet gown over all.[5] When fully attired and about to leave the Gatehouse, he was handed a cup of sack wine. After Raleigh had drunk, the bearer asked if he had liked it. "I will answer," replied Raleigh, his eyes twinkling, "as did the fellow who drank of St. Giles's bowl as he went to Tyburn: 'it is good drink, if a man might but tarry by it.' "[6] Then, the hour being eight o'clock, the sheriff and his assistants arrived and led him to the scaffold.

The King had deliberately chosen the early morning of this day, Lord Mayor's Day, for the execution with the hope, as Aubrey says, "that the pageants and fine shows might draw away the people from beholding the tragedy of one of the gallantest worthies that ever England bred."[7] But many people learned that a greater pageant, a more exciting show, was to take place elsewhere. Hence when Raleigh limped to the scaffold, his

---

[4] Tounson's narrative is in *ibid.*, 489-92. See also Thompson, *Ralegh*, 375-76.
[5] Oldys' *Ralegh*, in *Works*, I, 557.  [6] *Chamberlain Letters*, II, 177.
[7] Aubrey, *Brief Lives*, II, 189.

head thrown proudly back and Tounson walking by him, a large crowd had collected, including the Earls of Arundel, Doncaster, and Oxford. A number of nobles waited on horseback, others with their ladies stood at windows, while around the scaffold clustered a multitude of others. One of these last was a follower of Buckingham's whom the execution was to change into one of the most redoubtable opponents ever to confront the Stuart monarchy: Sir John Eliot, later Vice-Admiral of Devon, who was to die in the Tower a victim of James's son, Charles I.

As he approached the scaffold, Raleigh noticed an old man with a very bald head standing in the crowd. It was a cold morning, and Raleigh asked the man why he was here and what he wanted. "Nothing but to see you, and to pray God to have mercy on your soul," the old man replied. Touched, Raleigh thanked him, removed a lace nightcap that he wore beneath his hat, and tossed it to him, saying, "Thou hast more need of it now than I."[8]

But for a little while Raleigh had need of every garment, for he still suffered from illness and the morning was so raw that the sheriff ordered a fire built and offered to let him come down to warm himself. Raleigh graciously declined on the grounds that his ague would soon come upon him again and people would think he quaked with terror. Then, turning to the throng that quieted as he waited, he mentioned his illness, asking his listeners that, if they perceived any weakness in him, they ascribe it to his condition rather than to fear. He expressed the wish that his voice would be strong enough to reach the Lords standing before the window in Sir Randall Carew's house, and said he would strain himself that they might hear. At this, Arundel called out, "We will come down to you." Threading their way through the crowd, the Lords climbed the scaffold itself, shook his hand, and stood by while he spoke.

Gratified, Raleigh went on with his address. It was significant that his concern was not with the original treason charge of 1603 on which he was being executed but with the more recent matters that had impelled the King to carry out the sentence. He was dying a victim to Spanish vengeance and to the pusillanimity and

---

[8] Birch, *Court and Times of James I*, II, 100.

spite of his own King, and few present were under any illusions about it, least of all Raleigh himself. He passionately denied that he had ever received a commission from the French Crown. He denied Manourie's statement that he had reviled the King— though if ever a man had cause to do so, it was Raleigh. While he had expressed his opinion to Manourie that he had trusted too much in the King's good will, his respect for monarchy as an institution and his concern for his family would have kept him from saying more about the monarch who had revealed his every plan to Spain and promised Spain his life if those plans miscarried. He ridiculed Stukely's accusation that he had told Lords Carew and Doncaster of his plan to escape and that he had informed Stukely that the two Privy Councillors intended to join him in France. He was especially scornful of Stukely's charge that he had offered him a bribe of £10,000 to be permitted to escape. It is possible that he did offer Stukely a bribe, though he denied it, but the amount was preposterous: "I never made him an offer of £10,000 or £1,000." Furthermore, said Raleigh scornfully, "If I had had half so much, I could have done better with it." He forgave Stukely, however, and hoped God would too. Then he took up the slanders in connection with the Guiana voyage, particularly the charge that he had not intended to return. Turning to Arundel on the scaffold near him, he asked him if it was not true that when Arundel begged him before sailing to return to England, whatever happened, he had promised that he would come back.

"So you did," Arundel spoke out boldly; "it is true."

With a word of apology to the sheriff for the delay, Raleigh now brought up a matter that had long troubled him and of which Tounson's mention of the Earl of Essex had reminded him. This was the old calumny that, during the execution of Essex, he had stood in a window disdainfully puffing tobacco smoke. Raleigh utterly repudiated the charge. Essex had been unable to see him since he had moved over to the Armory, and, far from feeling disdain, he had been sorry for the Earl. He regretted, moreover, that he had stood so far distant because he heard afterward that Essex had desired to see him and to be reconciled to him. "I confess," Raleigh said earnestly, "I was of a contrary faction. But I knew that my Lord of Essex was a

314

noble gentleman, and that it would be worse with me when he was gone. For those that set me up against him did afterwards set themselves against me, and were my greatest enemies."[9]

He had done what he could to vindicate his name in a marvelously effective speech, and now he prepared for his leave-taking by asking all to join with him in a prayer for pardon. His course, he acknowledged, had been one of vanity: "I have long been a seafaring man, a soldier, and a courtier, and in the temptations of the least of these there is enough to overthrow a good mind, and a good man." When asked his faith by Tounson, he replied that he died "in the faith professed by the Church of England. I hope to be saved, and to have my sins washed away, by the precious blood and merits of our Saviour Christ."

The last moments had now arrived. "I have a long journey," he said, "and must bid the company farewell." Taking leave of his friends and acquaintances on the scaffold, he turned to Arundel and, after thanking him for attending, requested him to entreat the King not to publish anything defamatory to him. It was a vain request, for James hastened to get out the *Declaration* when Raleigh was no longer alive to speak to it. The sheriff now cleared the scaffold of all save Raleigh, Tounson, and the executioner. Having given away to attendants his hat and whatever money he had in his pockets, Raleigh removed his gown and doublet and asked to see the ax. The gaping headsman making no move, Raleigh said, "I prithee, let me see it. Dost thou think that I am afraid of it?" The ax then being given him, he ran his thumb along its edge. Smiling, he said to the astounded sheriff, "This is a sharp medicine, but it is a sure cure for all diseases."

Such courage, such poise, was unparalleled, and has stirred men ever since. He was probably the only cheerful person present. In fact, Sir Dudley Carleton said that Raleigh's "happiest hours were those of his arraignment and execution." John

---

[9] The scaffold speech, with an account of Raleigh's behavior, is variously recorded. The basic sources are Archbishop Sancroft's report in the *Tanner MSS* of the Bodleian Library, Oxford, and the reports in the Public Record Office, *S.P. Dom.* (James I), 103/52 and 53. The speech, with variations, is printed in—among other places—Jardine, *Criminal Trials*, I, 503-08; *Works*, VIII, 775-80; Oldys' *Ralegh*, in *ibid.*, I, 558-63; Edwards, *Ralegh* (*Life*), I, 699-704; Harlow, *Raleigh's Last Voyage*, 305-10.

Eliot reported that even Raleigh's enemies were moved to admiration, while Thomas Lorkin told Sir Thomas Puckering that Raleigh "seemed as free from all manner of apprehension as if he had been come thither rather to be a spectator than a sufferer." The man's courage moved even the Spanish agent, Ulloa, to report to Madrid, "Ralegh's spirit never faltered, nor did his countenance change." Writing long afterward, but when the country was still under the spell of that October day, Francis Osborne remarked that Raleigh conducted himself "with so high and religious a resolution, as if a Roman had acted a Christian, or rather a Christian a Roman."[10]

But even fortitude and wit, though contributing to his lasting fame, could not hold back the ax. The executioner now spread his own cloak for Raleigh to kneel on, then knelt himself to ask his victim's forgiveness. Laying his hands on the man's shoulders, Raleigh forgave him in a hearty voice and said, "When I stretch forth my hands, despatch me."

As he prepared to lay his head on the block, someone asked him if he would not prefer to face east toward the land where the Lord had risen. Raising his head, Raleigh replied, "So the heart be right, it is no matter which way the head lieth." This reply expresses the man, who, worldling that he was, with the frailties that all men possess and perhaps more because of his eminence, was never sordid or mean and, while looking after his own interests, labored for his country's greatness. Still, to satisfy his friends, he faced the east. He refused, however, to let the executioner blindfold him: "Think you I fear the shadow of the ax, when I fear not the ax itself?"

For a moment he prayed silently; then he stretched out his hands. The executioner had never had such a gallant victim and could not bring himself to do his duty. Again Raleigh stretched out his hands, and again the headsman faltered.

"What dost thou fear?" asked Raleigh. "Strike, man, strike!"

The ax rose and fell twice, and the effusion of blood was so great that all marveled at the victim's vitality. As the executioner held up the head, not the customary applause but a

---

[10] For the above, see Thompson, *Ralegh*, 369; J. Forster, *Life of Sir John Eliot*, I, 34; Birch, *Court and Times of James I*, II, 100; Harlow, *Raleigh's Last Voyage*, 315; Osborne, *Traditional Memorials on the Reign of King James*, 429.

shuddering sigh swept over the throng, and a man from somewhere in its midst exclaimed in a loud and solemn voice, "We
have not another such head to be cut off."[11]

[11] Probably the most vivid accounts of the execution are John Pory's to Carleton, Oct. 31, 1618. PRO, *S.P. Dom.* (James I), 103/61; Chamberlain's to Carleton, Oct. 31, 1618. *Chamberlain Letters*, II, 175-78; and the Rev. Thomas Lorkin
to Sir Thomas Puckering, Nov. 3, 1618. Williams, *Court and Times of James I*,
II, 99-103. Archbishop Sancroft's account in the *Tanner MSS* at the Bodleian,
Oxford, and partially printed in *Works*, VIII, 775-80, is detailed and not without
color. See also the excellent synthesis in Jardine, *Criminal Trials*, I, 502-11, and
the article by W. S. Powell, "John Pory on the Death of Sir Walter Raleigh," in
*William and Mary Quarterly*, 3d series, IX (1952), 532-38.

# Appendix · Raleigh's Name

THE following seventy-three contemporary spellings of Raleigh's name have been compiled: Raleigh, Ralegh, Rawley, Raweley, Raulie, Rawlegh, Rawleigh, Rawleighe, Raleghe, Rawlye, Rawleie, Rawligh, Raileigh, Raughlie, Rauleigh, Raleighe, Raylie, Raghley, Raghlie, Rawleygh, Rawleyghe, Rawely, Ralighe, Raule, Rawlee, Rauley, Rawleye, Raulyghe, Rawlyghe, Ralleigh, Rawlighe, Rawleighe, Rauleighe, Raughlie, Rallegh, Rawlei, Rauly, Raughley, Raughly, Raylye, Rolye, Ralle, Raughleigh, Raleikk, Rale, Real, Reali, Ralego, Rahlegh, Raley, Raleye, Raleagh, Raleygh, Raleyghe, Ralli, Raughleye, Rauleghe, Raulghe, Raweleigh, Raylygh, Reigley, Rhaleigh, Rhaly, Rauley, Wrawly, Wrawley, Raleich—used by the French, Ralo and Ralle—used by the Venetians, Halley —used by the Dutch, Raulaeus and Raleghus—Latin versions. The Spaniards usually alluded to him by variations of his first name: Gualtero, Guatteral, and Gualteral.

To Cecil (who write "Cecyll"), Raleigh was Rawley, Raleigh, and Ralegh; to King James, he was Raulie and Raleigh; to his wife, Ralegh (except for her one use of Raleigh); to Henry Howard, Rawlegh and Rawlie; to the Lord Admiral, Rawlighe; to Cobham, Rawlye; to Stukely, Raligh.

Raleigh, himself, used several spellings. In 1578, he signed a deed as Rawleyghe, his brother Carew as Rawlygh, and his father as Ralegh. From June 9, 1584 until his death, his signature on all correspondence was Ralegh, the name that also appears in his books.

Oddly enough, as Stebbing pointed out, "The spelling Raleigh, which posterity has preferred, happens to be one he is not known to have ever employed."[1]

The pronunciation appears to be less in doubt. Though the spellings indicate variation in pronunciation, most of the English versions bear out the first syllable as "Raw" and the last

[1] For spelling, see Stebbing, *Ralegh*, 30-31; Thompson, *Ralegh*, 394.

as having the sound of "ly" (lee), with the accent on the first. Present members of the Trevelyan family in the North and West Country, and the Kerrs as well, use it as a baptismal name. They spell it Raleigh and pronounce it "Rawly."[2]

[2] *Notes and Queries*, cxcv (1950), 391, 481.

# Bibliography

*Additional MSS*, British Museum

American Historical Association, *Papers*, v

Andrews, C. M., *The Colonial Period of American History*, 4 vols., New Haven, 1934

Anthony, I., *Ralegh and His World*, New York, 1934

Aubrey, J., *Brief Lives*, ed. by A. Clark. 2 vols., Oxford, 1898

Bacon. *The Works of Francis Bacon*, coll. and ed. by J. Spedding, R. L. Ellis, and D. D. Heath. 15 vols., Boston, 1860

Bagwell, R., *Ireland under the Tudors*, 3 vols., London, 1885-1890

Battenhouse, R. W., *Marlowe's "Tamburlaine,"* Nashville, 1941

Birch, T., *Memoirs of the Reign of Queen Elizabeth*, 2 vols., London, 1754

———, *Court and Times of James I*, 2 vols., London, 1848

Black, J. B., *The Reign of Elizabeth, 1558-1603*, Oxford, 1936

Bowen, C. D., *The Lion and the Throne: The Life and Times of Sir Edward Coke*, Boston, 1956

Bradbrook, M. C., *The School of Night*, Cambridge, England, 1936

Brooke, C. F. T., *The Life of Marlowe*, New York, 1930

Brown, A., *The Genesis of the United States*, 2 vols., Boston, 1890

———, *The First Republic in America*, Boston, 1898

Brushfield, T. N., *The Bibliography of Sir Walter Ralegh*, 2nd edition. Exeter, 1908

Buchan, J., *Walter Ralegh*, Stanhope Historical Prize Essay, Oxford, 1897

Burrage, G., *The Early English Dissenters*, 2 vols., Cambridge, 1912

*Calendar of State Papers: Carew, Colonial, Colonial (America and West Indies), Domestic, Foreign, Ireland, Spanish, Venetian*

Camden, W., *Annales Regni Jacobi: Epistolae*, ed. by T. Smith, London, 1691

———, *Annales Rerum Anglicarum et Hibernicarum Regnante Elizabetha*, ed. by T. Hearne. 3 vols., London, 1717

Carew. *Letters of George Lord Carew to Sir Thomas Roe, 1615-1617*, ed. by J. Maclean. Camden Society, London, 1869

Carlyle, T., *Oliver Cromwell's Letters and Speeches*, Boston, 1885

Cayley, A., *Life of Sir Walter Raleigh*, 2 vols., London, 1806

Cecil. *Secret Correspondence of Sir Robert Cecil with James VI*, ed. by Lord Hailes, London, 1766

———, *Letters from Sir Robert Cecil to Sir George Carew*, ed. by J. Maclean. Camden Society, London, 1864

Cecil, A., *A Life of Robert Cecil, First Earl of Salisbury*, London, 1915

Chamberlain. *The Letters of John Chamberlain*, ed. by N. E. McClure. 2 vols., Philadelphia, 1939

Channing, E., *A History of the United States*, 6 vols., New York, 1906-1925

Chapman, G., *Poetical Works*, ed. by A. C. Swinborne. 3 vols., London, 1875

Cheyney, E. P., *A History of England from the Defeat of the Armada to the Death of Elizabeth*, 2 vols., New York, 1914-1926

Chidsey, D. B., *Sir Walter Raleigh*, New York, 1931

Chute, M., *Ben Jonson of Westminster*, New York, 1953

Collier, J. P., "New Materials for a Life of Sir Walter Raleigh," in *Archaeologia*, XXXIV, 1852; XXXV, 1853

——, in *Notes and Queries*, 3rd Series, V

Collins, A., *Letters and Memorials of State in the Reigns of Queen Mary, Queen Elizabeth, and King James*, 2 vols., London, 1746

Corbett, J. S., *Sir Francis Drake*, London, 1894

——, *Drake and the Tudor Navy*, 2 vols., London, 1899

——, *The Successors of Drake*, New York, 1933

Corney, B., *Curiosities of Literature Illustrated*, London, 1838

*Cotton MSS*, British Museum

Craven, W. F., *The Southern Colonies in the Seventeenth Century, 1607-1689*, Baton Rouge, 1949

Cust, L., "The Portraits of Sir Walter Ralegh," in *The Walpole Society*, VIII, 1920

Davies, G., *The Early Stuarts, 1603-1660*, Oxford, 1937

Davies, R. T., *The Golden Century of Spain*, London, 1937

Dee. *The Private Diary of Dr. John Dee*, ed. by J. O. Halliwell. Camden Society, London, 1842

D'Ewes, S., *The Journals of All the Parliaments during the Reign of Queen Elizabeth, Both of the House of Lords and House of Commons*, London, 1682

Devereux, W. B., *Lives and Letters of the Devereux, Earls of Essex*, 2 vols., London, 1853

*Dictionary of National Biography*

D'Israeli, I., *Curiosities of Literature*, 4 vols., Boston, 1859

Dodd, W. E., *The Old South*, New York, 1937

Edwards, E., *The Life of Sir Walter Ralegh, together with His Letters*, 2 vols., London, 1868

*Egerton Papers*, ed. by J. P. Collier. Camden Society, London, 1840

Ellis-Fermor, U. M., *Christopher Marlowe*, London, 1927

Elton, G. R., *England under the Tudors*, New York, 1954

Falls, C., *Elizabeth's Irish Wars*, London, 1950

Figgis, J. F., *The Divine Right of Kings*, Cambridge, 1914

Firth, Sir C., *Essays Historical and Literary*, Oxford, 1938

Fitzgerald, B., *The Geraldines*, New York, 1951

Floyd, D., *Observations of Statesmen and Favorites of England since the Reformation*, London, 1665

Foster, C. L., Identification of Raleigh's Gold Field, in *Quarterly Journal of the Geological Society*, 1869

Foreign Office *Blue Books* on Venezuela-British Guiana Boundary Dispute, 17 vols., London, 1897-1899

Forster, J., *Life of Sir John Eliot*, 2 vols., London, 1864

Foxe, J., *Acts and Monuments*, 3 vols., London, 1684

Frere, W. H., *The English Church in the Reigns of Elizabeth and James I*, London, 1904

Froude, J. A., *History of England from the Fall of Wolsey to the Defeat of the Spanish Armada*, 12 vols., New York, 1870-1874

——, *English Seamen in the Sixteenth Century*, London, 1895

Fuller, T., *The Worthies of England*, ed. by J. Freeman. London, 1952

Gardiner, S. R., "The Case against Sir Walter Raleigh," in *Fortnightly Review*, VII, May 1867, and New Series, I

——, "Documents Relating to Sir Walter Raleigh's Last Voyage," in *Camden Miscellany*, V

——, *Prince Charles and the Spanish Marriage, 1617-1623*, 2 vols., London, 1869

——, *History of England from the Accession of James I to the Outbreak of the Civil War*, 10 vols., London, 1883-1884

Goodman, G., *The Court of King James the First*, ed. by J. Brewer. 2 vols., London, 1839

Gorges, A., *A Larger Relation of the Said Island Voyage*, in S. Purchas, *Purchas His Pilgrimes*, Mac Lehose edition. 20 vols., Glasgow, 1907

Gosse, E., *Raleigh*, New York, 1886

Green, A. W., *Sir Francis Bacon, His Life and Works*, Denver, 1952

Hakluyt, R., *The Principal Navigations, Voyages, Traffiques and Discoveries of the English Nation*, Mac Lehose edition. 12 vols., New York, 1904

Halliwell, J. O., *Poetical Miscellanies*, Percy Society, London, 1848

Hannah, J., *The Poems of Sir Walter Raleigh . . . and Other Courtly Poets*, London, 1892

*Harleian MSS*, British Museum

Harlow, V. T. (ed.), *The Discoverie of Guiana*, London, 1928

——, *Raleigh's Last Voyage*, London, 1932

Harrison, D., *Tudor England*, 2 vols., London, 1953

Harrison, G. B., *Willobie His Avisa*, London, 1926

——, *The Life and Death of Robert Devereux, Earl of Essex*, New York, 1937

Hawks, F. L., *History of North Carolina*, 2 vols., Fayetteville, N.C., 1857-1858

Hazard, E., *Historical Collections*, 2 vols., Philadelphia, 1792

Historical Manuscripts Commission Reports: *Allen George Finch MSS, Salisbury MSS, Lord De L'Isle and Dudley MSS*

Holdsworth, W. S., *A History of English Law*, 13 vols., London, 1903-1952

Holinshed, R., *Chronicles of England, Scotland, and Ireland*, ed. by H. Ellis. 6 vols., London, 1807-1808

Howell, J., *Epistolae Ho-Elianae*, ed. by J. Jacobs. London, 1890

Howell, T. B., *State Trials*, 21 vols., London, 1816

Hume, D., *History of England*, 6 vols., Boston, 1868

Hume, M. A. S., *Philip II of Spain*, London, 1897

————, *Sir Walter Raleigh*, New York, 1926

Innes, A. D., *The Maritime and Colonial Expansion of England under the Stuarts*, London, 1932

James I. *Correspondence of King James VI of Scotland with Sir Robert Cecil*, ed. by J. Bruce. Camden Society, London, 1861

————, "A Counterblast to Tobacco," in R. S. Rait, *A Royal Rhetorician*, London, 1900

Jardine, D., *Criminal Trials*, 2 vols., London, 1832-1835

Jonson, B., *Works*, ed. by F. Cunningham. 9 vols., London, 1875

Jordan, W. K., *The Development of Religious Toleration in England*, 4 vols., Cambridge, Mass., 1932-1940

Knappen, M., *Tudor Puritanism*, Chicago, 1939

Knott, J., "Sir Walter Ralegh's 'Royal Cordial,' " in *American Medicine*, New Series, VI, 1911

Latham, A. M. C., "Sir Walter Raleigh's Farewell Letter to His Wife in 1603," in *Essays and Studies by Members of the English Association*, XXV, 1940

————, "Sir Walter Raleigh's Gold Mine," in *Essays and Studies by Members of the English Association*, New Series, IV, 1951

————, *The Poems of Sir Walter Ralegh*, Cambridge, Mass., 1951

Lewis, G. R., *The Stannaries*, Cambridge, Mass., 1908

Leycester. *Correspondence of Robert Dudley, Earl of Leycester*, ed. by J. Bruce. Camden Society, London, 1844

Lipson, E., *The Economic History of England*, 3 vols., London, 1931

McElwee, W., *The Murder of Sir Thomas Overbury*, London, 1952

McMillan, H., *Sir Walter Ralegh's Lost Colony*, Raleigh, N.C., 1907

Magnus, P., *Sir Walter Raleigh*, London, 1952

Manningham. *Diary of John Manningham*, ed. by J. Bruce. Camden Society, London, 1868

Marlowe, C., *Works*, London, 1850

Martins, J. P. O., *A History of Iberian Civilization*, trans. by A. F. G. Bell, Oxford, 1930

Mathew, D., *The Jacobean Age*, New York, 1938

Milton, J., *Complete Poetical Works*, Cambridge Edition, Boston, 1899

Naunton, Sir R., *Fragmenta Regalia*, London, 1870

Neale, J. E., "Peter Wentworth," in *English Historical Review*, XXXIX, 1924

———, "The Commons' Privilege of Free Speech in Parliament," in *Tudor Studies*, ed. by R. W. Seton-Watson, London, 1924

———, *Queen Elizabeth*, New York, 1934

———, *The Elizabethan House of Commons*, New Haven, 1950

———, *Elizabeth I and Her Parliaments, 1559-1581*, London, 1953

———, *Elizabeth I and Her Parliaments, 1584-1601*, New York, 1958

*Notes and Queries*

Oldys, W., *Life of Sir Walter Ralegh*, in Volume I of Oxford edition (1829) of Raleigh's *Works*

Oppenheim, M. (ed.), *The Naval Tracts of Sir William Monson*, Naval Records Society. 5 vols., London, 1902-1914

Osborne, F., *Some Traditional Memorials on the Reign of King James*, in *Advice To A Son*, London, 1673

Overbury, Sir T., *Trial of Sir Walter Ralegh*, in *Cotton MSS*, British Museum

Parks, G. B., *Richard Hakluyt and the English Voyages*, New York, 1928

*Patent Rolls*

Pemberton, H., Jr., *Shakspere and Sir Walter Ralegh*, Philadelphia, 1914

Percy, E., *The Privy Council under the Tudors*, Oxford, 1907

Pollard, A. F., *Tudor Tracts, 1532-1588*, based on E. Arber's *An English Garner*. Ed. by T. Seccombe. 12 vols., New York, 1903

———, *The Evolution of Parliament*, London, 1920

Pope-Hennessy, Sir J., *Ralegh in Ireland*, London, 1883

Porter, C. W., III, "What Became of the Lost Colonists?" in *American Heritage*, IV, No. 2, Winter 1953

Powell, W. S., "John Pory on the Death of Sir Walter Raleigh," in *William and Mary Quarterly*, 3rd series, IX, 1952

*Privy Council, Acts of*

*Privy Council Registers, Elizabeth and James I*

Quinn, D. B., *The Voyages and Colonizing Enterprises of Sir Humphrey Gilbert*, 2 vols., London, 1940

———, *Raleigh and the British Empire*, New York, 1949

———, *The Roanoke Voyages*, 2 vols., London, 1955

Raleigh, Sir W., *The Works of Sir Walter Ralegh*, 8 vols., Oxford, 1829

Read, C., *Mr. Secretary Walsingham and the Policy of Queen Elizabeth*, 3 vols., Oxford, 1925

———, "Good Queen Bess," in R. L. Schuyler and H. Ausubel, *The Making of English History*, New York, 1952

———, *Mr. Secretary Cecil and Queen Elizabeth*, New York, 1955

Rodd, R., *Sir Walter Raleigh*, London, 1904

Rowse, A. L., *Sir Richard Grenville*, London, 1937

Rowse, A. L., *The England of Elizabeth, the Structure of Society,* New York, 1951

————, *The Expansion of Elizabethan England,* New York, 1955

Rymer, T., *Foedera,* 20 vols., London, 1704-1722

St. John, J. A., *Life of Sir Walter Raleigh,* 2 vols., 1868

Sanderson, W., *The Lives and Reigns of Mary Queen of Scotland and James the Sixth, King of Scotland,* London, 1656

Schomburgk, Sir R. H. (ed.), *The Discoverie of Guiana,* Hakluyt Society, London, 1848

Scott, W. R., *The Constitution and Finance of English, Scottish and Irish Joint-Stock Companies to 1720,* 3 vols., Cambridge, England, 1912

Shakespeare, W., *Complete Works,* Harvard Edition, Boston, 1886

Shirley, J. W., "Sir Walter Raleigh's Guiana Finances," in *Huntington Library Quarterly,* XIII, 1949

Sidney, A., *Works,* London, 1767

*Sloane MSS,* British Museum

Smith, L. C., *Life and Letters of Sir Henry Wotton,* 2 vols., Oxford, 1907

Sorenson, F., "Sir Walter Raleigh's Marriage," in *Studies in Philology,* XXXIII, 1936

Spedding, J., *The Life and Times of Francis Bacon,* 2 vols., Boston, 1878

————, *The Letters and Life of Francis Bacon Including All His Occasional Works,* 7 vols., London, 1861-1874

Spenser, E., *Works,* London, 1869

*State Papers,* Public Record Office. *Domestic,* Elizabeth I and James I; *Ireland,* Elizabeth I

Stebbing, W., *Sir Walter Ralegh,* Oxford, 1891

Stephen, Sir H. L., "The Trial of Sir Walter Raleigh," in *Transactions of the Royal Historical Society,* 4th series, II, 1919

Stowe, J., *Annals,* London, 1605

Strachey, L., *Elizabeth and Essex,* London, 1928

Strathmann, E. A., *Sir Walter Ralegh, A Study in Elizabethan Skepticism,* New York, 1951

Stukely, Sir L., *Apology,* in Volume VIII of Oxford edition (1829) of Raleigh's *Works*

Sully. *Memoires de Sully,* 6 vols., Paris, 1814

Tannenbaum, S. A., *The Assassination of Christopher Marlowe,* New York, 1928

*Tanner MSS,* Bodleian Library, Oxford

Taylor, E. G. R., *The Original Writings and Correspondence of the Two Richard Hakluyts,* 2 vols., London, 1935

Thompson, E., *Sir Walter Ralegh, Last of the Elizabethans,* New Haven, 1936

Townshend, H., *Historical Collections, An Exact Account of the Last Four Parliaments of Elizabeth*, London, 1680

Trevelyan, G. M., *England under the Stuarts*, New York, 1914

United States Commission on Boundary between Venezuela and British Guiana, *Report*, 9 vols., Atlanta, 1896-1897

Vere, Sir F., *Commentaries*, in C. H. Firth, *Stuart Tracts, 1603-1693*, based on E. Arber's *An English Garner*. Ed. by T. Seccombe. 12 vols., New York, 1903

Waldman, M., *Sir Walter Raleigh*, London, edition of 1950

Webster, J., *Dramatic Works*, ed. by W. Hazlitt. 4 vols., London, 1857

Wernham, R. B., "Queen Elizabeth and the Portugal Expedition of 1589," in *English Historical Review*, LXVI, 1951

Williams, R. F., *The Court and Times of James the First*, 2 vols., London, 1848

Williams, T., "The Surroundings of Ralegh's Lost Colony," in *American Historical Association Papers*, 1895

Williamson, H. R., *Sir Walter Raleigh*, London, 1951

Williamson, J. A., *The English Colonies in Guiana and on the Amazon, 1604-1668*, Oxford, 1923

———, *The Age of Drake*, London, 1938

Willson, D. H., "The Earl of Salisbury and the 'Court' Party in Parliament, 1604-1610," in *American Historical Review*, XXXVI, 1931

———, *The Privy Councillors in the House of Commons, 1604-1629*, Minneapolis, 1940

———, *King James VI and I*, New York, 1956

Winwood, Sir R., *Memorials of Affairs of State in the Reigns of Q. Elizabeth and K. James I*, ed. by E. Sawyer. 3 vols., London, 1725

Wood, A., *Athenae Oxonienses*, ed. by P. Bliss. 6 vols., Oxford, 1813-1820

Wotton, Sir H., *Reliquiae Wottoniae*, London, 1685

# Index

de Acuna, Don Diego Sarmiento (Count Gondomar), Spanish ambassador, 270, 272, hatred of WR and ascendancy over James, 258-60; proposes marriage of Charles and Infanta, 260; opposes WR, 260-61; acquires intelligence on WR's Guiana voyage, 262-63; obtains assurance of WR's execution, 284-86
——, Don Palomeque, 277, 278, 279
Adelantado, of Castile, 141, 148, 154, 163
Anne, Queen of England, 252, 255, 282, 307; befriends WR, 231; brings son to visit WR, 237; appeals for WR's life, 296-97
Aremberg, Count, 192, 193, 196, 208, 209, 212, 213
Armada, the Spanish, 59, 60-62
Arundel, Earl of, 263, 265, 281, 283, 299, 313
Aubrey, John, 8, 9, 25, 82, 111, 190, 295
Azores, the, 144, 148, 149, 152, 153, 154, 155

Bacon, Anthony, 66, 107, 126
——, Sir Francis, 4, 5, 66, 101, 179, 215, 262, 297, 304, 305
Barry, Lord David, 17, 18, 269
de Berrio, Don Antonio, 109, 112, 113, 277
Blount, Charles, Lord Mountjoy, 63, 145, 149, 161, 165, 182, 203
——, Sir Christopher, 149, 151, 152, 163, 167, 168, 169, 171
Boyle, Lord Richard, 269, 310
Brooke, George, 193, 194, 208, 219
——, Henry, Lord Cobham, 143-44, 162, 166, 169, 174, 181, 184, 185, 192, 193, 198, 206, 207, 208, 209, 210, 213, 214, 218, 220, 226, 228; description of, 175; Crown's statement of his connection with Bye Plot, 193-94; writes WR, 199-200; connection with WR, 203-04; says WR asked for a Spanish pension, 212; sentence commuted to imprisonment, 223-25

Buckingham, Duke of, see Villiers, George
Burghley, Lord, see Cecil, William
Burrough, Sir John, 90, 91, 96
Bye Plot, 193-94, 204

Cadiz, 3, 4, 65, 144, 247; expedition to, 125-38
Carew, Sir George, Lord Carew, 66, 84, 95, 132, 148, 160, 166, 184-85, 188, 256, 262, 270, 282, 285, 286, 307
Carleton, Sir Dudley, 217, 218, 225, 235, 250, 315
Carr, Robert, Earl of Somerset, 233, 234, 235, 237, 250, 251, 252, 253, 254, 255, 256
Cecil, Sir Robert, Earl of Salisbury, 91, 93, 96, 100, 101, 110, 160, 165, 166, 168, 170, 171, 196, 209, 210, 212, 219, 223, 226, 227, 228, 254, 255; races WR to Plymouth, 97-98; forms partnership with WR and Essex, 139-40; analysis of character and motives, 142-43; decries WR to Essex, 146-47; scotches Essex conspiracy, 169; unpopularity, 173; scolds Parliament, 177; conspires for accession of James VI of Scotland and destroys WR, 181-92; leaves WR to the law, 200-01; accepts Spanish pension, 212-13, 257; suggests James give Sherborne to Carr, 233; death, 251; WR's alleged epitaph on, 251-52
——, William, Lord Burghley, 19, 26, 43, 69, 76, 89, 91, 98, 99, 107, 158, 181, 209
Chamberlain, John, 161, 165, 217, 225, 235, 250
Chapman, George, 121
Cobham, Lord, see Brooke, Henry
Coke, Sir Edward, Attorney General, vii-viii, 101, 218, 228, 297, 302, 305, 306; prosecutes WR at treason trial, 203-15
Cottrell, Edward, 199, 212, 293
Criminal Procedure, 195-96, 214-15, 218

The Library of Congress has catalogued this book as follows:

Wallace, Willard Mosher, 1911—Sir Walter Raleigh. Princeton, N.J., Princeton University Press, 1959. 327 p. illus. 25 cm. Includes bibliography. 1. Raleigh, Sir Walter, 1552?-1618. DA86.22.R2W33(923.942)59—9677 ‡ Library of Congress